D0889663

THEORIES OF
Information
BEHAVIOR

Edited by
Karen E. Fisher
Sanda Erdelez
and
Lynne (E. F.) McKechnie

ASIST Monograph Series

Published for the American Society for Information Science and Technology by

Medford, New Jersey

Third Printing, August 2009

Theories of Information Behavior

Copyright © 2005 by American Society for Information Science and Technology

All rights reserved. No part of this book may be reproduced in any form or by any electronic or mechanical means, including information storage and retrieval systems, without permission in writing from the publisher, except by a reviewer, who may quote brief passages in a review. Published by Information Today, Inc., 143 Old Marlton Pike, Medford, New Jersey 08055.

Publisher's Note: The author and publisher have taken care in preparation of this book but make no expressed or implied warranty of any kind and assume no responsibility for errors or omissions. No liability is assumed for incidental or consequential damages in connection with or arising out of the information contained herein.

Many of the designations used by manufacturers and sellers to distinguish their products are claimed as trademarks. Where those designations appear in this book and Information Today, Inc. was aware of a trademark claim, the designations have been printed with initial capital letters.

Library of Congress Cataloging-in-Publication Data

Theories of information behavior / edited by Karen E. Fisher, Sanda Erdelez, and Lynne (E.F.) McKechnie.
    p. cm. -- (ASIST monograph series)
  Includes bibliographical references and index.
  ISBN 1-57387-230-X
  1. Information behavior. 2. Information retrieval. 3. Research. 4. Information resources. 5. Information science. I. Fisher, Karen E., 1966-
II. Erdelez, Sanda, 1960- III. McKechnie, Lynne. IV. Series.
  ZA3075.T465 2005
  020'.72--dc22

                                  2005010420

Printed and bound in the United States of America

President and CEO: Thomas H. Hogan, Sr.
Editor-in-Chief and Publisher: John B. Bryans
Managing Editor: Amy M. Holmes
VP Graphics and Production: M. Heide Dengler
Cover Designer: Michele Quinn
Book Designer: Kara Mia Jalkowski
Proofreader: Pat Hadley-Miller
Indexer: Sharon Hughes

In memory of Elfreda A. Chatman

Contents

List of Figures xiii

List of Tables xv

Acknowledgments xvii

Preface xix

Chapter 1   An Introduction to Metatheories,
              Theories, and Models 1
              Marcia J. Bates

Chapter 2   What Methodology Does
              to Theory: Sense-Making
              Methodology as Exemplar 25
              Brenda Dervin

Chapter 3   Evolution in Information
              Behavior Modeling
              Wilson's Model 31
              T. D. Wilson

The Theories

1   Affective Load 39
      Diane Nahl

2   Anomalous State of Knowledge 44
      Nicholas J. Belkin

3   Archival Intelligence 49
      Elizabeth Yakel

4   Bandura's Social Cognition 54
      Makiko Miwa

5   Berrypicking 58
     Marcia J. Bates

6   Big6 Skills for
     Information Literacy 63
     Carrie A. Lowe and Michael B. Eisenberg

7   Chang's Browsing 69
     Shan-Ju L. Chang

8   Chatman's Information Poverty 75
     Julie Hersberger

9   Chatman's Life in the Round 79
     Crystal Fulton

10   Cognitive Authority 83
     Soo Young Rieh

11   Cognitive Work Analysis 88
     Raya Fidel and Annelise Mark Pejtersen

12   Collective Action Dilemma 94
     Marc Smith and Howard T. Welser

13   Communicative Action 99
     Gerald Benoît

14   Communities of Practice 104
     Elisabeth Davies

15   Cultural Models of Hall
     and Hofstede 108
     Anita Komlodi

16   Dervin's Sense-Making 113
     Tonyia J. Tidline

17   Diffusion Theory 118
     Darian Lajoie-Paquette

18   The Domain Analytic Approach
     to Scholars' Information Practices 123
     Sanna Talja

19 Ecological Theory of Human
   Information Behavior 128
   Kirsty Williamson

20 Elicitation as Micro-Level
   Information Seeking 133
   Mei-Mei Wu

21 Ellis's Model of Information-
   Seeking Behavior 138
   David Ellis

22 Everyday Life Information Seeking 143
   Reijo Savolainen

23 Face Threat 149
   Lorri Mon

24 Flow Theory 153
   Charles Naumer

25 General Model of the Information
   Seeking of Professionals 158
   Gloria J. Leckie

26 The Imposed Query 164
   Melissa Gross

27 Information Acquiring-
   and-Sharing 169
   Kevin Rioux

28 Information Activities in Work Tasks 174
   Katriina Byström

29 Information Encountering 179
   Sanda Erdelez

30 Information Grounds 185
   Karen E. Fisher

31 Information Horizons 191
   Diane H. Sonnenwald

32   Information Intents 198
Ross J. Todd

33   Information Interchange 204
Rita Marcella and Graeme Baxter

34   Institutional Ethnography 210
Roz Stooke

**35   Integrative Framework for
Information Seeking and Interactive
Information Retrieval** 215
Peter Ingwersen

36   Interpretative Repertoires 221
Pamela J. McKenzie

**37   Krikelas's Model of
Information Seeking** 225
Jean Henefer and Crystal Fulton

**38   Kuhlthau's Information
Search Process** 230
Carol Collier Kuhlthau

39   Library Anxiety 235
Patricia Katopol

40   Monitoring and Blunting 239
Lynda M. Baker

**41   Motivational Factors for
Interface Design** 242
Carolyn Watters and Jack Duffy

42   Network Gatekeeping 247
Karine Barzilai-Nahon

43   Nonlinear Information Seeking 254
Allen Foster

44 Optimal Foraging 259
JoAnn Jacoby

**45 Organizational Sense Making
and Information Use** 265
Anu MacIntosh-Murray

46 The PAIN Hypothesis 270
Harry Bruce

**47 Perspectives on the Tasks in
which Information Behaviors
Are Embedded** 275
Barbara M. Wildemuth and Anthony Hughes

48 Phenomenography 280
Louise Limberg

49 Practice of Everyday Life 284
Paulette Rothbauer

50 Principle of Least Effort 289
Donald O. Case

**51 Professions and Occupational
Identities** 293
Olof Sundin and Jenny Hedman

52 Radical Change 298
Eliza T. Dresang

53 Reader Response Theory 303
Catherine Sheldrick Ross

54 Rounding and Dissonant Grounds 308
Paul Solomon

55 Serious Leisure 313
Jenna Hartel

56 Small-World Network Exploration 318
Lennart Björneborn

57   Nan Lin's Theory of Social Capital......... 323
Catherine A. Johnson

58   The Social Constructionist Viewpoint
on Information Practices 328
Kimmo Tuominen, Sanna Talja, and Reijo Savolainen

59   Social Positioning....................... 334
Lisa M. Given

60   The Socio-Cognitive Theory of
Users Situated in Specific Contexts
and Domains 339
Birger Hjørland

61   Strength of Weak Ties.................... 344
Christopher M. Dixon

62   Symbolic Violence 349
Steven Joyce

63   Taylor's Information Use
Environments 354
Ruth A. Palmquist

64   Taylor's Question-Negotiation 358
Phillip M. Edwards

65   Transtheoretical Model of the
Health Behavior Change 363
C. Nadine Wathen and Roma M. Harris

66   Value Sensitive Design 368
Batya Friedman and Nathan G. Freier

67   Vygotsky's Zone of Proximal
Development........................... 373
Lynne (E. F.) McKechnie

68   Web Information Behaviors of
Organizational Workers 377
Brian Detlor

69   Willingness to Return.................... 382
Tammara Combs Turner and Joan C. Durrance

70 **Women's Ways of Knowing** 387
Heidi Julien

71 **Work Task Information-Seeking
and Retrieval Processes** 392
Preben Hansen

72 **World Wide Web
Information Seeking** 397
Don Turnbull

About the Editors 401

Index 403

List of Figures

Chapters

Figure C2.1   Sense-Making Methodology's
central metaphor 28

Figure C3.1   The information user and the
universe of knowledge 32

Figure C3.2   Information need and seeking 33

Figure C3.3   A revised general model of
information-seeking behavior 34

Theories

Figure 2.1   The communication system of
interest to information science 45

Figure 7.1   Refined framework of browsing 70

Figure 11.1   The dimensions for analysis in
cognitive work analysis 90

Figure 19.1   Ecological model of information
seeking and use 129

Figure 20.1   Conceptual framework of the
elicitation process 134

Figure 22.1   The ELIS model 145

Figure 24.1   How the complexity of consciousness
increases as a result of flow experiences 155

Figure 25.1   A model of the information
seeking of professionals 160

Figure 29.1   Position of opportunistic acquisition
of information and information
encountering within the conceptual
model of information behavior 180

Figure 29.2   A functional model of information
encountering 181

Figure 30.1   Information grounds and information behavior 187

Figure 31.1   Flow of reflections and/or evaluations in human information behavior 193

Figure 31.2   A representative information horizon of a software engineer 194

Figure 31.3   A study participant's graphical representation of their information horizon 195

Figure 35.1   General model of cognitive information seeking and retrieval 216

Figure 37.1   Krikelas's model of information seeking 227

Figure 38.1   Kuhlthau's Information Search Process 231

Figure 42.1   Illustrative model of network gatekeeping 252

Figure 43.1   Nonlinear model of information-seeking behavior 255

Figure 44.1   Optimal foraging model of an information "diet" 260

Figure 44.2   Individual resource map of human behavioral ecology scholar showing core-periphery structure 261

Figure 65.1   A spiral model of the stages of change 364

Figure 65.2   The temporal dimension as the basis for the stages of change 365

Figure 68.1   Web information behaviors of organizational workers 378

Figure 71.1   Conceptual framework of IS&R tasks embedded in work task 393

List of Tables

Theories

Table 6.1   Comparison of information skills
process models 64

Table 6.2   The Big6 Model of information
problem solving 65

Table 7.1   Dimensions and elements in the
taxonomy of browsing 72

Table 11.1   Examples of questions to ask for
each dimension of cognitive work
analysis 91

Table 32.1   Information intents and manifestations
of changes in knowledge structures 201

Table 33.1   The two-way information interchange
in relationships and roles of information
providers and information users 207

Table 41.1   Design implications 244

Table 42.1   Traditional gatekeeping vs. network
gatekeeping 249

Acknowledgments

Theories of Information Behavior is a collaborative work of the information behavior community. We extend our deepest thanks to the 85 contributing authors who made this guide possible. We also thank graduate student assistants Scott Fields, Chris Pusateri, and Peter Emonds-Banfield from the Information School and the Department of Technical Communications at the University of Washington, and Mickey Coalwell and Donghua Tao of the School of Information Science and Learning Technologies at the University of Missouri, who helped to organize and carry out this project. We are indebted to the Institute of Museum and Library Services (IMLS) for its financial support.

Finally, we wish to acknowledge the immeasurable legacy of Professor Elfreda A. Chatman, a dear friend and esteemed mentor, teacher, and colleague who led the way in information behavior theory development and appreciation. In recognition of Elfreda's generous and profound work with students, royalties from publication will be used to support future activities of ASIST SIG USE.

Preface

"Working with conceptual frameworks and empirical
research has never been easy." (Chatman, 1996, p. 205)

Conceptual work is the greatest and most constant challenge for
many researchers. *Theories of Information Behavior* purports to facilitate theory building and use, to make conceptual engagement easier
than when Elfreda A. Chatman—one of the most influential theoretical scholars in information behavior—penned the above statement.
This guide provides authoritative entries for metatheories, theories,
and models of information behavior. We believe it will be helpful to
researchers, students, and practitioners as a ready reference guide to
conceptual frameworks relevant to information behavior research.

In recent decades scholars have used many terms to refer to varied
aspects of information behavior. The mid- and late 1990s flurry of theoretical activity coincided with emerging consensus about the name of
this subdiscipline within library and information science (Pettigrew,
Fidel, & Bruce, 2001, pp. 44–45). In the first comprehensive textbook
devoted to information behavior, Case (2002, p. 76) states that information behavior "is a term whose time has come" because it "captures a
broader range of information related phenomena, many of which are
"receiving fresh attention." While some researchers use "information
behavior" narrowly to refer only to information seeking activities, a
majority follow Wilson's (1999, p. 249) encapsulation that information
behavior is "the totality of human behavior in relation to sources and
channels of information, including both active and passive information-
seeking, and information use." It was along this line that Pettigrew, et
al., (2001, p. 44) defined information behavior as "how people need,
seek, give and use information in different contexts." Building on these
definitions, for the purposes of this handbook, we conceptualize information behavior as including how people need, seek, manage, give, and
use information in different contexts.

This book is preceded by several synergistic activities by the co-editors
and colleagues. Its origins stem from the "Theory use in information
science" project by McKechnie and Pettigrew (now "Fisher")
(Pettigrew & McKechnie, 2001), which earned a 1999 Research

Award from the Association for Library and Information Science Education (ALISE); the "Conceptual frameworks in information behavior" chapter in the 2000 *Annual Review of Information Science & Technology* by Pettigrew, Fidel, and Bruce; and the workshop on conceptual frameworks for studying information behavior at the 2002 Conceptions of Library and Information Science (CoLIS4) conference in Seattle, organized by Erdelez and Fisher. However, the focal point for the creation of the book was the 3rd Symposium of the Special Interest Group on Information Seeking and Use (SIG USE) at the 2003 Conference of the American Society for Information Science and Technology (ASIST), organized by Fisher and Erdelez, where more than 40 researchers discussed 23 theories of information behavior. All the above activities were greatly influenced and inspired by the Information Seeking in Context (ISIC) conferences, held biannually in Europe since 1996.

Information behavior researchers are among the highest users of theory within the library and information science research (Pettigrew & McKechnie, 2001). Also, theory use in information behavior is growing, with an increasing number of theories being developed from within the field. Continued growth of theory development is evident in 72 metatheories, theories, and models included herein, with 2.7 percent (2) being drawn from computer science, 4.1 percent (3) from the humanities, 31.0 percent (26) from the social sciences and 51.2 percent (43) from library and information science.

This book is intended as a researcher's guide, a practical overview of both well-established and newly proposed conceptual frameworks that one may use to study different aspects of information behavior. An unprecedented international effort by 85 scholars from 10 countries (Australia, Canada, Denmark, England, Finland, Ireland, Japan, Sweden, Taiwan, and the U.S.), each of the book's 72 entries follows a similar format. In addition to discussing origins of the theory, its propositions, methodological implications and its use, authors also provide links to other related conceptual frameworks and key authoritative primary and secondary references.

We asked ASIST 2003 SIG USE Symposium participants to write a 1,500 word contribution to the book about the theory they had presented at the symposium. All authors received several versions of the list of theories with the names of their contributors, and have helped us with suggestions for other theories and authors to be included. This collaborative snowballing approach to content development resulted in a comprehensive guide to the current conceptual frameworks in information behavior research. All entries underwent editorial peer review and, where necessary, assessment by other subject experts.

Individual entries in this guide are preceded by three introductory papers. The contribution by Marcia Bates expands upon her keynote address presented at the 2003 SIG USE Research Symposium in which she defines and explains the key theoretical concepts in LIS-related information behavior research. Brenda Dervin's contribution explicates the connections and mutual influences between theory and method. T. D. Wilson's engaging overview describes the over two-decade-long process of continuing growth and development of his theoretical model of information behavior. Together the three papers capture the key concepts, the theory-method connections and the process of theory development that set the context and provide a thoughtful introduction to the individual entries in the guide.

The Contents provide an overall picture of the guide. Following the introductory chapters, the individual entries are organized alphabetically by title. An integrated index provides access to the content by theory title, author, names of the individuals who developed the theories, broad information behavior concepts addressed and, where appropriate, methods associated with the use of the theories. References included in each of the entries point the reader to further resources.

As a book about information behavior, we felt it was important to structure the text so that *Theories of Information Behavior* could address the many potential information needs, management, seeking, use, and giving strategies that individuals from diverse contexts might bring to the book. Thus, for example, researchers wanting to know how a particular theory has been used in information behavior research could use the index and/or table of contents to find entries with references and to identify selected relevant studies. Doctoral students trying to identify a theory or model to use in their research could use the index to access theory by broad information behavior concepts or associated methods. Practitioners seeking to enrich their work through theoretical understanding could read all or selected relevant portions of the book. Researchers from outside of LIS, seeking a concise, clear, and authoritative description of some information behavior theory, could use the index to find a particular entry.

We welcome suggestions for improvement of this guide. In particular, we would appreciate recommendations for additional entries, updates to existing entries and new potential contributing authors. We also invite feedback about the content of entries and their structure; the organization of the overall guide; and access tools to facilitate the use its use. A page on the ASIST SIG USE Web site (www.asis.org/SIG/SIGUSE/) is our venue for input and other synergistic activities that will improve future editions and further advance the use of theory in information behavior research.

Karen E. Fisher
The Information School,
University of Washington, Seattle, WA

Sanda Erdelez
School of Information Science & Learning Technologies,
University of Missouri, Columbia, MO

Lynne (E. F.) McKechnie
Faculty of Information & Media Studies,
University of Western Ontario, London, ON

Case, D. O. (2002). *Looking for information: A survey of research on information seeking, needs, and behavior*. San Diego, CA: Academic Press.

Chatman, E. (1996). The impoverished life-world of outsiders. *Journal of the American Society for Information Science, 47*, 193–206.

Pettigrew, K., Fidel, R., & Bruce, H. (2001). Conceptual frameworks in information behavior. *Annual Review of Information Science and Technology, 35*, 43–78.

Pettigrew, K., & McKechnie, L. (2001). The use of theory in information science research. *Journal of the American Society for Information Science & Technology, 52*, 62–73.

Wilson, T. D. (1999). Models in information behaviour research. *Journal of Documentation, 55*(3), 249–270.

Wilson, T. D. (2000). Human information behavior. *Informing Science, 3*(2), 49–55.

Chapter 1

An Introduction to Metatheories, Theories, and Models

Marcia J. Bates
Department of Information Studies
University of California, Los Angeles, USA
mjbates@ucla.edu

INTRODUCTION

The objective of this chapter is to provide a general introduction to some key theoretical concepts of use in library and information science (LIS) research. First, the three terms in the title—metatheory, theory, and model—are defined and discussed. Next, an extended example is provided of a case in which a researcher might consider and test various models or theories in information-seeking research. Next, metatheories are considered at greater length, and the distinction is made between nomothetic and idiographic metatheories. Finally, 13 metatheoretical approaches in wide use in LIS are described. Explanatory texts are referenced, as well as example studies using each approach. The discussion is necessarily brief and simplifying.

DEFINITIONS

It is important, first, to distinguish the terms metatheory, theory, and model. These concepts are often confused and used interchangeably. They should not be, as understanding the distinctions among them can help in thinking about theoretical aspects of LIS.

- *Metatheory*: A theory concerned with the investigation, analysis, or description of theory itself. (Webster's Unabridged Dictionary)

1

- *Theory*: (a) The body of generalizations and principles developed in association with practice in a field of activity (as medicine, music) and forming its content as an intellectual discipline.... (Webster's Unabridged Dictionary) (b) A system of assumptions, accepted principles, and rules of procedure devised to analyze, predict, or otherwise explain the nature or behavior of a specified set of phenomena. (American Heritage Dictionary, 1969). (See also Reynolds, 1971.)
- *Model*: A tentative ideational structure used as a testing device.... (American Heritage Dictionary, 1969). (See also Lave & March, 1975.)

Metatheory can be seen as the philosophy behind the theory, the fundamental set of ideas about how phenomena of interest in a particular field should be thought about and researched (see also Wagner & Berger, 1985; Vakkari, 1997). The term has not been used much in LIS, but it is rapidly becoming more important to our understanding. In earlier years, the underlying philosophy behind research in the field could be identified as coming from few directions—from a general humanities approach and a general scientific approach. In recent years, however, more and more metatheoretical approaches have been developed within the field and borrowed from other fields. The result has been that we now have a confusion of many approaches competing for attention.

The concept of a metatheory has a lot of overlap with the term "paradigm," which was given its modern understanding in science by Thomas Kuhn (1996). In the terms used here, Kuhn considered a paradigm to be the metatheory, the theory, the methodology, and the ethos, all combined, of a discipline or specialty. So paradigm would have a broader meaning than metatheory. At the same time, metatheory is absolutely core to any paradigm, and is defining of a paradigm in many senses.

Theory, as defined in definition (a), can be thought of as the entire body of generalizations and principles developed for a field, as in "the theory of LIS." Second, and more of interest for this paper, is the concept of a single theory. A theory is a system of assumptions, principles, and relationships posited to explain a specified set of phenomena. Theories often carry with them an implicit metatheory and methodology, as in the "rules of procedure" in definition (b). However, for most purposes, the core meaning of theory centers around the idea of a developed understanding, an explanation, for some phenomenon.

Models are of great value in the development of theory. They are a kind of proto-theory, a tentative proposed set of relationships, which can then be tested for validity. Developing a model can often help in working through one's thinking about a subject of interest. Indeed, there is not always a sharp dividing line between a model and a theory about the same phenomenon. Models sometimes stand as theoretical beacons for years, guiding and directing research in a field, before the research finally matures to the point of producing something closer to a true theory.

In science, a classic sequence of development has been characterized as "description, prediction, explanation." That is, the first task when studying a new phenomenon is to describe that phenomenon. It is difficult to think about something if you know very little about it. So description comes first. Second, once one knows something about a phenomenon, it should be possible to predict relationships, processes, or sequences associated with the phenomenon. Third, based on the testing of predictions, one should be able to develop an explanation of the phenomenon, that is, a theory. Theories can always be overturned by later theories; even when a theory has been well tested it is always possible that later research will provide a more thorough, deeper explanation for the phenomenon of interest.

Models are most useful at the description and prediction stages of understanding a phenomenon. Only when we develop an explanation for a phenomenon can we properly say we have a theory. Consequently, most of "theory" in LIS is really still at the modeling stage.

In the next section, an example proto-theory, or model, is analyzed, and means of testing the model are discussed. However, some metatheories explicitly eschew the value and possibility of generalizing the studied reality of a situation in order to create a theory. Ethnomethodology, for example, "never bought into the business of theorizing, it was iconoclastic, it would not theorize foundational matters" (Button, 1991, pp. 4–5). Rather, ethnomethodologists "generally decline to theorize about the social world, preferring instead to go out and study it" (Ritzer, 2000, p. 75). At a minimum in the following discussion, one must assume a metatheoretical position that allows for and legitimates models and theories. So the following discussion cannot be applicable to every possible metatheoretical position.

EXAMPLE USING THESE TERMS

Let us take, as an example, the Principle of Least Effort. This is probably the most solid result in all of information-seeking research. Specifically, *we have found that people invest little in seeking information, preferring easy-to-use, accessible sources to sources of known high quality that are less easy to use and/or less accessible.* Poole (1985) did a meta-analysis of 51 information-seeking studies, in which he found this proposition strongly confirmed. (He also has a good discussion of theory in LIS.)

So ease of use and accessibility of information seem to be more important to people than quality of information. But what is the *explanation* for this phenomenon? Why are people unwilling to invest that little bit of extra energy in order to get information that they themselves would acknowledge is of better quality? We do not really have a theory. We have described the phenomenon; further, we have found this to be the case in many different environments with many different types of people, so it is a result that appears to be highly generalizable. Consequently, we can also confidently make predictions from these results. For example, we can predict that when we study a new group of people, they will probably also invest little energy in information seeking, and prefer easy-to-use, accessible resources.

So, through description and prediction we have modeled the Principle of Least Effort. Though we often represent models in diagrams that display relationships, we do not have to do so. In this case, our model can be described in a sentence (see the italicized statement above). (For some examples of models presented in diagram form, see Bates, 2002; Gaines, Chen, & Shaw, 1997; Metoyer-Duran, 1991; Wang & White, 1999; Wilson, 1999.) So the Principle of Least Effort is an observed behavior, one we have observed widely enough to confidently model as a principle. But we do not yet have an explanation—so we do not yet have a theory.

How can we move this research from being a model to being a theory? First, we can hypothesize various possible explanations based on work we find elsewhere in the field or in other fields. Here are some I have thought of:

1) People "satisfice" in all realms of life, including information seeking. The idea of satisficing comes from Simon (1976), who argued that in decision making, people make a good enough decision to meet their needs, and do not necessarily consider all possible, or knowable, options. Translated to the language of LIS, for example, using Dervin's concept of "Sense-Making" (Dervin, 1983, 1999), we could hypothesize that people make

sense of their situations based on what they know and can learn easily. Their Sense-Making need only be adequate to continue with life; it does not need to be so perfect or extensive as to enable them to make sense of everything.

2) People underestimate the value of what they do not know, and over-estimate the value of what they do know. People have difficulty imagin-ing what the new information would be that they do not know, while what they do know is vivid and real to them. Consequently, they under-invest in information seeking. See Gilovich, Griffin, & Kahneman (2002) and Kahneman & Tversky (2000) for work on distortions in deci-sion making and choice.

3) Gaining new knowledge may be emotionally threatening in some cases. Gregory Bateson once described what he called "value-seeking" and "information-seeking" (Ruesch & Bateson, 1968, pp. 178–179). In value-seeking, a person has an idea in mind of something that he or she wants. Suppose one wants some eggs and toast to eat, for example. One then goes out into the world, does various things involving chickens, grain, cooking, and baking, with the end result that one has a breakfast of eggs and toast. Thus, one has done things to parts of the world in order to make the world match the plan one has in mind. In information seek-ing, on the other hand, according to Bateson, the directionality is reversed; one acquires information from the world in order to impress it on one's own mind.

However, new knowledge can always bring surprises, sometimes uncomfortable ones. If "we are what we know," if our sense of self is based, in part, on our body of knowledge of the world, then to change that knowledge may be threatening to our sense of self.

4) Information is not tangible, and objects are. Intangible things seem less real to us, therefore less valuable. Consequently, we invest more in acquiring tangible than intangible things.

Each hypothesis above is not a complete explanation. For instance, *why* do people satisfice? However, if we were to test this satisficing hypothesis and we learned that people do satisfice in information seek-ing, we would have an explanation that tells us more than just the *observed fact* of least effort. We would then be able to place this result in the context of all the other research in other disciplines that has observed that people satisfice in a variety of circumstances, and could then draw on that research to develop tentative explanations (tentative theories) that go deeper than the satisficing explanation alone.

In fact, Simon's satisficing may be, in effect, another name for Zipf's Principle of Least Effort (1949). Poole (1985) believed his results fit well with Zipf's earlier work. Zipf had a more extensively conceptualized understanding of least effort, one that constitutes a preliminary explanation, i.e., theory, and which contributes to a better understanding of least effort than we usually articulate in LIS. To Zipf, according to Poole, least effort was technically the "least average rate of probable work" (Poole, 1985, p. 90). That is, people do not just minimize current work associated with some activity, because they could eventually do a total of much more work in the end. Rather, they make a considered estimate of all likely work associated with a given effort, now and in the future, and do the amount of work now that they estimate will best reduce their overall effort, now and later combined (Poole, 1985).

How could we test these four hypotheses listed? In each case one or more studies could be designed in order to attempt to discover which, if any, of these explanations is operating in people's information seeking. For example, in an experimental approach to Hypothesis 2, people could be placed in a realistic situation where they have certain information and do not have other information. They have to expend units in order to "purchase" additional clues or hints to solve the test problem. There are other ways they can expend those same units. The experimental subjects assign their units according to their best judgment. Afterward, they are given the information they did not have earlier. Do they now rate higher or lower the value of the information that they had not had in the test situation? On what basis do they assign value at each step of the experiment?

In an observational approach to Hypothesis 3, people could be studied in real information-seeking situations—suppose in three different types of situations: 1) finding information about a disease diagnosed in a family member, 2) researching a paper in a required course on a topic of little interest, 3) finding out more about a hobby or avocation (Hartel, in press). Searching could be observed and the subjects interviewed about their feeling reactions to their situation and the acts of information seeking in which they engage. Do they avoid new information or seek it eagerly? Are there signs of anxiety and threat around discovering new information? Do people have different responses to the different types of situation, and why?

In the example above, we started with a descriptive finding—the widely observed tendency of people to prefer easy-to-use and accessible information sources over harder to get, higher quality sources of information. This

"Principle of Least Effort" has been so widely observed that we were able to make confident predictions about where else it might appear as well. But we still had no explanation, no theory as to why this phenomenon occurs (except possibly in Zipf's original research, 1949). We hypothesized four possible explanations, and considered ways in which these theories could be tested. Testing might then lead to further tentative theories that would explain this phenomenon still more deeply.

SOURCES OF METATHEORIES

In the preceding section much was made of models and theories. What about metatheories? Where do they fit in? As Kuhn observed, in most natural sciences most of the time, there is a single predominant paradigm out of which researchers identify and test research questions. Metatheories about the nature of research and the desirable methods for each discipline are embedded in those paradigms. In the social sciences, however, it is more common to have a general paradigm for a field, which describes the domain of interest for that discipline—the operations of the mind for psychology, for example—but more than one metatheory, or philosophy of research, competing for the loyalties of researchers within that discipline. In the case of psychology, in the 1960s and 1970s there was a split between an older, behaviorist metatheory for the study of psychology (Skinner, 1992 reprint), and a newer, information processing approach (Chomsky, 1959; Anderson, 1995). The split went so deep that the latter approach came to be known by a different name, cognitive science. Over the last 10 to 15 years another metatheory, by the name of evolutionary psychology, has challenged the information processing approach (Barkow, Cosmides, & Tooby, 1992).

In the sciences, a new paradigm usually revolutionizes the field, that is, the new paradigm reconfigures all prior learning around a new core metatheory and body of research results. Examples have been plate tectonic theory in geology and molecular biology in biology. In the social sciences, however, several metatheories may continue side by side. Sometimes a metatheory will simply die out and other times it will grow and change, and still compete for the interest of researchers.

In the late 20th and early 21st centuries, there has been a proliferation of metatheories in the social sciences generally, and, certainly, in LIS as well. In our society, in general, old ways of thinking are breaking up and breaking down; supposed eternal verities are falling right and left, from the fall of the Berlin Wall and all that it meant about rigid social structures in East and West, to social boundaries that formerly split communities by race, gender, religion, and other long-standing, stable divisions. Even the eternal verities of forms of writing—the book, the journal, the newspaper article—are being shaken up in the new world of Internet information.

Under these circumstances, we should perhaps not be surprised that basic metatheoretical assumptions about what research is or should be are also breaking down and being challenged by newer approaches. I think it is also the case that different people have different cognitive styles, certain ways of thinking that are natural to them. We are all drawn to the sort of research and thinking that works best for us, that is most harmonious with the way our minds work. Wagner & Berger (1985) call these "orienting strategies."

In earlier, more rigid times, it tended to be the case that only certain orienting strategies were considered legitimate in a given field at one time. Heaven help the psychology doctoral student who wanted to take a qualitative approach back in the heyday of behaviorism, for example. Many talented people were forced out, simply because they had the wrong cognitive style for the intellectual spirit of the times. Now, there is generally more tolerance for different approaches, although there is still some tendency to argue that one's own preferred approach is the one true or best philosophy of research, and everything else is bunk.

I believe that the intensity of these struggles arises, in part, out of the different cognitive styles people have, which then draw them to corresponding different orienting strategies. It just feels so right to follow one's preferred approach that it just must be the case that the other guys are all wrong. However, I believe that every orienting strategy brings us something valuable, if we are only open to learn what it has to offer.

Thus, it is likely that there will continue to be several approaches in LIS to studying the phenomena of interest to our field. When one takes up a particular approach, however, it is important to understand the philosophy and some of the history behind the development of a particular research approach. That way, there will be a smooth and logically consistent passage from philosophy to theory and methodology.

THE NOMOTHETIC-IDIOGRAPHIC CONTRAST

First, we need to make a distinction between what are known as nomothetic and idiographic approaches to research. These two are the most fundamental orienting strategies of all.

- *Nomothetic* — "Relating to or concerned with the study or discovery of the general laws underlying something" (Oxford English Dictionary).

- *Idiographic* — "Concerned with the individual, pertaining to or descriptive of single and unique facts and processes" (Oxford English Dictionary).

The first approach is the one that is fundamental to the sciences. Science research is always looking to establish the general law, principle, or theory. The fundamental assumption in the sciences is that behind all the blooming, buzzing confusion of the real world, there are patterns or processes of a more general sort, an understanding of which enables prediction and explanation of the particulars.

The idiographic approach, on the other hand, cherishes the particulars, and insists that true understanding can be reached only be assembling and assessing those particulars. The end result is a nuanced description and assessment of the unique facts of a situation or historical event, in which themes and tendencies may be discovered, but rarely any general laws. This approach is the one that is fundamental to the humanities. (See an excellent discussion of these science/humanities theoretical differences in Sandstrom & Sandstrom, 1995; see also discussion in Bates, 1994.)

For the last couple of centuries, the social sciences have been the crossroads where these two approaches intersect, the ground over which the nomothetic and idiographic orienting strategies have fought. One of the common narratives of the 20th century was of the academic social science department, say, political science or economics, being invaded by newcomers with a mathematical or scientific approach to their subject, in opposition to the prior discursive, idiographic approach. In the late 20th century, that narrative was often reversed, when postmodernist theorists came into departments and superseded the more nomothetically oriented researchers who had been there previously.

LIS has not been immune to these struggles, and it would not be hard to identify departments or journals where this conflict is being carried out. My position is that both of these orienting strategies are enormously productive for human understanding. Any LIS department that definitively rejects one or the other approach makes a foolish choice. It is more difficult to maintain openness to these two positions, rather than insisting on selecting one or the other, but it is also ultimately more productive and rewarding for the progress of the field.

METATHEORIES IN LIS

The purpose of this section is to present brief descriptions of a number of the more popular metatheories that are being expressed in LIS these days. The arraying of these approaches in a common framework may be helpful for beginners in understanding the range of research approaches taken in LIS.

There are many metatheories operating in the field currently. There is disagreement between proponents of various metatheories, and there are also various interpretations and descriptions of any one metatheory. Furthermore, researchers become interested in new approaches as they appear in the field, and may change metatheories and methodologies during their career. Examples given below should be seen as just that, examples; researchers should not be assumed to be always unequivocally associated with a single metatheoretical approach.

It should also be understood that what is presented below is a *personal, idiosyncratic, and simplifying* selection. See Cool (2001); Hjørland (1998, 2000); Pettigrew, Fidel, & Bruce, (2001); and Talja, Tuominen, & Savolainen (in press) for other categorizations of metatheories.

For expositions and debates on metatheory and methodology in LIS, see Bar-Ilan & Peritz (2002); Bates, J. A. (2004); Bates, M. J. (1999); Case (2002); Crabtree et al. (2000); Dervin (1999, 2003); Dick (1995, 1999); Ellis (1992); Fidel (1993); Given & Leckie (2003); McClure & Hernon (1991); McKechnie (2000); Pettigrew & McKechnie, 2001; Powell (1997, 1999); Sandstrom & Sandstrom (1995, 1998); Sonnenwald & Iivonen (1999); Talja (1999, 2001); Thomas & Nyce (1998); Trosow (2001); Wang (1999); and Westbrook (1994).

With the description of each metatheory below, example applications are provided where possible, and textual sources explaining or elaborating on the various metatheories are also suggested. The listing begins with idiographic approaches in numbers 1–5, mixed approaches in numbers 6 and 7, and primarily nomothetic approaches in numbers 8–13.

1) A *historical* approach, in which understanding of the present is seen to arise out of an understanding of the past social, political, and economic events and processes, which have led to current conditions. For historical methods and issues, see Barzun & Graff's classic work (1992), as well as Appleby, Hunt, & Jacob (1994), and Rayward (1996). For examples of historical research in LIS, see Hildenbrand (1996), Maack (2000), and Wiegand & Davis (1994).

2) A *constructivist* approach, arising out of education and sociology, in which individuals are seen as actively constructing an understanding of their worlds, heavily influenced by the social world(s) in which they are operating. According to Kuhlthau (1993), educational constructivist theory built on the work of Dewey (1933, 1944), Kelly (1963), and Vygotsky (1978), among others, while, according to Ritzer (2000), sociological constructivist theory arose from Schutz (English translation 1967, original 1932), Berger & Luckmann (1990 reprint), and the closely related ethnomethodological work of Garfinkel (1967). Major proponents of this approach in LIS have been Dervin (1983, 1999) and Kuhlthau (1993).

3) A *constructionist or discourse-analytic* approach, with both humanities and social sciences roots, in which it is assumed that the discourse of a society predominately conditions the responses of individuals within that society, including the social understanding of information. According to Talja, Tuominen, & Savolainen (in press), constructionism sees "language as constitutive for the construction of selves and the formation of meanings." Further, "We produce and organize social reality together by using language." This metatheory arose from the work of Bakhtin (Holquist, 2002) and Foucault (1972), among others. Frohmann (1994) and Talja (1999) have expounded on the use of this approach in LIS. This approach has been applied in LIS by Budd & Raber (1996), Frohmann (2001), and Talja (2001), among others. A non-LIS, but highly relevant example can be seen in Hayles (1999).

4) A *philosophical-analytic* approach, in which the classical techniques of the discipline of philosophy, namely extremely rigorous analysis of ideas and propositions, are brought to bear on information-related matters. Certainly, the field of philosophy itself expresses and represents many different theoretical orientations and metatheories. However, despite the many differences among philosophers, there is a fairly universal and well-understood form of analysis and argumentation that is characteristic of the discipline as a whole. Philosophers who have come into LIS, or philosophers outside the field who have addressed LIS-related questions inevitably bring with them this mode of analysis and discourse. For a classic example of this, read Patrick Wilson's still-relevant discussion on the nature of the subject of a book (Wilson, 1968, pp. 69–92). See also Blair (2003), Cooper (1971), Dretske (1981), Fuller (2002), and Wilson (1977, 1983).

5) A *critical theory* approach, in which the hidden power relations and patterns of domination within a society are revealed and debunked

(Ritzer, 2000, p. 140ff). Michael Harris (1986) was an early practitioner in LIS. More recently, others have joined the debate, critiquing the roles of librarians, the kinds of research done in LIS, and so on. See Carmichael (1998), Chu (1999), Day (2001), Roma Harris (1992), Pawley (1998), Radford (2003), and Wiegand (1999).

6) An *ethnographic* approach, originating in anthropology, but now used throughout the social sciences, involving the use of a variety of field techniques, such as observation, documentation, and interviewing. These techniques are intended to enable the researcher to become immersed in a culture, identify its many elements, and begin to shape an understanding of the experience and world views of the people studied (Fielding, 1993). In LIS, see, for example, Chatman (1992), Kwasnik (1992), Pettigrew (2000), and Wilson & Streatfield (1981). A related, popular approach is grounded theory development (Glaser & Strauss, 1967). See Ellis (1993), Ellis & Haugan (1997), Kwasnik (1991), and Mellon (1986). Sandstrom & Sandstrom (1995) discuss the ways in which both nomothetically and ideographically oriented researchers have used ethnographic methods.

7) A *socio-cognitive* approach (Hjørland, 2002), in which both the individual's thinking and the social and documentary domain in which the individual operates are seen to influence the use of information. See also Jacob & Shaw (1998). Paisley presaged this viewpoint in his 1968 "Information needs and uses" review of scientists working within 10 social and information system contexts (Paisley, 1968). More recently, see Case (1991), Covi (1999), and Kwasnik (1991). The nature of context has been discussed in detail by Dervin (1997), and the nature of situation by Cool (2001). Because of the centrality in information studies of 1) information, 2) information technology, and 3) people's use of these, the interplay among these three elements is arguably at the heart of most social research in information studies.

Hjørland & Albrechtsen (1995) call the analysis of information and its social formation in a community of thought "domain analysis." Other roots of the domain analytic approach can be seen in the areas of historical and descriptive bibliography in librarianship (Bowers, 1994; Updike, 2001), as well as in recent developments around genre theory (Berkenkotter & Huckin, 1993; Vaughan & Dillon, 1998; Orlikowski & Yates, 1994).

The field of social informatics also focuses on the interactions among people, social environments, information technology, and documentary forms. See Bishop & Star's review (1996), as well as work by Kling &

McKim (2000), and Palmer (2001). This metatheory shares some of both the nomothetic and idiographic orientations.

8) A *cognitive* approach, arising out of cognitive science, in which the thinking of the individual person operating in the world is the dominating focus of research on information seeking, retrieval, and use (Bates, 1979; Belkin, 1990; Belkin, Oddy, & Brooks, 1982; Ellis, 1989; Ingwersen, 1992, 1999). See Newell & Simon (1972) and Anderson (1995) for expositions of this approach.

9) A *bibliometric* approach, in which the analysis of the statistical properties of information is seen to provide understanding of value for both the design of information provision and the theoretical understanding of social processes around information, including historical processes. The earliest theory was provided by Bradford (1948) and Zipf (1949). More recent major work has been done by Brookes (1968), Price (1986), Small (1999), and White & McCain (1998), among others. Much of this work has been made possible through the existence of citation indexes (Garfield, 1983).

10) A *physical* approach to information transfer, dating principally from the 1950s and 1960s interest in signaling and physical communication generated by the development of Claude Shannon's information theory (Cherry, 1966; Miller, 1951; Pierce, 1961; Shannon & Weaver, 1975; Wiener, 1961).

11) An *engineering* approach to information, in which it is assumed that human needs and uses of information can best be accommodated by successive development and testing of ingenious systems and devices to improve information retrieval and services. The fundamental test of validity for the engineering approach is an operational one, namely, "Does it work?" Thus a major method of developing new knowledge in engineering is through "proof of concept" work, in which an experimental system or device is developed and tested, improved, tested some more, and so on. For theory of engineering, see Dahlbom, Beckman, & Nilsson (2002) and Simon (1981). For applications in LIS, see Croft & Thompson (1987), Hendry & Harper (1997), Kraft & Petry (1997), Over (2001), and Salton & McGill (1983). Variations on this approach are found in artificial intelligence (Minsky, 1968; Russell & Norvig, 1995) and natural language processing (Allen, 1995; Chowdury, 2003; Liddy et al., 1993).

12) A *user-centered design* approach, in which the development and human testing of information organization and information system designs is seen as a path to both scientific understanding and improved

information access. User-centered design takes the "Does it work?" engineering question one step farther, and asks, "Does it work so well that people can concentrate on what they are doing rather than on operating the system or device?" Classic work in this area is by Norman (1990) and Nielsen (1993). A great deal of design work relevant to LIS goes on in human-computer interaction research (Carroll, 2002; Rogers, 2004). A number of people in LIS focus on user-centered design, for example, Ackerman (2000), Bates (1990, 2002), Dillon (1994, 1995), Hildreth (1989), and Marchionini (1995). See also Marchionini & Komlodi (1998).

13) An *evolutionary* approach, in which the insights of biology and evolutionary psychology are brought to bear on information-related phenomena (Barkow, Cosmides, & Tooby, 1992; Wright, 1994). This approach is just beginning to appear in LIS. See Bates (in press), Madden (2004), and Sandstrom (1994, 1999).

Each of the metatheories above is some part philosophy and some part methodology. However, the historical, philosophical-analytic, ethnographic, bibliometric, engineering, and design approaches are primarily methodology with some philosophy attached, while the others, the constructivist, discourse-analytic, critical theory, socio-cognitive, cognitive, physical, and evolutionary approaches are driven more by philosophical and theoretical orientations, which have methodological implications.

SUMMARY AND CONCLUSIONS

The objective of this chapter has been to introduce the concepts of metatheory, theory, and model, and distinguish them for the purposes of doing research in information seeking. An example result, the Principle of Least Effort, has been analyzed and discussed in relation to the three concepts. Methods of bringing this model closer to the status of a theory have been suggested.

The sources of metatheories in the social sciences have been discussed, and the nomothetic-idiographic distinction has been explained. Finally, 13 metatheories operating in LIS have been described. Sources for each metatheory and examples of its application have been presented.

ACKNOWLEDGMENTS

I wish to thank Karen Fisher and Sanda Erdelez for inviting me to present this paper, and Jenna Hartel for her very helpful suggestions on the manuscript.

Ackerman, M. S. (2000). The intellectual challenge of CSCW: The gap between social requirements and technical feasibility. *Human-Computer Interaction, 15*(2–3), 179–203.

Allen, J. F. (1995). *Natural language understanding* (2nd ed.). Menlo-Park, CA: Benjamin-Cummings.

American Heritage Dictionary of the English Language. (1969). Boston: Houghton-Mifflin.

Anderson, J. R. (1995). *Cognitive psychology and its implications* (4th ed.). New York: W. H. Freeman.

Appleby, J., Hunt, L., & Jacob, M. (1994). *Telling the truth about history.* New York: Norton.

Bar-Ilan, J., & Peritz, B. C. (2002). Informetric theories and methods for exploring the Internet: An analytical survey of recent research literature. *Library Trends, 50*(3), 371–392.

Barkow, J. H., Cosmides, L., & Tooby, J., Eds. (1992). *The adapted mind: Evolutionary psychology and the generation of culture.* New York: Oxford University Press.

Barzun, J., & Graff, H. F. (1992). *The modern researcher* (5th ed.). Fort Worth, TX: Harcourt Brace Jovanovich College Publishers.

Bates, J. A. (2004). Use of narrative interviewing in everyday information behavior research. *Library & Information Science Research, 26*(1), 15–28.

Bates, M. J. (1979). Information search tactics. *Journal of the American Society for Information Science, 30*(4), 205–214.

Bates, M. J. (1990). Where should the person stop and the information search interface start? *Information Processing & Management, 26*(5), 575–591.

Bates, M. J. (1994). The design of databases and other information resources for humanities scholars: The Getty Online Searching Project report no. 4. *Online and CD-ROM Review, 18*(6), 331–340.

Bates, M. J. (1999). The invisible substrate of information science. *Journal of the American Society for Information Science, 50*, 1043–1050.

Bates, M. J. (2002). The cascade of interactions in the digital library interface. *Information Processing and Management, 38*, 381–400.

Bates, M. J. (in press). Information, knowledge, data: An evolutionary framework for information science. *Journal of the American Society for Information Science and Technology.*

Belkin, N. J. (1990). The cognitive viewpoint in information science. *Journal of Information Science, 16*(1), 11–15.

Belkin, N. J., Oddy, R. N., & Brooks, H. M. (1982). ASK for Information Retrieval: Part I. Background and Theory. *Journal of Documentation, 38*(2), 61–71.

Berger, P. L., & Luckmann, T. (1990 reprint). *The social construction of reality: A treatise in the sociology of knowledge.* New York: Anchor Books.

Berkenkotter, C., & Huckin, T. N. (1993). Rethinking genre from a socio-cognitive perspective. *Written Communication, 10*(4), 475–509.

Bishop, A. P., & Star, S. L. (1996). Social Informatics of digital library use and infrastructure. *Annual Review of Information Science and Technology, 31*, 301–401.

Blair, D. C. (2003). Information retrieval and the philosophy of language. *Annual Review of Information Science and Technology, 37*, 3–50.

Bowers, F. T. (1994). *Principles of bibliographical description.* New Castle, DE: Oak Knoll Press.

Bradford, S. C. (1948). *Documentation.* London: C. Lockwood.

Brookes, B. C. (1968). Derivation and applications of the Bradford-Zipf distribution. *Journal of Documentation, 24*(4), 247–265.

Budd, J. M., & Raber, D. (1996). Discourse analysis: Method and application in the study of information. *Information Processing & Management, 32*(2), 217–226.

Button, G. (1991). Introduction: Ethnomethodology and the foundational respecification of the human sciences. In G. Button, (Ed.), *Ethnomethodology and the human sciences.* (p. 1–9). Cambridge, UK: Cambridge University Press.

Carmichael, J. V. J. (1998). *Daring to find our names: The search for lesbigay library history.* Westport, CT: Greenwood Press.

Carroll, J. M., Ed. (2002). *Human-computer interaction in the new millennium.* New York: ACM Press.

Case, D. O. (1991). Conceptual organization and retrieval of text by historians: The role of memory and metaphor. *Journal of the American Society for Information Science, 42*(9), 657–668.

Case, D. O. (2002). *Looking for information: A survey of research on information seeking, needs, and behavior.* New York: Academic Press.

Chatman, E. A. (1992). *The information world of retired women.* Westport, CT: Greenwood Press.

Cherry, C. (1966). *On human communication: A review, a survey, and a criticism* (2nd ed.). Cambridge, MA: MIT Press.

Chomsky, N. (1959). Review of B. F. Skinner, Verbal behavior. *Language, 35*, 26–57.

Chowdury, G. G. (2003). Natural language processing. *Annual Review of Information Science and Technology, 37*, 51–89.

Chu, C. M. (1999). Literacy practices of linguistic minorities: Sociolinguistic issues and implications for literacy services. *Library Quarterly, 69*(3), 339–359.

Cool, C. (2001). The concept of situation in information science. *Annual Review of Information Science and Technology, 35*, 5–42.

Cooper, W. S. (1971). Definition of relevance for information retrieval. *Information Storage and Retrieval, 7,* 19–37.

Covi, L. M. (1999). Material mastery: Situating digital library use in university research practices. *Information Processing & Management, 35*(3), 293–316.

Crabtree, A., Nichols, D. M., O'Brien, J., Rouncefield, M., & Twidale, M. B. (2000). Ethnomethodologically informed ethnography and information system design. *Journal of the American Society for Information Science, 51,* 666–682.

Croft, W. B., & Thompson, R. H. (1987). I3R—A new approach to the design of document-retrieval systems. *Journal of the American Society for Information Science, 38*(6), 389–404.

Dahlbom, B., Beckman, S., & Nilsson, G. B. (2002). *Artifacts and artificial science.* Stockholm: Almqvist & Wiksell International.

Day, R. E. (2001). *The modern invention of information.* Carbondale, IL: Southern Illinois University Press.

Dervin, B. (1983). Information as a user construct: The relevance of perceived information needs to synthesis and interpretation. In S. A. Ward & L .J. Reed (Eds.), *Knowledge structure and use: Implications for synthesis and interpretation.* (pp. 155–183). Philadelphia: Temple University Press.

Dervin, B. (1997). Given a context by any other name: Methodological tools for taming the unruly beast. In: Vakkari, P.; Savolainen, R.; & Dervin, B., (Eds.), *Information seeking in context: Proceedings of an international conference on research in information needs, seeking and use in different contexts* (pp. 13–38). London: Taylor Graham.

Dervin, B., (1999). On studying information seeking methodologically: The implications of connecting metatheory to method. *Information Processing and Management, 35*(6): 727–750.

Dervin, B. (2003). Human studies and user studies: A call for methodological inter-disciplinarity. *Information Research, 9*(I), paper 166. Retrieved March 12, 2004, from http://InformationR.net/ir/9-I/paper166.html

Dewey, J. (1933). *How we think.* Lexington, MA: Heath.

Dewey, J. (1944). *Democracy and education.* New York: Macmillan.

Dick, A. L. (1995). Library and information science as a social science: Neutral and normative conceptions. *The Library Quarterly, 65*(2), 216–235.

Dick, A. L. (1999). Epistemological positions and library and information science. *Library Quarterly, 69*(3), 305–323.

Dillon, A. (1994). *Designing usable electronic text: Ergonomic aspects of human information usage.* London: Taylor & Francis.

Dillon, A. (1995). Artifacts as theories: Convergence through user-centered design. *Proceedings of the ASIS Annual Meeting, 32:* 208–210.

Dretske, F. I. (1981). *Knowledge and the flow of information.* Cambridge, MA: MIT Press.

Ellis, D. (1989). A behavioural approach to information retrieval system design. *Journal of Documentation, 45*(3), 171–212.

Ellis, D. (1992). The physical and cognitive paradigms in information retrieval research. *Journal of Documentation, 48*(1), 45–64.

Ellis, D. (1993). Modeling the information-seeking patterns of academic researchers: A grounded theory approach. *The Library Quarterly, 63*(4), 469–486.

Ellis, D., & Haugan, M. (1997). Modeling the information seeking patterns of engineers and research scientists in an industrial environment. *Journal of Documentation, 53*(4), 384–403.

Fidel, R. (1993). Qualitative methods in information retrieval research. *Library & Information Science Research, 15*(3), 219–247.

Fielding, N. (1993). Ethnography. In N. Gilbert, Ed., *Researching social life.* (pp. 154–186). London: Sage.

Foucault, M. (1972). *The archaeology of knowledge.* London: Routledge.

Frohmann, B. (1994). Discourse analysis as a research method in library and information science. *Library & Information Science Research, 16*(2), 119–138.

Frohmann, B. (2001). Discourse and documentation: Some implications for pedagogy and research. *Journal of Education for Library and Information Science, 42*(1), 12–26.

Fuller, S. (2002). *Social epistemology* (2nd ed.). Bloomington: Indiana University Press.

Gaines, B. R., Chen, L. L. J., & Shaw, M. L. G. (1997). Modeling the human factors of scholarly communities supported through the Internet and World Wide Web. *Journal of the American Society for Information Science, 48*(11), 987–1003.

Garfield, E. (1983). *Citation indexing: Its theory and application in science, technology, and humanities.* Philadelphia: ISI Press.

Garfinkel, H. (1967). *Studies in ethnomethodology.* Englewood Cliffs, NJ: Prentice-Hall.

Gilovich, T., Griffin, D., & Kahneman, D., Eds. (2002). *Heuristics and biases: The psychology of intuitive judgment.* New York: Cambridge University Press.

Given, L. M., & Leckie, G. J. (2003). "Sweeping" the library: Mapping the social activity space of the public library. *Library & Information Science Research, 25*(4), 365–385.

Glaser, B., & Strauss, A. (1967). *The discovery of grounded theory: Strategies for qualitative research.* Chicago: Aldine.

Harris, M. H. (1986). State, class and cultural reproduction: Toward a theory of library service in the United States. *Advances in Librarianship, 14,* 211–252.

Harris, R. M. (1992). *Librarianship: The erosion of a woman's profession.* Norwood, NJ: Ablex.

Hartel, J. (in press). The serious leisure frontier in library and information studies: Hobby domains. *Knowledge Organization.*

Hayles, N. K. (1999). *How we became posthuman: Virtual bodies in cybernetics, literature, and informatics.* Chicago: University of Chicago Press.

Hendry, D. G., & Harper, D. J. (1997). An informal information-seeking environment. *Journal of the American Society for Information Science, 48*(11), 1036–1048.

Hildenbrand, S., Ed. (1996). *Reclaiming the American library past: Writing the women in.* Norwood, NJ: Ablex.

Hildreth, C. R. (1989). *Intelligent interfaces and retrieval methods for subject searching in bibliographic retrieval systems.* Washington, DC: Library of Congress Cataloging Distribution Service.

Hjørland, B. (1998). Theory and metatheory of information science: A new interpretation. *Journal of Documentation, 54*(5), 606–621.

Hjørland, B. (2000). Library and information science: Practice, theory, and philosophical basis. *Information Processing & Management, 36*(3), 501–531.

Hjørland, B. (2002). Epistemology and the socio-cognitive perspective in information science. *Journal of the American Society for Information Science and Technology, 53,* 257–270.

Hjørland, B., & Albrechtsen, H. (1995). Toward a new horizon in information science: Domain analysis. *Journal of the American Society for Information Science, 46,* 400–425.

Holquist, M. (2002). *Dialogism: Bakhtin and his world* (2nd ed.). New York: Routledge.

Ingwersen, P. (1992). *Information retrieval interaction.* London: Taylor Graham.

Ingwersen, P. (1999). Cognitive information retrieval. *Annual Review of Information Science and Technology. 34,* 3–52.

Jacob, E. K., & Shaw, D. (1998). Sociocognitive perspectives on representation. *Annual Review of Information Science and Technology, 33,* 131–185.

Kahneman, D., & Tversky, A., Eds. (2000). *Choices, values, and frames.* New York: Russell Sage Foundation.

Kelly, G. A. (1963). *A theory of personality: The psychology of personal constructs.* New York: W.W. Norton.

Kling, R., & McKim, G. (2000). Not just a matter of time: Field differences and the shaping of electronic media in supporting scientific communication. *Journal of the American Society for Information Science, 51*, 1306–1320.

Kraft, D. H., & Petry, F. E. (1997). Fuzzy information systems: Managing uncertainty in databases and information retrieval systems. *Fuzzy Sets & Systems, 90*(2), 183–191.

Kuhlthau, C. C. (1993). *Seeking meaning: A process approach to library and information services.* Norwood, NJ: Ablex.

Kwasnik, B. H. (1991). The importance of factors that are not document attributes in the organisation of personal documents. *Journal of Documentation, 47*(4), 389–398.

Kwasnik, B. H. (1992). A descriptive study of the functional components of browsing. In: *Engineering for human-computer interaction: Proceedings of the IFIP TC2/WG2.7 working conference on engineering for human-computer interaction, IFIP Transactions,* A–18: 191–203.

Kuhn, T. S. (1996). *The structure of scientific revolutions* (3rd ed.). Chicago: University of Chicago Press.

Lave, C. A., & March, J. G. (1975). *An introduction to models in the social sciences.* New York: Harper & Row.

Liddy, E. D., Jorgensen, C. L., Sibert, E. E., & Yu, E. S. (1993). A sublanguage approach to natural language processing for an expert system. *Information Processing & Management, 29*(5), 633–645.

Maack, M. N. (2000). "No philosophy carries so much conviction as the personal life": Mary Wright Plummer as an independent woman. *The Library Quarterly, 70*(1), 1–46.

Madden, A. D. (2004). Evolution and information. *Journal of Documentation, 60*(1), 9–23.

Marchionini, G. (1995). *Information seeking in electronic environments.* New York: Cambridge University Press.

Marchionini, G., & Komlodi, A. (1998). Design of interfaces for information seeking. *Annual Review of Information Science and Technology, 33*, 89–130.

McClure, C. R., & Hernon, P., Eds. (1991). *Library and information science research: Perspectives and strategies for improvement.* Norwood, NJ: Ablex.

McKechnie, L. E. F. (2000). Ethnographic observation of preschool children. *Library & Information Science Research, 22*(1), 61–76.

Mellon, C. A. (1986). Library anxiety-A grounded theory and its development. *College & Research Libraries, 47*(2), 160–165.

Metoyer-Duran, C. (1991). Information-Seeking Behavior of Gatekeepers in Ethnolinguistic Communities: Overview of a Taxonomy. *Library and Information Science Research, 13*(4), 319–346.

Miller, G. A. (1951). *Language and communication.* New York: McGraw-Hill.

Minsky, M. L., Ed. (1968). *Semantic information processing.* Cambridge, MA: MIT Press.

Newell, A., & Simon, H. A. (1972). *Human problem solving.* Englewood Cliffs, NJ: Prentice-Hall.

Nielsen, J. (1993). *Usability engineering.* Boston: AP Professional.

Norman, D. A. (1990). *The design of everyday things.* New York: Doubleday.

Orlikowski, W. J., & Yates, J. (1994). Genre repertoire: The structuring of communicative practices in organizations. *Administrative Science Quarterly, 39*(4), 541–574.

Over, P. (2001). The TREC interactive track: An annotated bibliography. *Information Processing & Management, 37*(3), 369–381.

Paisley, W. J. (1968). Information needs and uses. *Annual Review of Information Science and Technology, 3,* 1–30.

Palmer, C. L. (2001). *Work at the boundaries of science: Information and the interdisciplinary research process.* Boston: Kluwer.

Pawley, C. (1998). Hegemony's handmaid—The library and information studies curriculum from a class perspective. *The Library Quarterly, 68*(2), 123–144.

Pettigrew, K. E. (2000). Lay information provision in community settings: How community health nurses disseminate human services information to the elderly. *The Library Quarterly, 70*(1), 47–85.

Pettigrew, K. E., Fidel, R., & Bruce, H. (2001). Conceptual frameworks in information behavior. *Annual Review of Information Science and Technology, 35,* 43–78.

Pettigrew, K. E., & McKechnie, L. (2001). The use of theory in information science research. *Journal of the American Society for Information Science and Technology, 52,* 62–73.

Pierce, J. R. (1961). *Symbols, signals, and noise: The nature and process of communication.* New York: Harper.

Poole, H. (1985). *Theories of the middle range.* Norwood, NJ: Ablex.

Powell, R. R. (1997). *Basic research methods for librarians* (3rd ed.). Greenwich, CT: Ablex.

Powell, R. R. (1999). Recent trends in research: A methodological essay. *Library & Information Science Research, 21*(1), 91–119.

Price, D. J. D. (1986). *Little science, big science...and beyond*. New York: Columbia University Press.

Radford, G. P. (2003). Trapped in our own discursive formations: Toward an archaeology of library and information science. *The Library Quarterly, 73*(1), 1–18.

Rayward, W. B. (1996). The history and historiography of information science: Some reflections. *Information Processing & Management, 32*(1), 3–17.

Reynolds, P. D. (1971). *A primer in theory construction*. Indianapolis: Bobbs-Merrill.

Ritzer, G. (2000). *Modern sociological theory* (5th ed.). Boston: McGraw-Hill.

Rogers, Y. (2004). New theoretical approaches for human-computer interaction. *Annual Review of Information Science and Technology, 38*, 87–143.

Ruesch, J., & Bateson, G. (1968). *Communication: The social matrix of psychiatry*. New York: Norton.

Russell, S. J., & Norvig, P. (1995). *Artificial intelligence: A modern approach*. Englewood Cliffs, NJ: Prentice-Hall.

Salton, G., & McGill, M. J. (1983). *Introduction to modern information retrieval*. New York: McGraw-Hill.

Sandstrom, A. R., & Sandstrom, P. E. (1995). The use and misuse of anthropological methods in library and information science research, *The Library Quarterly, 65*(2), 161–199.

Sandstrom, A. R., & Sandstrom, P. E. (1998). Science and nonscience in qualitative research: A response to Thomas and Nyce. *The Library Quarterly, 68*(2), 249–254.

Sandstrom, P. E. (1994). An optimal foraging approach to information seeking and use. *The Library Quarterly, 64*(4), 414–449.

Sandstrom, P. E. (1999). Scholars as subsistence foragers. *Bulletin of the American Society for Information Science, 25*(3), 17–20.

Schutz, A. (1967). *The phenomenology of the social world*. Evanston, IL: Northwestern University Press.

Shannon, C. E., & Weaver, W. (1975). *Mathematical theory of communication*. Urbana, IL: University of Illinois Press.

Simon, H. A. (1976). *Administrative behavior: A study of decision-making processes in administrative organization* (3rd ed.). New York: Free Press.

Simon, H. A. (1981). *The sciences of the artificial* (2nd ed.). Cambridge, MA: MIT Press.

Skinner, B. F. (1992 reprint). *Science and human behavior*. New York: Classics of Psychiatry and Behavioral Sciences Library.

Small, H. (1999). A passage through science; Crossing disciplinary boundaries. *Library Trends, 48*(1), 72–108.

Sonnenwald, D. H., & Iivonen, M. (1999). An integrated human information behavior research framework for information studies. *Library & Information Science Research, 21*(4), 429–457.

Talja, S. (1999). Analyzing qualitative interview data: The discourse analytic method. *Library & Information Science Research, 21*(4), 459–477.

Talja, S. (2001). *Music, culture, and the library: An analysis of discourses.* Lanham, MD: Scarecrow Press.

Talja, S., Tuominen, K., & Savolainen, R. (in press). "Isms" in information science: Constructivism, collectivism and constructionism. *Journal of Documentation.*

Trosow, S. E. (2001). Standpoint epistemology as an alternative methodology for library and information science. *The Library Quarterly, 71*(3), 360–382.

Thomas, N. P., & Nyce, J. M. (1998). Qualitative research in LIS—redux: A response to a [re)turn to positivistic ethnography. *The Library Quarterly, 68*(1), 108–113.

Updike, D. B. (2001). *Printing types: Their history, forms, and use* (4th ed. expanded). New Castle, DE: Oak Knoll Press.

Vakkari, P. (1997). Information seeking in context: A challenging metatheory. In: P. Vakkari, R. Savolainen, & B. Dervin (Eds.), Information seeking in context: *Proceedings of an international conference on research in information needs, seeking and use in different contexts* (pp. 451–464). London: Taylor Graham.

Vaughan, M. W., & Dillon, A. (1998). The role of genre in shaping our understanding of digital documents. *Proceedings of the ASIS Annual Meeting, 35*, 559–566.

Vygotsky, L. (1978). *Mind in society: The development of higher psychological processes.* Cambridge, MA: Harvard University Press.

Wagner, D. G., & Berger, J. (1985). Do sociological theories grow? *American Journal of Sociology, 90*(4), 697–728.

Wang, P. L. (1999). Methodologies and methods for user behavioral research. *Annual Review of Information Science and Technology, 34*, 53–99.

Wang, P. L., & White, M. D. (1999). A cognitive model of document use during a research project. Study II. Decisions at the reading and citing stages. *Journal of the American Society for Information Science, 50*, 98–114.

Westbrook, L. (1994). Qualitative research methods: A review of major stages, data analysis techniques, and quality controls. *Library & Information Science Research, 16*(3), 241–254.

White, H. D., & McCain, K. W. (1998). Visualizing a discipline: An author co-citation analysis of information science, 1972–1995. *Journal of the American Society for Information Science, 49*, 327–355.

Wiegand, W. A. (1999). Tunnel vision and blind spots: What the past tells us about the present: Reflections on the twentieth-century history of American librarianship. *The Library Quarterly, 69*(1), 1–32.

Wiegand, W. A., & Davis, D. G., Eds. (1994). *Encyclopedia of library history*. New York: Garland.

Wiener, N. (1961). *Cybernetics: Or, control and communication in the animal and the machine* (2nd ed.). New York: MIT Press.

Wilson, P. (1968). *Two kinds of power: An essay on bibliographical control*. Berkeley, CA: University of California Press.

Wilson, P. (1977). *Public knowledge, private ignorance: Toward a library and information policy*. Westport, CT: Greenwood Press.

Wilson, P. (1983). *Second-hand knowledge: An inquiry into cognitive authority*. Westport, CT: Greenwood Press.

Wilson, T. D. (1999). Models in information behaviour research. *Journal of Documentation, 55*(3), 249–270.

Wilson, T. D., & Streatfield, D. R. (1981). Structured observation in the investigation of information needs. *Social Science Information Studies, 1*, 173–184.

Wright, R. (1994). *The moral animal: The new science of evolutionary psychology*. New York: Pantheon.

Zipf, G. K. (1949). *Human behavior and the principle of least effort: An introduction to human ecology*. Cambridge, MA: Addison-Wesley.

Chapter 2

What Methodology Does to Theory: Sense-Making Methodology as Exemplar

Brenda Dervin
School of Journalism and Communication
Ohio State University, USA
dervin.1@osu.edu

Popularly used, the term "theory" refers to mere conjecture or guess. The distance between this popular use and the use of the term in systematic study may seem far but in fundamental ways it is not as far as it seems. To illustrate, two common treatments of the term, albeit a fraction of the possibilities, will suffice. On the one hand, we have "theory" of the first kind—systematic propositional statements of the nature and characteristics of observed phenomena and the relationships between observed phenomena. This kind of theory—usually referred to as substantive theory—is theory that results from observation. On the other hand, we have "theory" of the second kind—theory that directs observings for it is widely agreed there is no observing, which is not guided by theory. Frequently referred to as metatheory, theory of the second kind is generally assumed to consist of philosophically grounded assumptions about the phenomena and about how to study it. Theory of the first kind is inexorably implicated in theory of the second kind and vice versa.

The implications of the juxtaposition of these two kinds of theory catapults us into a Kuhnian (1962) world where we must accept the idea that different observers whose observings are driven by different theories (type 2) are necessarily operating in different worlds and creating different theories (type 1) even while looking in the same direction from the same vantage point. This conclusion appears to undermine theory of the first kind. One can argue that it is at the juncture of these two kinds of theories that we find ourselves buried under mountains of discon-nected data and findings driven by mountains of different, sometimes incommensurate, theorizings presented as if theory of the first kind is the only kind operating.

Dervin's Sense-Making Methodology has been explicitly developed based on the premise that it is philosophically anchored methodological consideration, which builds the bridge between these two kinds of theory. In the context of this paper, this viewpoint assumes that methodological explication offers for the systematic study of information seeking and use (and more broadly all communicating processes) an avenue for under-standing how scholars move back and forth from theory of the first kind to theory of the second kind within theoretical discourses. Methodological explication can also, if well done, provide a common system of articulation with some degree of independence from the substantive interests of theory allowing the comparison of two substantive theories without having to couch one in terms of the other. This strength allows for comparison between theoretical discourses in a way that the results have a chance of adding up rather than merely piling up.

This kind of methodological explication can be called theory of the third kind—theory for methodology. The difficulty in comprehending the role that this approach to methodology can offer is that the term methodology is itself much used and abused. On the one hand, many—mostly those who favor quantitative approaches—collapse methodology into methods and, too frequently, into statistical methods. On the other, many—mostly those who favor qualitative approaches—collapse methodology into philosophic exami-nation. The former privilege theory of the first kind; the latter theory of the second. Few build methodological bridges between.

Dervin's Sense-Making Methodology attempts to begin to be theory of the third kind. The development of Sense-Making began in skeleton form in 1972, was first articulated as Sense-Making in 1983, and continues today (Dervin & Foreman-Wernet, 2003). Sense-Making is proposed as a generalizable approach to thinking about and studying human sense making and sense unmaking in its variant forms. Information seeking and use has been a primary substantive focus, among numerous others, including as examples: health communication, communicating in organi-zations, media reception, and dialogic communication.

Drawing primarily on the intersections of the writings of American and European theorists (of the second kind) in the fields of philosophy, sociology, psychology, education, cultural studies, communication, and feminist, cultural, and postmodern studies, Sense-Making rests on a fundamental set of philosophic assumptions about the nature of human Sense-Making (and sense unmaking) which, in turn, mandates a specific set of methodological moves.

These philosophic assumptions have been more fully explicated elsewhere. A subset will be presented here to illustrate how methodology opens up or closes down theoretical possibilities. Sense-Making Methodology mandates attention to a series of what might be called primitive terms—primitive in the sense that they are taken as the given foundation from which extrapolations are derived methodologically to build a bridge to method. In Sense-Making, the primitives include: time, space, horizon, gap, bridge, movement, power, constancy, and change.

These primitives are drawn together in the methodology's central metaphor, illustrated in Figure C2.1. The metaphor is designed as a highly generalizable "microscope" guiding the observation of communicating (for purposes here, information seeking and use). Sense-Making mandates that communicating be conceptualized as gap bridging—not in the purposive, problem solving sense (although that is one subset of all gap-bridgings) but in the sense of gap-bridging as a mandate of the human condition. Each new moment in time-space requires another gap-bridging step regardless of whether that step is manifested as habitual and unconscious; capricious and accidental; or invented and planned. Gap-bridging is posited as potentially changeable across time-space but in given time-space moments anchored in particular situational conditions with particular structural arrangements, experiential horizons, and flows of power/energy. As a person moves from time-space moment to time-space moment, gap-bridging is seen as both potentially responsive and potentially impervious to changing conditions.

Two major consequences of carrying these methodological assumptions into method will be pursued here. This first is the challenge Sense-Making offers to research designs that study information seeking and use as only habitual. In method, such studies tap into "usual" behaviors asking informants, for example, "How often do you use x?" or "When was the last time you used y?" Such studies also typically predict information seeking and use based on characteristics of users assumed to be constant across time-space (e.g., demographic and personality characteristics) or characteristics of situations assumed to be constant to all who experience these situations (e.g., domain or task).

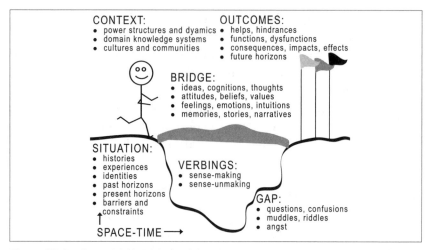

Figure C2.1   Sense-Making Methodology's central metaphor.

A study informed by Sense-Making does not challenge these research designs as wrong but rather as "not enough." Sense-Making mandates attention to information seeking and use as both potentially constant and potentially changeable across time-space. Likewise, it mandates attention to the conditions under which one would expect one or the other or both. As a methodological frame, then, Sense-Making proposes to provide an avenue for pursuing traditional studies of information seeking use and simultaneously opening up alternatives. The mandate to study time, space, and movement, for example, allows for the possibility of conceptualizing information seeking and use as habitually patterned and/or situationally/temporally patterned.

A second major consequence of carrying Sense-Making's methodological assumptions into method derives from mandated attention to flows of power/energy. Sense-Making assumes that movement through time-space is both facilitated by and constrained by flows of power. Given an assumption that a new moment in time-space makes change always possible even if not always probable, Sense-Making methodologically requires methods that allow the researcher to ask "Under what conditions would habit or constancy be found across time-space versus under what conditions would time-space anchored situational variation be found?"

By constructing interviewing methods that elicit informant reports of barriers and facilitators of information seeking and use, Sense-Making studies have been able to identify what is called the "render unto Caesar" hypothesis as one propositional generalization about information seeking and use. This proposition states that when external forces (e.g., such as economics) constrain information seeking and use alternatives, making some options less possible, then demographic attributes of users (conceptualized in Sense-Making as indices of societally imposed structural conditions) will predict better. When, however, external forces do not constrain (e.g., as when users evaluate information systems), then situational conditions of use will predict better. Again, a study informed by Sense-Making does not reject the demographic prediction. Rather it mandates attention to enlarged possibilities.

In the broadest sense, then, it can be said that methodology is the reflexive examination of how assumptions inscribe methods that open up research to some possibilities and constrain others. When interviewing method, for example, asks users for usual information-seeking behavior, method closes off the possibility of observing whether the "usual" is habitual, average, or caprice. It also closes off the possibility of observing information seeking and use patterns that change in response to changing situational conditions.

Too often, the methodological premises—or primitives—lurking behind social scientific research methods are unstated, buried in long histories of intragenre discourse. Unstated, or not, however, the primitives operate to both constrain and enable possible research attentions. What Sense-Making Methodology has attempted to do is build an explicit methodological bridge between method and the possibilities for constructing alternative theories of information seeking and use. Sense-Making assumes that theories of type 3 (theory for methodology) are required for reflexively addressing how theories of type 1 (substantive theories) are enabled and constrained by theories of type 2 (philosophical assumptions) and vice versa.

Carter, R. F. (2003). Communication, a harder science. In B. Dervin & S. Chaffee (Eds.), *Communication, a different kind of horse race: Essays honoring Richard F. Carter* (pp. 369–376). Cresskill, NJ: Hampton Press.

Dervin, B., & Foreman-Wernet. L., Eds. (2003). *Sense-Making Methodology reader: Selected writings of Brenda Dervin*. Cresskill, NJ: Hampton Press.

Kuhn, T. S. (1962). *The structure of scientific revolutions*. Chicago: University of Chicago Press.

Chapter 3

Evolution in Information Behavior Modeling: Wilson's Model

T. D. Wilson
Department of Information Studies
University of Sheffield, United Kingdom
t.d.wilson@shef.ac.uk

Wilson's various models of information behavior (Wilson, 1981, 1999b; Wilson & Walsh, 1996) were developed over a considerable period of time. The first set of models, published in 1981, had their origins in a doctoral seminar presentation at the University of Maryland in 1971, when an attempt was made to map the processes involved in what was known at the time as "user needs research."

That early, unpublished model contained the germ of the most frequently cited model in the 1981 paper, which set out the fundamental categories of causal factors that produce a "need for information" as well as the barriers that may prevent the person from taking action to seek information. As a result of his work on the INISS Project (Wilson & Streatfield, 1980) Wilson presented a series of interrelated models in his 1981 paper, which has become one of the most cited publications in the field.

The key model in that paper, however, was one that is not generally referred to, and is reproduced here as Figure C3.1. The figure suggests a three-fold view of information seeking: the context of the seeker, the "system" employed (which might be manual or machine and navigated either personally or by an intermediary), and the information resources that might be drawn upon. All of this is shown to exist within a "universe of knowledge" that might be drawn upon directly by the information seeker or the intermediary, through, for example, persons as embodiments

31

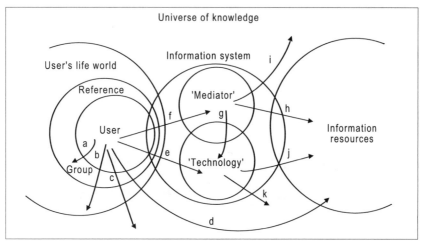

Figure C3.1   The information user and the universe of knowledge.
Note: From "On user studies and information needs," by T. D.
Wilson, 1981, *Journal of Documentation*, Copyright 1981 Emerald
Group Publishing. Adapted with permission.

of knowledge. Note that "technology" was interpreted widely, in the
general sense of anything that aids action: at the time, the application of
information technology to information seeking was in its infancy, and
neither the personal computer nor the World Wide Web existed. One of
the strengths of the model is that it continues to serve as a framework in
the present with as much validity as at the time of its conception.

The most cited model, however, was the development of that originally used in 1971, which is shown as Figure C3.2.

This model developed the idea of the personal, social role, and environmental context that may give rise to a need for information. Of particular
significance was the division of the needs that give rise to information-
seeking behavior into physiological, affective, and cognitive needs, and the
suggestion that information needs was an unhelpful concept for research
purposes and that the term "information-seeking behavior" should be
adopted as behavior is observable, whereas needs being internal mental
states, are not.

Curiously, the models presented in the 1981 paper, although frequently cited, were not elaborated upon to any significant extent by
other researchers. Consequently, when Wilson found himself free once
again to take up research into information-seeking behavior, there had

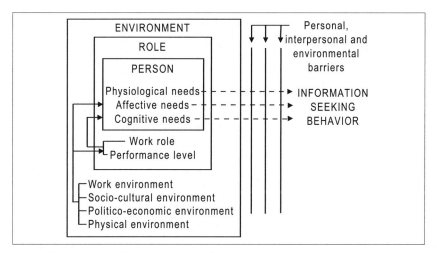

Figure C3.2   Information need and seeking.
   Note: From "On user studies and information needs," by T. D.
   Wilson, 1981, *Journal of Documentation*, Copyright 1981 Emerald
   Group Publishing. Adapted with permission.

been very little progress in developing a general model of information-seeking behavior.

At this point he obtained research support for a study of research on information-seeking behavior undertaken in a range of disciplines, since it had been evident to him that, over the years since his first attempt at modeling the process, the behavior of information users had become of increasing interest in areas such as information systems development, health information systems, consumer behavior, and other fields.

Examining this literature he found that the models from 1981 could be used as a framework to integrate studies from this diversity of fields. The result was a development of Figures C3.1 and C3.2 into a new general model of information-seeking behavior, reproduced as Figure C3.3. In addition to its publication as part of the research report (Wilson & Walsh, 1996), the model, together with a review of the related research, was published in the *Journal of Documentation* (Wilson, 1999b) and an earlier review was published in *Information Processing and Management* (Wilson, 1997).

Wilson's model is not derived from any theory proposed by other writers but from an analysis of human information behavior, partly *a priori*, but also from the detailed analysis of the information behavior of social

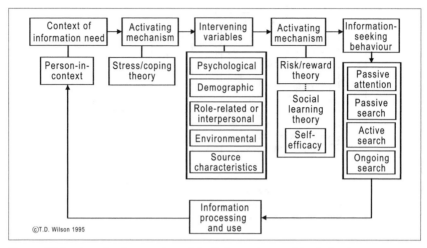

Figure C3.3   A revised general model of information-seeking behavior.

workers and their managers carried out as part of Project INISS. Various influences informed the construction of the model in its original form, particularly general systems theory and phenomenology, but the influences are not overt.

However, the latest version of the model directs attention to theory that might be used to explore various aspects. Thus, the decision to take action to satisfy a need for information is related to stress-coping theory (Folkman, 1984), while the decision to search information resources is associated with risk-reward theory (Settle & Alreck, 1989) and with the theory of self-efficacy (Bandura, 1977). It is also possible to relate various theories of learning to the "information processing and use" stage of the cycle shown in Figure C3.3. Probably the most popular approach in this area at present is "constructivist learning theory" (see, for example, (Steffe & Gale, 1995).   Wilson's model is a very general model and is not only hospitable to theory that might help to explain the more fundamental aspects of human behavior, but also to various approaches to information-seeking behavior and information searching. In one iteration of the model, Wilson incorporated Ellis's "behavioral characteristics" of information seeking (Ellis, 1989), which describes the activities of the information seeker engaged in the "active search" mode of information seeking. Similarly, Erdelez's (1997) "information encountering" may be seen as an elaboration of the 'passive attention' mode. Kuhlthau's (2004) treatment of the information search process is a detailed analysis of the stages in the active search for information, although not, of course, restricted to a single search episode. Dervin's (1996) Sense-Making theory can also be associated with Wilson's model, in that it deals with the perception of a need for information—the experienced "gap" in one's knowledge—and the steps taken to "bridge" the gap.

In other words, the model draws attention to the interrelated nature of theory in this field, whether drawn from other disciplines, or from with the research traditions of information science. The value of a model of this kind lies in drawing the attention of the researcher to the totality of information behavior and showing how a specific piece of research may contribute to an understanding of the whole. It has no pretensions to *explaining* everything to do with human information behavior, but it is *hospitable* to explanations set out by others and it prompts the researcher to ask the question, "Given my findings, what are the implications for these related areas?"

Wilson has also proposed that information-seeking behavior can be seen as goal-determined behavior and that the concept of problem solving provides a framework that can help to explain, for example, multiple search episodes, as the information seeker moves through the problem solving stages of *problem recognition, problem identification, problem resolution,* and *solution statement.* This model is also compatible with the 1996 framework, since it deals with the activities engaged in once the person has overcome the barriers to information seeking. These ideas are most fully elaborated in Wilson, et al., 2002.

Wilson's model has been cited by key authors in the field, including: Belkin, Borgman, Choo, Cole, Dervin, Ellis, Erdelez, Fidel, Ford, Ingwersen, Kuhlthau, Nilan, Pettigrew, Savolainen, Sonnenwald, Spink, Vakkari, and Wersig.

It is important to understand that Wilson's General Model has evolved over time and that it is necessary to understand the relationships among the various diagrams he has produced to illustrate his model. Thus, it should be understood that Figure C3.2 above is an elaboration of the box labeled "Person-in-context" in Figure C3.3. Consequently, no one model stands alone and in using the model to guide the development of research ideas, it is necessary to examine and reflect upon all of the diagrams in the 1981 paper as well as the 1996 model.

Wilson's General Model is less a theory than a theoretical framework: that is, although in its latest manifestation, theory plays a role, the Model is aimed at linking theories to action. It seems likely that the Model will continue to evolve as more and more researchers use it as a basis for thinking about the problems of human information behavior.

Bandura, A. (1977). Self efficacy: Towards a unifying theory of behavioral change. *Psychological Review, 84*, 191–215.

Dervin, B. (1996). *Chaos, order and Sense-Making: A proposed theory for information design.* In R. Jacobson (Ed.), Information design. Cambridge, MA: MIT Press.

Ellis, D. (1989). A behavioural approach to information retrieval design. *Journal of Documentation, 45*(3), 171–212.

Erdelez, S. (1997). Information encountering: A conceptual framework for accidental information discovery. In P. Vakkari, R. Savolainen, & B. Dervin (Eds.), *Information seeking in context: Proceedings of an international conference on research in information needs, seeking and use in difference contexts*, Tampere, Finland (pp. 412–421). London: Taylor Graham.

Folkman, S. (1984). Personal control and stress and coping processes: A theoretical analysis. *Journal of Personality and Social Psychology, 46*, 839–852.

Kuhlthau, C. C. (2004). *Seeking meaning: A process approach to library and information services.* (2nd ed.). Westport, CT: Libraries Unlimited.

Settle, R. B., & Alreck, P. (1989). Reducing buyers' sense of risk. *Marketing Communications*, January, 34–40.

Steffe, L., & Gale, J., Eds. (1995). *Constructivism in education.* Mahwah, NJ: Lawrence Erlbaum.

Wilson, T. D. (1981). On user studies and information needs. *Journal of Documentation, 37*(1), 3–15.

Wilson, T. D. (1997). Information behaviour: An interdisciplinary perspective. *Information Processing and Management, 33*(4), 551–572.

Wilson, T. D. (1999a). Exploring models of information behaviour: The 'Uncertainty' Project. In T. D. Wilson & D. K. Allen (Eds.), *Exploring the contexts of information behaviour: Proceedings of the 2nd international conference on information seeking in context*, August 12–15, 1998. Sheffield, UK (pp. 55–66). London: Taylor Graham.

Wilson, T. D. (1999b). Models in information behaviour research. *Journal of Documentation, 55*(3), 249–270.

Wilson, T. D., Ford, N. J., Ellis, D., Foster, A., & Spink, A. (2002). Information seeking and mediated searching, Part 2: Uncertainty and its correlates. *Journal of the American Society for Information Science and Technology, 53*, 704–715.

Wilson, T. D., & Streatfield, D. R. (1980). *You can observe a lot…: A study of information use in local authority social services departments.* Sheffield, UK: University of Sheffield, Department of Information Studies.

Wilson, T. D., & Walsh, C. (1996). *Information behaviour: An interdisciplinary perspective.* (British Library Research and Innovation Report No. 10). Sheffield, UK: University of Sheffield, Department of Information Studies.

The Theories

1
Affective Load

Diane Nahl
Information and Computer Sciences Department
Library and Information Science Program
University of Hawaii, USA
nahl@hawaii.edu

Information-seeking research and theory is focusing increasingly on the role of affect in information behavior (IB) and how it influences cognitive operations. Diane Nahl's research draws on the field of psychology, following the work of social-learning theorists such as Albert Bandura (1986), who contributed to the behavioral approach in cognitive psychology, and Erving Goffman (1974), who contributed to the behavioral approach in sociolinguistics, as well as Martin Seligman (1992) (positive psychology), Harold Garfinkle (1968) (ethnomethodology), and John Searle (1969) (speech act theory). Nahl's research on the role of affect in information behavior relates to the work of Nicholas Belkin (1980, 2000), Brenda Dervin (1992), Carol Kuhlthau (1993), T. D. Wilson (1984, 1999, 2000), Amanda Spink (2000), Sanda Erdelez (1997), and Rosalind Picard (1997), among others.

Affective load theory (ALT) is a social-behavioral perspective on the thoughts and feelings of individuals while engaged in information behavior (IB). ALT provides empirical methods for identifying affective states of users that disrupt ongoing cognitive operations (James & Nahl, 1986). Once a disruptive affective state is identified, coping assistance services (CAS) can be provided to encourage users to mitigate disruptive states to achieve task success. ALT identifies underlying habits of thinking and feeling while engaging in information behavior, and clarifies the details of information retrieval from a user perspective. There are three essential ideas in applying social-behavioral psychology to IB:

1) The mental activity of information users, both cognitive and affective, is defined as behavior (Martin & Briggs, 1986). For instance, "thinking of a search word" or "feeling motivated to finish a task" are behaviors. Global control of

the affective over the cognitive operates at general and specific levels. At the general level of control people possess motivational states such as optimism or pessimism prior to a search. At the specific level of control we experience micro-behaviors that involve search strategy such as inspecting a list, thinking of a synonym, or recalling an item that has been seen before. A search task or session involves hundreds of individual cognitive micro-behaviors, each one connected to an affective state that maintains or interrupts it (Nahl, 1997). Affective states are organized in a top-down hierarchy and can be reliably measured through concurrent self-reports about expectations, satisfactions, and acceptance during continuous cognitive activity.

2) Affective behavior initiates, maintains, and terminates cognitive behavior (Isen, Daubman & Gorgolione, 1987; Carver & Scheier, 2001). For instance, when searchers lose the motivation to continue a task, they begin thinking about something else. Or, if they unexpectedly find some new information they want, they switch activity midstream. The new affective behavior interrupts and takes over the ongoing activity and continues in a new direction with new cognitive activity. This managerial or directive function of affective behavior over cognitive, makes it desirable in information environments to employ self-monitoring techniques to keep track of the affective behavior of users (Nahl, 1996, 1998).

3) Affective behavior operates within a binary-value system: on/off or positive/negative. Cognitive behavior operates through a multivalue logic. Therefore, affective behavior is measured with bi-polar scales and cognitive behavior is measured with multiple-choice, matching or fill-in items. Content analysis and protocol analysis of concurrent verbal reports are used to identify affective and cognitive behavior patterns during search tasks (Nahl, 2001).

The behavioral approach to information use is attracting increasing interest among information scientists. However, sufficient attention is not given to the three essential elements outlined above. The focus has been on cognitive behavior and more recently, on how affective behavior is also important to consider. Nahl's social-behavioral theory of affective load makes explicit the need to create a methodological connection between each cognitive behavior and its affective support or control state. Affective load theory was developed by analyzing concurrent self-reports of searchers and learners in conjunction with quantitative ratings filled out by searchers while engaged in searching and problem-solving. To achieve high reliability, it is critical to obtain concurrent rather than recollected data. Nahl's ALT theory is emerging from a 20-year research program. One area of application has been to identify affective dimensions like self-efficacy and optimism that help searchers perform better. Currently ALT research focuses on how diverse affective behaviors interact to produce an effective coping style when searchers feel challenged by uncertainty.

ALT proposes that all information behavior involves affective states that provide specific goal-directionality and motivation to support cognitive activity. Affective load (AL) is operationally defined as uncertainty (U) multiplied by felt time pressure (TP). Uncertainty is defined as the combined degrees of irritation, frustration, anxiety, and rage (Nahl, 2004).

$$AL = U \text{ [irritation + frustration + anxiety + rage] x TP}$$

Affective load is high when people operate with ineffective cognitive behaviors. For example, cognitive ambiguity, uncertainty, or information overload attract affective behaviors that are negative and counterproductive to the searcher's goal. For instance, a search that appears to yield no relevant results after some attempts is cognitively disorienting, as represented by such thoughts as, "I'm no good at this" or "This is so frustrating!"

At other times, searchers are able to engage affective coping strategies when faced with cognitive load and uncertainty. For instance, "I'll just keep going until I find something" or "I'm positive I can find what I need in another database." These verbal expressions are standard and recurrent within a population of searchers, and because they are learned cultural habits, can be termed "learned affective norms" (LANs). Negative LANs disrupt cognitive strategies, interrupt the search, and often terminate it prematurely, while positive LANs provide persistence and integration to cognitive strategies. In general, negative LANs increase AL and appear in the form of uncertainty, anxiety, frustration, low expectations, pessimism, low self-efficacy, low task completion motivation, low satisfaction, low system acceptance, and other disruptive symptoms that interfere with a positive outcome. On the other hand, positive LANs decrease AL because they provide better coping strategies to manage ambiguity and cognitive load. Support and counseling interventions can be triggered when affective load rises above a specified level. Knowledge about the affective environ-ment of searchers will also be helpful in search instruction. More research is needed on how the affective information environment of searchers impinges on their cognitive activity to strengthen information system ser-vices and design.

Bandura, A. (1986). *Social foundations of thought and action: A social cognitive the-ory*. Englewood Cliffs, NJ: Prentice-Hall.

Belkin, N. J. (1980). Anomalous states of knowledge as a basis for information retrieval. *Canadian Journal of Information Science, 5*, 133–143.

Belkin, N. J. (2000). Helping people find what they don't know. *Communications of the ACM, 43*(8), 58–61.

Carver, C. S., & Scheier, M. F. (2001). Optimism, pessimism, and self-regulation. In E. C. Chang (Ed.), *Optimism and pessimism: Implications for theory, research, and practice* (pp. 31–51). Washington, DC: American Psychological Association.

Dervin, B. (1992). From the mind's eye of the user: The Sense-Making qualitative-quantitative methodology. In R. R. Powell (Ed.), *Qualitative research in informa-tion management* (pp. 61–84). Englewood, CO: Libraries Unlimited.

Erdelez, S. (1997). Information encountering: A conceptual framework for accidental information discovery. In P. Vakkari, R. Salvolainen, & B. Dervin, (Eds.), *Information seeking in context: Proceedings of an international conference on research in information needs, seeking and use in different contexts* (pp. 412–421). London: Taylor Graham.

Garfinkel, H. (1968). *Studies in ethnomethodology*. Englewood Cliffs, NJ: Prentice-Hall.

Goffman, E. (1974). *Frame analysis: An essay on the organization of experience*. New York: Harper & Row.

Isen, A. M., Daubman, K. A., & Gorgoglione, J. M. (1987). The influence of positive affect on cognitive organization: Implications for education. In R. E. Snow & M. J. Farr (Eds.), *Aptitude, learning, and instruction. Volume 3: Cognitive and affective process analyses* (pp. 143–164). Hillsdale, NJ: Lawrence Erlbaum.

James, L., & Nahl, D. (1996). Achieving focus, engagement, and acceptance: Three phases of adapting to Internet use. *Electronic Journal of Virtual Culture, 4*(1).

Retrieved March 25, 2004, from www.monash.edu.au/journals/ejvc/ejvcv4nI. james

Kuhlthau, C. C. (1993). *Seeking meaning: A process approach to library and information services*. Norwood, NJ: Ablex.

Martin, B., & Briggs, L. J., Eds. (1986). *Affective and cognitive domains: Integration for instruction and research*. Englewood Cliffs, NJ: Educational Technology Publications.

Nahl, D. (1996). The user-centered revolution: 1970–1995. In A. Kent & J. G. Williams (Eds.), *Encyclopedia of microcomputing. Volume 19* (pp. 143–200). New York: Marcel Dekker.

Nahl, D. (1997). Information counseling inventory of affective and cognitive reactions while learning the Internet. *Internet Reference Services Quarterly, 2*(2/3), 11–33.

Nahl, D. (1998). Learning the Internet and the structure of information behavior. *Journal of the American Society for Information Science, 49*, 1017–1023.

Nahl, D. (2001). A conceptual framework for defining information behavior. *Studies in Multimedia Information Literacy Education, 1*(2). Retrieved March 25, 2004, from www.utpjournals.com/jour.ihtml?lp=simile/issue2/nahlI.html

Nahl, Diane. (2004). Measuring the Affective Information Environment of Web Searchers. *Proceedings of the 67th annual meeting of the american society for information science & technology, 41*. Medford, NJ: Information Today.

Picard, R. W. (1997). *Affective computing*. Cambridge, MA: MIT Press.

Searle, J. R. (1969). *Speech acts: An essay in the philosophy of language*. London: Cambridge University Press.

Seligman, M. E. (1992). *Learned optimism: How to change your mind and your life*. New York: Pocket Books.

Spink, A. (2000). Toward a theoretical framework for information science. *Journal of Informing Science, 3*(2), 77–82.

Wilson, T. D. (1984). The cognitive approach to information-seeking behavior and information use. *Social Science Information Studies, 4*(2/3), 197–204.

Wilson, T. D. (1999). Models in information behavior research. *Journal of Documentation, 55*(3), 249–270.

Wilson, T. D., Ford, N. J., Ellis, D., Foster, A. E., & Spink, A. (2000). Uncertainty and its correlates. *The New Review of Information Behavior Research: Studies of Information Seeking in Context, 1*, 69–82.

2
Anomalous State of Knowledge

Nicholas J. Belkin
School of Communication, Information and Library Studies
Rutgers University, USA
nick@belkin.rutgers.edu

The concept of the *anomalous state of knowledge* (ASK) was proposed by Belkin (1977), within an explicitly communicative analysis of the fundamental problem of information science, as "the effective communication of desired information between human generator and human user" (Belkin, 1977, p. 22). Following Paisley and Parker (1965), Belkin understood that in the context of information science, this communication system is recipient-instigated and recipient-controlled. There exists a universe of texts that have been generated by a large number of human beings, and the actual communication begins when some person (the recipient) engages with one or more texts, thereby completing the communication system, and terminates it when some goal has been achieved. This is termed the linguistic level of communication, at which generators produce texts that users read. At the cognitive level, the texts are understood as being representations of the conceptual states of knowledge of their generators, as modified by their purposes, value and intentional and belief structures, and knowledge of potential recipients' states of knowledge. Belkin suggested that this underlying structure be considered the information associated with the text. He further proposed that the reason for initiating this communication system could be best understood at the cognitive level, as the recipient's recognition of a conceptual state of knowledge that is anomalous with respect to some goal, and the desire to resolve the anomaly. The two levels of the system are represented in Figure 2.1.

By *anomaly*, Belkin means that the user's state of knowledge with respect to a topic is in some way inadequate with respect to the person's ability to achieve some goal (later generalized as the ability to resolve a problematic situation) (Belkin, Seeger, & Wersig, 1983). *Anomaly* was

44

used explicitly to indicate that this state of inadequacy could be due not only to lack of knowledge, but many other problems, such as uncertainty as to which of several potentially relevant concepts holds in some situation.

ASK has obvious relationships to other proposals in information science, such as Taylor's (1968) "unconscious need," Wersig's (1971) "problematic situation," and Dervin's (1983) "gaps," but Belkin's ASK hypothesis differs from these other proposals in that

- It is an explicitly cognitive explanation of the general phenomenon.

- It suggests that anomalous states could be of different types.

- Some consequences of an operationalization of the concept have been tested in an empirical experiment (Belkin, 1977).

- Specific means to take it into account have been proposed and tested in the understanding and design of information retrieval systems (Belkin, 1980b; Belkin, Oddy, & Brooks, 1982; Belkin & Kwasnik, 1986).

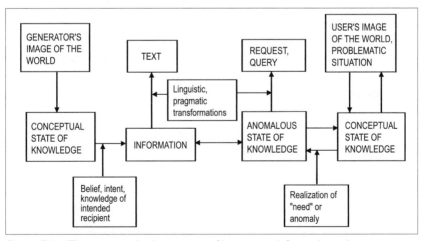

Figure 2.1   The communication system of interest to information science.
Note: Following "Anomalous states of knowledge as a basis for information retrieval," by N. J. Belkin, 1980, *Canadian Journal of Information Science,* 5, 133–143.

The general idea behind the ASK hypothesis is what was known as the *cognitive viewpoint*. This was succinctly explained by de Mey (1977, p. xvii): "The central point of the cognitive view is that any processing of information, whether perceptual or symbolic, is mediated by a system of categories or concepts which, for the information-processing device, are a model of his world."

Figure 2.1 indicates how the ASK hypothesis fits into the cognitive viewpoint. There, one can see that the communication system is under-stood as interactions between different states of knowledge, in particu-lar between the ASK and the information, the modified ASK and the gen-eral conceptual state of knowledge with respect to the topic or goal, and the problematic situation. This communication system is dynamic, in that any such interaction, by virtue of its possibility of modifying the user's image, leads to a different ASK, perhaps one closer to resolution of the problematic situation.

Belkin (1980a) pointed out that under the ASK hypothesis and its implications, for information retrieval (IR) purposes, it is inappropriate to ask a person to specify that which is required to resolve an ASK. The ASK should be represented in ways that are appropriate for representing that which a person doesn't know; and therefore, the normal IR retrieval model of ranking according to best match of query to document representation should be replaced by other techniques dependent upon type of ASK. Belkin (1980b) elaborated on these ideas, laying out the general ASK hypothesis and suggesting how it could be implemented in IR systems.

Combining the ASK hypothesis with Oddy's (1977) concept of IR without query formulation, Belkin, Oddy, and Brooks (1982) presented a general system design for an ASK-based IR system, and a method for elic-iting and representing ASKs. The representation technique was based on ideas of associative memory and its representation from cognitive psy-chology, in particular those of Deese (1965), Kintsch (1974), and Kiss (1975). In brief, the technique elicited so-called "problem statements" from users, and used a distance-sensitive co-occurrence analysis of this text to generate conceptual graphs, which were understood to be ASK representations. The same technique was used on document texts, the results of which were understood to be representations of the information associated with those texts. Later, Belkin and Kwasnik (1986) used this basic representational technique to develop methods for classifying ASKs according to their structural characteristics, in such a way as to suggest different retrieval techniques according to the different structures.

The ASK hypothesis has a clear relationship to information behavior in that it proposes a specific reason explaining why people engage in information-seeking behavior, and how that reason can be responded to through a person's interaction with information. Furthermore, it has been used to indicate how such interaction might best be supported through IR system design. The ASK hypothesis has also been a key element of the so-called cognitive viewpoint in information science, a turn in information science from system orientation to user orientation, which began in the mid- to late 1970s. Belkin (1990) and Ingwersen (2001) each provide evidence of the effect of this turn, and to some extent of the ASK hypothesis on theory and research in information science in general, and on information retrieval, and in the integration of information retrieval research with information behavior research in particular.

Belkin, N. J. (1977). *A concept of information for information science.* Unpublished doctoral dissertation, University College, University of London.

Belkin, N. J. (1980a). The problem of 'matching' in information retrieval. In O. Harbo & L. Kajberg (Eds.), *Theory and application of information research: Proceedings of the second international research forum on information science* (pp. 187–197). London: Mansell.

Belkin, N. J. (1980b). Anomalous states of knowledge as a basis for information retrieval. *Canadian Journal of Information Science, 5,* 133–143.

Belkin, N. J. (1990). The cognitive viewpoint in information science. *Journal of Information Science, 16,* 11–15.

Belkin, N. J., & Kwasnik, B. H. (1986). Using structural representations of anomalous states of knowledge for choosing document retrieval strategies. In F. Rabitti (Ed.), *1986 – ACM conference on research and development in information retrieval* (pp. 11–22). Pisa: IEI.

Belkin, N. J., Oddy, R. N., & Brooks, H. M. (1982). ASK for information retrieval. Parts I and 2. *Journal of Documentation, 38* (2), 61–71; 145–164.

Belkin, N. J., Seeger, T., & Wersig, G. (1983). Distributed expert problem treatment as a model for information system analysis and design. *Journal of Information Science, 5,* 153–167.

Dervin, B. (1983). Paper presented at the annual meeting of the International Communication Association, Dallas, TX. Retrieved April 27, 2004, from http://communication.sbs.ohio-state.edu/sense-making/art/artabsdervin83smoverview.html.

Deese, J. (1965). *The structure of associations in thought and language.* Baltimore: Johns Hopkins University Press.

Ingwersen, P. (2001). Cognitive information retrieval. *Annual Review of Information Science and Technology, 33,* 3–52.

Kintsch, W. (1974). *The representation of meaning in memory.* Hillsdale, NJ: Lawrence Erlbaum.

Kiss, G. (1975). An associative thesaurus of English: Structural analysis of a large relevance network. In A. Kennedy, & A. Wilkes (Eds.), *Long-term memory* (pp. 103–121). New York: Academic Press.

de Mey, M. (1977). The cognitive viewpoint: its scope and development. In M. de Mey, R. Pinxten, M. Poriau, & F. Vandamme (Eds.), *CC77: International workshop on the cognitive viewpoint* (pp. xvi–xxxii). Gent: University of Gent.

Oddy, R. N. (1977). Information retrieval through man-machine dialogue. *Journal of Documentation, 33,* 1–14.

Paisley, W. J., & Parker, E. B. (1965). Information retrieval as a receiver-controlled communication system. In *Education for information science* (pp. 23–31). London: Macmillan.

Taylor, R. S. (1968). Question-negotiation and information seeking in libraries. *College and Research Libraries, 29,* 178–194.

Wersig, G. (1971). *Information – Kommunikation – Dokumentation.* Pullach bei München: Verlag Dokumentation.

3
Archival Intelligence

Elizabeth Yakel
School of Information
University of Michigan, USA
yakel@umich.edu

Archival researchers are well-known for their use of primary sources of information, such as visual, textual, and aural archival and manuscript materials. Nevertheless, research concerning their information behavior (including the needs, seeking, and search strategies) lags behind other research on users' information behavior. On the one hand, this situation is potentially beneficial because one can take advantage of existing theories, such as berrypicking (Bates, 1989), foraging (Pirolli & Card, 1999), or sense making (Russell et al., 1993). The lack of focused research can be also detrimental to a deeper understanding of the work of archival researchers, because the above theories do not adequately explain the information behavior of users of archival materials. As long as knowledge of the information behavior of researchers using primary sources is lacking, the theory and models to respond to these individuals will be deficient. Archival intelligence (Yakel & Torres, 2003) proposes a first step in the formulation of a model defining the scope of information literacy for primary sources. This model seeks to change the current paradigm of "archival orientation" toward one focusing on archival information literacy.

In previous research focusing on the information needs of humanities scholars (e.g., Stieg, 1981; Wiberly & Jones, 1989), the emphasis has been on their use of published works and not on primary sources. More recent work (e.g., Cole, 2000) has begun to examine users' search processes regarding archival materials, but this work fails to explain much of the decision making that goes on before entry into the archives. While these theories should not be discarded, they need careful consideration and research as to how they can best be applied in the archival environment.

In addition to the information science community, the recent research in the educational psychology community has focused on primary sources. Wineberg (2001) and others have demonstrated the value of using primary sources in K-12 classrooms as a means of promoting critical thinking skills among the students. A research component has been incorporated into many social studies and history guidelines. As a result, teachers and their students are discovering digitized primary sources and physical archives (e.g., Robyns, 2001). Yet, in many cases teaching critical thinking skills is based exclusively on predefined document sets and students are not taught the information literacy skills to search for, select, and identify the most appropriate records on their own. The classroom exercises are also frequently combined with an "archival orientation" that focuses on teaching students how to use one archives for the current class project. This instructional approach does little to promote lifelong learning or the independent ability to use primary sources.

The model of Archival Intelligence (Yakel & Torres, 2003) proposes several dimensions of conceptual knowledge researchers need to know in the search, selection, and use phases of primary source research. The dimensions to archival intelligence are:

- Knowledge of archival theory, practices, and procedures

- Strategies for reducing uncertainty and ambiguity when unstructured problems and ill-defined solutions are the norm

- Intellective skills or the ability to understand the connection between representations of documents, activities, and processes with the actual object or process being represented

These larger conceptual areas can be further outlined. Knowledge of archival theory, practice, and procedures involves: 1) recognizing archival terminology and conceptual understanding of archives; 2) internalization of rules; and 3) the ability to assess one's own knowledge and that of the reference archivist. These three areas cover a broad range of knowledge and skills that appear to be germane to using primary sources and navigating the institutions in which the archives are housed effectively.

Since most inquiries involving primary sources represent unstruc-tured problems, developing strategies for reducing uncertainty and ambiguity in archives is essential. Two of these strategies are developing search tactics as a means of structuring ill-structured problems and the ability to ask questions of the archives staff as well as of the records themselves. Reitman (1965) notes that an unstructured problem is one that has "one or more parameters the values of which are left unspecified as the problem is given to the problem solving system" (p. 141). In archives, the existence of evidence is often not known, search and retrieval systems are complex, and/or the evidence requires interpreta-tion and may be ambiguous. Search strategies for the same query will vary from repository to repository due to differences in institutional structure, recordkeeping practices, and available records. For example, researching the origin of women's athletics at two universities would require the use of different access tools, consultation of varying records, and assessing diverse types of evidence (trustees' minutes, athletic office records, correspondence from the Dean of Women). The best evidence in one repository may differ considerably from that in another. Furthermore, many archival queries result in ill-structured solutions as the sources are interpreted and reinterpreted.

Intellective skills encompass the ability to understand representations of documents, activities, and processes (Zuboff, 1988, pp. 75–80). These skills are an important part of the development of an overall framework for problem solving in archives. There are several dimensions of intellective skills, among them the ability to plan an overall research strategy and understanding how a surrogate leads to or represents a primary source. A researcher has to make meaningful connections while advancing though the research process and develop the ability to act effectively on those connec-tions. In particular, the ability to visualize collections through representa-tions is becoming increasingly critical as the number of online surrogates increases. In the online environment, researchers may encounter multiple versions of the same record or collection. For example, at the University of Michigan, one can potentially access five separate representations of the same manuscript collection at two separate levels of granularity (a MARC record and an Encoded Archival Description [EAD] finding aid) through the Library of Congress OCLC, RLIN, and the local digital library. How researchers make sense of complex and overlapping archival access systems is unknown and an important feature of archival intelligence.

Further research is needed to refine this model and build a theory of information behavior vis-à-vis primary sources. Two pressing questions dominate:

1) Investigations are needed to develop a better understanding of researcher's information behavior when conducting studies involving primary sources. This includes basic research into information needs and analysis of the most effective search strategies for primary sources in the online environment.

2) Action research needs to be done to develop, implement, and evaluate educational offerings focused on addressing information literacy for primary sources.

In both of these areas there is much that can be tested and applied from the information science and educational psychology literatures. Ideally, these studies would incorporate a variety of qualitative and quantitative approaches to explore information behavior surrounding primary sources in great depth as well as with sufficient breadth with which to make generalizations.

Archival intelligence is a model for information literacy education in archives that applies information-seeking research to an understudied area: primary sources. As it develops from model to theory, it would have to be tested by studying diverse users and information needs in the array of environments in which primary sources exist. These include traditional and digital archives, microfilm reading rooms, and libraries with published primary sources. Also, because archival intelligence encompasses the range of information behaviors, such as needs, seeking, and selection, theory developed out of this model would have to consider other theories, such as cognitive authority and relevance. In the increasingly digital world, primary sources are becoming more visible, used, and mainstreamed in all libraries. Promoting information literacy for primary sources is a natural extension of other efforts in libraries and information centers.

Bates, M. (1989). The design of browsing and berrypicking techniques for the online search interface. *Online Review 13*, 407–424.

Cole, C. (2000). Name collection by Ph.D. history students: Inducing expertise. *Journal of the American Society for Information Science, 51*, 444–455.

Pirolli, P., & Card, S. K. (1999). Information foraging. *Psychological Review 106*, 643–675.

Reitman, W. R. (1965). *Cognition and thought*. New York: Wiley.

Robyns, M. C. (2001). The archivist as educator: Integrating critical thinking skills into historical research methods instruction. *American Archivist, 64*, 363–384.

Russell, D. M., Stefik, M. J., Pirolli, P., & Card, S. K. (1993). The cost structure of sensemaking. In Arnold, B., van der Veer, G., & White T. (Eds.), *Proceedings of the SIGCHI conference on human factors in computing systems*, April 24-29, 1993, Amsterdam, The Netherlands (pp. 269–276). New York: ACM Press.

Steig, M. (1981). The information of [sic] needs of historians. *College and Research Libraries, 42*, 549–560.

Wiberley, S. E., Jr., & Jones, W. G. (1989). Patterns of information seeking in the humanities. *College & Research Libraries, 50*, 638–645.

Wineburg, S. (2001). *Historical thinking and other unnatural acts: Charting the future of teaching the past*. Philadelphia: Temple University Press.

Yakel, E., & Torres, D. A. (2003). AI: Archival intelligence and user expertise. *American Archivist, 66*, 51–78.

Zuboff, S. (1988). *In the age of the smart machine: The future of work and power*. New York: Basic Books.

4
Bandura's Social Cognition

Makiko Miwa
R & D Division
National Institute of Multimedia Education, Japan
miwamaki@nime.ac.jp

Albert Bandura created social learning theory in the 1970s to empha-size the significance of observational learning. He maintained that most human behavior is learned by modeling. As the theory developed and expanded its scope to include psychological phenomena of motivational and self-regulatory mechanisms, Bandura renamed it "social cognitive theory." The new name emphasizes the social origins of much human thought and action, as well as the influential causal contribution of thought processes to human motivation, affect, and action.

Central to Bandura's theory, and particularly useful for a study of human information behavior, are three premises:

1) Triadic reciprocal causation posits that behavioral, cognitive, and other environmental influences all operate interactively as determinants of each other.

2) Multiple levels of goals assumes that goals are cognitively generated future events which motivate present human behavior. Bandura (1989) incorporates multiple levels of goals to explain how higher-level distal goals of general prin-ciples control lower-level goals of context-specific plan.

3) Self-efficacy proposes that people generate their thoughts, behavior, and affective states and that these, in turn, affect the course their own thoughts, behavior, and affective states, and that these, in turn, affect the courses of action people choose to take, the amount of effort they put forth, their resis-tance to failure, and the level of accomplishment they achieve.

Numerous studies in a variety of domains adopted Bandura's social cog-nitive theory as a general theory or metatheory to explain and/or analyze

54

human behavior in the context of everyday life. Wilson (1996) developed several models of human information seeking and information behavior and integrated them with models developed by other authors into a more general framework, generating a variety of research strategies. His 1996 model of information behavior adopts self-efficacy as a part of the activating mechanism of information seeking in order to explain why some information needs do not invoke information-seeking behavior.

Ren (1999) investigated uses of a variety of government information sources by small business managers in the State of New Jersey. She found that respondents with higher self-efficacy in using a particular information source are likely to use the source. Ren also found that executives with higher Internet self-efficacy used the Internet more frequently for government information searches than others.

Miwa (2000) conducted telephone interviews with 62 AskERIC users and analyzed their information-seeking processes. By adopting the conceptualization of multiple levels of goals from Bandura's social cognitive theory, she identified several occurrences of modification in users' goals during their information-seeking processes. Her findings underscore the dynamic nature of information-seeking processes.

Savolainen (2001) proposed a concept of *network competence* in the context of information seeking. He defined network competence as "the mastery of four major areas: knowledge of information resources available on the Internet, skilled use of the ICT tools to access information, judgment of the relevance of information, and communication" (p. 211). Savolainen developed his model of network competence by adopting the concept of self-efficacy from Bandura's social cognitive theory. The model relates four major factors of network competence: self-efficacy, outcome expectations, affective factors (e.g., anxiety), and experiences received from information seeking on the Internet. Savolainen emphasizes the significance of associations between network competence and self-efficacy in finding information on the Internet.

While Bandura and his colleagues used experimental methods in developing the theory, it can also be used as a general framework for naturalistic inquiry in data collection and analysis, as demonstrated by Miwa (2000). The theory can also serve as a framework for survey research as performed by Ren (1999), and for generating and/or synthesizing domain-specific models for information seeking and information behavioral research as demonstrated by Wilson (1999) and Savolainen (2001).

Social cognitive theory is a general theory or metatheory applicable to various types of everyday human behavior including information behavior. The theory has been tested and verified in a variety of contexts and applied not only in psychology but also in numerous domains including information studies. The theory is capable of capturing internal and external notions of social constraint. The major strength of this theory in information behavioral research seems to be its applicability to a variety of contexts and settings, particularly within everyday information behavior. Thus, the theory may help draw a big picture of human information behavior.

Though Bandura and his colleagues employed experimental design in developing and testing social cognitive theory, it might be difficult to apply experimental design in human information behavioral research incorporating the theory. This is mainly because the cognitive and affective states of humans seeking information are not directly observable. Information-seeking behavior is initiated unexpectedly when people perceive a gap or an anomalous state of knowledge. Thus, it might not be easy to employ direct observational technique in collecting naturalistic data of human information behavior incorporating social cognitive theory.

More research is needed to develop a general model of human information seeking and/or behavior in everyday life. Social cognitive theory may be a useful tool in conceptualizing and designing information behavioral research as well as in analyzing empirical data. For example, *triadic reciprocal causation* may be useful in developing a framework to be used in capturing a variety of cognitive, affective, and social factors associated with human information behavior in everyday life settings. *Multiple levels of goals* may be useful in differentiating task goals and IR goals in studying IR interaction. It may also be useful in capturing modification of goals in information-seeking processes. Finally, the concept of *self-efficacy* may have explanatory power for different levels of performance in information seeking and problem solving.

Bandura, A. (1986). *Social foundation of thought and action*. Englewood Cliffs, NJ: Prentice-Hall.

Bandura, A. (1989). Self-regulation of motivation and action through internal standards and goal systems. In A. P. Lawrence (Ed.), *Goal concepts in personality and social psychology* (pp. 19–85). Hillsdale, NJ: Lawrence Erlbaum.

Bandura, A. (1997). *Self-efficacy: The exercise of control.* New York: W. H. Freeman and Company.

Miwa, M. (2000). *Use of human intermediation in information problem solving: A users' perspective.* Syracuse, NY: ERIC Clearinghouse on Information and Technology.

Ren, W. (2001). Self-efficacy and the search for government information. *Reference & User Services Quarterly, 38*(3) 283–291.

Savolainen, R. (2002). Network competence and network information seeking on the Internet: from definitions towards a social cognitive model. *Journal of Documentation, 58*(2) 211–226.

Wilson, T. D., & Walsh, C. (1996). *Information behaviour: An interdisciplinary perspective.* Sheffield, UK: University of Sheffield.

5
Berrypicking

Marcia J. Bates
Department of Information Studies
University of California, Los Angeles, USA
mjbates@ucla.edu

The act of searching for information is, in itself, a very important part of the general behavior of information seeking. In the 1970s and 1980s much attention in library and information science was given to searching techniques. New online systems were being developed, and there was a recognized need for more sophistication in thinking about the searching process. Bates (1979a & b) wrote about information search tactics and produced the first *Annual Review of Information Science and Technology* chapter on search techniques (1981). Searching techniques needed to be quite sophisticated for a number of the systems developed in those years, and textbooks and compendia of searching methods appeared (e.g., Armstrong & Large, 1988; Harter, 1986).

The needs of the search process raised important questions in information seeking and information retrieval research as well. Despite the obvious connections between the research in these two areas, the two communities of researchers did not have as much to do with each other as would have been desirable. On the one hand, information-seeking research was demonstrating the complex factors involved in human efforts to find information; on the other hand, information retrieval research concentrated on testing and improving computer retrieval algorithms. In the information retrieval (IR) environment, it was not uncommon to work with standard, invented queries and standardized relevance assessments on those queries. Often, no actual user and no real search queries were involved.

Further, IR research was almost entirely organized around the single query. That is, an information search was assumed to consist of one use of an information system, in order to ask one question. The universal model for the information search in IR research was the case where the user would submit a query to an information system, the system would respond with an answer, the user might modify the query formulation to improve the system response, or the system itself would modify the query based on user interest in retrieved articles (so-called "relevance feedback"), and then, when the best search formulation had been found for that one, same query, the searcher would print out the records (usually assumed to be bibliographic citations), and walk away. One query, one use.

In the 1980s, however, more and more research was appearing that demonstrated how people really search for information. In particular, more work was published on the information-seeking behavior of social scientists (e.g., Ellis, 1989), and humanities scholars (Stone, 1982). The one-stop model of online searching seemed poorly fitted to the more gradual and complex information gathering associated with those disciplines. Furthermore, in the late 1970s and in the 1980s, the online searching world was dominated by database vendors such as DIALOG and LEXIS-NEXIS. Librarian intermediaries who searched databases would log on to one of these vendors' systems, and then search on one or more of the databases offered by the vendor—one-stop shopping, as it were. The mind-set in both research and practice at the time was overwhelmingly organized around the idea of trained librarian intermediaries getting everything in one search and with one search language. The idea of searching for many different types of information in a single search session at a computer, and in many types of sources (not only in bibliographic or full text databases), was still seen only dimly on the far horizon, and was not front and center in researchers' or practitioners' thinking.

The development of online catalogs in the 1980s, however, began to shake up these assumptions. First, online catalogs were designed for the nonlibrarian end-user. Virtually no skilled training could be assumed. Second, combining different kinds of databases and interfaces began to be a realistic possibility in the late 1980s, as libraries loaded other databases, sometimes with very different interfaces, into their catalogs.

Bates drew on all these developments to argue that real information searching does not always work in the one query/one use way that had been assumed, and that, furthermore, with the development of more sophisticated computer systems than had been possible in earlier years, we could now design for the way that people really search. In an article titled "The design of browsing and berrypicking techniques for the online search interface" (Bates, 1989), she laid out a model of the berry-picking search, and then proposed a variety of design features that users of online systems might like to have to accomplish their searching goals.

The berrypicking model differs from the traditional information retrieval searching model in four ways. Each will be discussed in turn:

1) *Nature of the Query.* According to Bates, real-life queries *change and evolve during the course of searching*, specifically, people:

> [M]ay begin with just one feature of a broader topic, or just one relevant reference, and move through a variety of sources. Each new piece of information they encounter gives them new ideas and directions to follow and, consequently, a new conception of the query. At each stage they are not just modi-fying the search terms used in order to get a better match for a single query. Rather the query itself (as well as the search terms used) is continually shifting, in part or whole. (1989, pp. 409–410)

2) *Nature of the Overall Search Process.* Bates said:

> [A]t each stage, with each different conception of the query, the user may identify useful information and refer-ences. In other words, the query is satisfied not by a single final retrieved set, but by a series of selections of individual references and bits of information at each stage of the ever-modifying search. (1989, p. 410)

Bates called this bit-at-a-time retrieval *berrypicking*, by analogy with picking huckleberries in the forest, as she had done in prior years when living in Washington state.

3) *Range of Search Techniques Used.* Bates pointed out that the usual model of subject searching in databases, which dominated the thinking at the time in the field, was only one of many techniques people might use online, and do use offline. In addition to *subject searching* in biblio-graphic databases, people also do *footnote chasing* (moving backward through the literature by following up endnotes and footnotes), *citation*

searching (moving forward through the literature by using citation indexes to see who has cited a given item or author), *journal run* (identifying a central journal in a subject area of interest and reviewing its contents pages), *area scanning* (browsing the materials collocated with other items already located), and *author searching* (searching for other works by an author already located) (Bates, 1989, p. 412). The techniques are not limited to this set.

4) *Domain Searched.* The approach taken above to searching necessarily implies that people search in different sources than we had usually thought of in information science research—in many other places besides bibliographic databases, as the searcher's ever-shifting berrypicking search moves from source to source, technique to technique.

As of this writing in spring 2004, the initial article on berrypicking (Bates, 1989) had been cited 148 times, according to the "ISI Web of Knowledge" citation databases (isiknowledge.com). Authors have used the article in addressing a wide range of information seeking and information system design questions, including many human-computer interface issues, as well as in work on the nature of browsing, and on information searching tactics. Bates addressed additional possible approaches to information system design that were sensitive to searching techniques in Bates (1990). She recently reanalyzed the original six techniques suggested (feature 3 mentioned previously) in terms of the gigantic search domain of the World Wide Web, and linked the analysis to the Bradford Distribution. Specifically, she suggested that the six techniques were each optimal for different regions of the distribution of relevant documents that there are on a subject in a domain (Bates, 2002). She also analyzed searching behavior in a joint paper with Suresh Bhavnani, in which the techniques and theories of cognitive science were applied to the information searching process (Bhavnani & Bates, 2002).

Finally, many of Bates' suggestions have been taken up in the world of the practice of information system design, where products and capabilities are introduced in vendors' systems and put up on the Web or incorporated into other information systems. It is impossible to know the extent to which these information system changes were influenced by Bates' work, or were redeveloped independently. However, the high citation count suggests that knowledge of the paper has been widespread.

Armstrong, C. J., & Large, J. A., Eds. (1988). *Manual of online search strategies*. Aldershot, England: Gower.

Bates, M. J. (1979a). Information search tactics. *Journal of the American Society for Information Science, 30*(4), 205–214.

Bates, M. J. (1979b). Idea tactics. *Journal of the American Society for Information Science, 30*(5), 280–289

Bates, M. J. (1981). Search techniques. *Annual Review of Information Science and Technology, 16*, 139–169.

Bates, M. J. (1989). The design of browsing and berrypicking techniques for the online search interface. *Online Review, 13*(5), 407–424.

Bates, M. J. (1990). Where should the person stop and the information search interface start? *Information Processing & Management, 26*(5), 575–591.

Bates, M. J. (2002). Speculations on browsing, directed searching, and linking in relation to the Bradford Distribution. In H. Bruce, R. Fidel, P. Ingwersen, & P. Vakkari (Eds.), *Emerging frameworks and methods: Proceedings of the fourth international conference on conceptions of library and information science* (CoLIS4) (pp. 137–150). Greenwood Village, CO: Libraries Unlimited.

Bhavnani, S., & Bates, M. J. (2002). Separating the knowledge layers: Cognitive analysis of search knowledge through hierarchical goal decompositions. *Proceedings of the 64th Annual Meeting of the American Society for Information Science & Technology, 39*, 204–213.

Ellis, D. (1989). A behavioural approach to information retrieval system design. *Journal of Documentation, 45*(3), 171–212.

Harter, S. P. (1986). *Online information retrieval: Concepts, principles, and techniques*. Orlando: Academic Press.

ISI Web of Knowledge. Retrieved June 9, 2004, from http://isiknowledge.com

Stone, S. (1982). Humanities scholars: Information needs and uses. *Journal of Documentation, 38*(4), 292–313.

6

Big6™ Skills for Information Literacy

Carrie A. Lowe
American Library Association, USA
clowe@alawash.org

Michael B. Eisenberg
The Information School
University of Washington, USA
mbe@u.washington.edu

Information literacy, defined as the ability to "recognize when information is needed and...locate, evaluate and use effectively the needed information" (American Library Association Presidential Committee on Information Literacy, 1989, p.1), is clearly the new basic skill set of the 21st century. New South Wales Department of Education's (n. d.) *information process*, Kuhlthau's (1993) *information seeking*, Stripling and Pitts's (1988) *research process*, and Irving's (1985) *study and information skills* guide educators as they incorporate information literacy skills in curricular context. These and other information literacy models underscore the fact that although there are specific skills that create information problem-solving, these steps are iterative and flexible (Eisenberg and Brown, 1992).

Research as well as practice shows that successful problem solving involves a series of steps or stages. Kuhlthau (1993) uncovered a series of steps that typically occurs in successful information searching. There are similarities between Kuhlthau's information search process steps and the stages of various models of information literacy (see Table 6.1). These information process models provide a road map for implementation and instruction of information literacy skills in the curriculum.

Among the information processing models shown in Table 6.1, a prominent position belongs to the Big6 approach developed by Mike Eisenberg and Bob Berkowitz (1990). The Big6 guides learners as they

Table 6.1   Comparison of information skills process models.

Kuhlthau Information Seeking	Eisenberg/Berkowitz Information Problem-Solving (The Big 6 Skills)	AASL/AECT Information Literacy Standards	Pitts/Stripling Research Process	New South Wales Information Process
1. Initiation 2. Selection 4. Formulation (of focus)	1. Task Definition 1.1 Define the problem 1.2 Identify info requirements	1. Formulation/analysis of information need	1. Choose a broad topic 2. Get an overview of the topic 3. Narrow the topic 4. Develop thesis/ purpose statement	Defining
3. Exploration 5. Collection (investigating info on (gather info on the the general focused topic) topic)	2. Info seeking strategies 2.1 Determine range sources 2.2 Prioritize sources	2. Identification/appraisal of likely sources	5. Formulate question to guide research 6. Plan for research & production	Locating
	3. Location & access 3.1 Locate sources 3.2 Find information	3. Tracing/locating indiv. resources 4. Examining, selecting & rejecting individual resources	7. Find, analyze, evaluate resources	Selecting
6. Presentation	4. Information use 4.1 Engage (read, view, etc.) 4.2 Extract info	5. Interrogating/using individual resources 6. Recording/storing information	8. Evaluate evidence take notes/compile bib	Organizing
7. Assessment (of outcome/ process)	5. Synthesis 5.1 Organize 5.2 Present	7. Interpretation, analysis, synth. and evaluation of information 8. Shape, presentation, and communication of information	9. Establish conclusions/ organize in outline 10. Create and present final product	Presenting
	6. Evaluation 6.1 Judge the product 6.2 Judge the process	9. Evaluation of the assignment	(Reflection point - is the paper/project satisfactory)	Assessing

embark on information problem-solving activities, and provides educators with a framework for teaching the research process and including information technology skills in the curriculum. It was developed from practice, observation, and work by Eisenberg and Berkowitz in a number of different teaching and learning situations and across grade and student age groups.

The Big6 Skills comprise a unified set of information and technology skills that taken together form a process. The process encompasses six stages from task definition to evaluation (see Table 6.2).

Many information problem-solving models provide a set of specific activities, or an outline of isolated skills, however, these models may also encourage a lockstep strategy that forces one specific method of problem solving and decision making. While similar to the other models, the Big6 approach includes a systematic set of activities. It also provides a broad-based, logical skill set that can be used as the structure for developing a curriculum, or as the framework for a set of distinct problem-solving skills. For example, the Big6 provides to teachers a definitive set of skills that students must master in order to be successful in any learning context. For students, the Big6 provides a guide to dealing with assignments and tasks as well as a model to fall back on when they experience difficulties. In a way, the Big6 creates "metacognition"—an awareness by students of their mental states and processes during information problem solving.

Table 6.2   The Big6 model of information problem solving.

---

1. Task Definition:
    1.1 Define the problem.
    1.2 Identify the information needed.

2. Information Seeking Strategies:
    2.1 Determine all possible sources.
    2.2 Select the best sources.

3. Location and Access:
    3.1 Locate sources.
    3.2 Find information within sources.

4. Use of Information:
    4.1 Engage (e.g., read, hear, view).
    4.2 Extract relevant information.

5. Synthesis:
    5.1 Organize the information from multiple sources.
    5.2 Present information.

6. Evaluation:
    6.1 Judge the result (effectiveness).
    6.2 Judge the process (efficiency).

Copyright 1987 Eisenberg and Berkowitz.

When Big6 is used as the framework for the completion of an information problem, classroom teachers and library media specialists work together to guide students through the project, from choosing a topic (Big6 #1, *task definition*) to self- and peer-assessment (Big6 #6, *evaluation*). Research has shown that an active, well-funded library media program has a measurable impact on student achievement (Lance, Welborn, & Hamilton-Pennell, 1992; Lance, Rodney, & Hamilton-Pennell, 2000); therefore, the kind of collaboration that Big6 creates provides students with the environment for success.

Although Big6 was developed in the field of library and information science, it can be applied to any information situation—academic, work—even everyday information problems, needs, and situations. This flexibility is facilitated by a number of important themes that character-ize the Big6:

1) Its process can be applied with students of all ages, and across all grade levels (K–20).

2) It perceives technology skills as integral to the information problem-solving process, by providing a broad, top-down structure for an integrated information and technology skills curriculum.

3) It is not always a linear, step-by-step process, but encourages a variety of alternative strategies such as jumping around, branching off, or looping back.

4) It provides a curriculum for integrating information literacy instruction with all subject area curricula.

5) It reflects critical thinking as an information problem-solving process.

6) Its process includes necessary elements for solving problems and completing tasks.

While the Big6 model holds potential for the study of human informa-tion behavior, so far most of the research on Big6 has been informal and anecdotal. For example, it has been suggested that the steps that com-prise Big6 are used by successful people every day; what Big6 does is pro-vide guidelines for teaching these skills to children and others who have not mastered them yet. Other informal research has shown that Big6 provides a useful framework for teaching technology skills, and that teaching these skills in the context of information problem solving results in better retention of knowledge (see Eisenberg, M. B., & Berkowitz, R. E., 1999 and 2000; Eisenberg, M. B., & Johnson, D, 2002; Eisenberg, M., Lowe, C., & Spitzer, K., 2004).

A recent action study by Berkowitz (n. d.) provides evidence of the advantages of Big6 skills approach. As a library media specialist in a New York State high school, Berkowitz collaborated with a social studies teacher whose students were performing poorly on the state's Regents exams (passing at the rate of 53 percent). Working together, they taught students to use the Big6 and to extend these skills to a testing situation.

The outcome of this intervention was that the next group of students passed the Regents exam at the rate of 91 percent.

Another recent Big6 study (Wolf, Brush, & Saye, 2003) looked at a class of middle school students assigned to research the African-American civil rights movement. In this project, the researchers instructed the students in the use of Big6 as a metacognitive scaffold. The researchers found that after instruction in Big6, the students were able to tackle complex information problems such as the research project with greater success. They also found that the students came to rely upon Big6 for making decisions about current and future activities related to the project. Future research on Big6 in an IB context could benefit from the use of a wide range of methodologies beyond the observation and short surveys employed in this study.

The Big6 approach is consistent with other models and standards of information literacy. Its special value comes from the ideas, resources, and strategies that go beyond the model itself. The flexibility of the Big6 and the richness of material supporting the Big6 (see www.big6.org) makes it highly adaptable to a range of educational systems and approaches in the U.S. and globally. Educators and IB researchers can focus on the Big6 to better understand information literacy and the process of integrating information skills instruction into K–20 educational systems and curriculum as well as into business and public sector contexts.

American Library Association. (1989). *Presidential Committee on Information Literacy. Final Report.* Chicago: American Library Association.

Berkowitz, B. (n. d.). *Research study: The Big6™ and student achievement - Report of an action research study.* Retrieved February 21, 2004, from www.big6.com/showarticle.php?id=11

The Big6 skills information problem-solving approach (n. d.). Retrieved February 21, 2004, from www.big6.com

Eisenberg, M. B., & Berkowitz, R. E. (1990). *Information problem-solving: The Big Six skills approach to library & information skills instruction.* Norwood NJ: Ablex.

Eisenberg, M. B., & Berkowitz, R. E. (1999). *Teaching information & technology skills: The Big6 in elementary schools.* Worthington, OH: Linworth.

Eisenberg, M. B., & Berkowitz, R. E. (2000). *Teaching information & technology skills: The Big6 in secondary schools.* Worthington, OH: Linworth.

Eisenberg, M. B., & Johnson, D. (2002). *Computer skills for information problem-solving: learning and teaching technology in context.* ERIC Digest EDO-IR-96-04. Syracuse, NY: ERIC Clearinghouse on Information and Technology.

Eisenberg, M. B., & Brown, M. K. (1992). Current themes regarding library and information skills instruction: Research supporting and research lacking. *School Library Media Quarterly, 20*(2), 103–109.

Eisenberg, M., Lowe, C., & Spitzer, K. (2004). *Information literacy: Essential skills for the information age* (2nd ed.). Westport, CT: Libraries Unlimited.

Irving, A. (1985). *Study and information skills across the curriculum.* London: Heinemann Educational Books.

Kuhlthau, C. C. (1993). *Seeking meaning: A process approach to library and information services.* Greenwich, CT: Ablex.

Lance, K. C., Rodney, M. J., & Hamilton-Pennell, C. (2000). *How school librarians help kids achieve standards: The second Colorado study.* San Jose, CA: Hi Willow.

Lance, K. C., Welborn, L., & Hamilton-Pennell, C. (1992). *The impact of school library media centers on academic achievement.* Denver, CO: Department of Education.

New South Wales Department of Education. (n. d.). *Information skills in the school.* Retrieved February 21, 2004, from www.schools.nsw.edu.au/schoollibraries/resources/policy.htm

Stripling, B., & Pitts, J. (1988). *Brainstorms and blueprints: Teaching library research as a thinking process.* Westport, CT: Libraries Unlimited.

Todd, R. (1995). Integrated information literacy skills instruction: Does it make a difference? *School Library Media Quarterly, 23*(2), 133–139.

Wolf, S., Brush, T., & Saye, J. (2003). The Big Six information skills as a metacognitive scaffold: A case study. *School Library Media Research, 6.* Retrieved February 21, 2004, from www.ala.org/ala/aasl/aaslpubsandjournals/slmrb/slmrcontents/volume62003/bigsixinformation.htm

7
Chang's Browsing

Shan-Ju L. Chang
Department of Library and Information Science
National Taiwan University, Taiwan
sjlin@ntu.edu.tw

Browsing is a commonly observed form of human information behavior. As a concept, it appears in many different disciplines with various meanings (Chang & Rice, 1993). Browsing as an important part of human information behavior has been observed and investigated in the context of information seeking in the library in general and has assumed a greater importance as an information search strategy in human-machine interaction in particular. However, conceptualization of browsing has been problematic because its nature is not well understood.

In order to understand the notion of browsing and provide the descriptive data for studying browsing, Chang (1995) first analyzed the literature to develop a preliminary model of browsing. This model was modified based on the findings from empirical observations and interview data from 33 users of three different library settings (including academic, public, and special libraries) to derive a descriptive conceptual framework for understanding browsing phenomena.

The resultant framework, based on the empirical evidence, makes explicit some unclear concepts associated with browsing in the literature, such as "vagueness" of goal or object, and clarifies the role of knowledge. It provides an analytical language, through characterization of the browsing process, for systematic description of various types of browsing behavior and for better articulation of what Herner (1976) calls "the levels of browsing." Chang's study contributes to the literature by identifying the five contexts that motivate people to browse and systematically describes the situations in which various types of browsing take place, which result in nine specific patterns of browsing.

Research in browsing by Chang (1995) documents why, how, and what people browse in terms of four underlying dimensions: behavior, motivation, cognition, and resource. Chang developed a taxonomy of browsing with empirical evidence on a further set of four subdimensions: scanning, goal, object, and form. Along with a second set of four subdimensions, movement, purpose, knowledge, and focus, nine patterns of browsing were identified. Together with a follow-up study (Chang, 2000), as shown in Figure 7.1, Chang proposes a multidimensional framework for understanding the influences on the process of browsing as well as the consequences of browsing.

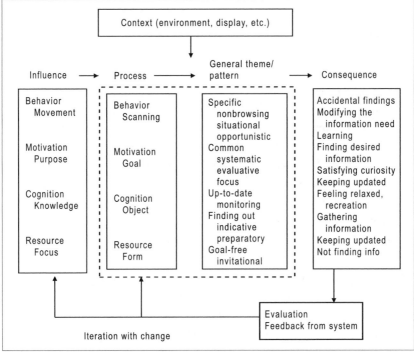

Figure 7.1   Refined framework of browsing.

Note: From *Accessing and Browsing Information and Communication* (p. 255), by R. E. Rice, M. McCreadie, and S-J. L . Chang, 2001, Boston, MA: MIT Press. Copyright 2001 by MIT Press. Adapted with permission.

This framework shows that movement, purpose, knowledge, and focus in the behavioral, motivational, cognitive, and resource dimensions, respectively, influence the browsing process in which people engage. In turn, the browsing process (in scanning, goal, object, and form dimensions) helps to determine the general themes and specific patterns of browsing.

The four dimensions that can be utilized to describe the process of browsing refer to:

1) The level of scanning activity

2) The specificity of information provided by the resource

3) The definiteness or specificity of the patron's goal

4) The specificity of the object sought

Scanning as a nonverbal behavior (there is no need to express the intent of one's actions in words) is considered a browsing activity, especially when it involves the more attentive acts of identifying, selecting, and examining. Behaviorally, browsing is increasingly easier to recognize as the level of scanning involvement increases—that is, when a patron's behavior involves selecting and examining an item after looking through a series of items.

The *resource scanned* refers to a series of information items under consideration. Four levels of a resource are identified according to the specificity of information provided for examination.

The *goal* dimension involves various degrees of open-endedness to the criteria for valid information acquisition, from intent to locate, evaluate, keep up, learn, and satisfy curiosity. The object dimension refers to what a patron seeks or expects while scanning a resource. The object can range from seeking a specific item, (or items sharing some common characteristics) to something general. Table 7.1 illustrates the elements of each dimension and shows the taxonomy of browsing. Thus, a given browsing activity can be described according to the level of scanning, the kind of resource scanned, and the type of goal and object.

Chang identifies nine specific patterns of browsing within each of five general themes:

1) *Looking for a specific item* – reveals situational browsing and opportunistic browsing

2) *Looking for something with common characteristics* – includes systematic browsing, evaluative browsing, and focus browsing

3) *Keeping up-to-date* – monitoring browsing

4) *Learning or finding out* – includes indicative browsing and preparatory browsing

5) *Goal-free* – invitational browsing

The patterns of browsing are characterized by the type of browsing that the patron engages in, along with four other criteria—movement (directed, interrupted, or undirected), knowledge (of location and content; high or low), purpose (to support or incidental), and focus (structure or content of a resource scanned).

For example, situational browsing is characterized by examining other unknown items during the process of locating a specific item, once the general area containing the needed item is identified. The type of browsing involved in this case can be described examining information objects to evaluate items with common characteristics. Opportunistic browsing is differentiated from situational browsing because it is characterized by scanning other items "incidental to the original purpose" during the process of locating a specific, intended item. Preparatory

Table 7.1   Dimensions and elements in the taxonomy of browsing.

Scanning	Resource	Goal	Object
Looking for	Meta-information	Locate	Specific item
Identifying	Object (whole)	Evaluate	Common items
Selecting	Object (part)	Keep up	Defined location
Examining	Information	Learn	General
		Satisfy curiosity	None
		Be entertained	

Note: From *Accessing and Browsing Information and Communication* (p. 295), by R. E. Rice, M. McCreadie, & S-J. L. Chang, 2001, Boston, MA: MIT Press. Copyright 2001 by MIT Press. Reprinted with permission.

browsing is characterized by learning something not specified. That is, no specific information or logical information object is sought. Rather, an information object known to the patron as having potentially interesting articles is scanned to look at whatever appears of interest is characteristic of this pattern. As another example, invitational browsing is characterized by scanning information or information objects to satisfy intrinsic motivation with no stated goal in mind. Often a given path of a resource area is followed (e.g., scanning sections of a newspaper or bookshelf sequentially). Browsing is invitational in that there is no specified objective to look for or learn about; the goal is open-ended to the extent that it is determined almost completely by external objects such as the appearance of books.

According to Chang, browsing, in essence, is an examination of unknown items of potential interest by scanning or moving through an information space in order to judge the utility of the items, to learn about something of interest in the item, or to satisfy curiosity about something. Browsing is often associated with the vagueness of information objects sought in order to make a value judgment. The nature of browsing is fundamentally evaluative and inclusive. At the micro-level, the nature of a browser's goal and specificity of object sought are the two most important factors influencing the way people browse.

Chang's research suggests that the concept of browsing is multifaceted. It serves as a search strategy when people are exposed to many alternatives to look for useful or interesting documents, to locate information items not considered beforehand or not found in the bibliographic tools. It also serves as a screening technique to help people decide what not to read, to filter out an unknown item of potential interest or use, which is actually not interesting or useful after examination. Browsing also serves as a viewing pattern in that the browser intends to identify something of potential interest to read by glancing through or "reading" the unknown items encountered in the process, but stops reading as soon as the item fails to hold the browser's interest. Such an evaluative viewing process can often result in a learning effect simply because of the opportunity of encountering the unknown. Finally, browsing is also a recreational activity that people engage in to satisfy an intrinsic need for enjoyment or diversion.

The characterization of browsing as an examination of unknown items, with scanning or moving through an information space, seems to explain why people constantly browse—because they are often surrounded with unknown items in our complex and fast-changing world. This includes all kinds of information objects and information, or even meta-information.

The implication of Chang's browsing framework and taxonomy for system design is that information systems can and should be designed to support various patterns of browsing. System development also needs to include personal attributes and "browsability" in its criteria for evaluation. In practical terms, Chang's work suggests that information providers (e.g., libraries) should arrange physical layout and displays in a way that encourages both successful and enjoyable browsing. Future research may test the browsing framework in alternative settings, such as shopping malls or Web sites on the Internet.

Chang, S-J. L., & Rice, R. E. (1993). Browsing: A multidimensional framework. *Annual Review of Information Science and Technology, 28*, 231–276.

Chang, S-J. L. (2001). Browsing and communication (Chapters 9–15). In: R. E. Rice, M. McCreadie, & S-J. L. Chang. *Accessing and browsing information and communication*. Boston, MA: MIT Press.

Chang, S-J. L. (2000). Research on browsing behavior in the libraries: An empirical analysis of consequences, success, and influences. *Journal of Library and Information Studies* (National Taiwan University), no.15, 37–68.

Chang, S-J. L. (1995). Toward a multidimensional framework for understanding browsing (Doctoral dissertation, Rutgers University, 1995). *Dissertation Abstracts International, 57*, 494.

Herner, S. (1970). Browsing. In *Encyclopedia of library and information science* (Vol. 3, pp. 408–415). New York: Marcel Dekker.

8
Chatman's Information Poverty

Julie Hersberger
Department of Library and Information Studies
University of North Carolina at Greensboro, USA
jahersbe@uncg.edu

Elfreda Chatman's theory of information poverty first appeared in print in the March 1996 volume of the *Journal of the American Society for Information Science*. Chatman had been publishing articles for many years that examined information needs and information-seeking behaviors of marginalized populations. In a keynote presentation at the opening of the *Information Seeking in Context (ISIC) 2000 Conference*, she explained the historical events underpinning development of her theories of information poverty, life in the round and normative behavior (Chatman, 2000). Chatman traced the evolution of many of her previous studies into three new middle-range theories that better explained her lifelong observations of information seeking by various populations in an everyday life context.

Regarding the theory of information poverty, Chatman explains: "I began my inquiries several years ago by wanting to discover: what constitutes a poverty lifestyle? On the surface this is a simple, almost elementary question. However, its answer has driven me to several conceptual frameworks and even the creation of several of my own" (Chatman, 2000, p. 4).

The theory of information poverty is set within the larger conceptual framework of information insiders and outsiders or what Chatman refers to as "the sociology of knowledge" (Chatman, 1996, pp. 194–197). What Chatman is describing here is what sociologists and anthropologists have for decades debated as the *emic* and *etic* approach to social science study. For an excellent article that explains the complexities of these analytical distinctions see Sandstrom (2004).

Following several studies, but in particular her study on the information world of aging women, Chatman did not find the expected results of information sharing in a homogeneous population. Social network theory did not satisfactorily explain this lack of information exchange. As a result, Chatman developed her theory of information poverty that established four key concepts: secrecy, deception, risk-taking, and situational relevance, each of which may be invoked as self-protective behaviors during the information-seeking process. Chatman (1996, p. 195) cites Bok's definition of secrecy as "intentional concealment...the overall intent of secret information is the idea that it will protect a person from unwanted intrusion into private space."

In terms of deception, Chatman suggests that "deception is a deliberate attempt to play-act, that is, to engage in activities in which our personal reality is consciously being distorted. It is a process meant to hide our true condition by giving false and misleading information" (Chatman, p. 196). Risk-taking is conceptualized as "an attribute affecting the acceptance of an innovation based on our perception of whether it is worthwhile or not. It does not seem to merit consideration if, weighed against personal or negative cost, the result would be negative" (Chatman, 1996, p. 196). Situational relevance is conceptualized as being consistent with the term "utility" (Chatman, 1996, p. 201).

From these four key concepts, six propositions were derived:

1) The information poor perceive themselves to be devoid of any sources that might help them.

2) Information poverty is partially associated with class distinction.

3) Information poverty is determined by self-protective behaviors, which are used in response to social norms.

4) Both secrecy and deception are self-protecting mechanisms due to a sense of mistrust regarding the interest or ability of others to provide useful information.

5) A decision to risk exposure about our true feelings is often not taken due to a perception that negative consequences outweigh benefits.

6) New knowledge will be selectively introduced into the information world of poor people. A condition that influences this process is the relevance of that information in response to everyday problems and concerns (Chatman, 1996, pp. 197–198).

Chatman notes that the six propositions "...represent a collective rather than individualistic model of need. As a theoretical framework, their purpose is to describe an impoverished information world" (Chatman, 1996, p. 197). Chatman (1996, p. 197) posits that:

> ...our membership in a particular social group contributes to information poverty. How? Because we can experience a need for information but are hindered from seeking it. Thus, we engage in self-protective behaviors to keep others from sensing our need. These behaviors are meant to hide our true crisis in an effort to appear normal and to exhibit acceptable coping behaviors.

Chatman's work has been extensively cited in the LIS literature. The theory of information poverty has been cited mainly by scholars examining contexts in which information seekers practice some sort of protective behavior, which, as a result, affects their access to useful or helpful information. In studies using Chatman's propositions as an analytical framework with the everyday information world of the homeless, Hersberger (2002/2003) and Hersberger, Pettigrew, & James (2000) found that some of the six statements were supported while others were not. As Chatman writes, "The value of propositions to theory construction lies in their ability to be tested, thereby strengthening or weakening the theory" (1996, p. 198).

One major flaw in Chatman's work here is her misuse of the term "social network theory." Scholars in this area are very assertive in maintaining that there is no central social network theory; rather, there are many. Scott (2000) states:

> It is undoubtedly the case that that social network analysis embodies a particular theoretical orientation towards the *structure* of the social world and that it is, therefore, linked with structural theories of action. But it is unlikely that any one substantive theory should be regarded as embodying the essence of social network analysis. The point of view...is that social network analysis is an orientation towards the social world that inheres in a particular set of *methods*. It is not a specific body of formal or substantive social theory. (Scott, 2000, p. 37)

Lin's theory of social capital or Granovetter's theory of strong and weak ties might also be useful to scholars wishing to examine social networks as information networks. Furthermore, Scott's handbook on social network analysis is another useful resource for explaining the basics of social network analysis. Still, Chatman's four core concepts and six propositions posed in the theory of information poverty do work better perhaps as a conceptual framework or an analytical framework until more theory testing occurs.

The theory of Information Poverty, therefore, may prove useful in future LIS studies, particularly those investigating information seeking by individuals who hold memberships in various marginalized groups.

Chatman, E. A. (2000). Framing social life in theory and research. *The New Review of Information Behaviour Research, 1*, 3–18.

Chatman, E. A. (1996). The impoverished life-world of outsiders. *Journal of the American Society for Information Science, 47*, 193–206.

Chatman, E. A. (1992). *The information world of aging women*. Westport, CT: Greenwood Press.

Chatman, E. A. (1983). *The diffusion of information among the working poor*. Unpublished doctoral dissertation, University of California, Berkeley.

Granovetter, M. S. (1982). The strength of weak ties: A network theory revisited. In P. V. Marsden & N. Lin (Eds.), *Social structure and network analysis*. Beverly Hills, CA: Sage.

Granovetter, M. S. (1973). The strength of weak ties. *American Journal of Sociology, 78*, 1360–1380.

Hersberger, J. A. (2002/2003). Are the economically poor information poor? Does the digital divide affect the homeless and access to information? *The Canadian Journal of Information and Library Science, 27*(3), 44–63.

Hersberger, J. A., Pettigrew, K. E., & James, L. (2000, April). *Social capital as embedded in social networks of homeless populations*. Paper presented at Sunbelt XXI, Vancouver, B.C., Canada.

Lin, N. (2001). *Social capital: A theory of social structure and action*. Cambridge, UK: Cambridge University Press.

Sandstrom, P.E. (2004). Anthropological approaches to information systems and behavior. *Bulletin of the American Society for Information Science and Technology, 30*(3), 12–16.

Scott, J. (2000). *Social network analysis* (2nd ed.). London: Sage.

9
Chatman's Life in the Round

Crystal Fulton
Department of Library and Information Studies
University College Dublin, Ireland
Crystal.Fulton@ucd.ie

The theory of life in the round represents a culmination of Elfreda Chatman's research during the 1980s and 1990s, which has focused on understanding information behavior through the social factors influencing that behavior. Of utmost importance to Chatman was exploring how ordinary people experience information in connection with everyday needs. She found that one's context was the determining factor of one's perspective on information and, therefore, shaped an individual's use or non-use of information. "Life in the round" offers a means to gaining in-depth insight into people's information behavior in that context.

Chatman put forth her theory in her 1999 article, "A Theory of Life in the Round." A "life in the round" is a "public form of life in which things are implicitly understood" (Chatman, 1999, p. 212), where members are concerned with their small world, the creation and support of social roles within that world, and information that can be used there. Currently applied in such research projects as Hersberger's exploration of the information needs of the homeless and the IBEC Life in the Round Project (IBEC, 2003), Chatman's theory continues to hold value for researchers exploring information behavior in a particular small-world context.

Chatman's ideas about life in the round have their roots in various sociological theories which influenced her research into everyday information behavior and assisted her with formulating the key concepts underpinning her theory (1998, 1999). For instance, Merton's (1972) research provided the basis of Chatman's use of the terms *insiders* and *outsiders* and informed her ideas of how insiders and outsiders respond to information problems (Chatman, 1996). Ultimately, Chatman's research into the social world of women prisoners led to her final development of a theory of life in the round.

Four concepts are central to the theory: *small world, social norms, social types*, and *worldview* (Chatman, 1999). A *small world* is a society or world in which members share a common worldview. Chatman (1999) notes that within a small world, members determine what is, and what is not, important, and which sources can be trusted. Living in the round has a particular effect upon information behavior: since "life in the round" is routine, information seeking beyond that world is neither needed nor wanted.

Social norms are standards of acceptable behavior in a given context. Using the works of such researchers as Tónnies (1957), Douglas (1970), Whyte (1981), and Angulo (1990), Chatman builds a picture of social norms as patterns, which give balance or order to a small world (1998; 1999). In the small world, information shapes collective behavior. Whereas insiders see their codes of behavior as normative, routine, and as fitting shared meanings, outsiders to the group cannot relate, because they do not share the same social meanings. Within a given social context, an individual seeks information, because he or she shares a common need with his or her homogenous social group (Pendleton & Chatman, 1998).

Social norms created and supported within the group determine labels applied to certain individuals or *social types*. The term refers to one's classification in terms of ability to acquire and use information. In her prison study, Chatman observed that inmates assigned social labels to other women inmates according to certain distinguishing characteristics. Through classification, individuals are assigned a social role and provide a standard by which to evaluate public behavior. For instance, in the prison study, *brides* were new prisoners, who were housed in a separate area of the prison, before being integrated into the general inmate population. These brides often partnered themselves with another social type, the *studs*, who offered protection, but also acted as information gatekeepers (Pendleton & Chatman, 1998).

Worldview is the collective of common beliefs, customs, and language of small world members, by which they evaluate behavior and interpret the world. This outlook causes members to accept information that comes from other insiders, but to suspect and reject information originating outside that world (Chatman, 1999; Pendleton & Chatman, 1998).

Using the key concepts noted above, Chatman offers six propositional statements, which constitute her theory of "life in the round":

> *Proposition 1*: A small-world conceptualization is essential to a "life in the round" because it establishes legitimized others (primarily insiders) who set boundaries on behavior.
>
> *Proposition 2*: Social norms force private behavior to undergo public scrutiny. It is this public arena that deems behavior—including information-seeking behavior—appropriate or not.
>
> *Proposition 3*: The result of establishing appropriate behavior is the creation of a worldview. This worldview includes language, values, meaning, symbols, and a context that holds the worldview within temporal boundaries.
>
> *Proposition 4*: For most of us, a worldview is played out as life in the round. Fundamentally, this is a life taken for granted. It works most of the time with enough predictability that, unless a critical problem arises, there is no point in seeking information.
>
> *Proposition 5*: Members who live in the round will not cross the boundaries of their world to seek information.
>
> *Proposition 6*: Individuals will cross information boundaries only to the extent that the following conditions are met: 1) the information is perceived as critical, 2) there is a collective expectation that the information is relevant, and 3) a perception exists that the life lived in the round is no longer functioning. (Chatman, 1999, 2000)

Observing life in the round, then, allows the researcher deeper understanding of information behavior in that small world. Members of the small world determine what information is, as well as how to access and use this information. As Chatman (1999) notes, the collective view of what is relevant is central to understanding how the small world operates. Thus, the theory shows us that information behavior is about constructing meaning. Critically, location or context facilitates this construction of meaning, since members assess the importance or relevance of things in their everyday lives.

Although the workings of a particular world are not transferable to another context, because behavior observed is context-specific, "life in the round" provides a useful framework for studying and working with various groups. For instance, life in the round can be used to identify stimuli that prompt a member of a small world to consider seeking information through an external source, thereby offering information service providers insight into the information worlds of their clientele and supporting their planning of effective information services. "Life in the round," then, offers a helpful approach to our understanding of information behavior, shifting the emphasis in exploring that behavior from a focus on information needs to social context.

Angulo, J. de. (1990). *Indians in overalls*. San Francisco, CA: City Light Books.

Chatman, E. A. (1999). A theory of life in the round. *Journal of the American Society for Information Science, 50*, 207–217.

Chatman, E. A. (2000). Framing social life in theory and research. *The New Review of Information Behaviour Research, 1*, 3–17.

Chatman, E. A. (1996). The impoverished life-world of outsiders. *Journal of the American Society for Information Science, 47*, 193–206.

Douglas, J. D. (1970). *Understanding everyday life: Toward the reconstruction of sociological knowledge*. Chicago: Aldine.

IBEC. (2003). *"Life in the round" and the homeless: Information flow, human service needs, and pivotal interventions (2003-2004)*. Retrieved January, 3, 2004, from http://ibec.ischool.washington.edu/ibecCat.aspx?subCat=Life%20in%20the%20Round&cat=Projects

Merton, R. K. (1972). Insiders and outsiders: A chapter in the sociology of knowledge. *American Journal of Sociology, 78*, 9–47.

Pendleton, V. E., & Chatman, E. A. (1998). Small world lives: Implications for the public library. *Library Trends, 46*, 732–751.

Tónnies, F. (1957). *Community and society*. C. P. Loomis, (Ed. and Trans.). East Lansing, MI: Michigan State University Press.

Whyte, W. F. (1981). *Street corner society*. Chicago: University of Chicago Press.

10
Cognitive Authority

Soo Young Rieh
School of Information
University of Michigan, USA
rieh@umich.edu

Patrick Wilson (1983) developed the cognitive authority theory from social epistemology in his book, *Second-hand Knowledge: An Inquiry into Cognitive Authority*. The fundamental concept of Wilson's cognitive authority is that people construct knowledge in two different ways: based on their first-hand experience or on what they have learned second-hand from others. What people learn first-hand depends on the stock of ideas they bring to the interpretation and understanding of their encounters with the world. People primarily depend on others for ideas as well as for information outside the range of direct experience. Much of what they think of the world is what they have gained second-hand.

Wilson (1983) argues that all that people know of the world beyond the narrow range of their own lives is what others have told them. However, people do not count all hearsay as equally reliable; only those who are deemed to "know what they are talking about" become cognitive authorities. Wilson coined the term *cognitive authority* to explain the kind of authority that influences thoughts that people would consciously recognize being proper. Cognitive authority differs from *administrative authority* or the authority vented in a hierarchical position.

Wilson makes several points about cognitive authority. First, it involves a relationship of at least two people. Thus having cognitive authority differs from being an expert, as a person can be an expert although unrecognized. Second, cognitive authority is a matter of degree; a little or a lot of it can be possessed. Third, cognitive authority is relative to a sphere of interest. On some questions, a person may speak with authority; but on other questions with none at all. Fourth, cognitive authority clearly relates to credibility: "The authority's influence on us is thought proper because he is thought credible, worthy of belief"

(p. 15). That is, cognitive authorities are among those regarded as credible sources of information.

Wilson claims that it is not always individuals in whom people recognize authority. Cognitive authority can be also found in books, instruments, organizations, and institutions. Wilson discusses various external tests for recognizing a text's cognitive authority. The first consideration is recognition of authorship: "We can trust a text if it is the work of an individual or group of individuals whom we can trust" (p. 166). Wilson states that personal cognitive authority involves only "present reputation and accomplishments up to now" (p. 167). The second consideration is that cognitive authority can be associated with a publisher: a publishing house, a single journal, publication sponsorship, and published reviews, all can acquire this authority. The third consideration is found in document type. For example, a standard dictionary has authority in its own right; people do not concern themselves about the names of compilers in reference books. The fourth and final consideration is the recognition of a text's content as plausible or implausible and bestows or withholds authority accordingly. Wilson is particularly concerned with the instant recognition: "a text usually has one chance to capture our attention; reading a few words of it may be enough to discourage us from continuing on to reading the whole thing" (p. 169). Wilson considers cognitive authority as one of the quality control components in information retrieval.

Cognitive authority has recently received renewed attention in information science research. Rieh (2000, 2002) employs this theory to examine the concept of quality and authority in the Web from the perspective of information-seeking behavior. The results of Rieh's study tends to validate Wilson's theory by demonstrating that Web searchers make judgments of quality and authority primarily based on their knowledge (domain knowledge, system knowledge), in addition to characteristics of sources (URL domain, type, reputation, single-collective, author/creator credentials) and characteristics of information objects (type, title, content, organization/structure, presentation, graphics, functionality). The subjects in Rieh's study often select Web pages when there is some indication of source authority based on their own experience, other people's recommendations, or something that they have heard. Rieh notes that the subjects often refer to "other people" who apparently serve as cognitive authorities; these can include friends, colleagues, doctors, or academics.

The subjects' cognitive authorities are also newspapers, journal articles, and even television advertisements.

Fritch and Cromwell (2001) present a theoretical model for gathering and assessing Internet information based on Wilson's cognitive authority theory. They argue that traditional measures of authority present in a print environment are lacking on the Internet and there is an increasing need for evaluating the authority of Internet information. They provide specific criteria to be considered, suggesting four primary filters for ascribing cognitive authority: filter for document, filter for author, filter for institution, and filter for affiliation.

McKenzie (2003) takes a constructionist approach to the theory of cognitive authority, arguing that descriptions of cognitive authority may be understood not as accurate representations of beliefs or attitudes but rather everyday fact constructions. She examines the issues of authoritative knowledge in the information seeking of pregnant women and analyzes the language they use to create cognitive authority descriptions in relation to discursive action. McKenzie concludes: "constructionist discourse analytic methods are particularly appropriate for identifying the specific strategies used by participants in creating their cognitive authority descriptions" (p. 283).

Wilson's conceptualization of cognitive authority provides numerous implications for information behavior research. When people look for information, they interact with texts or information systems. Each information medium (book, journal, newspaper, or Web) has its own quality control mechanisms. Consequently, there are a number of aspects of quality that can be recognized. The aspects of quality are, however, not always consistent: people may find a text that seems to be clearly written but is inaccurate; stimulating but unsound. In such cases, they rely on credibility, a chief aspect of quality, by asking "Can one believe what the text says, or can one at least take it seriously?" (Wilson, p. 171). When people find a source for which they are looking, they appropriately ask: do I need to look further, or can I take this source as settling the matter? If at this point people are already convinced of the source's authority, the question is already answered. But, if people are unfamiliar with the source, the question is likely to arise explicitly.

Wilson's theory indicates that in recognizing cognitive authorities people have bases or reasons for judgments of authority. Whatever their reasons that other people or materials deserve cognitive authority, people may not be able to describe their reasons on a quantitatively measurable scale. People can only justify their assessment of authority by citing indirect bases. Therefore, to understand cognitive authority, information behavior researchers must ask open rather than closed questions. Rieh (2000, 2002) finds that evaluation of cognitive authority is subjective, relative, and situational rather than objective, absolute, and universally recognizable. As McKenzie (2003) points out, it is also important to understand people's judgments of cognitive authority and bases for such judgments not on the level of verbal expressions but on the deeper cognitive levels.

The theory of cognitive authority closely relates to the notion of relevance in information retrieval. In tradition information retrieval, the problem of relevance judgment and selection of information has long been discussed within the context of topical relevance; e.g., in terms of whether the query topic matches the document topic. In the 1990s, however, a number of empirical studies about relevance have revealed that people use substantially more diverse relevance criteria than mere topicality when making relevance judgments (Mizzaro, 1997). Rieh's research (2000, 2002) implies that the theories of relevance judgment and criteria can be advanced by examining specific primary factors, such as information quality and cognitive authority.

Authority issues are currently receiving much attention not only in information science but also in other fields including education, human-computer interaction, and computer science (e.g., Fogg, 2003). However, researchers who have studied information quality and Web credibility problems from outside of the information science field rarely cite Wilson's cognitive authority theory or any other theories and models of information behavior. The time seems to be right for information behavior researchers to discuss the dissemination of information behavior theories beyond their own information science field.

Fogg, B. J. (2003). Prominence-Interpretation theory: Explaining how people assess credibility online. *Proceedings of ACM CHI 2003 Conference on Human Factors in Computing Systems*, 722–723. New York: ACM Press.

Fritch, J. W., & Cromwell, R. L. (2001). Evaluating Internet resources: Identity, affiliation, and cognitive authority in a networked world. *Journal of the American Society for Information Science and Technology, 52,* 499–507.

McKenzie, P. J. (2003). Justifying cognitive authority decisions: Discursive strategies of information seekers. *The Library Quarterly, 73,* 261–288.

Mizzaro, S. (1997). Relevance: The whole history. *Journal of the American Society for Information Science, 48,* 810–832.

Rieh, S. Y. (2000). Information quality and cognitive authority in the World Wide Web (Doctoral dissertation, Rutgers University, New Brunswick, NJ, 2000). *Dissertation Abstracts International, 61,* 3809.

Rieh, S. Y. (2002). Judgment of information quality and cognitive authority in the Web. *Journal of the American Society for Information Science and Technology, 53,* 145–161.

Wilson, P. (1983). *Second-hand knowledge: An inquiry into cognitive authority.* Westport, CT: Greenwood Press.

11
Cognitive Work Analysis

Raya Fidel
The Information School
University of Washington, USA
fidelr@u.washington.edu

Annelise Mark Pejtersen
Cognitive Systems Engineering Center
Risø National Laboratory, Denmark
AMP@risoe.dk

Cognitive work analysis (Vicente, 1999) is a work-centered conceptual framework developed by Rasmussen, Pejtersen, & Goodstein (1994) to analyze cognitive work. The purpose of cognitive work analysis (CWA) is to guide the design of technology for use in the work place. It is unique because of its ability to analyze real-life phenomena while retaining the complexity inherent in them. When applied to information behavior, the approach guides the analysis of human-information interaction in order to inform the design of information systems.

CWA's theoretical roots are in general systems thinking, adaptive control systems, and Gibson's ecological psychology, and it is the result of the generalization of experiences from field studies that led to the design of support systems for a variety of modern work domains, such as process plants and libraries. In the context of Information Science, the concept *information system* refers to any system, whether intellectual or computerized, that facilitates and supports human-information interaction. Thus, a library as a whole could be considered an information system, and so could a reference desk, the Web, an online public access catalog (OPAC), or a cataloging department.

Unlike the common approach to the design of information systems—design and development first and evaluation later—CWA evaluates first the system already in place, and then develops recommendations for design. The evaluation is based on the analysis of information behavior in context. CWA has been successfully applied to the evaluation and design of information systems and collaboratories. For example, it guided the development of the first retrieval system for fiction called BookHouse (Pejtersen, 1989; Rasmussen et al., 1994; Pejtersen, 1992). Based on the analysis of reference interviews in public and school libraries, Pejtersen developed a fiction retrieval system, with a graphical user interface, in which users can look for books by a variety of attributes, such as the subject, historical period, mood, and the cover design. It serves children and adults as well as library catalogers. The system also caters to various strategies: users can just browse without any particular attribute in mind, look for a specific book, or look for books that are similar to one they liked. More recently, CWA was used to analyze data collected in a study of Web searching by high school students (Pejtersen & Fidel, 1998; Fidel et al., 1999). In this study, the framework proved to be very powerful in helping to uncover the problems that students experienced when using the Web to search for information, and offered recommendations for designs that can alleviate such problems. Pejtersen and her colleagues have recently completed the COLLATE project that will support multi-institutional collaboration in indexing and retrieval among the national film archives of Germany, Austria, and the Czech Republic (Albrechtsen et al., 2002, Hertzum et al., 2002).

Cognitive work analysis considers people who interact with information "actors" involved in their work-related actions, rather than as "users" of systems. Focusing on information behavior on the job, CWA views human-information interaction in the context of human work activities. It assumes that in order to be able to design systems that work harmoniously with humans, one has to understand:

- The work actors do
- Their information behavior
- The context in which they work
- The reasons for their actions

Therefore, CWA focuses simultaneously on the task actors perform, the environment in which it is carried out, and the perceptual, cognitive, and ergonomic attributes of the people who do the task. A graphic presentation of the framework is given in Figure 11.1.

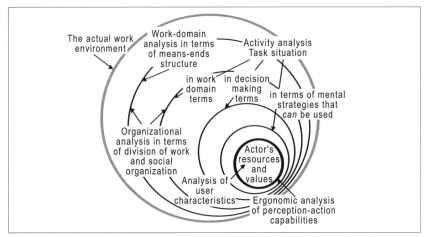

Figure 11.1   The dimensions for analysis in cognitive work analysis.

In this presentation each set of attributes mentioned in Figure 11.1 is designated with a circle and is considered a dimension for analysis. Thus, each dimension is a host of attributes, factors, or variables, depending on the purpose and method of a study.

In addition to the dimensions for analysis, CWA provides several templates to support both analysis and modeling. These templates are particularly suitable for the analysis of complex and dynamic phenomena. To illustrate the content of each dimension, Table 11.1 provides a few examples of questions one may want to ask when analyzing each dimension.

Although the dimensions are laid out in a certain order, employing them in actual projects follows no fixed sequence. Because of the interdependence among the dimensions, a researcher moves from one dimension to another in an iterative process. The path of this movement is determined by the particular problem at hand, and also by pragmatic considerations.

The dimensions presented by CWA represent the constraints on information seeking, starting with the individual resources and values of the actor to the external environment of the work place. For some dimensions, a dimension creates the constraint for the one nested within it. Thus, the work environment affects how a work place is operating, and this mode of operation shapes the task that an actor performs. The task, in turn, affects the decisions that an actor makes, and these decisions

Table 11.1   Examples of questions to ask for each dimension of cognitive work analysis.

Dimension	Examples of Questions to Ask in Analysis
Environment	What elements outside the organization affect it?
Work domain	What are the goals of the work domain? The constraints? The priorities? The functions? What physical processes take place? What tools are employed?
Organizational analysis	How is work divided among teams? What criteria are used? What is the nature of the organization, hierarchical, democratic, chaotic? What are the organizational values?
Task analysis in work domain terms	What is the task (e.g., design a new software product)? What are the goals of the task that generated an information problem? Constraints? The functions involved? The tools used?
Task analysis in decision making terms	What decisions are made (e.g., what metaphor to use for the interface)? What information is required? What sources are useful?
Task analysis in terms of strategies that can be used	What strategies are possible (e.g., browsing, the analytical strategy)? What strategies does actor prefer? What type of information is needed? What information sources does actor prefer?
Actor's resources and values	What is the formal training of the actor? Area of expertise? Experience with the subject domain and the work domain? Personal priorities? Personal values?

influence seeking behavior. In addition, the actor's characteristics have an effect on seeking behavior and so does the social organization of the work place. CWA assumes that while one can describe information behavior without taking these constraints into account, the best way to analyze information behavior is through an in-depth understanding of these constraints. Work analysis is, therefore, an analysis of the constraints that shape information behavior.

Because CWA investigates information behavior in context, individual studies create results that are valid for the design of information systems in the context investigated, rather then for the design of general information systems. Results from a variety of studies, however, can be combined and generalized to inform the design of other information systems.

Cognitive work analysis has several distinct attributes that are useful for the study of human-information interaction and for the design of information systems. Most importantly, it provides for a holistic approach that makes it possible to account for several dimensions simultaneously. In addition, the framework facilitates an in-depth examination of the various dimensions of a context. A study of a particular context is, therefore, a multidisciplinary examination with the purpose of understanding the interaction between people and information in the work context. These two attributes make the framework a powerful guide for the evaluation and design of information systems for the context under investigation because in reality all dimensions—personal, social, and organizational— play a role simultaneously and interdependently.

Lastly, while the framework is based on a set of conceptual and epistemological constructs, it provides a structure for the analysis of human-information interaction, without subscribing to specific theories or models. Sanderson (2003) explained that "The scientific foundations of CWA are various—a 'conceptual marketplace' as Rasmussen described it—because they have been appropriated to fulfill a practical need." One can employ a wide variety of theories, methods, or tools that may be deemed helpful for the analysis of a specific situation. This flexibility turns the focus of an investigation to the phenomenon under study, rather than to the testing and verification of models and theories, or to the employment of a particular methodology. At the same time, CWA has built-in mechanisms to carry out rigorous and systematic research.

Albrechtsen, H., Pejtersen, A. M., & Cleal, B. (2002). Empirical work analysis of collaborative film indexing. In H. Bruce et al. (Eds.), *Emerging frameworks and methods: Proceedings of the fourth international conference on conceptions of library and information science* (pp. 85–108). Greenwood Village, CO: Libraries Unlimited.

Churchman, C. W. (1979). *The systems approach*. New York: Dell.

Fidel, R. et al. (1999). A visit to the information mall: Web searching behavior of high school students. *Journal of the American Society of Information Science, 50,* 24–37.

Hertzum, M. et al. (2002). An analysis of collaboration in three film archives: a case for collaboratories. In H. Bruce et al. (Eds.), *Emerging frameworks and methods: Proceedings of the fourth international conference on conceptions of library and information science* (pp. 69–84). Greenwood Village, CO: Libraries Unlimited.

Pejtersen, A. M. (1985). Implications of users' value perception for the design of a bibliographic retrieval system. In J. C. Agrawal, & P. Zunde (Eds.), *Empirical foundations of information and software science* (pp. 23–37). New York: Plenum.

Pejtersen, A. M. (1989). *The BOOK House: Modeling user needs and search strategies as a basis for system design*. Roskilde, Risø National Laboratory. (Risø report M-2794).

Pejtersen, A. M. (1992). The Book House: An icon based database system for fiction retrieval in public libraries. In B. Cronin (Ed.), *The marketing of library and information services 2* (pp. 572–591). London: Aslib.

Pejtersen, A. M., & Fidel, R. (1998). *A framework for work-centered evaluation and design: A case study of IR on the Web*. Report for MIRA, Grenoble: France.

Rasmussen, J., Pejtersen, A. M, & Goodstein, L. P. (1994). *Cognitive systems engineering*. New York: Wiley.

Sanderson, P. M. (2003). Cognitive Work Analysis. In J. Carroll (Ed.), *HCI models, theories, and frameworks: Toward an interdisciplinary science*. New York: Morgan Kaufmann.

Vicente, K. J. (1999). *Cognitive work analysis*. Mahwah, NJ: Lawrence Erlbaum.

12
Collective Action Dilemma

Marc Smith
Microsoft Research, USA
masmith@microsoft.com

Howard T. Welser
Department of Sociology
University of Washington, USA
twelser@u.washington.edu

A social dilemma occurs when actors seek a collective outcome, yet each actor's narrow self-interest rewards her or him for not contributing to that group goal. Ironically, behavior that is reasonable at the individual level leads to a situation where all parties are worse off. Social dilemmas are unified by the presence of this deficient equilibrium, that is, a stable outcome that is less preferred for all actors, but it is nonetheless stable because no individual would gain by unilaterally changing their behavior.

The study of social dilemmas and collective action emerged from the intersections of economic theory with sociology and political science. Early pioneers include VonNeumann and Morgenstern (1944), Olson (1965), and Hardin (1968). This interdisciplinary effort has also integrated insights from psychology (Rabin, 1993), social psychology (Yamagishi, 1986), and evolutionary biology (Maynard Smith, 1998), and fostered the development of evolutionary game theory (Gintis, 2000). The research is unified by the formulation of abstract definitions of the nature of actors and the constraints in which they interact.

There are two classes of social dilemmas especially relevant to information behavior: the free rider problem and the tragedy of the commons. These dilemma situations refer to opposite sides of the same coin. In the free rider problem actors are tempted to not contribute to a group good, while in the tragedy of the commons actors are tempted to consume a good without consideration of how their use degrades that good. The free rider problem arises when actors want to enjoy a collective good, without contributing the resources necessary to create or maintain it.

The seminal statements come from extensions of the rational actor model (derived from economics) to political and social problems of collective action (Olson, 1965), theories of group solidarity (Hechter, 1987), and the enforcement of norms (Coleman, 1990). The free rider problem is seen as a pervasive challenge for any collective good providing group, and is especially problematic when contribution is voluntary and groups are informal. This is often the case in online groups, so studying provision of collective goods in these settings promises to bring new insight into this general question.

The tragedy of the commons (Hardin, 1968; Ostrom, 1990) occurs when individual consumption of a collective good degrades the quality of that resource for all. When the resource is large none of the individuals feel the negative effects of their own actions, thus they have no incentive to curtail their own consumption (Yamagishi, 1995). The tragedy of the commons highlights different ways that consumption of a resource interferes with the ability of others to use that resource. Bandwidth consumption due to excessive downloading is a clear example in the online setting (Huberman, Rajan, & Lukose, 1997). However, one of the major strengths of electronic resources is that they greatly reduce problems of rivalness (only one person can read a book at a time), degradation (Web pages don't wear out), and crowding (for most uses additional users do not noticeably degrade the quality of online information resources). However, there are online social spaces like Usenet groups, e-mail lists, and blogs that may have a social carrying capacity where excessive use by some may degrade the resource for others.

Both of these dilemmas can be modeled under the scientific metaphor of strategic interactive games (Von Neumann & Morgenstern, 1944), in which the prisoners' dilemma is the most common model. The prisoners' dilemma and allied game theoretic models formalize the conflict between individual and collective interests as a set of payoffs that are contingent on the behavior of the parties involved.

The baseline prediction in collective action dilemmas is that the deficient equilibrium will dominate in the absence of mechanisms that alter the payoff structure. Identifying and explaining the operation of such mechanisms has been the subject of a wide range of research. Contribution, cooperation, and trust are more likely to emerge when actors know that they will interact in the future, i.e., repeat games cast a "shadow of the future" (Murnighan & Roth, 1983). Reputation effects are reason this shadow affects dilemma situations. Actors "do the right thing" in order to protect their reputation, an important mechanism for generating trust in online settings (Kollock, 1999). In-group membership due to identities based on roles or on group affiliation can foster contribution when embedded in social ties (Snow, Zurcher, & Exland-Olson, 1980). Social ties, that is, the connections between individuals, are an important reason that people contribute to collective goods (McAdam & Paulson, 1993). Finally, selective incentives, in the form of valued goods (especially social incentives like approval), are only available to those that contribute and are important foundations for sustaining contribution (Coleman, 1990; Hechter, 1987). In the absence of the mechanisms like those described above, cooperation and contribution are harder to sustain, and are more likely to devolve into defection.

Millions of people interact daily in online spaces collectively generating knowledge capital, social capital, and communion with one another. Newsgroups, e-mail lists, Web boards, blogs, wikis, IM, and chat are all socio-technical networked systems that support collective action and are the hosts of many kinds of collective institutions. The ability of these communities to transform interaction into collective goods is dependent on mechanisms that encourage contribution while inhibiting defection. There are some clear lessons. Because online identities are cheap and ephemeral, positive reputation systems, where people earn a "good name" through time-consuming and long-term investment, are far more effective at overcoming collective action dilemmas than negative reputation systems (Kollock, 1999; Friedman & Resnick 2001). Contribution to collective goods in online settings is facilitated by systems that allow participants to compete for status as skilled, voluminous, or otherwise virtuous contributors (Kollock & Smith, 1996). However, because these status systems can emerge around any performance limiting criteria they are as likely to encourage detrimental behavior (like trolling) as virtuous helping behavior. The lesson for the management of information systems is that managers need to shape the criteria on which evaluation of status is based, so that those criteria reinforce the contribution needs of the group.

Collective action dilemma research tradition suggests several methodological lessons: 1) researchers should identity individual and collective interests, should describe how situations enable and constrain different behavioral options, and should identify mechanisms that alter the value that actors derive from both contribution and defection in online settings; 2) study in online contexts facilitates the use of multiple methods of analysis, including comparisons of qualitative descriptions of interaction, descriptions of the social structure, as well as formal models of the interests and constraints involved in the situation; 3) this approach recommends comparison across situations while identifying how general dilemma models, as well as general mechanisms, alter contribution.

Computer mediated collective action systems have been used by millions of individuals to collectively create millions of novel practices and artifacts with interesting properties. Many of these systems currently resist meaningful analysis and systematic observation because such features were not initial design goals and computational resources were scarcer than they are now. Given rapid changes in the costs of computation, storage, and bandwidth, it is increasingly possible to process the significant volumes of data many of these systems generate. As a result there is a significant opportunity to map large-scale patterns of collective action and empirically model its dynamics across large populations at low cost and with high fidelity.

Collective action dilemma models encourage the use of a bottom-up approach to understanding social systems. This perspective points to a range of technologies and possible social applications with profound implications for society. Human capacity for cooperation is at the core of our societies and the framework for our daily experience. Changes in the nature of collective action reach to the core of the fabric of the social world. Dilemma models highlight the points of conflict and articulate the opportunities for populations that succeed in overcoming the obstacles to collective action.

Coleman, J. S. (1990). *Foundations of social theory.* Cambridge, MA: The Belknap Press of Harvard University Press.

Friedman, E., & Resnick, P. (2001). The social cost of cheap pseudonyms. *Journal of Economics and Management Strategy, 10*(2), 173–199.

Gintis, H. (2000). *Game theory evolving: A problem-centered introduction to modeling strategic behavior.* Princeton, NJ: Princeton University Press.

Hardin, G. (1968). The tragedy of the commons. *Science, 162,* 1243–1297.

Hechter, M. (1987). *Principles of group solidarity*. Berkeley, CA: University of California Press.

Huberman, B. A., & Lukose, R. M. (1997). Social dilemmas and Internet congestion. *Science, 277*, 535–537.

Kollock, P. (1999). The production of trust in online markets. In E. J. Lawler, M. Macy, S. Thyne, & H. A. Walker (Eds.), *Advances in group processes*. Greenwich, CT: JAI Press.

Kollock, P., & Smith, M. (1996). Managing the virtual commons: cooperation and conflict in computer communities. In S. C. Herring (Ed.), *Computer mediated communication: Linguistic, social, and cross-cultural perspectives* (pp. 226–242). Philadelphia, PA: John Benjamins Publishing.

Maynard-Smith, J. (1998). *Evolution and the theory of games*. Cambridge: Cambridge University Press.

McAdam, D., & Paulson, R. (1993). Specifying the relation between social ties and activism. *American Journal of Sociology, 99*, 640–667.

Murnighan, J. K., & Roth, A. E. (1983). Expecting continued play in prisoner's dilemma games. *Journal of Conflict Resolution, 27*(2), 279–300.

Olson, M. (1965). *The logic of collective action*. Cambridge, MA: Harvard University Press.

Ostrom, E. (1990). *Governing the commons: The evolution of institutions for collective action*. New York: Cambridge University Press.

Rabin, M. (1993). Incorporating fairness into game theory and economics. *The American Economic Review, 83*(5), 1281–1302.

Snow, D., Zurcher L., & Ekland-Olson, S. (1980). Social networks and social movements: A microstructural approach to differential recruitment. *American Sociological Review, 45*, 787–801.

Von Neumann, J., & Morganstern, O. (1944). *The theory of games and economic behavior*. Princeton, NJ: Princeton University Press.

Yamagishi, T. (1995). Social dilemmas. In K. S. Cook, G. A. Fine, & J. S. House (Eds.), *Sociological perspectives on social psychology* (pp. 311–335). Boston: Allyn and Bacon.

Yamagishi, T. (1986). The Structural goal/expectation theory of cooperation in social dilemmas. In E. J. Lawler (Ed.), *Advances in group processes* (pp. 51–87). Greenwich, CT: JAI Press.

13
Communicative Action

Gerald Benoît
Graduate School of Library and Information Science
Simmons College, USA
gerald.benoit@simmons.edu

The theory of communicative action is part of Jürgen Habermas's (b. 1928) long study of society and the loci of power within society. Originally part of the Frankfurt School's efforts to study Kantian reason within a Marxist environment, Habermas expanded some ideas found in Mead and Peirce to emphasize the theory of behavior and analysis of language. He theorizes that blind pursuit of rationality, inappropriate application of scientific methods, and philosophies of language that place issues of acceptability and truth outside the realm of actual speakers overlook the way people use language in the social sphere to reach understanding and coordinate action.

Indeed, most of Habermas's writings emphasize discourse ethics and the concept of justice in a democracy. For the study of information-seeking behavior his program is valuable for exploring language use, the host of influences upon speakers and hearers called the "lifeworld," the expression of cultural values, and, most significantly, providing a model for "communicative competence." Through his analysis of language, we see a model of how language can be used to control others, to bring out interpretations that favor one side over the other, to "distort communication" and "colonize" others' lifeworld by one's own agenda. He provides, too, an insight into ways we can examine language use to coordinate our actions with others and to expose efforts at colonization.

The foundation for his work is available in English as *The Theory of Communicative Action*, volumes 1 and 2. He applies his theory to epistemology (*Knowledge and Human Interests*), hermeneutics, legal systems (*Between Facts and Norms*), politics and modern life (*The Philosophical Discourse of Modernity*), etc. Certainly one sees the influences of pragmatism and critique of science in his work and it is for

99

those reasons that his definitions of the behaviors that are "knowledge constitutive" are popular both in system design and in subjective decision making.

"Habermas differentiates three primary generic cognitive areas in which human interest generates knowledge. These areas determine categories relevant to what we interpret as knowledge. That is, they are termed 'knowledge constitutive'—they determine the mode of discovering knowledge and whether knowledge claims can be warranted. These areas define cognitive interests or learning domains, and are grounded in different aspects of social existence—work, interaction and power" (MacIsaac, 2004). Habermas defines three types of knowledge:

1) *Work* – acting and using language "instrumentally," typically based in the empirical-analytic sciences

2) *Practical* – human social interaction, or communicative action, governed by consensual norms, reciprocal expectations, propositions are valid only "in their intersubjectivity of the mutual understanding of intentions," the historical-hermeneutic disciplines

3) *Emancipatory* – self-knowledge or reflection, involving recognizing one's own and others' motivations and the correct reasons for one's problems

Because the expansive theory is complex only parts have been tried in real-world situations, although his expression of speech acts is favored by some computer scientists and system analysts. One of the earliest proponents was Flores et al. (1986), whose "Coordinator" computer system analyzed speech acts of people working on a shared project. As part of computer-supported cooperative work and human-computer interaction, the theory has been appropriated to study the use of computers and cognition (Winograd & Flores, 1986) and the impact on office work (Auramäki, Lehtinen, & Lyytinen, 1988; De Michelis & Grasso, 1994; Dietz, 1994; Janson & Woo, 1995).

As pertains directly to information seeking and information behavior, the theory has been applied to (a) theories of meaning, (b) information transfer, and (c) information systems design. The goal of information seeking is to provide resources appropriate to the information seekers and it is the question of what is appropriate that makes the theory so appealing. Casting information seeking as a communicative action raises questions of interpretation, meaning, truth, and responsible agency. For instance, information retrieval (IR) consists of a document collection, query representation, matching algorithm, and presentation (Baeza-Yates & Ribeiro-Neto, 1999). The behavior of the IR system is, to a critical theoretic reading, self-validating because the assertions made by the interaction (through the interface, the design decisions are made by the computer- or information scientist) are not warranted. Habermas's expression of speech act theory means each proposition is open to a shared method of evaluation, which supports the types of knowledge described above. Specifically, unless a speaker is intentionally trying to influence a hearer's interpretation or otherwise control the outcome, the "speaker" (both human or computer) must be willing to offer a warrant for the proposition that includes truth, truthfulness, sincerity, and normative right.

Such a perspective of information systems and information-seeking behavior raises the question of defining the actual object of information systems work. Adapting Garcia and Quek (1997), are information systems design and use technological or social issues? Does the information system's creation and use suggest an organization, a data system, or a social system? These questions, along with the empiricist foundation for justifying the use of decontextualized linguistic tokens and weighted frequencies for retrieval, raise concerns about the role of logic, meaning, and truth in information seeking (Peregrin, 1997; Benoît 1998).

Furthermore, the questions have sparked work on several specific facets: information transfer (Ferreira Novellino, 1998), human-computer interaction, interface design, and data models. Benoît (2001) demonstrated how speech act theory can be integrated into IR systems and the differences the model makes to end-user interpretation. By revealing relevance criteria through the interface, that is, including means to interact with the IR system in ways that play out the elements of speech acts Habermas recommends, end-users clarify linguistic confusions. By sharing the designer's decisions about system behavior and relevance evaluations, or—as Habermas would express it, providing the warrant—end-users can better avoid "distorted communication" to arrive at decisions appropriate for their own lifeworld.

The theory is also related to reader-response theory, hermeneutics, phenomenology, and particularly pragmatics (*On the Pragmatics of Communication*). The issues Habermas raises about relevancy and consent inform one's reading of Putnam's fact/value dichotomy (2002), Quine's pursuit of truth (1990), and empiricism. Habermas's theory is also in opposition to Searle's model of speech acts and society (1969, 1998), and reading both provides insight into language that maps directly to IR evaluation.

In summary, the theory recommends itself to any arena of human-human and human-computer interaction where issues of meaning construction, social performance, and application of knowledge in the public sphere are valued. A close reading also provides an operationalized foundation for evaluating human-human and human-computer information behaviors.

Auramäki, E., Lehtinen, E., & Lyytinen, K. (1988). A speech-act-based office modeling approach. *ACM Transactions on Information Systems, 6*(2), 126–152.

Baeza-Yates, R., & Ribeiro-Neto, B. (1999). *Modern information retrieval.* Reading, MA: Addison-Wesley.

Benoît, G. (1998). Information seeking as communicative action. (Doctoral dissertation, University of California, Los Angeles, 1998). *Dissertation Abstracts International, 59,* 3258.

Benoît, G. (2001, January). Critical theory as a foundation for pragmatic information systems design. *Information Research 6*(2). Retrieved May 4, 2004, from http://InformationR.net/ir/6-2/paper98.html

De Michelis, G., & Grasso, M. A. (1994). Situating conversations within the language/action perspective: the Milan conversation model. *Proceedings of the 1994 ACM conference on computer supported cooperative work* (pp. 89–100). New York: ACM.

Dietz, T., & Stern, P. C. (1995). Toward a theory of choice: Socially embedded preference construction. *Journal of Socio-Economics, 24,* 261–279.

Ferreira Novellino, M. S. (1998). Information transfer considering the production and use contexts: Information transfer language. Retrieved May 3, 2004, from www.db.dk/Nyt/BibNyt/1998nr2/brazil.htm

Flores, F., Graves, M., Hartfield, B., & Winograd, T. (1988). Computer systems and the design of organizational interaction. *ACM Transactions on Information Systems, 6*(2), 153–172.

Garcia, L., & Quek, F. (1997). Qualitative research in information systems: Time to be subjective? In A. S. Lee, J. Libenau, & J. I. DeGross (Eds.), *Information systems and qualitative research* (pp. 542–568). London: Chapman and Hall.

Habermas, J. (1971). *Knowledge and human interests*. Boston: Beacon.

Habermas, J. (1984–1987). *The theory of communicative action*. T. McCarthy (Trans.). Boston: Beacon.

Habermas, J. (1996). *Between facts and norms: Contributions to a discourse theory of law and democracy*. Cambridge, MA: MIT Press.

Habermas, J. (1987). *The philosophical discourse of modernity: Twelve lectures*. Cambridge, MA: MIT Press.

Habermas, J. (1998). *On the pragmatics of communication*. (M. Cooke, Ed.). Cambridge, MA: MIT Press.

Janson, M. A., Woo, C. C., & Smith, L. D. (1993, August). Information systems development and communicative action theory. *Information and Management, 25*(2), 59–72.

MacIsaac, D. (1996). The critical theory of Jürgen Habermas. Retrieved May 3, 2004, from Buffalo State, State University of New York Web site: http://physicsed. buffalostate.edu/danowner/habcritthy.html

Oeller, W. (1998, November 19). Negotiation in interaction. *Linguist List 9.1645*. Retrieved May 4, 2004, from www.linguistlist.org/issues/9/9-1645.html

Peregren, J. (1997). Language and its models: is model theory a theory of semantics? *Nordic Journal of Philosophical Logic, 2*(1), 1–23.

Putnam, H. (2002). *The collapse of the fact/value dichotomy and other essays*. Cambridge, MA: Harvard University Press.

Quine, W. V. (1990). *Pursuit of truth*. Cambridge, MA: Harvard University Press.

Searle, J. R. (1969). *Speech acts: an essay in the philosophy of language*. London: Cambridge University.

Searle, J. R. (1998). *Mind, language and society: Philosophy in the real world*. New York: Basic.

Winograd, T., & Flores, F. (1998). *Understanding computers and cognition: A new foundation for design*. Norwood, NJ: Ablex.

14
Communities of Practice

Elisabeth Davies
Faculty of Information and Media Studies
The University of Western Ontario, Canada
edavies2@uwo.ca

Communities of practice is social epistemology in two senses: First, communities of practice are where knowledge is created and resides (Lave & Wenger, 1991) and second, in pursuit of a common practice, individual members are attuned to one another. Learning is the focus of communities of practice, specifically, learning as social participation. Communities of practice theory originated in research into situated learning when educational anthropologist Jean Lave investigated cognition (Lave, 1988). Lave discovered that people in everyday life, for example, shopping for groceries, use what they have learned—arithmetic—in different ways depending upon the particular situation they find themselves in. Cognition, according to Lave, is "distributed—stretched over, not divided among—mind, body, activity, and culturally organized settings (which include other actors)" (Lave, 1988, p. I).

When Lave teamed up with Etienne Wenger to write *Situated Learning: Legitimate Peripheral Participation* (1991), "communities of practice" were an integral part of their developing theory of situated learning. Individuals learn, they posited, through the process of becoming a full participant in a sociocultural practice, such as midwifery, meat-cutting, or attending Alcoholics Anonymous meetings. Lave and Wenger identified "legitimate peripheral participation" as the way newcomers learn the practice in which they are engaged. Not only do newcomers learn to be practitioners from other members, the newcomers' identities are shaped as they learn the practice (Brown & Duguid, 1991).

Wenger went on to write *Communities of Practice* (1998) in order to expand on the idea of social learning. Essentially, a community of practice is the site where collective learning is accumulated into social practices (Wenger, 2000). Wenger (1998, 2000) asserts that in order for communities of practice to exist, three elements must be present:

1) Members must understand what the community is for; that is, the members must feel a sense of *joint enterprise* and accountability.

2) *Mutual engagement* arises when members have time to build trust and relationships with one another through regular interactions.

3) Members will develop a *shared repertoire* of stories, language, etc. that embodies the distinctive knowledge of the community and allows members to negotiate meaning.

Because members are unlikely to identify themselves collectively as a community of practice, certain indicators can be used to help recognize a community of practice including: evidence of sustained relationships; rapid flow of information and propagation of innovation; knowing what others know, what they can do, and how they can contribute specific tools, representations, and other artifacts; shared stories, inside jokes; and a shared discourse reflecting a certain perspective on the world (Wenger, 1998).

There is no formula for creating a community of practice, no amount of time or number of members that is "right." Nor does there seem to be a limit to the number of communities of practice to which an individual can belong. Originally, communities of practice were described as informal groups and were not a synonym for a work group or team or unit, etc. This distinction has faded recently in some of Wenger's and other management-oriented writers' contributions to the business and management literature (e.g., Wenger, 2000) in which organizations are encouraged to nurture or even "create" communities of practice.

Wenger's social theory of learning is positioned at the intersection of social theories of meaning and power on one axis, and collectivity and subjectivity on another axis. This intersection bears the most resemblance to other theories such as symbolic interactionism, cultural-historical activity theory, and critical psychology.

Communities of practice are discussed in the field of Education, often towards the end of creating online communities in distance education. Davenport & Hall (2002) wrote a thorough literature review of the ways in which communities of practice have been used in the fields of Information Science and Knowledge Management, in particular.

Information Science has recognized the community-building possibilities of the theory especially in studies of computer-supported cooperative work. The Knowledge Management field has also made wide use of the theory in both its theoretical and practitioner-oriented articles. Library Science's use of communities of practice has been less visible with the exception of the special libraries/knowledge management area.

Communities of practice have potential applications in two major streams of information behavior research: everyday life and professional or workplace studies. It might be argued that Library and Information Science (LIS) studies of professionals' information behavior have been applications of communities of practice theory before it was so named. Recent doctoral research focusing on a public defender's office (Hara, 2000) and humanities scholars (Neumann, 2002) are examples of the application of communities of practice theory in information behavior.

Following on Davenport & Cronin's (1998) call for LIS workplace studies to consider "the world of work *per se*, not [...] 'information seeking,' 'information needs,' 'information uses,' and 'information use environments' " (p. 266), the idea of situated learning and social practices could enter the LIS field through studies in which delineating preferred information channels and sources is not the main goal. Communities of practice theory is particularly strong for information behavior researchers in its focus on situatedness or context. The idea of overlapping communities and the various types of boundary work requires coexistence and cooperation, and the relationship between identity and practice, or being and doing.

Some issues that may discourage researchers include the difficulty in operationalizing important concepts. Very few concepts are defined straightforwardly, although they are described at length. The presence of seeming tautologies, for example "communities of practice produce their practice" (Wenger, 1998, p. 80) requires that the potential researcher accept the reflexivity both of the theory and of much of the writing about it.

Communities of practice were theorized following ethnographic research that included participant observation and interviewing. A community of practice is complex, multilayered, and sometimes geographically dispersed. It is fitting for a theory that recognizes the multiple viewpoints characteristic of participation in a community of practice to

rely heavily upon the methods of qualitative research. The phenomeno-
logical underpinnings of qualitative research are clearest when acknowledging the multiple realities (Lincoln & Guba, 1985) of participants'
lives. Information behavior researchers are committed to qualitative
methods, so it seems reasonable to expect that, with the emergence of
communities of practice theory in LIS doctoral research and the emphasis on the full range of work practices in workplace studies, communities
of practice theory will be seen more often in future information behavior
research.

Brown, J. S., & Duguid, P. (1991). Organizational learning and communities-of-practice:
    Toward a unified view of working, learning, and innovation. *Organization Science*,
    2(1), 40–57. Retrieved February 23, 2004, from www2.parc.com/ops/members/
    brown/papers/orglearning.html.

Davenport, E., & Cronin, B. (1998). Some thoughts on "just for you" service in the con-
    text of domain expertise. *Journal of Education for Library and Information
    Science, 39,* 264–274.

Davenport, E., & Hall, H. (2002). Organizational knowledge and communities of prac-
    tice. In B.Cronin (Ed.), *Annual review of information science and technology, 36*
    (pp. 171-227). Medford, NJ: Information Today.

Hara, N. (2000). Social construction of knowledge in professional communities of prac-
    tice: Tales in courtrooms (Doctoral dissertation, Indiana University, Bloomington,
    2000). *Dissertation Abstracts International, 61,* 953.

Lave, J. (1988). *Cognition in practice: Mind, mathematics, and culture in everyday
    life.* Cambridge, UK: Cambridge University Press.

Lave, J., & Wenger, E. (1991). *Situated learning: Legitimate peripheral participation.*
    Cambridge, UK: Cambridge University Press.

Lincoln, Y. S., & Guba, E. G. (1985). *Naturalistic inquiry.* Newbury Park, CA: Sage.

Neumann, L. J. (2002). Communities of practice as information systems: Humanities
    scholars and information convergence. (Doctoral dissertation, University of Illinois,
    Urbana-Champaign, 2002). *Dissertation Abstracts International, 62,* 3607.

Wenger, E. (1998). *Communities of practice: Learning, meaning, and identity.*
    Cambridge, UK: Cambridge University Press.

Wenger, E. (2000). Communities of practice: The key to knowledge strategy. In E. L.
    Lesser, M. A. Fontaine, & J. A. Slusher (Eds.), *Knowledge and communities* (pp.
    3–51). Boston, MA: Butterworth Heinemann.

15
Cultural Models of Hall and Hofstede

Anita Komlodi
Department of Information Systems
University of Maryland, USA
komlodi@umbc.edu

Hall (1959, 1966, 1976, 1984) and Hofstede (1980, 2001) derived two of the most popular models of culture. These models serve the purpose of describing a person's cultural context, usually in terms of communication and social relationships. Hofstede and Hall describe "culture" along several dimensions, which, in turn, constitute their models. Hofstede's approach originated from surveys with IBM employees around the world; Hall's work resulted from his international communication training experience and cultural anthropological research. While these culture models provide a good foundation for studying differences between groups, their inherent biases should be acknowledged. Both models have been developed in Western cultures and exhibit the biases of these cultures, except for one of Hofstede's dimensions described below.

Both models were developed to define dimensions along which cultures can be both described and differentiated. The models have been widely used in information technology fields (information systems, human-computer interaction) as the basis for comparing behavior across cultures. As an example, Callahan (2004) provides an overview of cultural differences impacting the use of technology and resulting variations in the design of user interfaces. However, the application of the theories in studies of information behavior (IB) has been limited, and very few cross-cultural comparisons of information-seeking behavior exist (Iivoneen & White, 2001; Duncker, 2002; Komlodi et al. 2004). In the few studies that do exist, models of culture are not considered when comparing behavior: the results are valuable for understanding variations in IB, but a basic understanding of cultural differences affecting IB is missing. Studying behavior from the cultural model starting point can enable researchers to address this question in a novel, structured way, building on existing culture models to explore cultural differences in IB.

The *level of context* in communication is Hall's (1959, 1966, 1976, 1984) most often applied dimension. It examines how much information is conveyed by the circumstance of a given situation and the group's cultural unconscious and shared knowledge versus explicitly in the message itself. A *high context* culture places more emphasis on the unspoken meaning of a given situation than on the actual message (very little information is included in the communicated message). Cultures with *low-context* interaction place much more importance on the explicit message transmitted. Without including the complete message in this explicit transmission of information, the meaning is lost or vague. North American and Northern European cultures tend to be low context, where messages specify many details and not much information is assumed in the context. Hall's *time* dimension is also often applied. *Time* concepts vary greatly from culture to culture, and Hall defined the two extremes of this dimension: polychronic and monochronic. *Polychronic time* is a circular, renewable resource in which multiple happenings can take place at the same time. Every activity has its natural time to occur and deadlines are less important (or not important at all) than completing tasks. *Monochronic time* is linear, in which usually one event happens at a time. Deadlines are important and time is not renewable, once the time for an activity has passed it cannot be recovered. Time concepts of cultures impact the way tasks are planned and executed and so do *action chains*. *Actions chains* describe sequences of actions that need to be completed before a goal is accomplished. Both action chains themselves and adherence to them differ across cultural groups. The last two dimensions describe characteristics of communication in various groups. The s*peed of messages* describes the frequency and pace of messages members of various cultures find acceptable. Some cultures are used to faster-paced messages than others. Television commercials play an important role in the United States and they create expectations of fast, short messages. If messages are communicated at a speed that the given culture is not used to, they may not achieve their desired effect. The dimension of *information flow* addresses how long it takes a message to travel through an organization and produce the desired effect. Hall's research demonstrated that high-context cultures, where relationships and information are valued more than schedules, tend to have very fast information flow while low-context cultures tend to be much slower.

Hofstede (1980, 2001) developed a cultural model consisting of five dimensions that seek to differentiate culture. *Power distance* describes perceptions of equality and inequality by members of various cultures. A low power distance society tends to be considerably more open to challenging the status quo of superiors. People in a low power distance culture deemphasize socio-economic differences. The high power distance society tends to support inequality within the society. The dimension of *individualism/collectivism* ranks cultures based on the individual or collectivistic orientations of their members. In individualistic societies, goals and accomplishments center around the individual, while in collectivistic societies the common goal and collaborative action dominate. In groups oriented toward collectivistic goals, the individual is sheltered by the group and owes loyalty to it. *Uncertainty avoidance* describes the "extent to which the members of a culture feel threatened by uncertain or unknown situations" (Hofstede 1981, p. 113). Members of cultures ranking high on this dimension do not tolerate situations with limited information and embedded vagueness and they seek certainty and long-term planning. Members of groups with low uncertainty avoidance figures do not become anxious when faced with uncertain situations and lack of rules. The *feminine/masculine* orientation of a culture speaks to the value system of a culture. Cultures with a masculine orientation emphasize values that have traditionally been related to the male gender role in Western cultures: masculine assertiveness and competition, career advancement, and financial accomplishment. Cultures ranking high on the femininity index place in the center those values traditionally associated with the female role: nurturance, family, concern for relationships, and quality of life. Finally, *long/short-term orientation* of societies describes future- versus history-orientation of the society. This final dimension was added later and was aimed at reducing the Western bias of the model. This dimension is based on Confucius' teaching and at the long-term end of the scale includes values such as persistence, thrift, respect of status, and a sense of shame. At the other end of the scale, there is personal steadiness and stability, protecting "face," respect for tradition, and reciprocation of greetings and favors.

Information seeking and use are important user tasks supported by computerized information systems. There is a long tradition of studying IB in electronic environments, however, the study of the impact of end-user national culture on the use of information systems to find, retrieve, and use information is very limited. This area of research is becoming more and more important as the users of many search systems access electronic systems from all over the world and often have to use the same user interface (e.g., Web search engines, online database systems). As noted at the beginning of this paper, the existing cross-cultural studies of IB often do not consider culture models. The application of these models to the study of IB has been limited, however, they are more often used in related fields.

Hofstede's model is popular among scholars of information systems and human-computer interaction. Researchers of information technology have applied Hofstede's theory to studying cultural differences in the management and classification of information systems, although cultural comparisons in information systems development, operations, and use have received limited attention (Ford et al., 2003). Cross-cultural usability experts applied Hofstede's dimensions to the design and understanding of user interfaces (e.g., Evers, 2001) and Web design (e.g., Gould & Marcus, 2000). Even though culture models have been applied in these related fields, they were often not considered in the cultural comparisons of IB.

Two attempts at relating culture models to IB and identifying potential interactions between them have been identified. Steinwachs (1999) examined the impact of culture on four elements of IB: the sender, the recipient, the information itself, and the channel of communication. She applied Hofstede's first four dimensions to study these elements. She concluded that all these elements of IB are deeply embedded in the cultural context and thus impacted by it, and provided recommendations to information intermediaries based on cultural differences in IB. In recent research (Komlodi & Carlin, in press) we relate both Hofstede's and Hall's models to an abstract model of information seeking to identify potential areas of impact. Strong and weak potential impact areas of cultural dimensions on information-seeking steps were identified. The previously discussed applications of culture models to the study of IB are proposed as the foundation for future cross-cultural studies of IB.

Cultural comparisons of IB can greatly benefit from the application of culture theories, as these help not just identify but also explain potential areas of differences in IB. Most of the existing cross-cultural IB research reports differences in behavior, without examining cultural variables to identify why these differences occur. A more thorough study of the impact of culture on IB will lead to deeper understanding of behavior and enable the designers of search systems to create interfaces that will be more usable by users from different cultural backgrounds.

Evers, V. (2001). *Cultural aspects of user interface understanding*. Doctoral Dissertation. Institute of Educational Technology, the Open University, London, England.

Callahan, E. (2004). Interface design and culture. In B. Cronin (Ed.), *Annual review of information science & technology, 39* (pp. 257–310) Medford, NJ: Information Today.

Duncker, E. (2002). Cross-cultural usability of the library metaphor. *Proceedings of the IEEE/ACM Joint Conference on Digital Libraries (JCDL '02)*, 223–230.

Ford, D. P., Connelly C. E., & Meister, D. B. (2003). Information systems research and Hoftsede's *Culture's Consequences*: An uneasy and incomplete partnership. *IEEE Transactions on Engineering Management, 50*(1), 8–25.

Gould, E., & Marcus A. (2000). Crosscurrents: Cultural dimensions and global Web user-interface design. *Interactions, 7*(4), 32–46.

Hall, E. T. (1959). *The silent language*. Garden City, NY: Doubleday.

Hall, E. T. (1966). *The hidden dimension*. Garden City, NY: Doubleday.

Hall, E. T. (1976). *Beyond culture*. Garden City, NY: Doubleday.

Hall, E. T. (1984). *The dance of life: The other dimension of time*. Garden City, NY: Doubleday.

Hofstede, G. H. (1980). *Culture's consequences: International differences in work-related values* (1st ed.). Beverly Hills, CA: Sage.

Hofstede, G. H. (2001). *Culture's consequences: Comparing values, behaviors, institutions, and organizations across nations* (2nd ed.). Thousand Oaks, CA: Sage.

Iivonen, M., & White, M. D. (2001). The choice of initial web search strategies: A comparison between Finnish and American searchers. *Journal of Documentation 57*, 465–491.

Komlodi, A., Weimin H., Jofoldi, H., Kessel, R., Riggs, T., Liang, C., & Haidar, T. (2004). Cross-cultural comparison of Web searching behavior. In M. Khosrow-Pour (Ed.), *Proceedings of the 15th international conference of the information resources management association* (pp. 1169–1170) Hershey, PA: IRM Press.

Komlodi, A., & Carlin, M. (in press). Identifying cultural variables in information-seeking behavior. *Americas Conference on Information Systems 2004*, New York, NY.

Steinwachs, K. (1999). Information and culture: The impact of national culture on information processes based on the theories of sociologist Geert Hofstede. *Journal of Information Science, 25*, 193–204.

16
Dervin's Sense-Making

Tonyia J. Tidline
School of Library and Information Studies
University of Alabama, USA
ttidline@slis.ua.edu

Brenda Dervin's Sense-Making is a conceptual tool of broad applicability for use in understanding the relationship of communication, information, and meaning. Sense-Making, (capitalized to distinguish the methodology from "sense making," which encompasses the phenomenon of making and unmaking sense) is integral to understanding how human beings derive meaning from information. In library and information science (LIS), Sense-Making methodology is associated with a shift in research emphasis from information *sources* to information *users* (Dalrymple, 2001). This shift was accomplished by conceiving of "information seeking and use" as "modes of communication practice" (Savolainen, 1993, p. 13).

Within various disciplines, including Communication and LIS, the methodology has been used to study information seeking associated with myriad settings and services, including libraries, information systems, media systems, Web sites, public information campaigns, classrooms, and counseling services. Sense-Making has also served to help understand intrapersonal, interpersonal, small group, organizational, national, and global communication practices, and has been used in tandem with constructivist, critical, cultural, feminist, postmodern, and communitarian research viewpoints (see Sense-Making Methodology Site in the references at the end of the chapter).

Sense-Making frequently has been operationalized through time-line and neutral questioning interview techniques. The former asks participants to describe their information-seeking sequence and analyzes the results using the situation-gaps-uses schema traditionally connected with the methodology. The latter—neutral interview strategy—guides users in expressing information needs in their own (instead of the information professional's) words, and has been applied to reference interview models.

(For a succinct description of the significance of "situations-gaps-uses" and neutral interviewing techniques in LIS, see Savolainen,1993.)

Sense-Making has come a long way since its introduction to LIS. An early, frequently cited Sense-Making study deemed it useful for delineating situations, gaps, and "everyday" needs associated with information seeking and use (Dervin, 1976). Ten years later, the methodology was central to a call for a "paradigm shift" to invoke the user (rather than system) point of view in information-seeking research (Dervin & Nilan, 1986). At the end of the last century, Sense-Making was touted as a "mature" methodology, accompanied by a recommended suite of data collection and analysis techniques. Most recently and specifically related to LIS is a growing interest in "information behavior," and the methodology has been directed toward understanding contexts and processes of information need, seeking, and use. Progressing from early analysis of the situations, gaps, and uses surrounding a human information "need," the methodology now stresses *verbing* (Dervin, 1993), which could allow LIS scholars to transcend simple classification and achieve holistic understanding of information activity.

Sense-Making has great utility for shifting researchers' focus from categorization to process, a focus that might better reflect the intricacies of information behavior. The concept of information behavior transforms distinct notions of need, seeking, and use into unified investigation of the processes by which people become informed. Interest in information process has been accompanied by growing interest in context, as reflected in the growing area of "Information Seeking in Context" (Kuhlthau, 1999; Talja, Keso, & Pietiläinen, 1999) and in the recognition that human beings do not compartmentalize their lives, expressed in Savolainen's (1995) concept of Everyday Life Information Seeking.

The Sense-Making methodology stresses individual rather than collective understanding. As a result, Sense-Making may seem to be inadequate for explaining group and organizational information exchange and communication processes. However, any misapprehension that Sense-Making is limited to individual "cognition" can be alleviated by a review of current Sense-Making tenets, which are extensive in their consideration of the dynamic influence of time, space, cognition, affect, power, culture, and individual and collaborative Sense-Making.

Any difficulty in understanding the scope and promise of Sense-Making for LIS research might not be located with the principles it entails, but with understanding how to operationalize the methodology for studying group activity. Certainly past focus on scripted interviews used for collecting and analyzing data from individuals could contribute to this circumstance. Using various approaches might alleviate such difficulties. Specifically, "qualitative" or interpretive research allows for the methodology to be applied in ways that foster broader application. By combining Sense-Making with other theories and expanding ideas about how to study and report information behavior, LIS researchers can use the methodology to its maximum advantage. For example, some other theories that fit naturally with Sense-Making principles include Erdelez's Information Encountering; Miller's Monitoring and Blunting; Nahl's Affective Load; Hall's Cultural Model; and sense making as developed in accordance with the work of Wieck and Checkland.

Sense-Making methodology offers a structure for deciphering information behavior. Its principles, particularly its emphasis on verbing, can accommodate multiple variables (those of time, space, affiliation, or affinity) easily neglected in information seeking and use research. The methodology has typically been associated with structured interview methods (even "neutral" questioning enforces a framework of discussion), which short-circuit its interpretive potential. Despite its customary alliance with certain perspectives and methods, Sense-Making can be paired with other epistemological agendas. Interpretive (as opposed to the less useful term "qualitative"; see Hathaway, 1995) research using narrative analysis is one way to maximize Sense-Making's explanatory power.

For example, the concept of bricolage enables researchers to blend an array of strategies ideal for deciphering the complexities of information behavior (Denzin & Lincoln, 1998; Kinchloe, 2001). Bricolage requires the researcher to draw on a deep understanding of the vast store of research philosophies and methods and select those best suited to her research aims of the moment. In the recent research study by Tidline (2003) on the information properties of visual art, Sense-Making methodology offered the best framework for learning and reporting how people can be informed by art. The traditional models of Sense-Making with their prescribed interview structure did not fit the enlarged depiction of information behavior reflected in the study. However, fitting narrative analysis with Sense-Making principles, operationalized through open-ended interviews, allowed the researcher to capitalize on the human "proclivity to organize experience in terms of plots" (Ochs & Capps, 1996, p. 26).

A mixture of Sense-Making, narrative analysis, and reflexive assessment could contribute to organic understanding of human information behavior. This is because, as Dervin claims "a focus on verbings offers a different entry for the search for systematic understandings of the human condition. Instead of focusing on elusive, ever-changing and constantly challenged nouns, Sense-Making mandates a focus on the *hows* (emphasis added) of human individual and collective Sense-Making and sense-unmaking, on the varieties of internal and external cognizings, emotings, feelings, and communicatings that make, reinforce, challenge, resist, alter, and reinvent human worlds" (1999, p. 731). Verbing compels that we emphasize the process of being informed instead of persistently trying to define information as a discrete entity (or noun). Because humans tell stories that reveal cognitive and affective motivations and contextualize information behavior, Sense-Making and narrative analysis offer potential for discovering new vistas of information behavior.

Corbin J. M., & Strauss, A. (1998). *Basics of qualitative research: Techniques and procedures for developing grounded theory* (2nd ed). Thousand Oaks, CA: Sage.

Dalrymple, P. W. (2001). A quarter century of user-centered study: The impact of Zweizig and Dervin on LIS research. *Library and Information Science Research*, 23(2), 155–65.

Denzin, N. K., & Lincoln, Y. S. (1998). *The landscape of qualitative research: Theories and issues*. Thousand Oaks, CA: Sage.

Dervin, B. (1983, May). *An overview of Sense-Making research: Concepts, methods, and results to date*. Paper presented at the International Communication Association Annual Meeting, Dallas.

Dervin, B. (1992). From the mind's eye of the user: The Sense-Making qualitative-quantitative methodology. In J. D. Glazier, & R. R. Powell (Eds.), *Qualitative research in information management* (pp. 61–84). Englewood, CO: Libraries Unlimited.

Dervin, B. (1993). Verbing communication: Mandate for disciplinary invention. *Journal of Communication*, 43(3), 0021–9916.

Dervin, B. (1999). On studying information seeking methodologically: The implications of connecting metatheory to method. *Information Processing and Management 35*, 727–750.

Dervin, B., & Foreman-Wernet, L., Eds. (2003). *Sense-Making Methodology reader: Selected writings of Brenda Dervin.* Cresskill, NJ: Hampton Press.

Dervin, B., & Nilan, M. (1986). Information needs and uses. *Annual Review of Information Science and Technology, 21*, 19–38.

Hathaway, R. S. (1995). Assumptions underlying quantitative and qualitative research: implications for institutional research. *Research in Higher Education, 36*, 535–562.

Kincheloe, J. L. (2001). Describing the bricolage: Conceptualizing a new rigor in qualitative research. *Qualitative Inquiry, 7*, 679–692.

Ochs, E., & Capps, L. (1996). Narrating the self. *Annual Review of Anthropology, 25*, 19–43.

Savolainen, R. (1993). The Sense-Making theory: Reviewing the interests of a user-centered approach to information seeking and use. *Information Processing & Management, 29*, 13–28.

Savolainen, R. (1995). Everyday life information seeking: Approaching information seeking in the context of "way of life." *Libraries & Information Science Research, 17*, 259–294.

Sense-Making Methodology Site. Retrieved March 17, 2004, from http://communication. sbs.ohio-state.edu/sense-making/default.html

Talja, S., Keso, H., & Pietiläinen, T. (1999). The production of context in information seeking research: A metatheoretical view. *Information Processing and Management, 35*, 751–763.

Tidline, T. J. (2003) *Making sense of art as information.* Unpublished doctoral dissertation, University of Illinois, Urbana-Champaign.

17
Diffusion Theory

Darian Lajoie-Paquette
Faculty of Information and Media Studies
The University of Western Ontario, Canada
dlajoiep@uwo.ca

Although its main principles were in use earlier, *diffusion of innovations theory* (diffusion theory) was first formally articulated by Everett M. Rogers in the early 1960s. Areas of research where this theory has been applied include agriculture, health, teaching and learning, marketing and management, and, in the recent past, communication innovations involving new technologies, such as the Internet and e-mail. The four main elements of diffusion theory are embodied in a deceivingly simple definition: Diffusion is the process by which an *innovation* is *communicated through channels over time* among members of a *social system* (Rogers, 2003).

An *innovation* is an idea, practice, or object that is perceived as new by an individual or other unit of adoption (Rogers, 2003). Knowing of an innovation creates uncertainty in the mind and the potential of a new idea impels an individual to learn more about the innovation. Once information-seeking activities reduce uncertainty about expectations to a comfortable level, a decision concerning adoption is made. If adopted, further evaluation about the effects of the innovation is carried out. Thus, the innovation-decision process is essentially an information-seeking and processing activity in which an individual is motivated to reduce uncertainty about relative advantages and disadvantages of an innovation (Rogers, 2003).

The main questions typically asked are: What is the innovation?; How does it work?; Why does it work?; What are its consequences?; and, What will be its advantages and disadvantages in my situation? (Rogers, 2003).

It should not be assumed that all innovations are equivalent units of analysis. While consumer innovations such as cell phones and DVD players require only a few years to reach widespread use, other new ideas, such as the metric system or auto seat belts, require decades to reach popular use.

According to Rogers (2003), the following perceived characteristics of innovations help to explain their different rates of adoption:

- *Relative advantage*, or the degree to which an innovation is perceived as better than the former idea. This may be measured in economic terms, but social prestige, convenience, and satisfaction are also important factors.

- *Compatibility*, or the degree to which an innovation is perceived as being consistent with the existing values, past experiences, and needs of potential adopters. An idea that is incompatible with the values and norms of a social system will not be adopted as rapidly as an innovation that is more compatible.

- *Complexity*, or the degree to which an innovation is perceived as difficult to understand and use. Simple ideas are diffused more rapidly than innovations requiring development of new skills and understanding.

- *Trialability*, or the degree to which an innovation may be experimented with before adoption. New ideas that can be tested in increments will generally be adopted more quickly than those that cannot.

- *Observability*, or the degree to which the results of an innovation are visible to others. The easier it is to see the results of an innovation, the more likely it is to be adopted.

Diffusion is a particular type of communication in which the message content is concerned with a new idea. The essence of the diffusion process is the information exchange through which one individual communicates a new idea to others. At its most elementary form, the process involves an innovation, an individual with knowledge of or experience with the innovation, another individual with no knowledge of or experience with the innovation and, finally, a communication channel connecting the two individuals. A communication channel is the means by which messages transfer between individuals. Channels may include mass media such as radio, television, newspapers, the Internet, or interpersonal channels such as face-to-face exchanges.

Time is a crucial element in three aspects of the diffusion process: 1) the innovation-decision process by which an individual passes from first knowledge of an innovation through to its adoption or rejection; 2) the innovativeness of an individual, that is, the timeliness with which an innovation is adopted compared with other members in the system; and, 3) the rate of adoption of an innovation, usually measured as the number of members of the system who adopt the innovation in a given time period.

In the innovation-decision process, an individual passes from *knowledge* (first knowledge of an innovation) to *persuasion* (formation of an attitude toward the innovation) to *decision* (the decision to adopt or reject) to *implementation* (actual use of the innovation) and finally to *confirmation* (commitment to adopt). A social system, as defined by Rogers (2003), is a set of interrelated units engaged in joint problem solving to accomplish a common goal. The units of a social system may be individuals, informal groups, organizations, or subsystems. Social structure affects diffusion in several ways through the system's own set of norms, its established internal behavior patterns, as well as its opinion leaders who are able to influence attitudes or behavior.

As innovations tend to be related to technologies it is not surprising that library and information science research on diffusion theory has focused on technology, particularly the Internet and various digital tools that have emerged in the past decade. White's (2001) survey of 140 American academic libraries used diffusion theory to analyze the use of academic digital reference services, focusing on the extent and rate of diffusion, the characteristics of libraries in each adopter category, and the re-invention of the innovation during implementation. Starkweather and Wallin (1999) conducted focus group sessions and personal interviews to explore faculty attitudes regarding the increasing computerization of academic library information resources. Brown's (2001) study of music scholars examined the use and perceptions of helpfulness of electronic mail and electronic discussion groups by music scholars using diffusion theory to describe and assess scholars' level of agreement with statements concerning relative advantages and compatibility of e-mail and electronic discussion groups to the research process. A study by Marshall (1990) used diffusion theory to predict the level of implementation of end-user online searching.

Two examples of library and information science diffusion theory research that does not involve computer technology are found in PhD dissertations on the influence of American librarianship on librarianship in other countries. Rochester (1990) examined American influence, as facilitated by the Carnegie Corporation of New York in the 1930s, on librarianship in New Zealand. Maack (1986) focused on the impact of American librarianship on the diffusion of the philosophy and practice of librarianship in France.

The research of Elfreda Chatman stands out in its examination of diffusion of innovations theory as it relates to those whom she calls informationally disadvantaged. Chatman (1986) attempted to test diffusion theory in a study of the awareness, use, and diffusion of an innovation in a job environment of the working poor. In this case, the innovation was information itself, an unusual approach in the field of diffusion research. Chatman (1987) also looked at opinion leadership in a low-income environment, the diffusion of information within this milieu, and the role opinion leaders play as disseminators of new information related to employment.

Possibilities for future information behavior research using diffusion theory research abound. Many more groups of people, many different information uses, and many more information channels remain totally unexplored.

Brown, C. D. (2001). The role of computer-mediated communication in the research process of music scholars: An exploratory investigation. *Information Research*, 6(2). Retrieved February 15, 2004, from http://informationr.net/ir/6-2/paper99.html

Chatman, E. A. (1986). Diffusion theory: a review and test of a conceptual model in information diffusion. *Journal of the American Society for Information Science*, 37, 377–386.

Chatman, E. A. (1987). Opinion leadership, poverty, and information sharing. *RQ*, 26, 341–353.

Maack, M. N. (1986). Americans in France: Cross-cultural exchange and diffusion of innovations. *Journal of Library History*, 21, 315–333.

Marshall, J. (1990). Diffusion of innovation theory and end-user searching. *Library and Information Science Research*, 12(1), 55–69.

Rochester, M. K. (1990). *The revolution in New Zealand librarianship: American influence as facilitated by the Carnegie Corporation of New York in the 1930s.* Report based on a Ph.D. Dissertation. Halifax, NS: Dalhousie University, SLIS.

Rogers, E. M. (2003). *Diffusion of innovations* (5th ed.). New York: Free Press.

Starkweather, W. M., & Wallin, C. C. (1999). Faculty response to library technology: Insights on attitudes. *Library Trends, 47,* 640–668.

White, M. D. (2001). Diffusion of an innovation: Digital reference service in Carnegie Foundation master's (comprehensive) academic institution libraries. *Journal of Academic Librarianship, 27*(3), 173–187.

18
The Domain Analytic Approach to Scholars' Information Practices

Sanna Talja
Department of Information Studies
University of Tampere, Finland
sanna.talja@uta.fi

The term d*omain analysis* was introduced by Hjørland and Albrechtsen (1995) who argued that it is more fruitful to view domains (specialties, disciplines, or discourse communities) as basic units of analysis rather than focus on "users" in a generalized and context-independent manner. The domain analytic approach is not new, however; the history of social science research on scholars' information practices in various fields goes back to the 1930s, culminating in the many classic papers presented in the 1958 International Conference on Scientific Information (Bates, 1971). Thus, from the very beginning, studies on scholars' information practices have represented a more sociologically and contextually oriented line of research in comparison to, for instance, information search behavior studies.

The work of Diana Crane (1972), Herbert Menzel (1959), Thomas Allen (1977), William Paisley (1968; Parker & Paisley, 1966), William Garvey (1979), and others are classics of "domain analytic" research because they embed scholars' information practices within the overarching context of disciplinary differences, with the goal of forming holistic understandings of scholarly communities' work and communication practices.

However, as noted by Palmer (1999), Bates (2002), and Hjørland (2002), the development of a more systematic domain analytic approach for explaining scholars' information practices is still in its infancy. While numerous studies have shown that there are major field differences in scholars' work and information practices, and that these differences are likely to persist in the electronic era, (Kling & Covi, 1997; Kling & McKim, 2000) few studies have attempted to develop a comprehensive understanding of the epistemic and other factors that underlie these differences.

Hjørland (2002) argues that epistemic schools are the most generalizable explanatory models of information practices. He distinguishes between four epistemic schools (empiricism, rationalism, historicism, and pragmatism) and outlines what kind of knowledge is considered relevant in each school. In the school of historicism, for instance, background knowledge about preunderstandings, theories, historical developments and evolutionary perspectives are considered to be relevant, whereas "low priority is given to decontextualized data," and "intersubjectively controlled data are often seen as trivia." (p. 269). Although Hjørland does not link the epistemic schools with specific fields, his categorization aptly informs about differences in the nature of research within the schools, and about the general context of information seeking. However, in addition to epistemic positions, scholars' information practices are affected by factors such as degree of inter- and multidisciplinarity (Bates, 1996; Palmer, 1999), and field size (Bates, 2002).

In a study of the adoption and use of e-journals and databases across four domains (history, nursing science, environmental biology, and literature and cultural studies), Talja and Maula (2003) explain the variation in scholars' information-seeking practices by the following interrelated domain factors:

- Field size (density of the universe of relevant documents)
- Degree of scatter
- Primary relevance criteria (topical/paradigmatic)
- Book versus article orientation

The hypothesis that variation in scholars' search methods is directly related to field size was developed by Bates (2002). According to Bates,

- Research areas with high numbers of topically relevant materials are best searched by browsing.
- Research areas with middling numbers of topically relevant materials are best searched by directed subject searches.
- Research areas with very sparse ("needle in a haystack") numbers of relevant items are best searched by linking (chaining from seed documents).

Bates thus suggests that both the oversupply and scarcity of topically relevant materials makes directed searching—conducting descriptor-based subject searches in databases whose materials have been indexed, catalogued, and classified—an unproductive search technique, and that scholars in densely and sparsely populated research areas will rely more on browsing and linking techniques.

The distinction between low-scatter domains and high-scatter domains was originally made by Mote (1962). According to Mote, low scatter domains are those in which the underlying principles are well-developed, the literature is well organized, and the width of the subject area is relatively limited and clearly defined. In high scatter domains, the subject area is wider, the number of different research topics is greater, and the literature is less clearly organized or unhelpfully organized in the light of scholars' research interests and problems. Scholars in low-scatter fields are served by a small number of highly specialized journals, whereas in high-scatter fields, relevant materials are distributed across several disciplines and published in a large number of different journals (Packer & Soergel, 1979). Inter- and multidisciplinary fields are typically high scatter domains in the sense that the researcher must typically cross several disciplines to locate all relevant materials (Bates, 1996).

The well-known fact that humanities scholars often prefer to use browsing and chaining as techniques for identifying relevant literature is also related to relevance criteria and the nature of the research object. Talja and Maula (2003) distinguish between topical and paradigmatic relevance as primary relevance criteria. In fields where research objects and problems can be constructed differently from diverse viewpoints, information seekers commonly attach their search strategies to particular *conversations* or paradigms. The choice of theories or methodological approaches may limit or widen the range of materials considered as relevant independently of the topic or phenomenon studied. In natural sciences, research objects are usually more stable and standardized, and searches are more commonly focused on the phenomenon or substance being studied.

Previous research (Kling & Covi, 1997) also shows that scholars' search techniques differ in fields where books carry the most prestige and are regarded as the most important sources, as compared to fields where peer-reviewed articles are considered as the most important sources. Scholars in fields where articles are the main publication channel will rely more on formal scanning, that is, directed searching, whereas scholars in fields where books carry the most prestige are often "author-filterers" in search of like-minded colleagues (Walsh & Bayma, 1996).

Although most scholars will use a mix of different search strategies such as directed searching, browsing, and chaining, there are clear differences in the relative importance of these methods across fields. Humanities scholars can discover essential theoretical ideas from literatures previously alien to them, but serendipitous findings for natural scientists are of a different nature, because they rarely conduct searches outside their own specialties.

Talja and Maula's study was a small-scale comparative qualitative study, providing a basis on which to conduct further research on the predictive power of factors such as field size, scatter, primary relevance criteria, and book vs. article orientation. Talja's and Maula's empirical findings support the overall hypothesis that these factors have clear impacts on the patterns of use of e-journals and databases. Contrary to the Bates hypothesis, however, Talja and Maula found that humanities scholars working in sparsely populated research areas (such as Finnish literature) used manual and Web browsing and information encountering as their primary search methods. Humanities scholars working in densely populated research areas (such as media and cultural studies) chose some cognitive authorities (books or authors) and proceeded by linking to identify relevant works by using theoretical suitability or similarity as their primary selection criterion.

The domain analytic approach that identifies and explains significant field differences in scholars' information practices differs considerably from—and therefore complements—Ellis' well-known research phases model that identifies similarities in patterns of information seeking across fields. Domain analytic studies can significantly help in endeavors to support scholarly communities and improve their access to scientific literature.

Allen, T. J. (1977). *Managing the flow of information: Technology transfer and the dissemination of technical information within the R & D organization.* Cambridge, MA: MIT Press.

Bates, M. J. (1971). *User studies: A review for librarians and information scientists.* ERIC Document Reproduction Service No. ED 047–738.

Bates, M. J. (1996). Learning about the information seeking of interdisciplinary scholars and students. *Library Trends, 45,* 155–164.

Bates, M. J. (2002). Speculations on browsing, directed searching, and linking in relation to the Bradford distribution. In H. Bruce, R. Fidel, P. Ingwersen, & P. Vakkari (Eds.), *Emerging frameworks and methods: Proceedings of the fourth international conference on conceptions of library and information science (CoLIS4)* (pp. 137–149). Greenwood Village, CO: Libraries Unlimited.

Crane, D. (1972). *Invisible colleges: Diffusion of knowledge in scientific communication.* Chicago: University of Chicago Press.

Garvey, W. D. (1979). *Communication: The essence of science.* Oxford: Pergamon Press.

Hjørland, B. (2002). Epistemology and the socio-cognitive perspective in information science. *Journal of the American Society for Information Science and Technology, 53,* 257–270.

Hjørland, B., & Albrechtsen, H. (1995). Toward a new horizon in information science: domain-analysis. *Journal of the American Society for Information Science, 46,* 400–425.

Kling, R., & Covi, L. (1997). Digital libraries and the practices of scholarly communication. Retrieved March 3, 2004, from www.slis.indiana.edu/kling/SCIT/SCIT97.htm.

Kling, R., & McKim, G. W. (2000). Not just a matter of time: Field differences and the shaping of electronic media in supporting scientific communication. *Journal of the American Society for Information Science, 51,* 1306–1320.

Menzel, H. (1959). Planned and unplanned scientific communication. *Proceedings of the international conference on scientific information.* Washington, DC: National Academy of Sciences-Natural Research Council.

Mote, L. J. B. (1962). Reasons for the variation of information needs of scientists. *Journal of Documentation, 18,* 169–175.

Packer, K. H., & Soergel, D. (1979). The importance of SDI for current awareness in fields with severe scatter of information. *Journal of the American Society for Information Science, 30,* 125–135.

Paisley, W. (1968). Information needs and uses. In C.A. Cuadra (Ed.), *Annual Review of Information Science and Technology, 3* (pp. 1–30). Chicago: Encyclopedia Britannica.

Palmer, C. L. (1999). Aligning studies of information seeking and use with domain analysis. *Journal of the American Society for Information Science, 50,* 1139–1140.

Parker, E. W., & Paisley, W. J. (1967). *Scientific information exchange at an interdisciplinary behavioral science convention.* Stanford, CA: Stanford Institute for Communication Research.

Talja, S., & Maula, H. (2003). Reasons for the use and non-use of electronic journals and databases: a domain analytic study in four scholarly disciplines. *Journal of Documentation, 59,* 673–691.

Walsh, J. P., & Bayma, T. (1996). Computer networks and scientific work. *Social Studies of Science, 26,* 661–703.

19
Ecological Theory of Human Information Behavior

Kirsty Williamson
School of Information Management and Systems, Monash University
School of Information Studies, Charles Sturt University, Australia
kirsty.williamson@sims.monash.edu.au

With Bates's (2002) "Towards an integrated model of information seeking and searching," a breath of fresh air blew into the debate about theories of information seeking and searching. Her theory attempted to be encompassing while bringing together many layers of understanding of human life and gave also particular prominence to the notion that information is not always purposefully sought. Bates gave equal emphasis to the active and passive in her "modes of information seeking" and that "it is not unreasonable to guess that we absorb perhaps 80 percent of all our knowledge through simply being aware, being conscious and sentient in our social context and physical environment" (p. 4).

The ecological theory for the study of human information behavior (ecological theory) by Williamson develops Williamson's (1998) model of information seeking and use (see Figure 19.1), which emerged from a large-scale study focusing on older people and everyday life information. This model emphasizes that, at least in the field of everyday life information, information is often incidentally acquired rather than purposefully sought. While concepts such as "gaps" (e.g., Dervin & Nilan, 1986), "uncertainty reduction" (e.g., Kuhlthau, 1993), and "anomalous states of knowledge" (e.g., Belkin, 1978) are appropriate for the study of purposeful information seeking, not all information-related behavior is purposeful. Williamson chose the term "incidental information acquisition" as a result of the influence of P. Wilson (1977) who suggested that people find information unexpectedly as they engage in other activities, with information acquisition becoming an "incidental concomitant." Other researchers who have given prominence to this concept are Erdelez (1997) who used the term "information encountering," and

Savolainen (1995) who saw everyday life information seeking as manifesting itself in the "monitoring of daily life world" (p. 317). Williamson (1998) also believed that people monitor their world for relevant information, but suggested that some needs are "unconscious" becoming recognized only when relevant information is discovered.

The concept of incidental information acquisition may have been neglected because it is difficult to explore empirically. Williamson (1998) used three in-depth interviews with each of 202 participants to gain extensive understanding of the processes involved. Nevertheless, incidental information acquisition remains a concept that should be further

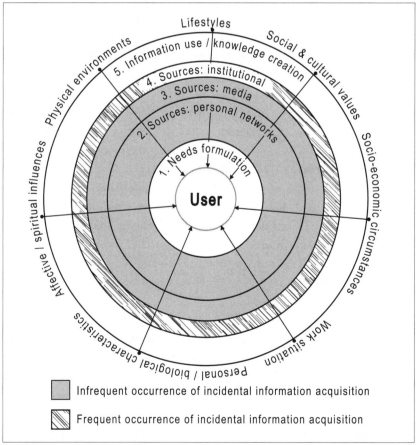

Figure 19.1   Ecological model of information seeking and use.

explored. It is particularly important to the study of the use of sources of information and information systems.

While the shift of focus from information systems to users (Dervin & Nilan, 1986) has been loudly applauded, there is a need for an acknowledged compromise position and for at least some of the focus to move to the *relationship* between information types/sources/systems and the information seeker/user. After all, it is from sources and systems that people usually seek or acquire information. As Talja (1997) stated, if the focus is shifted to the study of knowledge formations, "it is equally important to study the socio-cultural aspects and the ideological nature of the information systems, as it is to study the socio-cultural aspects of the users" (p.77). There is also a need to include information sources such as family, friends, and colleagues, who are not components of "information systems," but who play a significant role in incidental information acquisition. As Kari and Savolainen (2002) pointed out, although there have now been a large number of studies of information searching on the World Wide Web, the broader picture and the relationship with other sources of information is usually not considered.

Williamson explored concepts of both "purposeful information seeking" and "individual information acquisition" in an ecological framework which, inter alia, encompasses as influences on behavior several of the layers from Bates's (2002) integrated theory. The key influence for this framework was work by Hummert, Nussbaum, and Wiemann (1992), who argued that research about people must be grounded in a view of nature as *personal existence*. This means that human beings should not be conceptualized exclusively as either individual entities or socially constructed entities. Rather, they should be seen as self-creating, but within contexts that involve various kinds of biological and social circumstances and constraints.

In recent years, Williamson has undertaken many funded projects, which identified how her ecological model can be broadened and modified, to be useful to study information-related behavior beyond the everyday life area, and also for the study of user preferences for information types, e.g., visual/textual or scholarly/lay information. Her view is similar to that of Bates who postulated that the scientific, the cognitive, and the socially constructed metatheories all have value and a possible continuing role. Williamson has particularly used social constructionist theory

(Berger & Luckman, 1967) and personal constructivist theory (Kelly, 1963) to capture both shared and individual meanings—the consensus and the dissonance —about information seeking and use.

For example, in a study by Williamson and Manaszewicz (2002) the researchers set out to understand potential user perspectives in relation to a range of information issues on an online portal with breast cancer information. Several "ecological" elements were found to play a part, including promoting or impeding information seeking. Examples are biological factors/physical health, age, ethnicity, place of residence (city/country), stage of disease, and affective issues. The outcome is that information is being "tailored" to user needs through a portal—by the provision of "user-centric" resource descriptions and a metadata repository that links the self-selected profiles with specific information resources. This is an example of how information behavior researchers can work with metadata and technical experts to develop systems based on the information-related behavior of prospective users.

The major strength of the ecological theory is its flexibility to include all influences on behavior at any stage of the information-seeking or information-acquisition process. Examples of its use have involved many different academic and industry partnerships, topic areas, and target groups, e.g., online investors, people with disabilities, and members of the International Olympic Community (see Information and Telecommunications Needs Research Web site). A part, or parts of the concentric circle diagram, presented in Figure 19.1, can be used, as appropriate, and the influences on behavior can be selected and/or expanded according to the user group or groups involved.

Bates, M. (2002). Toward an integrated model of information seeking and searching. *The New Review of Information Behaviour Research, 3*, 1–15.

Belkin, N. J. (1978). Information concepts for information science. *Journal of Documentation, 34*, 55–85.

Berger, P. L., & Luckmann, T. (1967). *The social construction of reality: A treatise in the sociology of knowledge*. New York: Anchor Press.

Dervin, B., & Nilan, M. (1986). Information needs and uses. In M. E. Williams (Ed.), *Annual review of information science and technology, 21*, 3–33. White Plains, NY: Knowledge Industry Publications.

Erdelez, S. (1997). Information encountering: A conceptual framework for accidental information seeking. In P. Vakkari, R. Savolainen, & B. Dervin (Eds.), *Information Seeking in Context* (pp. 412–421). London: Taylor Graham.

Hummert, M. L., Nussbaum, J. F., & Wiemann, J. M. (1992). Communication and the elderly: Cognition, language and relationships. *Communication Research, 19*, 413–422.

Information and Telecommunications Needs Research. (n. d.). Retrieved February 10, 2004, from www.sims.monash.edu.au/research/itnr/

Kari, J., & Savolainen, R. (2002). Towards a contextual model of information seeking on the Web. In Working Papers of ISIC 2002, *Information seeking in context: The fourth international conference on information seeking in context* (pp. 488–513). Lisbon, Portugal: Universidade Lusiada.

Kelly, G. (1963). *The psychology of personal constructs*. Vols 1 & 2. New York: Norton.

Kuhlthau, C. (1993). A principle of uncertainty for information seeking. *Journal of Communication, 49*(40), 339–355.

Savolainen, R. (1995). Everyday life information seeking: Findings and methodological questions of an empirical study. In M. Hancock-Beaulieu & N. O. Pors (Eds.), *Proceedings of the 1st British-Nordic conference* (pp. 313-331). Copenhagen, Denmark: The Royal School of Librarianship.

Talja, S. (1997). Constituting 'information' and 'user' as research objects: A theory of knowledge formations as an alternative to the information man-theory. In P. Vakkari, R. Savolainen, & B. Dervin (Eds.), *Information Seeking in Context* (pp. 67–80). London: Taylor Graham.

Williamson, K. (1998). Discovered by chance: The role of incidental information acquisition in an ecological model of information use. *Library and Information Science Research, 20*(1), 23–40.

Williamson, K., & Manaszewicz, R. (2002). Breast cancer information needs and seeking: Towards an intelligent, user sensitive portal to breast cancer knowledge online. *New Review of Information Behaviour Research, 3*, 203–219.

Wilson, P. (1977). *Public knowledge, private ignorance*. Westport, CT: Greenwood Press.

20
Elicitation as Micro-Level Information Seeking

Mei-Mei Wu
Graduate Institute of Library and Information Studies
National Taiwan Normal University, Taiwan
meiwu@cc.ntnu.edu.tw

Elicitation, or "questioning" and "question-asking," is not only an important phenomenon in everyday communication, but also a salient concept in the areas of library reference services and information retrieval interaction. Elicitation was not a focus of systematic research until the 1960s, when the logic of questions and answers attracted researchers' attention (Wu, 1993). A bibliography compiled by Egli and Schleichert in 1976 reveals that in the 1960s, when the concepts of artificial intelligence and automatic query systems were introduced, the primary concern of elicitation research was the logic of questions and answers. The fundamental assumption of the logic of questions is that any question Q needs a logically true answer A as a presupposition (Belnap & Steel, 1976). This assumption, however, does not lend itself well to empirical observation. Goffman (1976) and Stenstrom (1984), for example, investigate the mundane conversation and both challenge the circular logic necessary when a question and a response are assumed as criteria for each other.

The next stage in the development of elicitation research belongs to psychology and the empirical aspects of elicitation in various social contexts (e.g., Belkin & Vickery, 1985; Dillon, 1990; Graessar & Black, 1985). Among the research topics addressed are the studies of comprehension, the internal cognitive process of asking a question and the provision of a proper answer (Galambo & Black, 1985), and the taxonomies for question forms and functions based on empirical observation (Kearsley, 1976). For example, Dillon (1990) suggests that prior to the act of asking a question, the speaker presupposes that the listener has the answer or should know the answer, which constitutes the first element,

133

the assumption. The question, including the processes of formation and the act of expression, is the second element. The answer that follows is the third element of an elicitation.

Wu (1993) proposes a conceptual framework for the elicitation process (see Figure 20.1) that applies Dillon's elicitation elements (assumption, question, and answer) and emphasizes the internally and externally driven forces that create the need for elicitation. In the framework, an elicitation is initiated either by a self-inquiry, which arises from information need, or by a situation, such as a desire to show one's social power, to seek self-identity, to improve a relationship, or to keep the conversation going. The second step is the formulation of an elicitation that relates to an individual's personal knowledge and experience. This step is followed by the act of expressing the elicitation. Studies in this area focus on the syntactic structure (grammatical forms), the semantic meaning (in an IR situation, the elicitation purposes), and the pragmatic meaning (the illocutionary act or the communicative function) of an elicitation. The next step is the comprehension of an elicitation by the other person, which leads to a reply or an answer. An optional step is feedback to the reply or a subsequent elicitation driven by another self-inquiry or situation. The identification of an

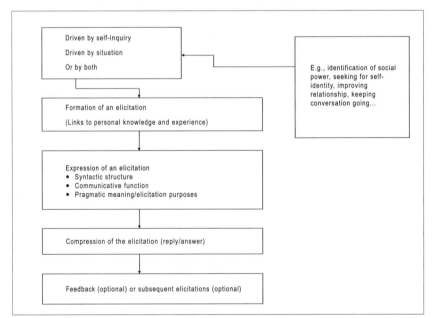

Figure 20.1   Conceptual framework of the elicitation process.

elicitation from a discourse is based on the syntactic structure (forms), the semantic meaning (purposes), the pragmatic intention (functions), and the speaker's assumption as to what the responding person knows (Wu, 1993).

Elicitation reflects social power and social roles, as suggested by Dillon (1990), in that, for example, a teacher asks more questions than a student, a doctor asks more questions than a patient, a policeman and judge ask questions, but a suspect and accused do not. Elicitation is a paramount concern of information retrieval researchers not only in question-answering retrieval system design, but also in understanding the patron's micro-level information-seeking behavior. Wu (1993) analyzed 38 patron-intermediary interaction dialogues in genuine information retrieval settings in academic libraries, and found that the total number of elicitations in an IR interaction dialogue has a significantly positive relationship with the length of interaction and with the number of utterances. The elicitation of intermediaries can be termed "pre-planned," because its frequency does not increase with the length of interaction. In contrast, a patron's elicitation is "situational" because its frequency does increase with the length of interaction. Patrons' individual characteristics, status, age, search experiences, and the intermediaries they interact with, all affect the frequency of the elicitation behavior.

Wu (1993) proposes that elicitation constitutes micro-level information-seeking (MLIS) behavior, suggesting that it may take many acts of elicitation to fulfill an overall goal of seeking a particular piece of information. Wu identifies patrons' elicitation purposes as cognitive, social, and communication related. She also found that two-thirds of patron elicitation purposes in an IR interaction regard outputs, terms, and search procedures, mostly cognitive need related. Because a patron elicitation increases with the length of interaction, the intermediaries may rely on the patron's MLIS to develop dynamic user models, which can be updated during the process of interaction.

By analyzing intermediaries' elicitation purposes, syntactic forms and communicative functions, three types of intermediary elicitation styles have been identified: 1) situational, 2) functional, and 3) stereotyped. To seek an explanation of the elicitation styles, three modes of *inquiring mind* are specified: 1) information problem detection, 2) query formulation process, and 3) database instructions (Wu & Liu,

2003). An inquiring mind refers to an individual's tendency to elicit certain threads of questions influenced by professional beliefs, individual characteristics, tasks, goals, and the interactive contexts in conversation. Given the commonly held assumption of the intermediary's role in modeling the user's information need, an interesting finding is that there are relatively few elicitations addressing detection of the patron's information problem in Wu and Liu's total of 30 patron-intermediary interaction dialogues collected in the real setting of both academic and research libraries. Wu and Liu (2003), however, report that the inquiring mind in information problem detection mode, directly modeling the user's information need, only occurs in one search interview across all 30 cases of interactions. This finding does not support the notion that the intermediary's professional identities form a user model by detecting or diagnosing the user's information need. It seems the institutional dialogue is a complex information-seeking process in which the participants manage their goals, tasks and activities through their use of language, which is influenced by not only their professional training but also their individual characteristics and perhaps environmental conditions. The question of how the intermediary's professional role is revealed in the reference or search interview needs a more comprehensive conceptual-analytic framework.

Overall, elicitation as an MLIS behavior provides a promising approach for addressing both practical and theoretical concerns of information behavior in patron-intermediary interaction. The MLIS framework facilitates various aspects of higher-level information seeking and as such can be applied to information seeker education on how to improve personal information behavior in asking effective questions. It can also be applied in training intermediaries in dynamic user modeling during elicitation, in asking effective questions, and in improving the professional identity of information services. Finally, more research is needed on the MLIS framework to understand its role within the broader framework of information behavior during patron-intermediary interaction.

Belkin, N. J., & Vickery, A. (1985). *Interaction in information systems: A review of research from document retrieval to knowledge-based systems.* Cambridge, UK: Cambridge University Press.

Belnap, N., & Steel, T. (1976). *The logic of questions and answers.* London: Yale University Press.

Dillon, J. T. (1990). *The practice of questioning*. New York: Routledge.

Egli, U., & Schleichert, H. (1976). Bibliography of the theory of questions and answers. In Belnap, N. & Steel, T. (Eds.), *The logic of questions and answers*. London: Yale University Press.

Galambo, J., & Black, J. B. (1985). Using knowledge of activities to understand and answer questions. In A. C. Graesser, & J. B. Black (Eds.), *The psychology of questions*. Hillsdale, NJ: Erlbaum.

Goffman, E. (1976). Replies and responses. *Language in Society, 5*, 257–313.

Graesser, A. C., & Black, J. B., Eds. (1985). *The psychology of questions*. Hillsdale, NJ: Erlbaum.

Kearsley, G. P. (1976). Questions and question-asking in verbal discourse: a cross-disciplinary view. *Journal of Psycholinguistic Research, 5*, 355–375.

Stenstrom, A. B. (1984). *Questions and responses in English conversation*. Malmö, Sweden: Gleerup.

Wu, M. M. (1993). Information interaction dialogue: A study of patron elicitation in the information retrieval interaction. (Doctoral dissertation, Rutgers University, New Brunswick, New Jersey, 1993). *Dissertation Abstracts International 54*, 1131.

21
Ellis's Model of
Information-Seeking Behavior

David Ellis
Department of Information Studies
University of Wales, United Kingdom
dpe@aber.ac.uk

The approach to modeling information-seeking behavior described here has its origin in a perceived absence of empirically based models of information-seeking behavior in information retrieval research (Ellis, 1984a, 1984b). The intention was to derive an empirically based model of the information-seeking behavior of academic social scientists that could inform the development of information retrieval systems and which might be of more general interest for the information studies field (Ellis, 1987, 1989a, 1989b, 1990). The principal theoretical premise of the study was that behavior offered a more tractable focus of study than cognition and that a behavioral approach to user modeling would be more feasible than the prevailing cognitive approaches in information retrieval research. The propositions of the theory were that underlying the complex patterns of information-seeking behavior were a relatively small number of different types of activity characterized as:

- *Starting* – activities characteristic of the initial search for information
- *Chaining* – following chains of citations or other forms of referential connection between material
- *Browsing* – semi-directed searching in an area of potential interest
- *Differentiating* – using differences between sources as a filter on the nature and quality of material examined
- *Monitoring* – maintaining awareness of developments in a field through the monitoring of particular sources

- *Extracting* – systematically working through a particular source to locate material of interest

The behavioral model itself consists of the relation between these characteristics or components. These can interact in various ways in different information-seeking patterns. It does not represent a set of stages or phases that any or all researchers follow when seeking information. The relation between the different characteristics can only be described in the most abstract and general terms unless there is reference to a particular information-seeking pattern at a particular time.

The original model has been extended and developed in studies of the information-seeking behavior of other groups of researchers, including English literature researchers (Smith, 1988), physicists and chemists (Ellis, Cox, & Hall, 1993), and engineers and research scientists in an industrial environment (Ellis & Haugan, 1997). In each case, the derivation of the categories and properties was inductive and followed the grounded theory approach (Ellis, 1993). Despite the differing disciplinary backgrounds of the different groups of researchers studied, there was considerable similarity in general and detail between them. In the study of English literature researchers Smith (1988) identified activities consistent with starting, chaining, and monitoring as well as other activities characteristic of surveying (familiarization with the literature of the area), selection and sifting (deciding which references to follow up and which to cite), and assembly and dissemination (drawing together material for publication and dissemination).

The study of the chemists identified activities consistent with starting, chaining, browsing, differentiating, monitoring, and extracting, as well as two other characteristics not highlighted in the study of the social scientists: verifying (checking that information is correct) and ending (characteristics of information seeking at the end of a project).

The study of the physicists employed different terminology to that of the social scientists but it was clear that the activities themselves could be closely mapped to the characteristics of the original model: initial familiarization (activities undertaken at the earliest stages of information seeking), chasing (following up citation links between material), source prioritization (ranking sources based on perceptions of their relative importance), maintaining awareness (activities involved in keeping up-to-date), and locating (activities engaged in to actually find the information).

Finally, the study of the engineers and researchers identified activities consistent with surveying, chaining, monitoring, browsing, extracting, and ending, as well as distinguishing (activities undertaken when information sources are ranked according to their perceived relative importance) and filtering (characterized by the use of criteria or mechanisms to make the information as relevant and precise as possible).

The methodological basis of all the studies was the grounded theory approach as originally developed by Glaser and Strauss (1967). The approach informed the choice of researchers to interview and the form of analysis employed. The methodological basis of the studies was the constant comparative method, employing theoretical sampling, and inductive analysis to develop the properties and categories of the models (Ellis, 1993). The basic research design and methodology can be replicated for studies of other groups without presupposition as to the outcome.

The model has been widely cited in the information-behavior literature, perhaps particularly, and most pertinently, in papers in the Information Seeking in Context Conferences (ISIC) in Sheffield, UK (1998) and Goteborg, Sweden (2000). More recently through an international research collaboration between the University of Sheffield, UK and the University of North Texas, USA (Spink et al., 2002a), the uncertainty in information seeking project has addressed behavioral, cognitive, and affective issues within the same research design, including studies in relation to the behavioral model into such questions as uncertainty and its correlates (Wilson et al., 2002), successive searching (Spink et al., 2002b), cognitive styles in information seeking (Ford et al., 2002), and user-intermediary interaction (Ellis et al., 2002).

The behavioral approach to user modeling outlined here does not address cognitive or affective aspects of information seeking. However, the range of different groups studied and the employment of a consistent methodological approach across the different studies, indicate that the approach represents a broadly based, robust, and widely applicable way of modeling the information-seeking behavior of researchers in both academic and industrial research environments.

Ellis, D. (1984a). The effectiveness of information retrieval systems: The need for improved explanatory frameworks. *Social Science Information Studies, 4*, 262–272.

Ellis, D. (1984b). Theory and explanation in information retrieval research. *Journal of Information Science, 8*, 25–38.

Ellis, D. (1987). *The derivation of a behavioral model for information system design.* Unpublished doctoral dissertation, University of Sheffield, England.

Ellis, D. (1989a). A behavioral approach to information retrieval system design. *Journal of Documentation, 45*, 171–212.

Ellis, D. (1989b). A behavioral model for information retrieval system design. *Journal of Information Science, 15*, 237–247.

Ellis, D. (1990). Database design and the generation, communication and utilization of information by academic social scientists. In M. Feeney & K. Merry (Eds.), *Information technology and the research process* (Proceedings of a conference held at the Cranfield Institute of Technology, Cranfield, 1989) (pp. 252–271). London: Bowker Saur.

Ellis, D. (1993). Modeling the information seeking patterns of academic researchers: A grounded theory approach. *Library Quarterly, 63*, 469–486.

Ellis, D., Cox, D., & Hall, K. (1993). A comparison of the information seeking patterns of researchers in the physical and social sciences. *Journal of Documentation, 49*, 356–369.

Ellis, D., & Haugan, M. (1997). Modeling the information seeking patterns of engineers and research scientists in an industrial environment. *Journal of Documentation, 53*, 384–403.

Ellis, D., Wilson, T. D., Ford, N. J., Foster A., Lam, H. M., Burton, R., & Spink, A. (2002). Information seeking and mediated searching: Part V. User intermediary interaction. *Journal of the American Society for Information Science and Technology, 53*, 883–893.

Ford, N. J., Wilson, T. D., Foster A., Ellis, D., & Spink, A. (2002). Information seeking and mediated searching: Part IV. Cognitive styles in information seeking. *Journal of the American Society for Information Science and Technology, 53*, 728–735.

Glaser, B. G., & Strauss, A. I. (1967). *The discovery of grounded theory: Strategies for qualitative research.* New York: Aldine.

Hoglund, L., & Wilson, T. D., Eds. (2000, 2001). *The new review of information behaviour research: Studies of information seeking in context.* (ISIC III. Proceedings of the third International Conference on Research on Information Needs, Seeking and Use in Different Contexts, August 2000, Goteborg, Sweden). London: Taylor Graham.

Smith, K. (1988). *An investigation of the information seeking behaviour of academics active in the field of English literature.* Unpublished master's thesis, University of Sheffield, England.

Spink, A., Wilson, T. D., Ford, N. J., Foster A., & Ellis, D. (2002a). Information seeking and mediated searching: Part I. Background and research design. *Journal of the American Society for Information Science and Technology, 53*, 2002, 695–703.

Spink, A., Wilson, T. D., Ford, N. J., Foster A., & Ellis, D. (2002b). Information seeking and mediated searching: Part III. Successive searching. *Journal of the American Society for Information Science and Technology, 53*, 2002, 716–727.

Wilson, T. D., & Allen, D. K., Eds. (1999). *Exploring the contexts of information behaviour.* (ISIC II. Proceedings of the second International Conference on Research on Information Needs, Seeking and Use in Different Contexts, August 1998, Sheffield, UK.). London: Taylor Graham.

Wilson, T. D., Ford, N. J., Ellis, D., Foster, A., & Spink, A. (2002). Information seeking and mediated searching: Part II. Uncertainty and its correlates. *Journal of the American Society for Information Science and Technology, 53*, 2002, 704–715.

22
Everyday Life Information Seeking

Reijo Savolainen
Department of Information Studies
University of Tampere, Finland
Reijo.Savolainen@uta.fi

The model of information seeking in the context of way of life (ELIS model) was developed in the mid-1990s by Reijo Savolainen (see Savolainen, 1995). The development of the model was primarily motivated by the need to elaborate the role of social and cultural factors that affect people's way of preferring and using information sources in everyday settings. It was hypothesised that even though individuals select and use various sources to solve problems or make sense of their everyday world, the source preferences and use patterns are ultimately socially conditioned. Thus, an attempt was made to approach the phenomena of ELIS as a combination of social and psychological factors.

The development of the ELIS model was also motivated by the elaboration of terminological issues of information-seeking studies and the need to specify the nature of ELIS, as compared to job-related information seeking. Although the model emphasizes the legitimate nature of the nonwork contexts, this was not interpreted as an attempt to create a dichotomy between the processes of job-related and "other" information seeking because job-related information seeking and ELIS complement each other.

The central point of departure of the model is *way of life,* which provides a broad context for investigation of individual and social factors affecting ELIS. Way of life is approached by drawing on the idea of *habitus* developed by Bourdieu (1984). Habitus can be defined as a socially and culturally determined system of thinking, perception, and evaluation, internalized by the individual. Habitus is a relatively stable system of dispositions by which individuals integrate their experiences and evaluate the importance of different choices, for example, the preference of information sources and channels. Savolainen (1995) defined the concept of way of life as "order of things," which is based on the choices that

143

individuals make, ultimately oriented by the factors constituting habi- tus. "Things" stand for various activities taking place in the daily life world, including not only job but also necessary reproductive tasks such as household care and voluntary activities (hobbies); "order" refers to preferences given to these activities. Correspondingly, people have a "cognitive order" indicating their perceptions of how things are when they are "normal." Through their choices individuals have practically engaged in a certain order of things, and it is in their interest to keep that order as long as they find it meaningful.

The major factors that may be used to operationalize the concept of way of life include the *structure of time budget*, described as a relation between working and leisure time; *models of consumption of goods and services*; and the *nature of hobbies*. Because the meaningful order of things might not reproduce itself automatically, individuals are required to take active care of it. This care may be called *mastery of life*; it is asso- ciated with pragmatic problem solving, especially in cases where the order of things has been shaken or threatened. Mastery of life is a gen- eral preparedness to approach everyday problems in certain ways in accordance with one's values. Information seeking is an integral compo- nent of mastery of life, which aim is to eliminate a continual dissonance between perceptions of "how things are at this moment" and "how they should be." Savolainen (1995) defined four major types of mastery of life (see Figure 22.1):

1) *Optimistic-cognitive mastery of life* is characterized by a strong reliance on positive outcomes for problem solving. Because problems are primarily conceived as cognitive, systematic information seeking from different sources and channels is indispensable.

2) *Pessimistic-cognitive mastery of life* approaches problem solving in a less ambitious way: There are problems that might not be solved optimally. Despite this the individual may be equally systematic in problem solving and in the information seeking which serves it.

3) *Defensive-affective mastery of life* is grounded on optimistic views concerning the solvability of the problem; however, in problem solving and information seeking affective factors

dominate. This means that the individual may avoid situations implying a risk of failure and requirements to actively seek information.

4) *Pessimistic-affective mastery of life* can be crystallized in the expression of "learned helplessness." The individual does not rely on his or her abilities to solve every day life problems. Systematic information seeking plays no vital role because emotional reactions and short-sightedness dominate problem-solving behavior.

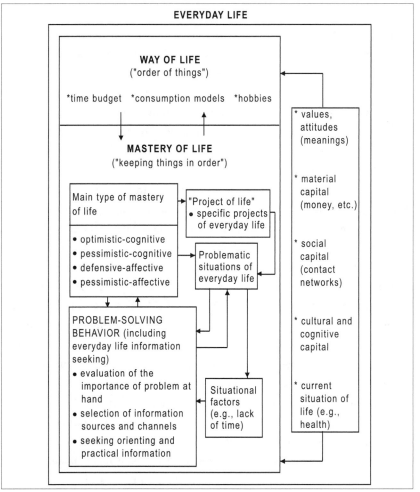

Figure 22.1   The ELIS model.

The model suggests that way of life ("order of things") and mastery of life ("keeping things in order") determine each other. Values, conceptions, and the current phase of life affect way of life and mastery of life. Equally important is the material, social, and cultural (cognitive) capital owned by the individual, providing "basic equipment" to seek and use information. The distribution of the different kinds of capital in relation to capital owned by others determines the total value of the material, social, and cultural capital, thus determining the basic conditions of way of life and mastery of life. However, way of life or mastery of life does not determine how a person seeks information in individual situations. As a constellation of everyday activities and their mutual valuation, way of life provides only general criteria for preferring and using various sources and channels so that the preferences are natural or even self-evident in the light of earlier choices. Similarly, mastery of life describes the tendency to adopt a certain information-seeking strategy in problem-solving situations. Hence, it is necessary also to devote attention to the specific features of the problem situation, for example, the repertoire of information sources available and the acuteness of the problem.

Savolainen (1995) utilized the above model in an empirical study conducted in Finland. The study focused on two groups, representing middle and working class. The study revealed that the habitus-related differences between social classes proved to be quite as expected regarding the nature of work, relationships between work and leisure, and nature of hobbies. The most distinctive differences were found in the nature of hobbies. The consumption models were more distinctive in the purchase of books, magazines, and newspapers. The empirical study strengthened the assumption that way of life directs information seeking in a significant way. Teachers were more eager to seek factual information from various media, and they took a more critical stand toward the supply of light entertainment from radio, television, newspapers, and magazines. However, the study also revealed that personal interest and current life situation affect media use. There appeared to be teachers not particularly interested in the culture or politics sections of newspapers; similarly, some workers preferred documentaries and other serious programs and took a critical view of entertainment.

In the case of seeking practical information the link to way of life appeared to be less evident, because this kind of ELIS is contextualized in specific problem-solving situations. Both workers and teachers preferred informal sources, primarily personal communication, whereas the utilization of formal channels remained surprisingly low. The teachers differed from workers most markedly regarding the utilization of contact networks. The concept of way of life was also used in Savolainen (1999), a study on the ways in which people prefer the Internet in ELIS. These studies indicated that qualitative methods (semistructured theme interviews and narratives of critical incidents) are most preferable since the analysis of the complex relationships between way of life, mastery of life, and information seeking requires nuanced and context-sensitive empirical data.

The ideas behind the ELIS model are related to a number of other models and theories. For example, Chatman's (2000) theory of normative behavior crystallizing the findings of her long research project and Williamson's (1998) ecological model of everyday life information seeking are relevant in this sense. The ELIS model has been cited widely as one of the approaches focusing on the specific issues of everyday life information seeking (e.g., Given, 2002; McKenzie, 2003; Pettigrew, Fidel & Bruce, 2001).

In summary, the ELIS model provides a holistic framework for social and psychological factors affecting people's source preferences in everyday contexts. The model could be developed by elaborating the concept of mastery of life and validating the types of mastery of life. For example, the types of mastery of life could be investigated empirically in relation to people's context-sensitive perceptions of their information-related competencies (Savolainen, 2002). In addition, the relationships between way of life, mastery of life, and ELIS could be thematized more clearly from the social constructionist viewpoint: how do people position themselves as information seekers and users in discourse and how do they construct the issues of way of life and mastery of life as contextual factors affecting ELIS?

Bourdieu, P. (1984). *Distinction. A social critique of the judgement of taste*. London: Routledge.

Chatman, E. A. (2000). Framing social life in theory and research. *The New Review of Information Behaviour Research, 1*, 3–17.

Given, L. M. (2002). The academic and the everyday: investigating the overlap in mature undergraduates' information-seeking behavior. *Library and Information Science Research, 24*, 17–29.

McKenzie, P. J. (2003). A model of information practices in accounts of everyday life information seeking. *Journal of Documentation, 59*, 19–40.

Pettigrew, K., Fidel, R., & Bruce, H. (2001). Conceptual frameworks in information behavior. In M.E. Williams (Ed.), *Annual review of information science and technology, 35* (pp. 43–78). Medford, NJ: Information Today.

Savolainen, R. (1995). Everyday life information seeking: Approaching information seeking in the context of "way of life." *Library and Information Science Research, 17*, 259–294.

Savolainen, R. (1999). Seeking and using information from the Internet: The context of non-work use. In T. D. Wilson & K. Allen (Eds.), *Exploring the contexts of information behaviour* (pp. 356–370). London: Taylor Graham.

Savolainen, R. (2002). Network competence and information seeking on the Internet: From definitions towards a social cognitive model. *Journal of Documentation, 58*, 211–226.

Williamson, K. (1998). Discovered by chance. The role of incidental information acquisition in an ecological model of information use. *Library & Information Science Research, 20*, 23–40.

23
Face Threat

Lorri Mon
The Information School
University of Washington, USA
lmon@u.washington.edu

Erving Goffman, an influential sociologist, explored the presentation of the self in social interactions, which has implications for the study of human behavior in intermediated information-seeking contexts. His work on *face threat* is encompassed within the larger body of his life's work in investigating the micro-sociology of face-to-face interactions to make visible the *interaction order* of interpersonal behavior in public and "behind the scenes." The performative aspects of self-presentation in Goffman's work have been described as *dramaturgy*, while the cognitive aspects of how individuals understand their expected roles within a situation and activity are discussed as *frame analysis*.

Goffman theorized that during all interpersonal interactions, individuals are engaged in a process of "impression management"—strategic maneuvers to obtain, share, or hide information that is either supportive to or destructive of a desired public self-image or "face." Goffman (1971) described the personal information that individuals control about themselves while in interaction with others as the "information preserve."

Goffman (1955) defined "face" as the public image of the self as indicated through socially approved attributes in accordance with expected social roles and behaviors. An individual's "face" is socially constructed through perceptions of both the individual and others. It is created from observations of behavior and other available evidence, and can be damaged by "face threatening acts," which attack or undermine the individual's positive public self-image. Threats to "face" include perceptions of loss of autonomy (being perceived by the self or others as unable or incapable) and perceptions of failure to maintain one's expected social role (and thus being perceived as having misrepresented the self). Threats range from direct and intentional attacks to unintended and subtle implications through

149

words or actions that challenge an individual's preferred role or publicly presented "face."

Threats or attacks on "face" must be countered through "face work." Goffman (1955) described "face work" as encompassing both the strategic ritual work in interpersonal interactions, which is designed to avoid damage to the "public face" of self and others, and also the remedial ritual work designed to repair damage to the projected self-image once a "loss of face" has occurred. Explanations and apologies are part of the ritual work of repairing "face threatening acts" in interpersonal interactions. Thus, the appearance of apologies or defensive explanations from users during feedback on information systems or interactions with information intermediaries can be seen as indicators signaling potential problems of "face threat" occurring in systems or services.

Tracy and Tracy (1998, 2002) used Goffman's concepts of "frame" and "face threat" in communications research as a framing theory for exploring information-gathering interactions between callers and 911 emergency calltakers. Questioning in the informational interview process was observed to present problems of face threat. Mokros, Mullins, and Saracevic (1995) utilized Goffman's work in information science as an influence in building a microanalytic approach for studying videotaped interactions between users and search intermediaries. Chatman (1999) referred to Goffman's work on the presentation of the self in interpreting the information behavior of women in a maximum-security prison. The theory was particularly useful for examining information behavior in discursive interactions.

Interactions are understood within contextual and socially determined frames of reference, within which some information is "framed in" while other information is "framed out." Mismatches between frames may cause interactional problems and misunderstandings between participants. Frames, roles, and shared societal understandings determine expectations and definitions of the activity and the situation, the etiquette of attention and inattention to actions and information, the keeping of strategic secrets in terms of information considered public or private, and how self-presentations are adapted to the existing information conditions in which they are performed.

Individuals engage in activities in situational contexts framed by expectations and social roles. Information seeking often occurs as a social activity within which the participants interact in defined roles such as information seeker ("patron," "user") and intermediary ("librarian," "expert"). The interaction is "framed" within each participant's expectations about the setting ("library"), participants' socially defined roles, and the appropriate actions for the encounter. Individuals may maintain multiple different public roles or "selves" at any one time, selectively presenting the "self" or performing the role appropriate for each particular audience. Individuals also may experience role conflict when audiences converge, and may chafe at or avoid information-seeking activities that require enacting face-threatening roles considered "beneath" them (such as "library patron" rather than "professor").

The face threat theory also offers strong potential for use in the study of online information behavior. Goffman (1961) described the "virtual" nature of the self and of the presentation of multiple different "selves" in differing contexts. Online information systems and services offer possibilities of designing self-presentation methods to better meet users' needs for controling public access to personal information. Designs that incorporate anonymity for users may offer new opportunities for reducing "face threat" in online interpersonal information-seeking interactions.

Goffman's face threat theory is compatible with discourse analysis and a micro-analytic approach that focuses on roles within the information-seeking interaction, situated activities, and overlapping or mismatched frames of reference. Grounded theory may be used in developing a contextually appropriate analysis of emergent factors and themes within the information-seeking interaction. While the theory has been applied in other fields, such as communications research, psychology, and sociology, despite the acknowledged influence of Goffman's works on various information science researchers (Chatman, 1999; Tuominen & Savolainen, 1997; Solomon, 1997; Mokros, Mullins & Saracevic, 1995), it has not yet been extensively utilized or tested within the information science field.

The Goffman face threat theory is most promising to research involving interpersonal interactions within information-seeking contexts which involve discourse. Information-seeking behaviors in intermediation have long been an area of interest to information science. Research has explored user behavior and intermediation interactions in libraries and other information-seeking contexts with a focus on understanding issues such as dissatisfaction, nonuse, and nonusers. Incorporating the "face threat" theoretical framework for examining information-seeking interactions would allow researchers to explore elements of information systems and services that may have unintended consequences in reducing demand and alienating users.

Brown, P., & Levinson, S. C. (1987). *Politeness: Some universals in language usage.* New York: Cambridge University Press.

Chatman, E. A. (1999). A theory of life in the round. *Journal for the American Society for Information Science, 50,* 207–217.

Goffman, E. (1955). On face-work: An analysis of ritual elements in social interaction. *Psychiatry: Journal for the Study of Interpersonal Processes, 18*(3), 213–231.

Goffman, E. (1961). *Encounters: Two studies in the sociology of interaction.* New York: Macmillan.

Goffman, E. (1974). *Frame analysis: An essay on the organization of experience.* Cambridge, MA: Harvard University Press.

Goffman, E. (1967). *Interaction ritual: Essays on face-to-face behavior.* New York: Anchor Books.

Goffman, E. (1971). *Relations in public: Microstudies of the public order.* New York: Basic Books.

Goffman, E. (1959). *The presentation of self in everyday life.* New York: Anchor Books.

Mokros, H., Mullins, L. S., & Saracevic, T. (1995). Practice and personhood in professional interaction: Social identities and information needs. *Library & Information Science Research, 17,* 237–257.

Solomon, P. (1997). Conversation in information-seeking contexts: A test of an analytical framework. *Library & Information Science Research, 19,* 217–248.

Tracy, K., & Tracy, S. J. (1998). Rudeness at 911. *Human Communication Research, 25,* 225–251.

Tracy, S. J. (2002). When questioning turns to face threat: An interactional sensitivity in 911 call-taking. *Western Journal of Communication, 66*(2), 129–157.

Tuominen, K., & Savolainen, R. (1997). A social constructionist approach to the study of information use as discursive action. In P. Vakkari, R. Savolainen, & B. Dervin (Eds.), *Information seeking in context: Proceedings of an international conference on research in information needs, seeking and use in different contexts* (pp. 81–96). London: Taylor Graham.

24
Flow Theory

Charles Naumer
The Information School
University of Washington, USA
Naumer@u.washington.edu

Flow Theory, developed by Mihaly Csikszentmihalyi, seeks to explain a mental state that occurs when a person becomes intensely engaged and absorbed in an activity. People in this mental state report experiencing feelings of great enjoyment and fulfillment. This theory has been applied in a number of fields as a way of improving human experience and increasing engagement in activities.

Csikszentmihalyi's research has focused on the study of what makes people happy, satisfied, and fulfilled, as well as the study of creativity and the qualities of experience associated with creativity. His work has focused on better understanding the nature of human experience as it relates to positive aspects of human behavior. Csikszentmihalyi is one of the pioneers in the field of positive psychology and the study of optimal human functioning. Positive psychology deviates from the prevailing model of categorization and treatment of human pathology by focusing inquiry on describing positive human experiences, such as optimism, well-being, hope, happiness, passion, and creativity. By understanding these aspects of human experience, positive psychology aims to inform the advancement and development of healthy individuals, families, and communities (Snyder, 2002).

Csikszentmihalyi created the theory of flow in the 1970s while attempting to develop a better understanding of the age-old question of when people feel the happiest (Csikszentmihalyi, 1975). His research on this topic led him to conclude that happiness is largely dependent on how people interpret the events of their lives. Happiness is not the result of external forces but of internal forces. Therefore, he contends that happiness can be cultivated and developed by learning to control inner experience. His research findings indicate that people who are able to control their inner experience are best able to determine the quality of their lives (Csikszentmihalyi, 1990).

Csikszentmihalyi's research examines the qualities of experience that lead to happiness and identifies conditions of optimal experience, which he defines as "flow." The mental state of flow is defined as a state in which people are so involved in an activity that nothing else seems to matter. In this mental state, the experience itself is so enjoyable that people will do it even at great cost, for the sheer sake of doing it (Csikszentmihalyi, 1990). The qualities of optimal experience are described as "a sense of exhilaration, a deep sense of enjoyment that is long cherished and that becomes a landmark in memory for what life should be like" (Csikszentmihalyi, 1990, p. 3). These moments occur when "a person's body or mind is stretched to its limits in a voluntary effort to accomplish something difficult and worthwhile" (Csikszentmihalyi, 1990, p. 3). Thus, optimal experience is something that is created or made to happen by an individual. Examples of people being in a state of flow include surgeons performing surgery, rock climbers scaling a mountain, or musicians performing a difficult piece of music.

To study flow, a new method was developed to measure the quality of subjective experience called the Experience Sampling Method (ESM). This technique involves asking people to wear an electronic paging device for a week and to write down how they feel and what they are thinking about whenever the pager signals (Csikszentmihalyi, 1990). The pager is activated about eight times each day at random intervals. Flow theory was based on studying over a hundred thousand such core sections of experience from different parts of the world.

Csikszentmihalyi's studies found that every flow activity provided a sense of discovery engendering a creative feeling of transporting the person into a new reality. In this mental state, the person was pushed to higher levels of performance leading to previously undreamed-of states of consciousness. The result of this experience meant that the self was transformed into a more complex entity.

Two of the most theoretically important dimensions of the experience are challenges and skills as represented on the two axes of Figure 24.1. The diagram demonstrates that when a person is engaging in a new task his or her skill level will be low and the challenge needed to engage the person will also be low for flow to occur. However, as the person's skill level increases the level of challenge will need to increase in order for the person to maintain a sense of flow. Conditions of flow will occur when there is a balance between the level of challenge and the required skill. Otherwise, when the level of challenge exceeds a person's skill level then anxiety may occur. Conversely, when the skill level exceeds the level of challenge then boredom may occur.

The relationship between challenge level and skill level is the second of eight conditions that Csikszentmihalyi identifies as making up the flow experience. These conditions are: 1) clear goals and immediate feedback; 2) equilibrium between the level of challenge and personal skill; 3) merging of action and awareness; 4) focused concentration; 5) sense of potential control; 6) loss of self-consciousness; 7) altered sense

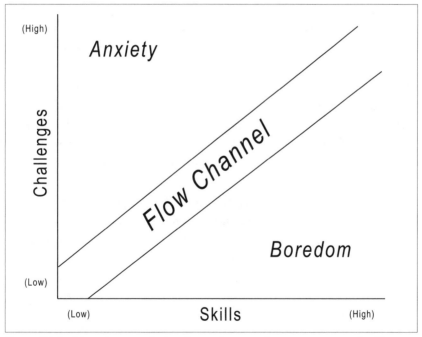

Figure 24.1   How the complexity of consciousness increases as a result of flow experiences.

Note: From **Flow: The psychology of optimal experience** (p. 74), by M. Csikszentmihalyi, 1990, New York: Harper & Row. Copyright 1990 by Harper & Row. Adapted with permission.

of time; and 8) experience becoming autotelic or self-rewarding (Csikszentmihalyi, 1993).

In addition to informing academic research, flow theory has been widely applied in a number of different fields. Educators have adopted Flow Theory as a means of informing teaching practices and developing effective learning environments that encourage learners to become highly engaged. Business leaders have used flow to develop management practices and business processes that facilitate high level engagement, as well as to develop products and services that are appealing to customers. The concept of flow has also been used as a way of rehabilitating juvenile delinquents, designing museum exhibits, and organizing activities in old people's homes (Csikszentmihalyi, 1990).

In the field of information science, the theory of flow has been mostly applied to system use and design. Several studies in the field of human computer interaction address issues regarding flow and user's interaction with computers. One such study examines users' flow experiences while surfing the Web (Chen, 1999). Another study examines information systems and their affect on quality of life (Artz, 1996). Of particular interest to information behavior may be Csikszentmihalyi's discussion of information theory and how new information that is processed by individuals creates either order or disorder in consciousness. He contends that if a piece of information creates order in consciousness, it supports conditions of flow and if it creates disorder in consciousness it inhibits flow from occurring (Csikszentmihalyi, 1990).

Flow theory's approach to the qualitative aspects of information behavior may be very useful in understanding human-information interaction. In addition to its application for system design it may also be useful in understanding information behavior in everyday contexts. The flow model and ESM methodology for studying human experience may facilitate further exploration into the aspects of experience that impact information behavior.

Artz, J. M. (1996). Computers and the quality of life: Assessing flow in information systems. *SIGCAS Computing Society, 26*, 7–12.

Chen, H., Wigand, R. T., & Nilan, M. (1999). Flow experiences on the Web. *Computers in Human Behavior, 15*, 454–608.

Csikszentmihalyi, M. (1975). *Beyond boredom and anxiety*. San Francisco: Jossey-Bass.

Csikszentmihalyi, M. (1982). Towards a psychology of optimal experience. In L. Wheeler (Ed.), *Annual Review of Psychology and Social Psychology, 3*, (pp. 13–36). Beverly Hills, CA: Sage.

Csikszentmihalyi, M. (1990). *Flow: The psychology of optimal experience*. New York: Harper & Row.

Csikszentmihalyi, M. (1993). *The evolving self: A psychology for the third millennium*. New York: HarperCollins.

Csikszentmihalyi, M., & Csikszentmihalyi, I., Eds. (1988). *Optimal experience: Psychological studies of flow in consciousness*. Cambridge, UK: Cambridge University Press.

Csikszentmihalyi, M., & LeFevre, J. (1989). Optimal experience in work and leisure. *Journal of Personality and Social Psychology, 56*, 815–822.

Larson, R., & Csikszentmihalyi, M. (1983). The experience sampling method. In H. T. Reis (Ed.), *Naturalistic approaches to studying social interaction: New directions of methodology in social and behavioral science, 15* (pp. 41–56). San Francisco: Jossey-Bass.

Snyder, C.R., & Lopez, S. J., Eds. (2002). *Handbook of positive psychology*. New York: Oxford University Press.

Trevino, L. K., & Webster, J. (1992). Flow in computer mediated communication. *Communication Research, 19*, 539–573.

Webster, J., Trevino, L. K., & Ryan, L. (1993). The dimensionality and correlates of flow in human computer interactions. *Computers in Human Behavior, 9*, 411–426.

25
General Model of the Information Seeking of Professionals

Gloria J. Leckie
Faculty of Information and Media Studies
The University of Western Ontario, Canada
leckie@uwo.ca

One of the central questions in research related to human societies revolves around why and how people do what they do, either individually or collectively. To answer these questions, one end of the theoretical spectrum includes what could be termed the metatheorists, such as Michel Foucault (1980), Pierre Bourdieu (1990), and Anthony Giddens (1984), whose work attempts to unravel largescale societal processes within which individuals are situated but not necessarily very visible. Toward the other end of the spectrum are theorists with a more finely grained and specialized theoretical perspective, such as Carol Kuhlthau (2004) and Elfreda Chatman (1999), who focus upon the microprocesses of daily life in particular cultural contexts and social settings. For these scholars, what happens to individuals as they construct their realities within the larger societal framework is of prime concern.

One of the areas of daily life that is of interest to this latter group of theorists is the specific processes that take place within the world of work. This is entirely understandable since human beings spend so much of their time in either paid or unpaid work, and so work is an area of life that is definitely worthy of indepth consideration. But what, exactly, is worth investigating about the work that people do? For one thing, quite a bit of effort has been invested in trying to understand what "work" is, what distinguishes one kind of work from another, who is likely to engage in that work and why, and what the doing of that work actually means. Abbott's treatise (1988) on what constitutes professionalism is one example, as is work done by Harris (1992) on the gendering of practice in library and information science (LIS) and by Latour and Woolgar (1986) on the documentary work of the laboratory.

158

A second area of investigation related to work has to do with the specifics of what people actually do in their jobs and how they do it. In the literature of LIS and other professionally oriented disciplines, there has been a strong interest in examining the information-seeking practices of practitioners within various fields of professional work. Studies have examined the information-seeking behaviors and information uses of librarians, academics, researchers, doctors, nurses, dentists, engineers, lawyers, and many others. These studies examine what information practices are embedded within professional work, how those information-related practices function to contribute to the work, and whether or not those practices can be improved or changed for the better.

Within LIS, early studies of information practices concentrated on scientists and other scholarly researchers, but with the early studies done by Wilson and Streatfield (1977) on the information-related practices of social workers in a government agency, the door was opened for studies of other, nonacademic professionals. The following three decades resulted in a plethora of studies about how different professional groups searched for, used, and integrated information sources into their work processes. At the same time, scholars from other professional groups were also doing studies about this same concern, but the literature was very scattered and lacked cohesion. Accordingly, Leckie, Pettigrew (now Fisher), and Sylvain (1996) conducted an extensive meta-review of the LIS literature and the literatures of a number of other professional fields with the aim of looking for patterns or trends in common across all of these studies. Five key findings emerged from the literature review:

1) Despite their training in a particular area of expertise, a professional often assumes a number of complex and different work roles (such as service provider, administrator, researcher, counselor etc.) as part of her/his work position.

2) These roles have a constellation of tasks associated with them.

3) The tasks required in each role are likely to prompt information needs and/or seeking.

4) There are intervening factors that may either facilitate or inhibit the finding and use of information for specific tasks.

5) It often takes more than one attempt to find the appropriate information (thus suggesting a feedback mechanism is at work).

What resulted from consideration of these common threads in the literature was a general model (see Figure 25.1) of how individuals from diverse professions search for and use information on the job.

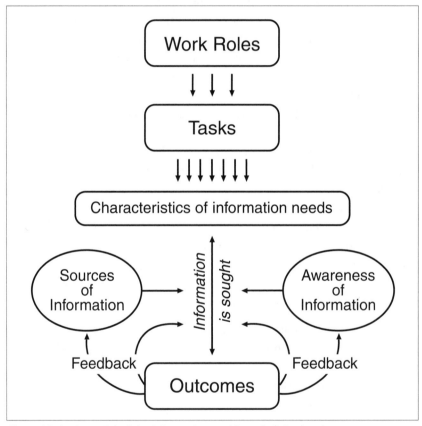

Figure 25.1   A model of the information seeking of professionals.

> **Note:** From "Modelling the information seeking of professionals: A general model derived from research on engineers, health care professionals, and lawyers," by G. J. Leckie, K. E. Pettigrew and C. Sylvan, 1996, *Library Quarterly*, 66, 161-193. Copyright 1996 by the University of Chicago Press. Adapted with permission.

The model suggests that only through a thorough understanding of complex work roles and their associated tasks will we be able to truly understand why, how, and when information seeking may occur. Leckie, Pettigrew, and Sylvain (1996) also concluded that information-seeking and information-related practices were more similar across diverse professions than previously had been thought.

The model assumes that the work prompting the roles and tasks takes place within some context which is specific to a particular work position. The larger context was deliberately left unidentified, and it was anticipated that contextual factors (such as the ideology and power relations of the organization), which might have an impact upon the work would be sketched in for the particular sites and workplaces being studied. So, for instance, in an engineering firm that is highly environmentally conscious, the social norms guiding the work of the firm would likely have an impact on the roles undertaken by particular engineers working within the firm, and this in turn could have a bearing on the types of information required and the ways in which such information was sought and used. To keep the model general enough to cover a variety of different professions and different types of work, the components of the model also were kept slightly vague.

Leckie, Pettigrew, and Sylvain (1996) determined that there were certain factors shaping the individual's information need (such as his/her status in the organization, years of experience, area of specialization etc.) and that these characteristics acted as a filter in the information-seeking process (i.e., characteristics of information needs). Once the information-seeking process had begun, other factors became important in the eventual success or failure of the seeking event, including all potential sources of information available (i.e., sources of information) and whether the individual had some knowledge of those sources and their likely usefulness (i.e., awareness of information). It was intended that these three components should be rather open-ended so that future researchers could fit a variety of factors into them. The end result of the seeking event was some sort of outcome, either moving the work forward (such as in the production of a report or provision of service) or requiring further information seeking for greater clarification (via the feedback loop).

Since the model was first published, it has been both praised and crit-icized, but nonetheless cited quite widely. In particular, two studies that have attempted to test and refine the model are noted here. Kwasitsu (2003) examined the information seeking of design and process engi-neers, and concluded that there was ample evidence that work tasks were the primary triggers of information seeking for engineers engaged in microchip design and manufacturing. The most comprehensive use of the model to date is by Wilkinson (2001) who tested it in her study of the information seeking of lawyers. In that study, Wilkinson proposed an extensive and important enhancement of the model to accommodate the particular ways in which her participants conducted their work. Her main refinements to the model were to make the organizational context and the demographic characteristics of the user more explicit and more directly linked to awareness of information and selection of sources.

Finally, the basic assumption (an understanding of roles and tasks is important because they are the primary impetus for work-related infor-mation practices) of the model seems to be supported by Vakkari (2003) in his review of task-based information seeking. He states that "studies have concentrated on search tasks rather than on the activities that trig-ger them... Taking the task into account seems to be a necessary condi-tion for understanding and explaining information searching..."

Abbott, A. (1988). *The system of professions: An essay on the division of expert labor*. Chicago: University of Chicago Press.

Bourdieu, P. (1990). *The logic of practice* (Richard Nice, Trans.). Cambridge, UK: Polity Press.

Certeau. M. de. (1984). *The practice of everyday life* (Steven Rendall, Trans.). Berkeley, CA: University of California Press.

Chatman, E. A. (1999). A theory of life in the round. *Journal of the American Society for Information Science, 50*, 207–217.

Foucault, M. (1980). *Power/knowledge: Selected interviews & other writing 1972–1977* (Colin Gordon, Ed., Colin Gordon, et al, Trans.). New York: Pantheon Books.

Giddens, A. (1984). *The constitution of society: Outline of the theory of structuration*. Berkeley, CA: University of California Press.

Harre, R., & Langenhove, L. van, Eds. (1999). *Positioning theory: Moral context of intentional action*. Oxford: Blackwell Publishers.

Harris, R. M. (1992). *Librarianship: The erosion of a woman's profession*. Norwood, NJ: Ablex.

Kuhlthau, C. (2004). *Seeking meaning: A process approach to library and information services* (2nd ed.). Westport, CT: Libraries Unlimited.

Kwasitsu, L. (2003). Information-seeking behavior of design, process and manufacturing engineers. *Library & Information Science Research, 25(4)*, 459–476.

Latour, B., & Woolgar, S. (1986). *Laboratory life: The construction of scientific facts*. Princeton, NJ: Princeton University Press.

Leckie, G., Pettigrew, K., & Sylvain, C. (1996). Modeling the information seeking of professionals: A general model derived from research on engineers, health care professionals and lawyers. *Library Quarterly, 66(2)*, 161–193.

Smith, D. (1999). *Writing the social: Critique, theory, and investigations*. Toronto: University of Toronto Press.

Vakkari, P. (2003). Task-based information searching. *Annual Review of Information Science and Technology, 37*, 413–464.

Wilkinson, M. A. (2001). Information sources used by lawyers in problem solving: An empirical exploration. *Library & Information Science Research, 23(3)*, 257–276.

Wilson, T. D., & Streatfield, D. R. (1977). Information needs in local authority social services departments: An interim report on project INISS. *Journal of Documentation, 33*, 277–293.

26
The Imposed Query

Melissa Gross
School of Information Studies
Florida State University, USA
mgross@lis.fsu.edu

Melissa Gross developed the *imposed query model* in the field of information science. The model is pragmatic in that it is based on observation of actual user behavior in public and school library settings. It describes and explains the imposed information-seeking process as comprised of six stages that follow the query from its initiation, transfer to, and transaction by the imposer's agent and ends with the imposer's evaluation of the agent's response to the query (Gross, 1995).

The basic premise of this model is that questions are of two types: self-generated and imposed. Self-generated questions arise from the context of a person's life and are pursued by the person who is asking the questions. Imposed questions occur when the person who constructs the question asks someone else to transact it.

Questions that are imposed upon and transacted by an agent have many opportunities for mutating away from their original intent over the course of their life cycle. The successful resolution of imposed queries depends on many variables. These include:

- Quality of question transfer from imposer to agent
- Characteristics of the agent, such as level of attained literacies (reading level, information-seeking skills, computer skills, communication skills, etc.), physical wellness, language, ability to empathize, and sense of ownership of the question
- Characteristics of the relationship between the imposer and the agent such as stereotypes and beliefs they have about each other as well as the cultural, psychological, and affective dimensions of the relationship including power dynamics between them

164

- Characteristics of the imposer, for instance, ability to communicate, cognitive skills, ability to elicit cooperation from the agent(s)

- Characteristics of the information intermediary (who may be a person, system, or resource) including professional competency, ability to recognize question type, stance of professional empathy, familiarity with the imposed query and the context that produced it, stereotypes and beliefs held about the imposer in a generic sense (for example, teachers) or in terms of a specific person (the fifth grade teacher, Mrs. Thomas), etc.

- Availability of resources, quality of available resources, appropriateness of resources to question, etc.

Several models and theories are central to the imposed query. Taylor's process of question formulation (1962), Belkin's anomalous state of knowledge (1980), and Dervin's Sense-Making theory (Dervin & Dewdney, 1986) are used to describe the origins of queries developed by the imposer and Shannon and Weaver's theory of communication (1975) provides a basis for discussing potential mutations in the imposed query that may occur as it is transferred from person to person and transacted over its life cycle.

The graphical model depicting the imposed query and describing this information-seeking behavior was first published in 1995. Research that tests and further explores the model began with a pilot study performed in a school library media center and focused on circulation transactions (Gross, 1997). The pilot was followed by a dissertation project that replicated the original study in three school library media centers and supplemented its quantitative approach with in-depth interviews with teachers, students, and the school library media specialist at the original pilot school. The results of this study support the finding that imposition is a verifiable information-seeking behavior and provide insights into the lifecycle of imposition in the elementary school context, including the origin and adoption of the roles of imposer and agent, and describes how elementary age children go about seeking information for imposed as well as self-generated information needs (Gross, 1999a, 2000a, 2004).

This work was followed by a series of papers that explore the implica-tions of the imposed query for the evaluation of library services (Gross, 1998), the performance of reference services with adults (Gross, 1999b), and the provision of information services for children (Gross, 2000b). In 2000, a secondary analysis of survey data collected in 13 pub-lic libraries in Southern California to assess user satisfaction with the public library and reference service was performed. User queries were categorized as self-generated or imposed based on the subject's view of whom he or she was seeking information for and analyzed to determine the prevalence of imposed queries at the adult reference desk in public libraries (Gross, 2001), to determine who the imposers and agents are in this information-providing environment (Gross & Saxton, 2001), and what affect question type might have on user assessments of satisfaction (Gross & Saxton, 2002). Recently, the imposed query model was employed to provide a framework in the investigation of children's com-puter use in an urban public library (Gross, Dresang, & Holt, in press).

In addition to these primary investigations that have sought to describe and explore the imposed query model, the imposed query has been cited extensively in theoretical and empirical work in the area of information behavior and is used to inform practice in the field of library and information science.

The imposed query has implications on other areas of information-seeking behavior that are waiting to be explored in future research. These include the areas of relevance, specifically the ability of people to make relevance judgments for someone else, library anxiety, collabora-tive information seeking, everyday information seeking, and the use of others in information seeking including people as resources as well as people as agents, mediators, and gatekeepers, and the selection and use of peer and other informants in both formal and informal contexts.

It may be that a useful connection can be made between the imposed query and the theory and methodology of Sense-Making as developed by Dervin and others (Dervin & Dewdney, 1986). In particular, there is much to explore in determining how individuals make sense or construct meaning for others and the relationship of this process to determinations of relevance and the identification of "right" answers. There are also connections to be made between the gift query described in imposed query research (1998) and the serendipitous information seeking described by Twidale, Nichols, and Paice (1997) and the information-sharing behavior reported by Erdelez and Rioux (2001). Connections of this type may eventually lead to a more unified view of collaborative information seeking. The idea of question type is also pertinent to studies investigating the grounded theory developed to explain library anxiety. It is not clear to what extent the experience of library anxiety (Mellon, 1986) is related to question type as the majority of studies in this area relate to class assignments, not self-generated information seeking.

Much is still unknown about imposed information seeking. In-depth study of the various relationships and environments that produce and respond to impositions are waiting to be studied as are many dimensions of this behavior such as the cultural, educational, gender, and socio-economic contexts of information seeking in order to fully explicate the role of imposition in information seeking. However, the imposed query has already demonstrated utility for informing practice and professional training in the area of reference services and reference evaluation. To date, research on the imposed query has been descriptive and exploratory in nature. More work is needed in order to discover the explanatory value of this model, which has already provided a new range of research questions for the field.

Belkin, N. J. (1980). Anomalous states of knowledge as a basis for information retrieval. *Canadian Journal of Information Science, 5*, 133–143.

Dervin, B., & Dewdney, P. (1986). Neutral questioning: A new approach to the reference interview. *RQ, 25*, 507–508.

Erdelez, S., & Rioux, K. (2000). Sharing information encountered for others on the Web. *The New Review of Information Behaviour Research 1*, 219–233.

Gross, M. (1995). The imposed query. *RQ, 35*, 236–243.

Gross, M. (1997). Pilot study on the prevalence of imposed queries in a school library media center. *School Library Media Quarterly, 25*, 157–166.

Gross, M. (1998). The imposed query: Implications for library service evaluation. *Reference & User Services Quarterly, 37*, 290–299.

Gross, M. (1999). Imposed queries in the school library media center: A descriptive study. *Library & Information Science Research, 21*, 501–521.

Gross, M. (1999b). Imposed versus self-generated questions: Implications for reference practice. *Reference and User Services Quarterly, 39*, 53–61.

Gross, M. (2000). Imposed and self-generated queries in the elementary school environment. In R. M. Branch & M. A. Fitzgerald (Eds.), *Educational media and technology yearbook 2000* (pp. 120–129). Englewood, CO: Libraries Unlimited, Inc.

Gross, M. (2000b). The imposed query and information services for children. *Journal of Youth Services in Libraries, 13*, 10–17.

Gross, M. (2001). Imposed information seeking in school library media centers and public libraries: A common behavior? *Information Research, 6*. Retrieved September 10, 2003, from www.shef.ac.uk/~is/publications/infres/6-2/paper 100.html

Gross, M. (2004). Children's information seeking at school: Findings from a qualitative study. In M. K. Chelton & C. Cool (Eds.), *Youth information seeking: Theories, models, and approaches*. Lanham, MD: Scarecrow Press.

Gross, M., Dresang, E. T., & Holt, L. E. (in press). Children's in-library use of computers in an urban public library. *Library & Information Science Research*.

Gross, M., & Saxton, M. L. (2002). Integrating the imposed query into the evaluation of reference: A dichotomous analysis of user ratings. *Library & Information Science Research, 24*, 251–263.

Gross, M., & Saxton, M. L. (2001). Who wants to know? Imposed queries in the public library. *Public Libraries, 40*, 170–176.

Mellon, C. A. (1986). Library anxiety: A grounded theory and its development. *College & Research Libraries, 47*, 160–165.

Shannon, C. E., & Weaver, W. (1975). *The mathematical theory of communication*. Urbana, IL: University of Illinois Press.

Taylor, R. S. (1962). The process of asking questions. *American Documentation, 13*, 392.

Twidale, M. B., Nichols, D. M., & Paice, C. D. (1997). Browsing is a collaborative process. *Information Processing & Management, 33*, 761–783.

27
Information Acquiring-and-Sharing

Kevin Rioux
Department of Library and Information Studies
University of North Carolina at Greensboro, USA
ksrioux@uncg.edu

Information acquiring-and-sharing (IA&S) refers to a set of com-bined behaviors and processes in which an individual:

- Cognitively stores representations of other people's information needs

- Recalls those needs when acquiring (in various contexts) information of a particular type or quality

- Makes associations between the information that s/he has acquired and someone s/he knows who s/he perceives to need or want this information

- Shares this information in some way

This emerging conceptual framework is based on Rioux's (2004) exploratory study of the general characteristics of IA&S in Internet-based environments. It is also informed by Rioux's (2000) work on SIF-FOW (*S*haring *I*nformation *F*ound *F*or *O*thers on the Web), which indicates that this process is an identifiable, natural, highly social, and pleasant information behavior that is supported by habituated e-mail based sharing strategies.

Rioux's close consideration of Erdelez's (1997) notion of information encountering provided one of the initial incentives for exploring IA&S behaviors. Rioux hypothesized that when an "information encounterer" unexpectedly "bumped into" what she or he perceived as useful or desir-able information, s/he would often believe that this information would also address the information needs of someone she or he knew. Subsequently the person would share the information.

This hypothesis was confirmed by Erdelez and Rioux (2000a), who provide evidence that some individuals do in fact frequently encounter information in Internet contexts that addresses their own information needs as well as those of others, and that this information is frequently shared in some way (typically via e-mail). The study furthermore indicates that Internet environments actually facilitate both information encountering and information acquiring-and-sharing.

Elements of IA&S have since been linked to notions of Web-based sharing tools (Erdelez & Rioux, 2000b) information agents (Gross & Saxton, 2001), third-party/proxy searching (Pettigrew et al., 2001), organizational knowledge, communities of practice, and distributed cognition (Davenport & Hall, 2002), social sharing (Talja, 2002), and the demographics of sharers (Case, 2002). Despite the breadth of these works, systematic and specific accounts of individual users' behaviors associated with IA&S are absent in the literature. This overlooked status is problematic because we cannot get a complete picture of individuals' information use behavior if we exclude relatively common IA&S behaviors.

One may assert that acquiring-and-sharing behaviors are fundamentally social behaviors, which may partially account for why information sharing in networked environments has been researched primarily as a *group* phenomenon rather than a specific information behavior enacted by *individuals*. Yet, current computing designs underscore the individualized nature of IA&S in Internet-based environments. Presently, most users access the Internet via a *personal* computer equipped with a *single-user* interface. Although many of these computers are networked in some way, they are designed to support one user at a time. Thus, IA&S behaviors in Internet environments often support group information needs, yet they are not typically enacted with other individuals or practiced as a part of a group.

In response to this area of opportunity for theory expansion, Rioux continues to build this IA&S framework. Perhaps the most developed examination of IA&S to date is Rioux's (Submitted) explanatory scheme that describes the cognitive and affective aspects of how users "store" and recall the information needs of others.

The scheme begins with the various types of communication/social interaction that users have with family, friends, colleagues, and acquaintances in various contexts. With low effort or consciousness on the part of the user, cognitive representations of these communications, the people involved, topics mentioned, needs mentioned or inferred, feelings experienced in these conversations, etc., are placed in *potential memory* during everyday communication events. These representations remain inert until what can be characterized as a *cognitive threshold* is breached. In the context of information acquisition in Internet-based environments, this breach occurs when a user acquires information of a certain quality (e.g., utility, novelty, interest) via the Web, a received e-mail, via an electronic list posting, etc.

Once the cognitive threshold is breached, a *cognitive trigger* is quickly activated. Users experience a variety of mental states that mimic sensory states as they recall cognitive representations stored in the potential memory space, and make associations between the information they have acquired and possible recipients of this information. These include mental images of recipients' faces and names and acquired/stored topics as well as mental "voices." This recall and association process then prompts information sharing behavior.

Although somewhat complex, this entire process is quite rapid and requires very little effort on the part of the user. In fact, users have very little top-of-mind awareness of these mental events, which suggests that they are in fact subconscious. When Rioux (2004) probed his respondents for comments on their affective states while engaged in this information behavior, they characterized the process as being quite pleasant and natural.

Information acquiring-and-sharing has implications for a number of information behavior topics. Among them:

- The notion that users acquire information in response to both their own needs and motivations as well as the needs and motivations of other people they know sets forth a holistic rather than an atomistic view of human experience.

- The information acquiring-and-sharing framework confirms the notion that information behavior phenomena are part of human communicative and social processes.

- This framework also acknowledges the importance of affect in information behavior, thus buttressing Kuhlthau's (1991) ISP model and other information behavior works that focus on the feelings and emotions experienced by users.

- IA&S also provides additional dimensions to theories and

works that focus on users' mental processes as they engage in information behavior (e.g., Dervin, 1993; Wilson, 1994).

- The framework also affirms an idea from Wilson's (1999) general model of information behavior, which holds that information seeking may involve other people and may involve information exchange.

- As the IA&S framework is developed, it will inform the practice of librarians and other information professionals tasked with developing, maintaining and improving corporate, distance learning, research, and general-use information systems.

- Social marketers and retail marketers may also be particularly interested in learning more about this behavior, which in effect extends and hones advertising, public health, and political campaigns.

Future development of the IA&S concept may include: studying IA&S among specific groups (e.g., teachers, expectant mothers, scientists), exploring "non-sharing" behaviors, and examining this IA&S from the perspective of the receiver. An in-depth study of the relationships and communication channels between information sharers and receivers would also be valuable.

Case, D. (2002). *Looking for information: A survey on research on information seeking, needs and behavior*. New York: Academic Press.

Davenport, E., & Hall, H. (2002). Organizational knowledge and communities of practice. *Annual Review of Information Science and Technology, 36*, 171–227.

Dervin, B. (1992). *An overview of Sense-Making research: Concepts, methods and results to date*. International Communications Association Meeting, Dallas, Texas.

Erdelez, S. (1997). Information encountering: A conceptual framework for accidental information discovery. In P. Vakkari, R. Savolainen, & B. Dervin (Eds.), *Information seeking in context: Proceedings of an international conference on research in information needs, seeking and use in different contexts* (pp. 412–421). London: Taylor-Graham.

Erdelez, S., & Rioux, K. S. (2000a). Sharing information encountered for others on the Web. *New Review of Information Behaviour Research, 1*, 219–233.

Erdelez, S., & Rioux, K. (2000b). Sharing tools on newspaper websites: An exploratory study. *Online Information Review, 24*(3), 218–228.

Gross, M., & Saxton, M. (2001). Who wants to know?: Imposed queries in the public library. *Public Libraries, 40*(3), 170–176.

Kuhlthau, C. C. (1991). Inside the search process: Information-seeking from the user's perspective. *Journal of the American Society for Information Science, 42,* 361–371.

Pettigrew, K., Fidel, R., & Bruce, H. (2001). Conceptual frameworks in information behavior. *Annual Review of Information Science and Technology, 35,* 43–78.

Rioux, K. S. (2000). Sharing information found for others on the World Wide Web: A preliminary examination. *Proceedings of the 63rd Annual Meeting of the American Society for Information Science,* 68–77.

Rioux, K. S. (2004). *Information acquiring-and-sharing in Internet-based environments: An exploratory study of individual user behaviors.* Unpublished doctoral dissertation, The University of Texas at Austin.

Rioux, K. S. (submitted). *"Storing" and recalling the information needs of others: An emerging conceptual framework of Internet users' perceived cognitive and affective states.* Manuscript submitted for publication.

Talja, S. (2002). Information sharing in academic communities: Types and levels of collaboration in information seeking and use. *New Review of Information Behaviour Research, 3,* 143–160.

Wilson, T. D. (1994). Information needs and users: Fifty years of progress? In B. C. Vickery (Ed.), *Fifty years of information progress: A Journal of Documentation review* (pp. 15–51). London: Aslib.

Wilson, T. D. (1999). Models of information behavior research. *Journal of Documentation, 5*(3), 249–270.

28
Information Activities
in Work Tasks

Katriina Byström
The Swedish School of Library and Information Studies
University College of Borås, Sweden
katriina.bystrom@hb.se

The theory of information activities in work tasks of varying complexity was developed by Byström and colleagues (Byström, 1999, 2002; Byström & Järvelin, 1995; Byström & Hansen, 2002) based upon their empirical research as well as on contributions from the fields of library and information science and organizational studies. The theory has been utilized, analyzed, and further developed by others (e.g., Ingwersen, Vakkari, Kuhlthau, Järvelin, and Wilson), and it connects with such frameworks as Ingwersen's Cognitive Information Retrieval Theory, Cognitive Systems/Work Analysis (Pejtersen and Fidel with colleagues), Taylor's Information Use Environments, Allen's Person-in-Situation Approach, Belkin's work on Interactive Information Retrieval, and Wilson's on Information Behavior.

"Information activities in work tasks" was developed to provide research results that readily relate to real-life work contexts where information activities occur. It thus focuses upon work tasks of varying complexity as its starting point to understanding information intensive, real-life contexts. These work tasks are divided into various sub-tasks as associated with naturally occurring, information seeking and information searching/retrieval (where the latter is viewed as a sub-task of the former). The unit of analyses is more specific than that in preceding studies of professionals' information behavior. Moreover, work tasks were traditionally viewed as either external (independent of the actor or user) or as internal (subordinate to the comprehension of the actor). To this and central to the theory, a third perception is added: tasks as social constructions formed in the interaction within their context. In this sense, Byström focuses on perceived tasks that mirror the social constraints in real-life work contexts and are thus a fruitful point of departure for empirical study of information activities. Indeed, studies focusing on perceived work tasks may make the relationship between context and information activities more tangible.

The theory's core builds upon the relationships between the information types sought and the information sources used where information, itself, is considered an abstract tool that enables a task to be completed. Byström chose a relatively simple classification for types of information used in problem solving. The original classes were somewhat modified, mainly by shifting the focus from "problems" to "tasks." In accordance with this shift, task information denotes a specific task at hand, and it is often presented in the form of facts (e.g., names, numbers, statements, and events). Domain information is applicable in several tasks of the same kind, and it comprises more general statements that may be factual (e.g., section of law) or interpretative (e.g., lawyer's opinion). Task-solving information is useful in several tasks of the same kind, and it focuses on how to perform a task. All these types of information are used in all tasks, but this does not mean that a task performer actually needs to acquire all of them. The strength of such a simple classification is that it is suitable for many settings, but simultaneously it obviously provides less detailed results on information types. Thus, a development of subcategories is recommended in future research.

For information channels and sources, the specific classification used was derived from the data; with channels Byström refers to (assumed) function to guide the task performer to sources that (are assumed to) provide the information sought, and that these functions may be present either separately or simultaneously. The main categories for channels and sources are people as information sources and documentary sources that later on have been completed with visits or events as information sources. These are completed with subcategories with respect to the studied context.

Information types sought and information channels/sources are further related to work tasks. Byström focuses on task complexity—in terms of a priori determinability—as a task quality studied, which has been recognized as an important task dimension in organizational studies. Tasks are divided into five categories of complexity depending on the task performer's perceived uncertainty about (information) requirements, process, and result of the task. The relationships between information types and channels/sources are studied on these different levels of task complexity. There is, however, no impediment to change task complexity to another quality and still use the rest of the theory's conceptual framework.

The relationships between information types and sources that the theory proposes—with empirical support—are: 1) in cases where no information is considered as necessary to acquire, it is received passively and mainly from documentary sources (e.g., through mechanisms built into the organizational routines); 2) sources for task information are typically people who are involved in the matter at hand, official documents and registers, although this type of information is occasionally sought even from experts and in meetings; 3) visits/events seem to be sources for task information (here the empirical material is rather limited); 4) domain information is readily available from literature and even from experts and in meetings; and 5) experts and meetings appear to be the most commonly utilized sources for task-solving information. The combination of information types acquired creates other kinds of relationships between information types and sources, such as: when more types of information are acquired; 6) more sources are utilized, but the variety among source types decreases; 7) the use of people inside the organization increases; and 8) the use of external documentary sources increases.

Task complexity frames the relationships between information types and source use. As perceived complexity of the task increases; 9) people tend to acquire more types of information; and 10) they are less certain to predict what types of information are necessary to acquire. The former will lead to the alterations that were described in the above relationships. Thus, the perceived task complexity has an indirect relationship to source use. However, task complexity modifies the source use even directly: 11) people in the role of experts are relied to an increasing extent for acquisition of all types of information as tasks are perceived as more complex.

The theory involves some methodological recommendations. Work task as a unit of analysis implies the process nature of the activities studied. Byström utilized task diaries as the main instrument for data collection. These task diaries focused on the perception of tasks by the task performer and her information activities during task performance process. A subsequent interview shortly after task completion is recommended. Interviews complete the self-recordings by allowing a greater extent of explanations and other supplementary information to surface. The combination of these methods is considered especially suitable for following the whole, often in time discontinuous, task performance processes.

This theory is now in an additional phase of development. To seek possibilities to combine the research fields of information seeking and retrieval has been a natural extension of the original theory (Byström & Hansen, 2002). Through Byström's and Hansen's empirical research the level of information-search tasks is now added to the conceptual framework. Information-search task consists of either information retrieval from electronic source(s) or consultation of any other type of source. Whereas the theory shifted the level of analysis from general to more specific (from jobs to work tasks) in work-related information-seeking studies, the opposite takes place in information retrieval studies. The act of retrieving information from an electronic channel/source is shifting level of analysis from specific to more general. This places IR-activities in relation to work tasks leading to two important consequences: IR-activities are connected to 1) a realistic goal, that is, the satisfactory conclusion of a work task, as well as 2) other IR-activities and/or consultation of other types of channels/sources. Accordingly, the central concept in IR research, relevance, is highlighted from an additional perspective. Since task complexity is related to the information activities on information-seeking level, it is also likely to be related to such activities on information-search level.

To conclude, the theory for Information Activities in Work Tasks has proved to be useful for studying information activities in real-life contexts. It increases our understanding of people's information activities in work situations, and it may be helpful for developing and designing information systems/management in work organizations. Its conceptual framework seems also suitable for bridging two important research areas in information studies, information seeking, and information retrieval, which form an emerging research area within library and information science. Furthermore, there is a potentiality to develop this theory in respect to a broader context (e.g., projects, business processes, and social contexts), where work tasks are seen as sub-tasks or sub-processes.

Byström, K. (1999). *Task complexity, information types and information sources: examination of relationships*. Unpublished doctoral dissertation, University of Tampere, Finland. Retrieved March 17, 2004, from www.hb.se/bhs/personal/katriina/kby-diss.pdf

Byström, K. (2002). Information and information sources in tasks of varying complexity. *Journal of the American Society for Information Science and Technology, 53,* 581–591.

Byström, K., & Hansen, P. (2002). Work tasks as units for analysis in information seeking and retrieval studies. In H. Bruce, R. Fidel, P. Ingwersen, & P. Vakkari (Eds.), *Emerging frameworks and methods: Proceedings of CoLIS4* (pp. 239–251). Greenwood Village, CO: Libraries Unlimited.

Byström, K., & Järvelin, K. (1995). Task complexity affects information seeking and use. *Information Processing and Management, 31,* 191–213.

29
Information Encountering

Sanda Erdelez

School of Information Science and Learning Technologies

University of Missouri–Columbia, USA

sanda@missouri.edu

The concept of information encountering (IE) was introduced into the information behavior literature by Erdelez (1997), based on her research of accidental acquisition of information among 132 information users in an academic environment (see http://infoencountering.com). While information behavior research has traditionally focused on how people actively seek information, Erdelez and several other authors, such as Williamson (1998) and Toms (2000), brought attention to opportunistic acquisition of information (OAI), which is a common behavior in a modern environment saturated with information and pervasive technologies for its processing and accessing.

Erdelez's initial research effort focused upon identifying and describing the characteristics of IE, defined broadly as a memorable experience of unexpected discovery of useful or interesting information. She proposed a conceptual framework for facilitating systematic study of IE with three key elements: characteristics of the information user, characteristics of the information environment, and characteristics of the encountered information. Erdelez also described four tentative categories of information users based on their perceptions of IE experiences: *super-encounterers*, *encounterers*, *occasional encounterers*, and *non-encounterers*.

In her follow-up work, Erdelez (2000) addressed the characteristics of the Internet and the Web as IE environments. The information richness of the Web and the ease of manipulation of electronic information might seem to be advantageous for IE. Erdelez, however, reported that this may be true only for users at the middle and lower end of the IE spectrum. The super-encounterers in her study reported a high level of apprehension about the Web as an IE environment. A related study by Erdelez

& Rioux (2000) explored the use of the Web for encountering information useful to other people.

Through the above empirical research, Erdelez confirmed that IE is an integral element of users' overall information behavior and a very rich topic for study. After additional conceptual refining, Erdelez recently identified IE as a specific type of OAI and defined it as *an instance of accidental discovery of information during an active search for some other information.* This view of IE, while narrower than the one presented in her initial study, allows for the presence of other types of OAI that yet need to be identified and defined. Figure 29.1 illustrates the nested position of IE in the context of OAI, and within information acquisition and information behavior in general. Figure 29.1 also indicates that OAI, as a type of information acquisition, is on the same hierarchical level as purposive information seeking. Such placement of OAI in relation to information seeking has been supported in several other models of information behavior, such as Wilson's model of information behavior (Wilson, 1999) and Williamson's (1998) ecological model of information use.

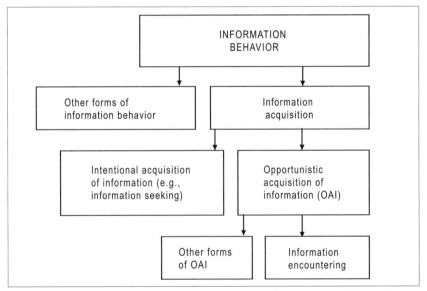

Figure 29.1   Position of opportunistic acquisition of information and information encountering within the conceptual model of information behavior.

Building upon the more specific definition of IE, Erdelez (2004) developed a functional model of IE, identifying several steps that occur during an IE experience: *noticing, stopping, examining, capturing,* and *returning* (see Figure 29.2).

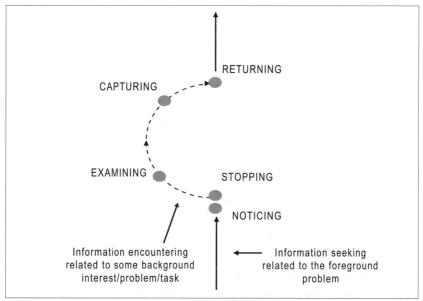

Figure 29.2   A functional model of information encountering.
   Note: This is an updated versions of the model from "Investigation of information encountering in the controlled research environment," by S. Erdelez, *Information Processing & Management* (2004).

The model assumes the existence of: 1) an initial information-seeking task that is related to the user's "foreground problem"; and 2) one or more "background interest/problems/tasks" that are not actively addressed by the user's information-seeking behavior. During an episode of information encountering, a switch occurs in users' attention from the foreground problem to the background problem.

Each step of the model involves a combination of cognitive, affective, and behavioral processes that may be applied as a user: 1) sees information potentially relevant to the background problem; 2) interrupts the original search process to examine the encountered information; 3) saves the information that is deemed to be worth saving; and 4) returns to the initial information search for the foreground problem. While the model presents one simplified and complete episode of IE, natural occurrences of IE come in many variations (e.g., interruptions and looping), which are influenced by the user's individual differences and the context of the overall situation.

Methodologies for studying IE and other types of OAI have been firmly based in qualitative approaches. Of key importance has been the capability of qualitative research—such as in-depth interviewing—to capture rich descriptions of users' OAI experiences and to create a shared conceptual understanding and openness of communication between the researcher and the respondents. Erdelez (1997) and Erdelez & Rioux (2000) also used surveys for both prescreening of the study participants and for the collection of more structured data about users' perceptions about their IE experiences. Some other researchers who also relied on a combination of qualitative research methods are Williamson (1998) and Foster and Ford (2002).

Building upon earlier efforts by Toms (2000) and Campos and de Figueiredo (2001), Erdelez (2004), in recent research, explored the possibility of studying IE in a controlled research environment. She attempted to induce IE in respondents, using a research setup that manipulated the presence of a trigger for IE experiences while controlling the user's background problem, foreground problem, and the information environment. Experimental research in IE could increase the understanding of the predictive power of various elements of Erdelez's conceptual framework, especially regarding the impact of individual differences and the characteristics of the information environment on the occurrence of an IE episode. However, many challenges in experimental research design and instrumentation would first need to be overcome.

Information encountering and the evolving methods for its study outline the still insufficiently explored territories of OAI, information acquisition, and information behavior in general. IE may also enrich conceptualization of several other evolving frameworks and theories of information behavior, such as:

- *Principle of least effort* (Zipf, 1949), especially in terms of showing that through IE, users are rewarded even when there is no apparent investment of effort to search for some information.

- *Everyday life information behavior,* as in Savolainen's (1995) everyday information seeking, Fisher, Durrance, and Hinton's (2004) information grounds, and Williamson's (1998) ecological model of information use, which demonstrates that everyday information needs become intertwined with work-related needs through IE.

- *Personal information management,* as in Jones (2004), which brings attention to similarities and differences in managing information acquired by encountering vs. purposeful information seeking.

- *Multi-processing in information behavior,* including research on multitasking information seeking and information searching processes by Spink et al. (2002) and the study of task switching and interruptions by Czerwinski et al. (2004).

Information encountering is not in itself a fully developed theory; however, the framework introduced by Erdelez for the study of IE promises to provide several key ingredients for theory building in information behavior research. A theory that builds upon the IE view of information behavior will need to accommodate the interplay between purposeful and opportunistic acquisition of information and may help explain information behavior in a natural and holistic way.

Campos, J., & de Figueiredo, A. D. (2001). Searching the unsearchable: Inducing serendipitous insights. In R. Weber, & C. Gresse (Ed.), *Proceedings of the workshop program at the fourth international conference on case-based reasoning,* ICCBR 2001, Technical Note AIC-01-003. Washington DC: Naval Research Laboratory, Navy Center for Applied Research in Artificial Intelligence.

Czerwinski, M., Horvitz, E., & Wilhite, S. (2004). A diary study of task switching and interruptions. In *Proceedings of the 2004 conference on human factors in computing systems* (pp. 175–182). New York: ACM Press.

Erdelez, S. (1997). Information encountering: A conceptual framework for accidental information discovery. In P. Vakkari, R. Savolainen, & B. Dervin (Eds.), *Information seeking in context: Proceedings of international conference on research in information needs, seeking and use in different contexts* (pp. 412–421). London: Taylor Graham.

Erdelez, S. (2000). Towards understanding information encountering on the Web. In D. H. Kraft (Ed.), *Proceedings of the 63rd annual meeting of the american society for information science* (pp. 363–371). Medford, NJ: Information Today.

Erdelez, S. (2004). Investigation of information encountering in the controlled research environment. *Information Processing & Management, 40,* 1013–1025

Erdelez, S., & Rioux, K. (2000). Sharing information encountered for others on the Web. *The New Review of Information Behavior Research, 1,* 219–233.

Fisher, K. E., Durrance, J. C., & Hinton, M. B. (2004). Information grounds and the use of need-based services by immigrants in Queens, NY: A context-based, outcome evaluation approach. *Journal of the American Society for Information Science and Technology, 55,* 754–766.

Foster, A. E., & Ford, N. (2002). Serendipity and information seeking: An empirical study. *Journal of Documentation, 59,* 321–340.

Jones, W. (2004). Finders, keepers? The present and future perfect in support of personal information management. *First Monday, 9*(3). Retrieved March 5, 2004, from www.firstmonday.org/issues/issue9_3/jones/index.html

Savolainen, R. (1995). Everyday life information seeking: Approaching information seeking in the context of "way of life." *Library and Information Science Research, 17,* 259–294.

Spink, A., Ozmultu, S., & Ozmultu, H. C. (2002). Multitasking information seeking and searching processes. *Journal of the American Society for Information Science and Technology, 53,* 639–652.

Toms, E. G. (2000). Understanding and facilitating the browsing of electronic text. *International Journal of Human-Computer Studies, 52,* 423–452.

Williamson, K. (1998). Discovered by chance: The role of incidental information acquisition in an ecological model of information use. *Library and Information Science Research, 20*(1), 23–40.

Wilson, T. D. (1999). Models in information behaviour research. *Journal of Documentation, 55,* 249–270.

Zipf, G. K. (1949). *Human behavior and the principle of least effort: An introduction to human ecology.* Cambridge, MA: Addison-Wesley.

30
Information Grounds

Karen E. Fisher
The Information School
University of Washington, USA
fisher@u.washington.edu

The theory of information grounds arose from Karen Pettigrew's (1998, 1999, 2000) field work at community foot clinics on how nurses, the elderly, and other individuals share human services information. Pettigrew drew upon Tuominen and Savolainen's (1997) social construc- tionist approach to define information grounds as synergistic "environ- ment[s] temporarily created when people come together for a singular purpose but from whose behavior emerges a social atmosphere that fos- ters the spontaneous and serendipitous sharing of information" (Pettigrew, 1999, p. 811).

According to Pettigrew (1998) and Fisher, Durrance, and Hinton (2004), information grounds are temporal: They can occur anywhere at any time in varied and often unexpected places. Yet they focus upon a primary, instrumental purpose, separate from information provision (viewed as a by-product of social interaction) such as receiving a ser- vice or product. Pettigrew's foot clinics, for example, were temporarily located in hospital auditoriums, common rooms in seniors' buildings, and the basements of churches or service clubs, yet the clinics were always attended by the same types of people: nurses, seniors, recep- tionists, and other people needing foot care. In this sense, information grounds are attended by identifiable social types—people or actors who are expected in that setting and play expected social roles, includ- ing those connected to information flow. Some actors, for example, may play heavier roles than others in disseminating information, facilitat- ing information flow through providing feedback or communicating information needs.

As people gather at an information ground, they engage in social inter- action, conversing about life, generalities, and specific situations that lead to serendipitous and sometime purposive, formal and informal sharing of information on varied topics. Actors may thus post information by themselves, and engage in two-person or group exchanges while simultaneously acting as requesters, intermediaries (or negotiators), or providers. Notably, information needs are not presented in ways documented in such formal settings as community information centers and public libraries. Although the process is similar in that people may present needs indirectly, and professionals may use communication techniques to identify the actual need, people rarely approach others and immediately say, "Where can I get x?" Instead, information needs emerge through casual interaction, through small talk, or just chit-chat. Sometimes people use these casual interactions purposefully to question someone about his or her knowledge of a subject in which the person may be experiencing difficulty, or to follow up on the outcomes of a previous information exchange. On other occasions, information is shared incidentally in a manner similar to that described by Erdelez (1997) and Williamson (1998). In other words, information is shared serendipitously without anyone expressing (or necessarily having) a need for that information. Proxy information seeking (when someone seeks information on behalf of someone else; also known as the "imposed query") further occurs at information grounds. Additionally, people report using and benefiting from information shared at information grounds in multiple ways, including the physical, social, affective, and cognitive dimensions.

Along these lines, information grounds are context rich: Many subcontexts from many perspectives are always at play, and together they form a whole or grand context (see Pettigrew 1999 for an in-depth discussion of context). In terms of the temporal sense, as members disperse, so does the information ground, at least until the next gathering. Meanwhile, new situations arise in people's lives, local and global events continue to occur, and people pick up new information to be shared at their next information ground.

Based on the foregoing, and following Chatman's (2000) approach to deriving theory, Fisher, Durance, and Hinton (2004a, pp. 756–757) described information grounds as comprising seven key concepts (see Figure 30.1). They derived the following propositional statements:

1) Information grounds can occur anywhere, in any type of temporal setting, and are predicated on the presence of individuals.

2) People gather at information grounds for a primary, instrumental purpose other than information sharing.

3) Information grounds are attended by different social types, most if not all of whom play expected and important, albeit different, roles in information flow.

4) Social interaction is a primary activity at information grounds such that information flow is a by-product.

5) People engage in formal and informal information sharing, and information flow occurs in many directions.

6) People use information obtained at information grounds in alternative ways, and benefit along physical, social, affective, and cognitive dimensions.

7) Many sub-contexts exist within an information ground and are based on people's perspectives and physical factors; together these sub-contexts form a grand context.

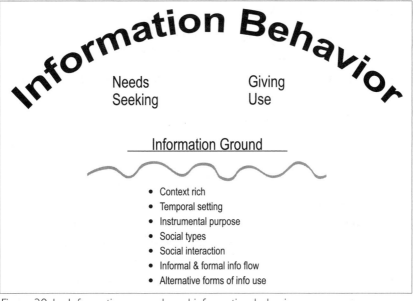

Figure 30.1   Information grounds and information behavior.

Recent research shows that information grounds occur in varied set-tings, including hair salons, barber shops, quilting bees, playgrounds, tat-too parlors, metro buses, restaurants and coffee shops, midwifery scenes, food banks, bike shops, Indonesian master huts, sport fields, coping and literacy skill classes for immigrants, story time hours at public libraries, waiting rooms in auto repair shops and medical offices, grocery store lineups, communal laundry rooms, ferries, and luggage carousels at air-ports (IBEC, 2004). Based on recent field work by Fisher and colleagues (2004b and 2005), the public's most common information grounds are places of worship and the workplace. Considerable research is needed on the nature of information grounds. As Fisher and colleagues explain, "the notion of IGs [information grounds] may be only newly proposed in the literature, but the phenomenon itself is not new, only its identification. Linked strongly with people's natural inclination of constructing and sharing information interpersonally and thus socially, IGs have been around since time immemorial and yet, little research—at least from an IB [information behavior] perspective—has explored their nature." In future work, Fisher and colleagues are deriving a typology that captures such nuances as:

- Focal activities
- Actor/social type roles
- Effects of information type (trivial vs. big decision information; insider vs. outsider)
- Motivation (voluntary vs. forced or hostage, e.g., choir groups vs. waiting rooms)
- Membership size and type (open vs. closed)

Research is also needed on how information needs are expressed and recognized as information grounds, how information is socially con-structed among different actors, how people's perceptions and participa-tion in information grounds change over time, the life cycles of information grounds (how they are created and sustained; what causes them to disap-pear or transform), and how they can be used to facilitate information flow, including how employers can alleviate the stressors of unemployment by helping laid-off employees establish or identify replacement informa-tion grounds that can facilitate the availability of information required during times of transition. In sum, information grounds have local and global impact because they occur across all levels of all societies as people create and utilize them to perform tasks in the course of daily life. The better we understand where information grounds are situated for different populations as well as how they emerge and function, the better we can design ways of facilitating information flow in them.

Chatman, E. A. (2000). Framing social life in theory and research. *New Review of Information Behaviour Research: Studies of Information Seeking in Context. 1,* 3–17.

Erdelez, S. (1997). Information encountering: A conceptual framework for accidental information discovery. In P. Vakkari, R. Savolainen, & B. Dervin (Eds.), *Information seeking in context: Proceedings of an international conference on research in information needs, seeking and use in different contexts*, August 14–16, 1996, Tampere, Finland (pp. 412421). London: Taylor Graham.

Fisher, K. E., Durrance, J. C., & Hinton, M. B. (2004a). Information grounds and the use of needbased services by immigrants in Queens, NY: A contextbased, outcome evaluation approach. *Journal of the American Society for Information Science & Technology, 55,* 754–766.

Fisher, K. E., Marcoux, E., Miller, L. S., Sanchez, A., & Cunningham, E. R. (2004b). Information behavior of migrant Hispanic farm workers and their families in the Pacific Northwest. *Information Research, 10* (Based on a paper given at the ISIC Conference, Dublin, 2004).

Fisher, K. E., Naumer, C. M., Durrance, J. C., Stromski, L., & Christiansen, T. (2005). Something old, something new: Preliminary findings from an exploratory study about people's information habits and information grounds. *Information Research, 10* (Based on a paper given at the ISIC Conference, Dublin, 2004).

IBEC. (2004). *Information Grounds.* Retrieved May 25, 2004, from http://ibec. ischool.washington.edu

Pettigrew, K. E. (1998). The role of community health nurses in providing information and referral to the elderly: A study based on social network theory (Doctoral dissertation, The University of Western Ontario, Canada, 1998). *Dissertation Abstracts International, 59,* 3683.

Pettigrew, K. E. (1999). Waiting for chiropody: Contextual results from an ethnographic study of the information behavior among attendees at community clinics. *Information Processing & Management, 35,* 801–817.

Pettigrew, K. E. (2000). Lay information provision in community settings: How community health nurses disseminate human services information to the elderly. *The Library Quarterly, 70,* 47–85.

Tuominen, K., & Savolainen, R. (1997). A social constructionist approach to the study of information use as discursive action. In P. Vakkari, R. Savolainen, & B. Dervin

(Eds.), *Information seeking in context: Proceedings of an international conference on research in information needs, seeking and use in different contexts.* August 14–16, 1996, Tampere, Finland (pp. 81–96). London: Taylor Graham.

Williamson, K. (1998). Discovered by chance: The role of incidental information acquisition in an ecological model of information use. *Library & Information Science Research, 20(1),* 23–40.

31
Information Horizons

Diane H. Sonnenwald
The Swedish School of Library and Information Science
Göteborg University and University College of Borås, Sweden
Diane.Sonnenwald@hb.se

The information horizons theoretical framework and methodology proposes a general, descriptive explanation of human information-seeking and
use behavior, and data collection and analysis techniques to explore human
information-seeking behavior in context. The framework and methodology are based on empirical studies of human information behavior in a
variety of contexts and builds on theories from several research traditions,
including information science and sociology.

Key ideas in the theoretical framework include the role of social networks and contexts in information behavior, the importance of understanding information behavior as a process, and the concept of an
"information horizon" that constrains and enables information-seeking
behavior. The framework suggests that certain types of data, which
have not been traditionally included in studies of information behavior,
are important. These data include: when and why people access (and do
not access) individuals and other information resources; relationships
among information resources; the proactive nature of information
resources; and the impact of contexts and situations on the information-
seeking process. A research methodology has been developed to collect
and analyze these types of data.

The methodology primarily consists of an interview during which
study participants are asked to provide a graphical and verbal articulation of their information horizon in a particular context. That is, each
study participant is asked to draw a map of his or her information horizons showing all information resources, including people, they typically
access when seeking information within a specific context. Each study
participant is also asked to describe the information resources and
explain their importance and role in the information-seeking process.

Techniques to analyze these data are drawn from social network and graph theory.

The information horizons theoretical framework and methodology have influenced a number of studies investigating information needs of high school students, graduate and undergraduate students, older adults, and professionals such as journalists, engineers, and scientists (e.g., Hultgren, 2003). It has also influenced computer science research, e.g., universal access and interface development (e.g., Maad, 2003).

A detailed discussion of information horizons theoretical framework is provided in Sonnenwald (1999) and Sonnenwald, Wildemuth, and Harmon (2001). This framework includes the five main propositions.

Proposition 1: Human information behavior is shaped by and shapes individuals, social networks, situations, and contexts. An individual, within a particular situation and context, may encounter an information need; the situation and context help determine the information need. Social networks also provide a lens that facilitates the identification and exploration of information needs. Furthermore, the individual, social network, situation, and context may help determine the information resources available to satisfy the need.

Proposition 2: Individuals or systems within a particular situation and context may perceive, reflect, and/or evaluate change in others, self, and/or their environment. Information behavior is constructed amidst a flow of such reflections and/or evaluations, in particular, amidst reflections and/or evaluations concerning a lack of knowledge. This process can be visualized as a linear process consisting of an initial perception of change and a series of reflections, or evaluations, and decisions or events (see Figure 31.1.) The process need not be linear; each phase can be dynamic in the sense it could be interrupted at any time, or interwoven among other processes. The reflections at each phase appear to be motivated by accommodation with self, others, and the environment, often with some form of dominance. For example, accommodation with self may include accommodating personal feelings such as uncertainty and confusion, and accommodation with others may include considering how others could affect your career.

Proposition 3: Within a context and situation is an "information horizon" in which we can act. When an individual decides to seek information, there is an information horizon in which they may seek

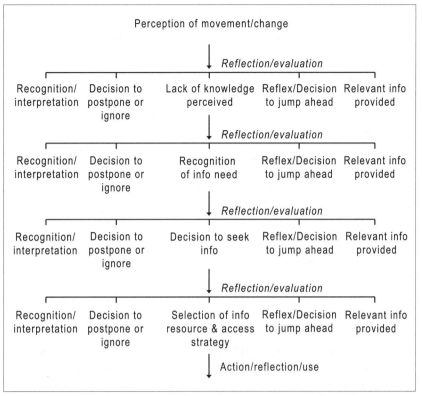

Figure 31.1   Flow of reflections and/or evaluations in human information behavior.

information. An information horizon may consist of a variety of infor-mation resources and relationships among these resources. Examples of resources are: social networks, including colleagues, subject matter experts, reference librarians, information brokers; documents, including broadcast media, Web pages, books; information retrieval tools, includ-ing computer-based information retrieval systems, bibliographies; and experimentation and observation in the world (see Figure 31.2).

Information horizons, and subsequently information resources, are determined socially and individually and may be different for different contexts even for the same individual. In some situations and contexts, an information horizon may be bounded by social economics and politics. Of course, individuals also shape their information horizons. For example, individual knowledge of possible resources and preferences may help

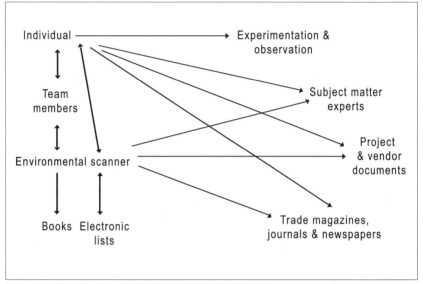

Figure 31.2   A representative information horizon of a software engineer.

determine an individual's information horizon. Furthermore, information resources in an information horizon may have knowledge of each other and the individual, and may recommend resources to satisfy an information need or lack of knowledge. In this way, an information resource may expand an individual's information horizon. Information resources may also proactively provide information based on their understanding of an individual's lack of knowledge or information need.

Proposition 4: Human information-seeking behavior may, ideally, be viewed as collaboration among an individual and information resources. It is bounded by an individual's information horizon. The goals of collaboration, in this sense, are the sharing of meaning and resolution of a lack of knowledge condition. Collaboration with (and among) information resources ideally includes reflexive interaction, and/or reflexive provisioning of information. Furthermore, collaboration often presupposes continuing relations. Collaboration among the individual and information resources will, of course, be bounded by the individual's information horizon for the given situation and context.

Proposition 5: Because information horizons consist of a variety of information resources, many of which have some knowledge of each other, information horizons may be conceptualized as densely populated spaces. In a densely populated solution space, many solutions are assumed, and the information-retrieval problem expands from determining the most efficient path to the best solution, to determining how to make possible solutions visible—to an individual(s) and to other information resources.

After a sample population and context for a research study have been identified, semi-structure interviews should be conducted with each study participant. During an interview, a participant should be asked to draw a map of his or her information horizon, i.e., all information resources, including people, he or she typically access when seeking information in the context that is the focus of the research study. Participants should also be encouraged to talk about and explain their drawing as they create it (Figure 31.3).

After the graphical representation of her or his information horizon has been created, each participant should be asked to describe incidents when it was very satisfying to seek information and very dissatisfying. Follow-up questions should be used to encourage the participant to provide details about each incident. These questions are based on the critical incident interview technique.

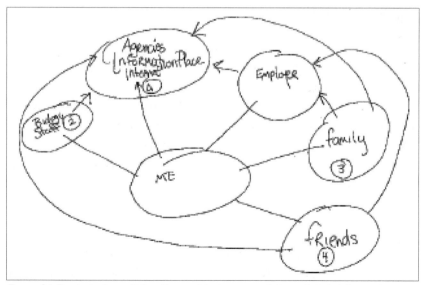

Figure 31.3   A study participant's graphical representation of their information horizon.

The concept of an information horizon map appears to be intuitive to a wide range of study populations, and the act of creating an information horizon map appears to help participants focus and verbalize their thoughts regarding information resources and their information-seeking processes. Interview questions help reduce the possibility of participants' omitting important information about resources. Thus the technique provides in-depth data that is not possible to obtain via questionnaires or computer logs. Because the maps are participants' synthesis of multiple information-seeking situations over time, the technique also provides data that cannot generally be obtained through observations or experiments.

A first step in analyzing the information horizon maps involves transferring the graphical representations to a matrix where the rows represent the information resources included in all participants' maps and the columns represent each participant. The cells of the matrix are populated with numbers that represent each participant's preferences or order of access among the information resources. When a participant's graphical drawing is unclear, the interview transcript should be consulted for clarification. The identification of all information resources is important and may bring to light new information resources not previously discussed in the literature.

The data in the matrix can be further analyzed to develop descriptive statistics regarding information resources used by the study population, and to discover patterns in information-seeking processes, trends among information resource preferences, and relationships among information resources. The results of such analysis identifies what resources are being accessed most and least frequently, which resources recommend other resources, and which resources are not connected with or never recommend other resources. Analysis of the oral interview data can help explain these relationships.

Hultgren, F. (2003). *Approaching the future: A study of school leavers' information seeking and use.* Unpublished PhD dissertation proposal, Göteborg University.

Maad, S. (2003). Universal access to multimodal ITV content: Challenges and prospects. In N. Carbonell, & C. Stephanidis (Eds.), *Universal access: Theoretical perspectives, practice and experience* (pp. 195–208). New York: Springer.

Sonnenwald, D. H. (1999). Evolving perspectives of human information behavior: Contexts, situations, social networks and information horizons. In T. D. Wilson, & D. K. Allen (Eds.), *Exploring the contexts of information behavior: Proceedings of the second international conference in information needs, seeking and use in different contexts* (pp. 176–190). London: Taylor Graham.

Sonnenwald, D. H., Wildemuth, B. M., & Harmon, G. (2001). A research method using the concept of information horizons: An example from a study of lower socio-economic students' information seeking behavior. *The New Review of Information Behavior Research, 2,* 65–86.

32
Information Intents

Ross J. Todd
School of Communication, Information and Library Studies
Rutgers University, USA
rtodd@scils.rutgers.edu

Developed by Ross Todd, this new theory is situated within the study of information utilization, and has its foundation in the cognitive view of information science, information-seeking behavior, information utilization, and knowledge representation. By focusing on the drivers and effects of information utilization, information intents assumes the "active-creative role of the user for the process of use, explicitly talking of cognitive transformation, knowledge conversion, adaptation, reformulation, or re-invention" (Wingens, 199, p. 37).

Historically, the study of information utilization has emerged from several different traditions, including sociology of knowledge, applied social science research, and more recently, human information behavior. It focuses on what people in a range of contexts do with information they seek out or have provided for them, and rests on the assumption that information has the potential to influence, to make a difference to their thoughts, actions, and emotions. Despite considerable empirical research into information utilization since the 1970s, the state of the art of theory building has remained low, and characterized by generalizations centering on the predominant classification of conceptual, instrumental, and symbolic utilization (Beyer & Trice, 1982). Accordingly, information intents theory was developed to provide a richer understanding of what happens in people's minds when they consume information.

Brookes' Fundamental Equation was employed as a general framework for elucidating information intents. Brookes argued that the "theoretical" pursuit of information science should be "the cognitive interactions between users and the public knowledge systems" (Brookes, 1980a, p. 248). He explicated this as an abstract "Fundamental Equation of Information Science," most commonly expressed as $K[S] + \Delta I = K[S + \Delta S]$ (Brookes, 1980b, p. 131).

Brookes saw the equation as an interactive cognitive process of what people already know, how what they know changes through selectively taking in information, and the effect of these changes.

Specifically, a person's existing knowledge structure K[S] is changed by an increment of information ΔI, and this modification has some effect, a changed knowledge structure K[S + ΔS] where ΔS indicates the modification effect. The same information ΔI may have different effects on different knowledge structures, the adjustments being shaped by perceptions, attitudes, and values, that is, people's frames of reference. Existing private knowledge is transformed as new information is continually selected and integrated, creating new knowledge structures. Information intents is posited as both driver and outcome of this cognitive transformation.

Information intents was explicated through an analysis of adolescent girls' existing knowledge about the drug heroin and how their knowledge was modified by exposures to information about it, and what were the cognitive effects of this modification. A quasi-experimental methodology involved baseline measures of existing knowledge, the introduction of staged exposures to information, and documenting and mapping of the sequence of knowledge structures. The information exposures were in the form of different, publicly available information about the nature and history of heroin, individual implications of heroin use, and community implications. Free generation written discourse and question-answering protocols were used to acquire knowledge at each phase, as well as perceptions of the process. Knowledge was mapped in the form of Conceptual Graph Structures (Graesser & Clark, 1985). These structures were analyzed across the exposures to derive the information intents and their corresponding manifestations of changes in knowledge structures.

The theory proposes that cognitive information utilization can be characterized by five information intents, which are both drivers and effects of information utilization. These are:

- *Get a complete picture* – to build an expanded, more complex picture: add specific detail; add new facets or dimensions to an existing idea; make new connections between existing ideas; trigger to remembering and recalling ideas not thought of at the time

- *Get a changed picture* – to make changes to existing ideas; correcting specific facts and broader perceptions

- *Get a clearer picture* – to see existing ideas and how these ideas are related together, with greater understanding and clarity

- *Get a verified picture* – to verify existing ideas when some doubt existed as to the certainty of these ideas, even though on surface the ideas appeared stated as certain

- *Get a position in a picture* – to express an opinion, state a viewpoint or estimation of constructed pictures as a personal value judgment guess, inference or conclusion

These intents are manifested in distinct patterns of changes to knowledge structures. The five information intents and manifestations are shown in Table 32.1.

The Theory of Information Intent posits that people engage with information in purposeful, deliberate, and selective ways to get expanded, and/or changed, and/or clearer and/or verified pictures, and/or by being able to state positions. As drivers and outcomes of information utilization, information intents enable people to move forward in their information endeavors, constructing new pictures that represent new understandings. This is not random acquisition, but one shaped by a desired cognitive intent in the context of individual frames of reference such as personal experience, existing knowledge, and current stage of life cycle.

This theory has been used in two recent studies. The first, *Student Learning Through Ohio School Libraries* (Todd & Kuhlthau, 2004), involved 13,123 students and 880 teachers. This study sought to identify how students benefit from school libraries through elaborating conceptions of "help" and providing a measure of these helps as perceived by students. One of the seven conceptual categories ("Using Information") focused on information intents. The study showed that the impact of the school library in enabling information utilization for knowledge construction ranked third highest of the seven categories of "helps," with helps related to getting information and using information technology ranking higher. The second study, currently underway, is tracking how

Table 32.1   Information intents and manifestations of changes in knowledge structures.

Information Intent	Manifestation of changes in knowledge structures

Get a complete picture	a) inclusive: adding specific instances, examples or types
	b) elaborative: building associative structures:
	  • property-oriented structures
	  • manner-oriented structures
	  • cause-oriented structures
	  • goal-oriented structures
	c) integrative: separate structures integrated more holistically

Get a changed picture	a) construction: building up a complete picture b) deconstruction: removing incorrect ideas c) reconstruction: replacing with more appropriate ideas
Get a clearer picture	a) explanation: tells how and tells why b) precision: appending information to add precision of detail
Get a verified picture	a) no change b) emphatic: repetition of ideas to add weight or emphasis c) inclusive: including more precise, specific ideas d) defensive: defend and reaffirm viewpoints
Get a position in a picture	a) reactive: expressions of agreement/disagreement b) formative: deriving personal conclusion based on facts c) potential positioning: foreseeing future use of facts d) predictive: predicting new events and states

students in 10 New Jersey schools utilize information in the school library for knowledge construction.

The theory provides a framework for understanding of the cognitive dimensions of how and why people utilize information in the process of constructing knowledge, and for describing the transformation of their knowledge structures through information utilization. It is applicable to understanding the cognitive drivers and outcomes of purposeful information utilization, and a cognitive effects approach to conceptualizing how libraries and information services help people.

A major difficulty with exploring cognitive information utilization is the problem of peering into people's minds. The methodology for elucidating information intents is workable, sensitive, and detailed enough to allow new concepts and perspectives to emerge. However, it is time consuming, demanding considerable time commitment and cognitive load on participants.

Information intents provides an approach to a stronger user-centered design of electronic information retrieval systems by providing a framework of an alternative set of categories of desired outcomes, which could be built in information systems as a central design feature. It could allow people to enter the system, not just in terms of content or document description, but also in terms of the desired cognitive intents they seek, such as wanting facts, opinions or viewpoints, arguments, explanations, or even wanting to identify misconception. It provides a new way of looking at the dialogue between users and information professionals from the perspective of understanding the kinds of cognitive intents and outcomes desired with a view to establishing a sharper understanding of user needs. The theory also provides opportunities for information literacy instructional design by focusing on developing cognitive processes and knowledge construction processes.

Beyer, J., & Trice, H. (1982). The utilization process: A conceptual framework and synthesis of empirical findings. *Administrative Science Quarterly, 27*, 591–622.

Brookes, B. (1974). Robert Fairthorne and the scope of information science. *Journal of Documentation, 30*(2), 139–152.

Brookes, B. (1980a). Measurement in information science: Objective and subjective metrical space. *Journal of the American Society for Information Science, 31*, 248–255.

Brookes, B. (1980b). The foundations of information science. Part I. Philosophical aspects. *Journal of Information Science, 2,* 125–133.

Graesser, A., & Clark, L. (1985). *Structures and procedures of implicit knowledge.* Norwood, NJ: Ablex.

Todd, R. J. (1999). Back to our beginnings: Information utilization, Bertram Brookes and the fundamental equation of information science. *Information Processing & Management, 35,* 851–870.

Todd, R. J. (1999b). Utilization of heroin information by adolescent girls in Australia: A cognitive analysis. *Journal of the American Society for Information Science, 50,* 10–23.

Todd, R., & Kuhlthau, C. (2004). *Student learning through Ohio school libraries: Background, methodology and report of findings.* Columbus, OH: OELMA.

Wingens, M. (1990). Toward a general utilization theory: A systems theory reformulation of the two-communities metaphor. *Knowledge: Creation, Diffusion, Utilization, 12*(1), 27–42.

33
Information Interchange

Rita Marcella and Graeme Baxter
Aberdeen Business School
The Robert Gordon University, United Kingdom
r.c.marcella@rgu.ac.uk and g.baxter@rgu.ac.uk

The Theory of Information Interchange by Marcella and Baxter evolved over a number of years from the research on government information service and citizen information behavior at a regional, United Kingdom, and European level. With a background in information science and communication research (e.g., work by Kuhlthau, 1991; Dervin, 1976; Ford, 1973; Wilson, 1981), the theory focuses on the importance of considering the roles and aims of both the information provider and the information user in assessing the effectiveness of, and potential improvements to, the information communication process.

A number of papers provide detail of the research evidence upon which the theory is based. The earliest of these involved an evaluation of the implementation of European information policy in the United Kingdom (Marcella & Baxter, 1997). It revealed the variety of contexts in which users might require information about the European institutions, while suggesting that individuals frequently lacked any motivation to seek such information or awareness that such information might be of value to them in their everyday lives. The study also highlighted a gulf between the European Commission's objective in developing information services and the perspective of a potential user who is most frequently apolitical. The European Commission focused largely on a desire to encourage a positive (political) response to Europe, if manifested or even disguised in an apparently altruistic desire to be more open and transparent in governing. The user's focus was on a personal value of information for making a decision, solving a problem, resolving a worry, or understanding a complex phenomenon (in line with Dervin, 1976). Moreover, the research suggested that each user might require this information in a range of different life contexts—educational, work-related, business, domestic, consumer-oriented, recreational, and political purposes. The latter are arguably the least potent motivators. In contrast, the European Commission conceptualized a public need for what might be very loosely and unhelpfully construed as "general citizen" information for which there was very little evidence of need.

A second project investigated service provision and information needs at the national U.K. level, characterized as an exploration of "citizen-ship information" (Marcella & Baxter, 1999; Marcella & Baxter, 2000a; Marcella & Baxter, 2000b; and Marcella & Baxter, 2001). It sought to develop a holistic understanding of the nature and use of citizenship information, its potential contribution to the individual's capacity to prosper and survive, and the ways in which access to information might support the democratic process and encourage participation. The study highlighted again the tendency for services and researchers to conceptu-alize citizenship information in a far more literal and limited way than might the citizens who simply wanted to know what they needed to know in order to deal with the demands that life might throw at them. There is an observable, indeed understandable, desire on the part of providers to place limits around what must be provided, a desire still manifest in providers' construction of public sector information in the context of freedom of access to information.

A further project (Marcella, Baxter, & Moore, 2002; Marcella, Baxter, & Moore, 2003) explored the impact of new information and communications technologies on use of parliamentary information. The results indicated that new technologies, while offering a means of widening access to some groups in the population, did little to overcome the barrier of apathy for those with little sense that such information might have real value to them.

Marcella and Baxter have drawn on the themes developed by Schutz (1946), which suggested that different persons in different situations may possess different world views and make different demands on information sources and services as a result. They argue that the evolu-tion of a body of well-informed citizens has been hindered, since Schutz developed his theories, by an increasing anonymity and isolation in social life, by the exponential growth in the amount of information available to the individual, and by the alternative modes of access possi-ble in its communication.

Information Interchange Theory is built upon the fundamental dichotomy between the information provider view and the user view. The provider seeks to generalize and work toward a baseline and poorly articulated state of 'informedness' necessary to survive and/or to respond positively to the public sphere. In contrast, the user acts in a variety of contextualized roles, and varies in his or her level of expertise or informedness prior to the interchange of information. The user view is multiple, rich, and complex, with a variation in motivation to become highly informed dependent on the urgency and significance of information need.

The theory conceptualizes the information user in an essentially post-modernist way, as an isolated and fragmented entity who may assume certain characteristics in particular life contexts. It calls for highly qualitative techniques in research design, techniques that offer opportunities to create rich pictures of individual complexity. More recently Marcella and Baxter have developed an innovative tool, the interactive electronically assisted interview, which enables the collection of data about information need and information-seeking behavior while prompting users to discuss freely and expand upon the relationship between information and their experience as "citizens."

Information Interchange Theory also helps to elucidate the nature of the relationship between provider and user in a highly critical and thoughtful manner. Table 33.1 illustrates these two-way relationships and roles of each of the information actors in interchange.

Information Interchange Theory recognizes the significance of the different roles and objectives of the information "actor" in holding, providing, withholding, accessing, and using information in a complex interaction between (at least) two parties with potentially conflicting conceptions of the purpose of the interchange process, where all actors are influenced by their context or agenda. It recognizes that information actors will demonstrate varying degrees of activity or passivity in differing information behavior contexts and that each actor may assume different roles and different levels of activity/motivation/informedness in varying life contexts.

While Information Interchange Theory recognizes individuality and complexity in the users of government information, the authors' research

Table 33.1   The two-way information interchange in relationships and roles of
information providers and information users.

Information provider		Information user
Seeks to create the "well-informed citizen."	← →	Seeks information of interest, practical use and benefit.
Seeks to promote positive response to certain messages.	→	Has little instrinsic desire to be informed as a citizen.
	←	Requires objective, unbiased information to enable sound decisions to be made.
Conceives of the user as a general stable and predictable citizen with standard requirements.	→ ← →	Displays complexity in individual level of informedness required.
	←	Shares some but few general stable characteristics with other users.
Values information about user response to information about government, in order to test public opinion.	→ ←	Sees limited value in providing information to government if there is no perceived benefit or response.
Demonstrates tension between desire to inform and mold opinion and desire to create well-informed citizens capable of formulating thoughtful opinions.	→ ← → ←	Increasingly finds much about government difficult to understand and is unconvinced about the benefits of increased understanding.
Is frequently issue-focused and message-focused.	← →	Is frequently issue-focused but increasingly cynical about messages.
Information provision seen as proactive and purposive.	← →	Information use tends to be highly reactive, ad hoc and unpredictable.

has also revealed that it is possible to draw some highly significant generalizable conclusions, such as:

- The finding that young people were less convinced of the importance of being able to access high-quality and reliable information

- The fact that better educated respondents tended to be more critical of their own capacity to locate high-quality information and more discerning about the limitations of the sources that were available to them

- The fact that it was highly questionable whether users (whether apparently expert or not) were in fact consistently able to judge the quality and extent of their own informedness

A most direct application of Information Interchange Theory is in the study of government information; however, it might also be used in studies of other sectors, such as business information and information literacy. In their current research, Marcella and Baxter have applied the theory to an examination of user information needs in the context of public sector organisations related to the implementation of Freedom of Information legislation in the U.K. The theory could be also applied in study of various types of information service to examine misalignments in service ethos and to develop a better understanding of the user perspective.

Dervin, B. (1976). The everyday information needs of the average citizen: A taxonomy for analysis. In M. Kochen, & J. P. Donohue (Eds.), *Information for the community* (pp. 19–38). Chicago: American Library Association.

Ford, G. (1973). Research in user behaviour in university libraries. *Journal of Documentation, 29*(1), 85–106.

Kuhlthau, C. C. (1991). Inside the search process: Information seeking from the user's perspective. *Journal of the American Society for Information Science, 42,* 361–371.

Marcella, R., & Baxter, G. (1997). European Union information: An investigation of need amongst public library users in 3 Scottish authorities. *Journal of Librarianship and Information Science, 29*(2), 69–76.

Marcella, R., & Baxter, G. (1999). The information needs and the information seeking behaviour of a national sample of the population in the United Kingdom. *Journal of Documentation, 55*(2), 159–183.

Marcella, R., & Baxter, G. (2000a). Information need, information seeking behaviour and participation with special reference to needs related to citizenship: Results of a national survey. *Journal of Documentation, 56*(2), 136–160.

Marcella, R., & Baxter, G. (2000b). The impact of social class and status on citizenship information needs. *Journal of Information Science, 26*(4), 239–254.

Marcella, R., & Baxter, G. (2001). A random walk around Britain: A critical assessment of the random walk sample as a method of collecting data on the public's citizenship information needs. *The New Review of Information Behaviour Research, 2*, 87–103.

Marcella, R., Baxter, G., & Moore, N. (2002). Theoretical and methodological approaches to the study of information need in the context of the impact of new information and communications technologies on the communication of parliamentary information. *Journal of Documentation, 58*(2), 185–210.

Marcella, R., Baxter, G., & Moore, N. (2003). Data collection using electronically assisted interviews in a roadshow: A methodological evaluation. *Journal of Documentation, 59* (2), 143–167.

Schutz, A. (1946). The well informed citizen: An essay, on the social distribution of knowledge. *Social Research, 13*, 463–478.

Wilson, T. D. (1981). On user studies and information needs. *Journal of Documentation, 37*(1), 3–15.

34
Institutional Ethnography

Roz Stooke
Faculty of Education
The University of Western Ontario, Canada
rkstooke@uwo.ca

Institutional Ethnography (IE) was developed during the 1980s by Dorothy Smith (1987, 1990a, 1990b) in response to her concerns about the standard sociological research practices of the time. IE is a qualitative approach that aims to provide a "sociology for people" (Smith, 1999). IE researchers take a standpoint in the everyday world to investigate linkages among activities carried out in local settings of everyday life and translocal processes of administration and governance (DeVault & McCoy, 2002, p. 751). The relevance of IE to library and information science (LIS) lies in its successful use by researchers, practitioners, and activists working together outside academic settings to address concerns about equity and social justice.

Smith first articulated the theories underpinning IE in the form of a critique of her own practice. As a feminist activist during the 1960s and 1970s she was troubled by the disjuncture she perceived between the embodied discourses in which she participated as a mother and the rational, impersonal discourses in which she participated as a sociologist. She recalls feeling an intense frustration with sociological concepts and categories that could not adequately describe her experiences as a mother, a frustration she attributes to the "gender subtext of the rational and impersonal" (1987, p. 4). In Smith's view, rational and impersonal discourse dominates social life in industrial societies such that its concepts and abstractions suppress the language of the domestic sphere and promote the view that the everyday world cannot be a "site for development of systematic knowledge" (Smith, 1990a, p.18). Smith contests this view. She coined the term "problematic of the everyday world" to denote "a set of puzzles that do not yet exist in the form of puzzles but are 'latent' in the actualities of the experienced world" (Smith, 1987, p. 91). She remains adamant, however, that the everyday world is "through and through socially organized" (Smith, 1999a, p. 65) and that the social organization of the everyday world is not wholly discoverable from within. IE studies therefore begin with the experiences of individuals or groups in a local setting, but they aim to "go beyond what can be known in any local setting" (Campbell & Gregor, 2002, p. 59).

The related concepts *social organization* and *social relation* are central to an understanding of IE's analytic project. *Social organization* combines Garfinkel's social ontology with Marx's materialist method. Like Garfinkel, Smith construes social life as an ongoing accomplishment of the actual practices of people carrying out work (broadly defined) in local settings. Invoking Marx, she then proposes that work carried out in local settings is linked by *social relations* (sequences of actions) to work carried out *extralocally* by people not necessarily known to one another. *Social relations* hook work in local sites to the work of *institutions*, complexes of relations organized around a specific function such as law, health care, or education. For example, when a librarian engages in a partnership with a local social agency, the librarian's outreach work is entered into *social relations* that link that work to work carried out in government offices, and sites of social policy making. It is important to note, however, that although *social relations* concert and coordinate, they do not determine what goes on in a setting. Moreover, although IE researchers acknowledge the powerful role played by discourses in mediating people's actions, they maintain that people are always active in determining what actually goes on in a situation.

DeVault and McCoy (2002, p. 755) identify a sequence of steps to which IE studies generally conform. They are: 1) identify an experience, 2) identify some of the institutional processes that are shaping the experience, and 3) investigate those processes in order to describe analytically how they operate as grounds of the experience. Many IE researchers gather empirical data in local settings using field methods such as interviews, participant observation, and document traces. IE data are not regarded as windows on subjective experience, however, but rather as sources of clues to the social organization of the setting.

There is always something missing from even very good experiential accounts made by people who live the events in questions .... To understand the workings of any setting involves learning how people, seemingly positioned outside the setting, are nevertheless active inside it. (Campbell & Gregor, 2002, p. 60)

There are no hard and fast rules for analysing data, but IE researchers aim to read them *relationally*. It is "rather like grabbing a ball of string, finding a thread, and then pulling it out"(DeVault & McCoy, 2002, p. 755) and, as one clue leads to another the pattern of extralocal relations shaping the local is finally brought into view. The individual IE studies do not aim to solve all aspects of a puzzle, but rather to contribute to an emergent "map" of the *extended relations* of a setting.

IE's potential to support information-seeking research is best demonstrated by characterizing information seeking as a textually mediated *work* process. IE researchers define *work* generously to include information-seeking activities in and outside organizational settings, and they attend to the ways in which people from all walks of life and in diverse situations activate and interact with texts to accomplish their *work*. But as Smith (1999b, pp. 45–46) explains, "[R]ather than explaining how and why people act (or behave) as they do, we would seek from particular experience situated in the matrix of the everyday/everynight world to explore and display the relations, powers, and forces that organize and shape it." What IE can contribute to information-seeking research is a set of strategies for working with the people who experience the issues and concerns taken up by researchers to jointly explicate how those people's efforts to access information and support are *socially organized*.

IE's potential to support LIS research can also be demonstrated by pointing to previously established similarities between librarianship and the human service professions (e.g., Harris, 1992). IE has been successfully employed by researchers and practitioners in human service professions to jointly explore issues of access to services. The studies take as a starting point the suggestion that frontline workers in human service professions may routinely, albeit unwittingly, carry out work that undermines their ability to actually help the people they set out to serve

(Campbell & Gregor, 2002; DeVault & McCoy, 2002) and they aim to explicate how such situations are accomplished. Librarians, like human service professionals, act as intermediaries between people and systems and in fulfilling their professional mandate, they too carry out work that undermines the democratic goals of their profession (Wiegand, 2003).

To date, no IE studies have been reported in LIS literature, but this author recently conducted an IE study examining the social organization of children's librarians' work in support of multi-agency initiatives for families with young children. Analysis of the data indicates that IE provides public service librarians with new ways to look at their practice. For example, the analysis points to work processes through which librarians' well-intentioned actions on behalf of all families with young children succeed in meeting the needs for information and support primarily of families from middle-class backgrounds. If, as Walter (2001, p. 113) contends, librarians must become politically active in order to advocate for the people they aim to serve, then practitioners too need research that is for them rather than about them. IE is a hitherto untapped resource to be harnessed in that project.

Campbell, M., & Gregor, F. (2002). *Mapping social relations: A primer in institutional ethnography.* Aurora, ON: Garamond.

DeVault, M. L., & McCoy, L. (2002). Institutional ethnography: Using interviews to investigate ruling relations. In J. F. Gubrium & J. A. Holstein (Eds.), *Handbook of interview research: Context and methods* (pp. 751–776). Thousand Oaks, CA: Sage.

Harris, R. M. (1992). *Librarianship: The erosion of a woman's profession.* Norwood, NJ: Ablex.

Smith, D. E. (1987). *The everyday world as problematic: A feminist sociology.* Boston, MA: Northeastern University Press.

Smith, D. E. (1990a). *The conceptual practices of power: A feminist sociology of knowledge.* Toronto, ON: University of Toronto Press.

Smith, D. E. (1990b). *Texts, facts and femininity: Exploring the relations of ruling.* London: Routledge.

Smith, D. E. (1999a). From women's standpoint to a sociology for people. In J. L. Abu-Lughod (Ed.), *Sociology for the twenty-first century: Continuities and cutting edges* (pp. 65–83). Chicago: University of Chicago Press.

Smith, D. E. (1999b). *Writing the social: Critique, theory, and investigations.* Toronto, ON: University of Toronto Press.

Walter, V. (2001). *Children and libraries: Getting it right.* Chicago: American Library Association.

Wiegand, W. (2003). Broadening our perspectives. *The Library Quarterly, 7*3(1), v–x.

35
Integrative Framework for Information Seeking and Interactive Information Retrieval

Peter Ingwersen
Department of Information Studies
Royal School of Library and Information Science, Denmark
pi@db.dk

The integration of perspectives and models of information seeking and information retrieval (IS&R) into a holistic conceptual framework for research is currently under development (Ingwersen & Järvelin, submitted). Epistemologically it is founded on the cognitive viewpoint (Belkin, 1990) and based on elements of the cognitive theory for interactive information retrieval (IIR) put forward by Ingwersen (1992, 1996, 2001). Intentionality in the form of perceived work and search tasks or non-job related interests is central as the rationale underlying IS&R (see, e.g., Vakkari, 2003).

The framework reflects the understanding that IS&R is a process of cognition for the information–seeking actor(s) or team in context. Algorithmic and IIR, as well as information seeking (IS), involve cognitive and emotional representations from a variety of participating actors. Such representations are seen as manifestations of human cognition, reflection, emotion, or ideas forming part of IS&R components and kinds of interaction in context—as shown in Figure 35.1.

The framework operates with several kinds of contexts. First, algorithmic and IIR processes cannot stand alone, but are nested in IS behavior as special cases of information behavior (Wilson, 1999). Algorithmic IR, that is, the study of the interaction between information objects and information technology-based algorithms (arrow 4 in Figure 35.1), has no real meaning without human information interaction with IR systems (arrows 2–3). IIR itself functions in the context of IS—but reversely IS becomes increasingly *also* meaningful only

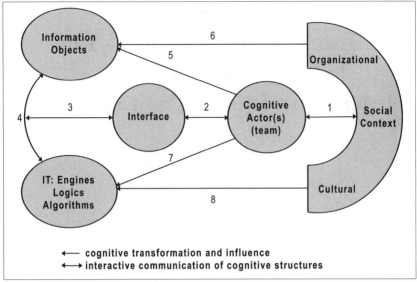

Figure 35.1   General model of cognitive information seeking and retrieval.
Note: From "The turn: The integration of information seeking and retrieval in context," by Ingwersen & Järvelin (Submitted). Arrow numbers refer to kinds of interaction or influence.

when considering the involvement of formal (algorithmic) IR engines and information structures. This is because progressively more informal communication channels become formalized due to the overpowering and integrative effects of modern IT. As information behavior (IB) is regarded, generation, acquisition, use, and communication of information—as well as information seeking—are affected. Typical information-seeking behavior is acquisition of information from knowledge sources, for instance, from a colleague, through (in)formal channels like social interaction in context (arrow 1), or via an IR system (arrows 2–4); IIR involves information acquisition via formal channels like the Internet, or from other organized sources. Information acquisition, use, and interaction are thus regarded central phenomena of IB, including IS&R.

Secondly, every information actor (or team of actors) operates in, and is influenced by, a dual contextual frame: that of the IT and information spaces surrounding the actor(s)—the systemic context on the left-hand side, Figure 35.1—and the socio-cultural organizational context to the right. By manifestations of practice the latter context influences over time the information space on the one hand (arrow 6) and the IT infra-structure (arrow 8) on the other. According to the framework, the study of one component (or an element), say interface functionality, should incorporate an awareness or direct involvement of the IT and informa-tion object components *as well as* of the searchers using the interface in some conceivable context. Potentially, all the other components thus influence the one under investigation.

Third, during interaction any actor is influenced by its past experi-ences (the historic context) and, *in turn*, actors influence their systemic and socio-cultural environment directly (arrows 1, 5, 7) and indirectly over time via other actors' information seeking and use of information. In this way, actors are shaping the change of scientific and professional domains, work and management strategies, trends of entertainment, or indeed the change of a paradigm. The framework strongly suggests the laboratory (Cranfield) model to become extended toward the searchers' interactive situation in context and increasingly involving dynamic non-binary relevance conceptions and realistic experimental settings. Similarly, the algorithmic components should be integrated in IS studies.

During the 1990s a number of conceptual models of the central phe-nomena and features of IS&R were developed, discussed, and *applied*, supporting the cognitive framework for IS&R. Kuhlthau's (1993) stage model for information searching fundamentally integrates affective char-acteristics, like uncertainty, confusion, and confidence with cognitive structures and actions. Saracevic's (1996) stratified model of IIR, later extended by Spink, Greisdorf, and Bateman (1998) also to cover regions of relevance, incorporated the algorithmic components into information interaction. Among others, Vakkari (2001, 2003), in traditional IR con-texts, and Wang, Hawk, and Tenopir (2000) studying the Web, applied Kuhlthau's model and cognitive approaches to their longitudinal empirical research. In a comprehensive investigation Bilal (2000) studied children's cognitive web IR patterns (2000). Vakkari (2001) produced a conceptual model of stages of work and search task performance. Byström and Järvelin (1995) empirically investigated work task complexity. They saw the perceived work task in context of experiences and work practice as the central phenomena behind information need development and IS. The higher the task complexity, the less the use of formal channels and sources. Many other studies (e.g., Ingwersen, 2001; Vakkari, 2003) analyzed or empirically investigated the interactivity connected to the arrows (1–4) in Figure 35.1. So far, however, the omission of best-match IR involvement in the research settings has been a typical limitation.

Since the Schamber, Eisenberg, and Nilan influential paper (1990), relevance has been regarded as a dynamic, multi-dimensional, and scalable phenomenon. Thanks to the above mentioned works and contributions by Cosijn and Ingwersen (2000) and Borlund (2003a) among many others, results from the softer IS&R research begin to penetrate into mainstream algorithmic IR experiments. For instance, Ruthven, et. al. (2003) made direct use of searcher behavior during IIR in order to adjust and test innovative relevance feedback algorithms. Novel performance measures, taking into account the dynamics of the IIR situation and applying graded relevance, have been proposed and tested experimentally recently (Kekäläinen & Järvelin, 2002). Borlund (2003b) proposed and tested a comprehensive cognitive IIR evaluation framework, based on simulated work tasks, in order to make experiments realistic and, at the same time, maintain experimental control.

The IS&R framework does not claim to cover IB as such. But it may contribute fresh perspectives for IB research, for example, by suggesting studies of relationships between information use and generation (arrows 2, 5–6). It is related to the Sense-Making theory, the social constructionist approach (Tuominen et. al., 2002), and probabilistic and plausible inference network models (Turtle & Croft, 1990). It emphasizes empirical tests of research hypotheses, that is, involving real-life situations and/or controlled simulations with test persons in realistic contexts, to apply combined data collection methods founded in the social sciences, and to use qualitative and statistically valid quantitative analysis methods.

Belkin, N. J. (1990). The cognitive viewpoint in information science. *Journal of Information Science: Principles and Practice, 16*(1), 11–15.

Bilal, D. (2000). Children's use of the Yahooligans! Web search engine: I. Cognitive, physical and affective behaviors on fact-based search tasks. *Journal of the American Society for Information Science, 51*, 646–665.

Borlund, P. (2003a). The concept of relevance in IR. *Journal of the American Society for Information Science and Technology, 54*, 913–925.

Borlund, P. (2003b). The IIR evaluation model: A framework for evaluation of interactive information retrieval systems. *Information Research, 8*(3). Retrieved March 16, 2004, from http://informationr.net/ir/8-3/paper152.html

Byström, K., & Järvelin, K. (1995). Task complexity affects information seeking and use. *Information Processing & Management, 31*, 191–213.

Cosijn, E., & Ingwersen, P. (2000). Dimensions of relevance. *Information Processing & Management, 36*, 533–550.

Ingwersen, P. (1992). *Information retrieval interaction*. London: Taylor Graham.

Ingwersen, P. (1996). Cognitive perspectives of information retrieval interaction: Elements of a cognitive IR theory. *Journal of Documentation, 52*(1), 3–50.

Ingwersen, P. (2001). Cognitive information retrieval. In: M. Williams (Ed.), *Annual Review of Information Science and Technology, 34*, 3–51.

Ingwersen, P., & Järvelin, K. (submitted). *The turn: The integration of information seeking and retrieval in context*. Manuscript submitted for publication.

Kekäläinen, J., & Järvelin, K. (2002). Using graded relevance assessments in IR evaluation. *Journal of the American Society for Information Science and Technology, 53*, 1120–1129.

Kuhlthau, C. C. (1993). *Seeking Meaning*. Norwood, NJ: Ablex.

Ruthven, I., Lalmas, M., & van Rijsbergen, C. J. (2003). Incorporating user search behaviour into relevance feedback. *Journal of the American Society for Information Science and Technology, 54*(6), 529–549.

Saracevic, T. (1996). Relevance reconsidered '96. In P. Ingwersen & N. O. Pors (Eds.), *Information science: Integration in perspective* (pp. 201–218). Copenhagen, Denmark: Royal School of Librarianship.

Schamber, L., Eisenberg, M. B., & Nilan, M. S. (1990). A re-examination of relevance: Toward a dynamic, situational definition. *Information Processing & Management, 26*, 755–776.

Spink, A., Greisdorf, H., & Bateman, J. (1998). From highly relevant to not relevant: Examining different regions of relevance. *Information Processing & Management, 34*, 599–621.

Tuominen, K., Talja, S., & Savolainen, R. (2002). Discourse, cognition and reality: Toward a social constrionist metatheory for library and information science. In H. Bruce, et al. (Eds.), *Emerging frameworks and methods* (pp. 217–284). Greenwood Village, CO: Libraries Unlimited.

Turtle, H., & Croft, W. B. (1990). Inference methods for document retrieval. *ACM-SIGIR Forum*, June, 1–24.

Vakkari, P. (2001). Changes in search tactics and relevance judgments in preparing a research proposal: A summary of findings of a longitudinal study. *Information Retrieval, 4*(3/4), 295–310.

Vakkari, P. (2003). Task based information searching. In B. Cronin (Ed.), *Annual Review of Information Science and Technology, 37*, 413–464.

Wang, P., Hawk, W. B., & Tenopir, C. (2000). Users' interaction with World Wide Web resources: an exploratory study using a holistic approach. *Information Processing & Management, 36*, 229–251.

Wilson, T. D. (1999). Models in information behavior research. *Journal of Documentation, 55*(3), 249–270.

36
Interpretative Repertoires

Pamela J. McKenzie
Faculty of Information and Media Studies
The University of Western Ontario, Canada
pmckenzie@uwo.ca

The *interpretative repertoire* is a theoretical and analytical concept used in some forms of discourse analysis. The term was developed by social psychologists, including Jonathan Potter and Margaret Wetherell, in response to the understanding among social psychologists that action results from processes operating within the heads of individuals. Such an understanding assumes that language and people are separate entities, and that language is a neutral medium between the social actor and the world. Accounts are therefore taken as transparent representations of events or mental states. Analysis within this paradigm relates to the truth or faithfulness of an account, or uses accounts as evidence of underlying processes. This analysis tends to look for similarities rather than variations within and across accounts, to aggregate accounts into categories such as "attitudes," and to downplay or discount the social situatedness of action.

A constructionist perspective, on the other hand, places an emphasis "on discourse as the vehicle through which the self and the world are articulated, and on the way different discourses enable different versions of selves and reality to be built" (Tuominen, Talja, & Savolainen, 2002, p. 273). Of critical importance is the assumption that "the things we hold as facts are materially, rhetorically, and discursively crafted in institutionalized social practices" (p. 278).

Potter and Wetherell's form of discourse analysis (described in detail in Potter & Wetherell, 1987; Potter, 1996; Wetherell, Taylor & Yates, 2001) is developed from the study of language use in a variety of disciplines. It builds on ethnomethodology, speech act theory, and semiology to explain how people use language to construct versions of the social world. Their perspective on discourse analysis recognizes that language allows for multiple versions of an event. This analysis is therefore concerned with the ways that individuals construct their versions to *do* things. In particular, a study of the variations in language use can shed light on the ways that speakers and writers construct their accounts and structure them to appear factual (the epistemological orientation of discourse), and the ways that they use accounts to serve rhetorical functions (the action orientation of discourse).

A constructionist perspective does not assume that an individual will represent people and events consistently over time. Rather, an individual is expected to develop a variety of different representations, depending on the function performed by the account. For example, one might tell two quite different stories when describing a night of youthful excess to a parent or to a room-mate. Regularity within the accounts of a single individual is therefore less interesting than the regularity that exists in the elements used by different speakers to describe the same person, event, or thing. Potter and Wetherell argue that a range of accounts of the same phenomenon will contain the same "relatively internally consistent, bounded language units which we have called...interpretative repertoires" (Wetherell & Potter, 1988, p. 171). The interpretative repertoire is a key component of this form of discourse analysis—as Wetherell and Potter (1988, p. 172) explain:

> Repertoires could be seen as building blocks speakers use for constructing versions of actions, cognitive processes, and other phenomena. Any particular repertoire is constructed out of a restricted range of terms used in a specific stylistic and grammatical fashion. Commonly these terms are derived from one or more key metaphors and the presence of a repertoire will often be signaled by certain tropes or figures of speech.

Identifying and analyzing interpretative repertoires is a major methodological component of discourse analysis. Data collection and analysis therefore revolve around several core requirements:

- Considering the account itself to be the primary object of research rather than seeing it as a transparent representation of an individual's attitudes and beliefs or the true nature of events

- Working with examples of language as it is actually used (transcripts or written texts) rather than summaries or paraphrases, and paying close attention to patterns in language use within examples
- Focusing on variations in the ways discourse is constructed, both within and across accounts, in order to begin to understand the epistemological and action orientations of specific versions

The work of Potter and Wetherell was developed for and has been used extensively in social psychology. It is therefore related to other constructionist approaches—such as positioning theory—in that discipline, as interpretative repertoires may be used to construct positions for one's self or others. This approach has also been used widely beyond social psychology. A search of Web of Science (February 9, 2004) identified a total of nearly 1,200 citations to the two central works explaining the use of interpretative repertoires (898 citations to Potter & Wetherell, 1987, and 278 to Potter, 1996). Recent studies citing these works and using the interpretative repertoire come from disciplines as diverse as management, forestry, addiction studies, women's health, and human-computer interaction. In information studies, Potter and Wetherell's work has been used to study the ways that accounts are constructed—for example, the ways that "technology" is reproduced as a series of interests (Jacobs, 2001) and the ways that authority claims are made, contested, and defended (McKenzie, 2003)—and the ways that information seeking and use can take discursive action (Tuominen & Savolainen, 1997).

As an analytic unit, the interpretative repertoire shows promise for those responding to calls for a constructionist metatheory in library and information science by Tuominen, Talja, and Savolainen (2002) and Tuominen and Savolainen (1997). Analyzing the interpretative repertoires used by information seekers can assist us in understanding the ways that information seeking and information sources are constructed in local discursive encounters. A study of the epistemological orientation of discourse may provide insights into the techniques speakers and writers use to evaluate information sources or information-seeking strategies. An analysis of the action orientation of discourse could show how information seekers within specific contexts justify their information behavior. Like other constructionist approaches, the use of interpretative repertoires has the potential to "[shift] the focus of research from understanding the needs, situations, and contexts of individual users to the production of knowledge in discourses, that is, within distinct conversational traditions and communities of practice" (Tuominen, Talja, & Savolainen, 2002, p. 273).

Jacobs, N. (2001). Information technology and interests in scholarly communication: A discourse analysis. *Journal of the American Society for Information Science & Technology, 52*, 1122–1133.

McKenzie, P. J. (2003). Justifying cognitive authority decisions: Discursive strategies of information seekers. *The Library Quarterly, 73*(3), 261–288.

Potter, J. (1996). *Representing reality: Discourse, rhetoric and social construction.* Thousand Oaks, CA: Sage.

Potter, J., & Wetherell, M. (1987). *Discourse and social psychology: Beyond attitudes and behaviour.* London: Sage.

Tuominen, K., & Savolainen, R. (1997). A social constructionist approach to the study of information use as a discursive action. In P. Vakkari, R. Savolainen, & B. Dervin (Eds.), *Information seeking in context: Proceedings of an international conference in information needs, seeking and use in different contexts* (pp. 81–96). London: Taylor Graham.

Tuominen, K., Talja, S., & Savolainen, R. (2002). Discourse, cognition, and reality: Toward a social constructionist metatheory for library and information science. In H. Bruce, R. Fidel, P. Ingwersen, & P. Vakkari (Eds.), *Emerging frameworks and methods: CoLIS 4. Proceedings of the fourth international conference on conceptions of library and information science* (pp. 271–283). Greenwood Village, CO: Libraries Unlimited.

Wetherell, M., & Potter, J. (1988). Discourse analysis and the identification of interpretive repertoires. In C. Antaki (Ed.), *Analyzing everyday explanation: A casebook of methods* (pp. 168–183). Newbury Park, CA: Sage.

Wetherell, M., Taylor, S. & Yates, S. J., Eds. (2001). *Discourse theory and practice: A reader.* London: Sage.

37
Krikelas's Model of Information Seeking

Jean Henefer and Crystal Fulton
Department of Library and Information Studies
University College Dublin, Ireland
Jean.Henefer@oceanfree.net and Crystal.Fulton@ucd.ie

James Krikelas proposed his model for information-seeking behavior in his landmark article, "Information-Seeking Behavior: Patterns and Concepts" (1983). While extensively cited over the last two decades, the model has been criticized for its simplicity and for its inherent character as a "library search model" (Case, 2002, p. 122). The latter observation is understandable, when one considers both Krikelas's professional background as an academic librarian and the bibliographic, system-oriented paradigm that dominated the period during which he conducted his studies. In fact, if one studies Krikelas's work from this historical perspective, his model in many respects can be viewed as signaling a turning point in the field of user studies, establishing new criteria to guide our research into information seeking, as well as laying the groundwork for the development of models and theories of information behavior in the years to come.

Krikelas developed his model in an effort to unify the field of user studies, one that he described as lacking a single theoretical approach. He was concerned by the recurring failure in library and information science to establish a distinction between use studies and user studies and the difficulties encountered in reaching a consensus on how we define information. It is in addressing this latter point that Krikelas takes his first major step away from the traditionalist approach. He dismisses the tendency to equate information with use of records or the literature as too narrow and conceptualizes information as any stimulus that affects one's certainty (a definition that encompasses the potential of information to create, as well as reduce, uncertainty), a point echoed by Dervin and Nilan (1986). Krikelas's reconsideration of information allowed for

225

the use of a range of possible sources including personal memory, inter-personal communication, individual impressions, and observations. Underpinning this holistic view of information is his belief that it is the individual user who defines for him or herself what is information. Krikelas acknowledges that if one accepts this view of information, then a problem arises for the researcher: how can one study the internal processes of an individual reducing uncertainty? He contends that observing information-seeking behavior in isolation will not provide reliable data, but must be accompanied by a clear understanding of the purpose behind the behavior. It is this recognition of the need to explore the various factors at work in the information world of the user that makes Krikelas's model important in the development of an alternative research approach to the traditional paradigm.

In order to accommodate the possible range of purposes affecting information seeking, and, in a real sense, information behavior as a whole, Krikelas presents three information activities as the foundation of his model: information gathering, information seeking, and information giving (Figure 37.1). To draw distinctions between the three possible activities, he explores the concept of information needs. Need is defined as a state of uncertainty recognized by the individual. Krikelas eschews the idea of unconscious needs as irrelevant to active information seeking, adopting instead a two-tiered analysis consisting of immediate needs and deferred needs. Information seeking is a response to what the individual perceives as an immediate need; information gathering is associated with deferred needs. In explaining the purpose behind information gathering (e.g., the accumulation of stimuli to be retained for future possible use), Krikelas cites as examples of information gatherers, scientists or academics keeping abreast of developments in their field who will store the stimuli in personal files or their memories for future reference. However, he does extend information gathering beyond this rather specialized view to include the observation that people on a day-to-day basis casually engage in information gathering at some level (consciously or indeed unconsciously) and suggests that the purpose behind this type of activity is an instinctive human drive to create an array of mental constructs (referred to as "a cognitive environmental 'map' ") to deal with uncertainty (Krikelas, 1983, p. 9). While Krikelas accepts that this kind of information activity is difficult to monitor, because it is fundamentally

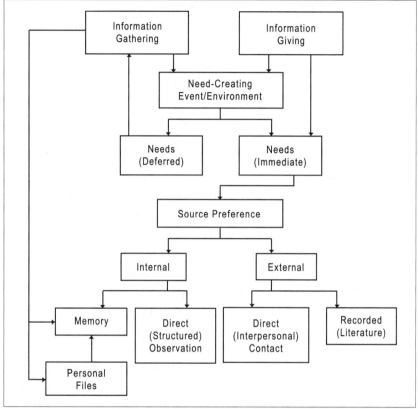

Figure 37.1   Krikelas's model of information seeking.
Note: From "Information-seeking behavior: Patterns and concepts," by J. Krikelas, 1983, *Drexel Library Quarterly*, 19, p. 17. Copyright 1983 by College of Information Science and Technology, Drexel University. Reprinted with permission.

internalized, he includes information gathering in his model, contributing a further dimension to our understanding and appreciation of human information behavior.

Returning to the subject of immediate information needs, Krikelas strives to develop a more in-depth understanding of the nature of needs. Drawing upon studies conducted on information needs (e.g., Warner, Murray, & Palmour, 1973; Chen & Hernon, 1981), Krikelas raises the point that a meaningful proportion of the population will say that they have no information needs. The environment in which one works or in which one lives will have a bearing on the type of information one needs as well as on how one defines that need. Additionally, need might arise from an isolated event. An awareness of the multiplicity and diversity of elements creating needs is, he contends, important in predicting information-seeking behavior. Krikelas continues his analysis of needs by making the distinction between "discrete" and "continuous" needs and states that an individual may employ entirely different information-seeking behaviors based on the nature of the particular problem. He concludes that while the nature of the individual's work environment and personality are important determinants of their information-seeking behavior, it is really the nature of the problem itself and the individual's perception of its urgency that will be most predictive of their activity.

On the basis of this analysis of information needs, Krikelas's model explores two aspects of information seeking: the categorization of sources and the reasons why individuals prefer certain sources. Krikelas extends the traditional concept of information source by including both internal and informal resources in his model of information seeking. With respect to the issue of source selection, he observed that, in most instances, individuals will rely on internal sources or, put another way, sources they create themselves. These include drawing upon one's own experience, accessing information stored in one's memory or personal files, or in some cases by observing the world around them. It is, however, the second category of source selection, the external resource, which he studies in more detail. When individuals make the decision to go outside themselves to find information, they will either seek the needed stimuli from a personal or impersonal resource. Krikelas describes this as the difference between direct contact with an individual who is perceived to have the needed information and indirect contact with materials (books, journals, documents, etc.) that may contain the required information. Once the decision is made to seek information from an external source, it is the direct, human source that is most preferred.

In analyzing the motives for source selection in information seeking, Krikelas develops an order of preference, with convenience, as opposed to accuracy, being the underlying principle. Information seekers will prefer to obtain their information from an individual who they know, who can be consulted with a minimum of effort, and who is believed to have the requisite knowledge (although in reality they may not have accurate information). Should this type of personally acquainted, direct source be unavailable, the information seeker will try to find an individual who is recognized by others as someone who will have the information. Krikelas contends that, in most cases, it is only when these two direct, personal approaches to information seeking are unsuccessful that the information seeker turns to the impersonal, material resources to satisfy his or her information need.

While Krikelas's focus is primarily information seeking, he does anticipate the analysis of information behavior by including information gathering and information giving in his model. The latter is described as "the act of disseminating messages" (1983, p. 13) that can be part of the process of information gathering or information seeking, depending on the nature of the individual's need. Krikelas's model marks a dynamic shift from the traditional approach to user studies by providing a more complex, rich analysis of the nature of information seeking, as well as establishing that our research interests must go beyond the specific act of information seeking to incorporate other facets of human information behavior.

Case, D. O. (2002). *Looking for information: A survey of research on information seeking, needs and behavior.* San Diego, CA: Academic Press.

Chen, C., & Hernon, P. (1981). *A regional investigation of citizens' information needs in New England.* Washington, DC: Department of Education.

Dervin, B., & Nilan, M. (1986). Information needs and uses. *Annual Review of Information Science and Technology, 21,* 3–33.

Krikelas, J. (1983). Information-seeking behavior: Patterns and concepts. *Drexel Library Quarterly, 19,* 5–20.

Warner, E. S., Murray, A. D., & Palmour, V. E. (1973). *Information needs of urban residents.* Washington, DC: Department of Health, Education and Welfare. Division of Library Programs.

38
Kuhlthau's Information Search Process

Carol Collier Kuhlthau
School of Communication, Information and Library Studies
Rutgers University, USA
kuhlthau@scils.rutgers.edu

The objective of library and information services and systems is to provide access to sources, information, and ideas. Enhanced access encompasses intellectual as well as physical access. Physical access addresses the location of sources and information. Intellectual access addresses interpretation of information and ideas within sources. The Information Search Process addresses intellectual access to information and ideas, and the process of seeking meaning.

The development of the Information Search Process as a conceptual framework is the result of two decades of empirical research that began with a qualitative study of secondary school students and the development of the initial model in 1983. This model was verified and refined through quantitative and longitudinal methods of diverse library users in 1989 and further developed in case studies continuing on to 2001 (Kuhlthau, 2004). Longitudinal methods were applied extensively, with data collected at three points during the process of information seeking using interview techniques to elicit personal accounts. All participants were real people with real tasks requiring extensive information seeking in libraries and information systems.

Based on George Kelly's personal construct theory, the Information Search Process depicts information seeking as a process of construction. The model describes common patterns in users' experience in the process of information seeking for a complex task that has a discrete beginning and ending, and requires construction and learning to be accomplished. Thoughts, feelings, and actions are described in six stages:

1) *Initiation* – a person becomes aware of a lack of knowledge or understanding, making uncertainty and

apprehension common.

2) *Selection* – a general area, topic, or problem is identified and initial uncertainty often gives way to a brief sense of optimism and a readiness to begin the search.

3) *Exploration* – inconsistent, incompatible information is encountered and uncertainty, confusion, and doubt frequently increase.

4) *Formulation* – a focused perspective is formed and uncertainty diminishes as confidence begins to increase.

5) *Collection* – information pertinent to the focused perspective is gathered and uncertainty subsides as interest and involvement in the project deepens.

6) *Presentation* – the search is completed, with a new understanding enabling the person to explain his or her learning to others, or in some way to put the learning to use.

People experience the Information Search Process holistically, with an interplay of thoughts, feelings, and actions (Figure 38.1). These studies were among the first to investigate the affective aspects or the feelings of a person in the process of information seeking along with the cognitive and physical aspects. One of the most surprising findings that was evident in

Stages	Task Initiation	Topic Selection	Prefocus Exploration	Focus Formulation	Information Collection	Search Closure	Starting Writing
Feelings	uncertainty	optimism	confusion, frustration, doubt	clarity	sense of direction/ confidence	relief	satisfaction or dissatisfaction
Thoughts		ambiguity — — — — — — — → specificity					
		Increase interest — — — — — — →					
Actions		seeking relevant information — — — ► seeking pertinent information					

Figure 38.1   Kuhlthau's Information Search Process.

Note: From *Seeking meaning: A process approach to library and information services*, 2nd edition (p. 82), by C. C. Kuhlthau, 2004, Westport, CT: Libraries Unlimited. Copyright by Carol Collier Kuhlthau. Adapted with permission.

the exploration stage was the discovery of a sharp increase in uncertainty and decrease in confidence after a search had been initiated. However, this experience is one of the most recognizable when people are presented with the model. Information seeking is a process of seeking meaning, not just finding and reproducing information. This process of construction involves exploration and formulation and rarely proceeds directly from selection to collection. The holistic experience influences the decisions and choices a person makes throughout the process of information seeking.

Within this task model the process of information seeking from the user's perspective may be thought of as a sequence of choices based on four criteria: task, time, interest, and availability. The person in the midst of seeking information is concerned with the task to be accomplished, the time allotted, personal interest, and information available. These criteria offer an alternative way of understanding relevant judgments in the context of a sequence of choices within the stages of the Information Search Process. People in the course of information seeking were found to base choices on these questions: Task: What am I trying to accomplish? Time: How much time do I have? Interest: What do I find personally interesting? Information available: What information is available to me? One or more of these may predominate at any given time.

Since an important element in theory building is to state findings and patterns revealed through extensive research as a conceptual premise, the conceptual premise proposed from the model of the Information Search Process is stated as an "uncertainty principle" for library and information services and systems. This uncertainty principle states that uncertainty is a cognitive state that commonly causes affective symptoms of anxiety and lack of confidence. Uncertainty and anxiety can be expected in the early stages of the process. The affective symptoms of uncertainty, confusion, and frustration are associated with vague, unclear thoughts about a topic or question. As knowledge states shift to more clearly focused thoughts, a parallel shift occurs in feelings of increased confidence. Uncertainty due to a lack of understanding, a gap in meaning, or a limited construct initiates the process of information seeking. The uncertainty principle is expanded by six corollaries, each of which offers an explanation of a particular component of the

Information Search Process: process, formulation, redundancy, mood, prediction, and interest.

The axiom that information reduces uncertainty is not necessarily the person's experience in information seeking. In certain situations information actually increases uncertainty. This research reveals that prior to formulation people are likely to experience heightened uncertainty in the face of unique, incompatible, inconsistent information that requires construction and interpretation to be personally understood. It seems helpful for people to *expect* uncertainty to increase during the exploration stage of the process rather than thinking that increased uncertainty is a symptom that something has gone wrong. The expectation that information reduces uncertainty initially may be at odds with the person's experience in actual situations of information seeking. These findings indicate the need for considering uncertainty as a natural, essential characteristic of information seeking as a sign of the beginning of learning and creativity. Uncertainty is a concept that offers insight into the user's quest for meaning within the Information Search Process.

How can library and information services and systems be responsive to the stages of the Information Search Process? The concept of a zone of intervention drawn from Vygotsky's zone of proximal development has been introduced for diagnosing a user's need for assistance and support. The zone of intervention is that area in which a user can do with guidance and assistance what he or she cannot do alone or can do only with difficulty. Intervention in this zone enables the person to move along in the information-search process. Intervention outside of this zone is intrusive on the one hand and overwhelming on the other. Intervention on both sides of the zone of intervention is inefficient and unnecessary.

Taken together, the stages of the Information Search Process, uncertainty principle, and concept of a zone of intervention proposes a conceptual framework for understanding information seeking as a process of construction from the user's perspective (Kuhlthau, 2004). The conceptual framework is based on the experience and behavior of people involved in extensive research projects that need to be accomplished in a prescribed period of time. People using libraries and information systems to accomplish complex tasks that require them to gain new understandings commonly experience increased uncertainty and decreased confidence in the early phases of information seeking. Increased uncertainty in the Information Search

Process indicates a zone of intervention for librarians, information professionals, and information system designers. The conceptual framework of the Information Search Process also challenges researchers to look beyond the query to the inquiry to discover ways to enhance intellectual access that leads to learning, creativity, and innovation.

Kelly, G. (1963). *A theory of personality: The psychology of personal constructs.* New York: W. W. Norton.

Kuhlthau, C. (2004). *Seeking meaning: A process approach to library and information services (*2nd edition). Westport, CT: Libraries Unlimited.

Vygotsky, L. (1978). *Mind in society: The development of higher psychological processes.* Cambridge, MA: Harvard University Press.

39
Library Anxiety

Patricia Katopol
The Information School
University of Washington, USA
pfk@u.washington.edu

The theory of library anxiety was developed by Constance Mellon and explicated in *Library anxiety: A grounded theory and its development* (Mellon, 1986). Mellon worked with academic librarians and English composition faculty in a two-year-long project that sought to integrate library research skills with composition classes. As part of the study, students were questioned about their research processes for class assignments. Instead of talking about their difficulties in searching for information, Mellon found that students talked about their feelings about the library itself. They reported feeling lost, afraid to approach the library staff, and unable to find their way around the library. Mellon labeled these collected feelings of discomfort *library anxiety*.

Students with library anxiety exhibited a type of anxiety that manifested itself as a sense of powerlessness when beginning an information search that required using the library. This powerlessness was due to an inability to navigate the library and a feeling of inferiority when they compared their library skills to those of other students. Students with library anxiety were unable to determine how they should begin their reference search and were unable to find the materials they needed in the library. They were also hesitant to ask library staff the questions that might allay their anxiety and improve their skills for fear of appearing inadequate.

While these findings were not new to librarians, the faculty was generally unaware of the problem. By defining and labeling the students' problems as library anxiety, Mellon was able to convey to faculty outside of the library that these behaviors constituted problems that needed to be addressed. She likened this situation to an awareness by faculty that some students had anxious feelings about math or test-taking, but it was not until these feelings were labeled math anxiety or test anxiety that constructive steps were taken to deal with them. Mellon suggested that using methods similar to those that successfully decrease other types of anxieties might decrease library anxiety. For example, the anxiety should be recognized as legitimate, and the anxious person provided with experiences in which he or she can be successful (Mellon, 1986).

In addition to introducing the theory, *Library anxiety: A grounded theory and its development* contributed to the development and encouragement of qualitative research in information science. Mellon appealed for the use of qualitative research as it provided a deeper insight into information behavior and the information-related events under study. By using the participants' own words regarding their information behavior to inform the study, a truer picture of the behavior is revealed.

Over the years, the theory of library anxiety has benefited from a number of contributions. While Mellon studied undergraduates, behaviors constituting library anxiety have been shown in graduate students as well (Jiao & Onwuegbuzie, 1998). Other work has shown that library anxiety was more than just a collection of the behaviors of normally anxious individuals (those having trait anxiety), but was held by students without trait anxiety, necessitating additional study on the specific phenomenon of library anxiety (Jiao & Onwuegbuzie, 1999). In the public library environment, Liu presented information behavior of immigrants and minorities that appears to have the same general characteristics as library anxiety (Liu, 1995). The Library Anxiety Scale was developed as an attempt to quantify feelings about the library (Bostick, 1993). It notes five dimensions of library anxiety: barriers with staff, affective barriers, comfort with the library, knowledge of the library, and mechanical barriers.

While library anxiety continues to be a useful theory for explaining a particular type of information behavior, it is a creature of its time, placing the library as central for student information-gathering and research activities. The Multidimensional Library Anxiety Scale was developed in order to correct some of the limitations of the original Library Anxiety Scale and expand on the types of information behavior to which the theory might apply (Van Kampen, 2004). For example, gender, online source preferences, and use of off-campus information resources were added to the original scale. Both scales are useful additions to studies of information behavior; however, they may not adequately allow for the participant voice that Mellon found so meaningful in her work.

As students attending American colleges and universities come from increasingly diverse backgrounds, the theory of *stereotype threat* from psychology may be a useful addition to the theory. Stereotype threat manifests itself as a fear of being seen as reinforcing a negative stereotype (Steele, 1999). While everyone suffers from it at some time, stereotype threat is a particular problem for black students. Many students, white and black, hesitate to ask a question at the reference desk for fear of appearing foolish. However, black students may believe that asking a question will somehow prove to the librarian that the student is not qualified to be at the university—that the student does not possess the requisite skills or knowledge because of his or her race. Stereotype threat, coupled with the traditional elements of library anxiety, may disproportionately inhibit black students from having useful and positive library experiences. Research is needed on how stereotype threat and library anxiety may affect the information behavior of other minorities.

As library anxiety has been updated to include factors of gender, use of electronic resources, etc., it may be usefully applied to situations outside of the library, such as information behavior in the workplace. Such behavior is often explained by theories of organizational behavior or communications (Morrison, 1993, 2002). The information behavior of new employees, unfamiliar with workplace resources and afraid of appearing incompetent by asking about them, may be very similar to the behavior of students exhibiting library anxiety. Researchers examining this behavior from an organizational or communications perspective might benefit from adapting elements of library anxiety to their theories on information behavior in the workplace.

Mellon confirmed what librarians have always known about the overwhelming tangle of fears and concerns that prohibit students from effectively engaging in library research. She pointed out and explained the problem for faculty and school administrators, so they could take measures for helping students to successfully overcome their anxiety (Van Scoyoc, 2003). Participatory research methods, such as action research, that can include librarians, faculty, and students, help to integrate research and practice in the field, creating real-life solutions that may reduce this specific anxiety (Jiao & Onwuegbuzie, 1999).

Library anxiety remains a strong theory that helps to explain information behavior, not just in undergraduates, but in an expanding universe of
actors, such as immigrants, new hires, and even graduate students, who
find themselves lost in an unfamiliar information world.

Bostick, S. L. (1993). The development and validation of the library anxiety scale in
   research in reference effectiveness. In M. E. Murfin & J. B. Whitlatch (Eds.),
   *Proceedings of a preconference sponsored by the Research and Statistics
   Committee, Management and Operation of Public Services Section, Reference and
   Adult Services Division, American Library Association, San Francisco, June 26,
   1992* (pp. 1–7). Chicago: ALA.

Jiao, Q., & Onwuegbuzie, A. (1998). Perfectionism and library anxiety among graduate students. *Journal of Academic Librarianship, 24*(5), 365–371.

Jiao, Q. G., & Onwuegbuzie, A. J. (1999). Is library anxiety important? *Library
   Review, 48*(6), 278–282.

Liu, M. (1995). Ethnicity and information seeking. In J. B. Whitlatch (Ed.), *Library
   users and reference services* (pp. 123–134). New York: Haworth Press.

Mellon, C. (1986). Library anxiety: A grounded theory and its development. *College &
   Research Libraries, 47*, 160–165.

Morrison, E. (1993). Newcomer information seeking: Exploring types, modes, sources,
   and outcomes. *Academy of Management Journal, 36*, 557–589.

Morrison, E. (2002). Information seeking within organizations. *Human
   Communication Research, 28*(2), 229–242.

Steele, C. (1999). Thin ice: "Stereotype threat" and black college students. [Electronic
   version]. *The Atlantic Monthly, 284*, 44–54.

Van Kampen, D. J. (2004). Development and validation of the multidimensional library
   anxiety scale. *College & Research Libraries, 65*, 28–34.

Van Scoyoc, A. M. (2003). Reducing library anxiety in first-year students. *Reference &
   User Services Quarterly, 42*(4), 329–341.

40
Monitoring and Blunting

Lynda M. Baker
Library and Information Science Program
Wayne State University, USA
aa0838@wayne.edu

Suzanne M. Miller, a psychologist, developed her monitoring-and-blunting (M&B) theory through her research on stress and information behavior. She has published in many psychology journals, such as the *Journal of Personality and Social Psychology*, *Health Psychology*, and *Journal of Consulting and Clinical Psychology*. Chapters describing M&B may be found in *Coping and health* (Miller, 1980), *Learned resourcefulness* (Miller, 1990), and *Personal coping: Theory, research, and application* (Miller, 1992).

M&B theory is based on an earlier theory of avoidance and vigilance, which was developed to explain people's information-seeking behavior during stressful or aversive situations. The theory posits that, when faced with an aversive event, people differ in their preference for information. Monitors are the people who seek information to keep apprised of the threat-related situation because knowing "what is happening" helps to decrease their stress. Blunters use distracting behavior to avoid information about a stressful event because it increases their stress levels. They may, however, seek information after the stressful event has passed (Baker, 1994).

M&B theory has been used in psychology, medicine, nursing, and library and information science. It is very relevant to information behavior. On a daily basis, people deal with stressful events in both their personal and work environments. Although most theories/models describe information seeking as situationally based, they do not differentiate between a stressful or non-stressful situation. M&B theory fills the gap in the research on information behavior by providing insight into information seeking as a coping mechanism in times of stress. It acknowledges that each person is unique in her/his desire for information.

Miller (1987) developed the Miller Behavioral Style Scale (MBSS) to measure one's self-reported coping style. The MBSS is composed of four short stress-evoking scenarios: having dental work done; being held hostage in a public building; hearing rumors of being laid off from work; and experiencing a deep dive during an air flight. Four monitoring and four blunting statements follow each scenario. Respondents are asked to choose all the statements that best describe their reactions to the particular scenario. Their score is calculated by summing the number of both monitoring and blunting responses and then subtracting the blunting score from the monitoring score. The mean or median is used to divide respondents into monitors (scores above the mean/median) or blunters (scores below the mean/median).

M&B seems to be related to and support both Krikelas's (1983) information-seeking model and Dervin's (1992) Sense-Making model. The former includes both immediate information seeking, as well as the collecting of information to satisfy deferred information needs. The monitors would fall into the first category, while blunters could fit into the second one. M&B also relates to the Sense-Making model because both monitors and blunters seek information, albeit in different time frames.

One of the strengths of M&B theory is that it provides an explanation of the different information-seeking strategies people use to cope with stress. It may explain why some people want very detailed information, while others prefer scant information about a threatening event. One weakness identified by Steptoe (1989) concerns the scenarios used in the MBSS in that people may find it difficult to determine how they would react to situations they have not experienced. Another factor that the M&B does not take into account is the information-seeking behavior of people who continually face stress, such as people with chronic diseases. For example, in her study of women with multiple sclerosis, Baker (1994) found that although monitors wanted more information than did blunters, the distinction tended to blur over time. Blunters, who had multiple sclerosis for more than two years, sought information which suggests that as they became more accustomed to the disease and its exacerbations, they did not view information as stressful.

One possible future use of M&B theory would be to study people in a variety of stressful situations, such as students doing school assignments, which could connect M&B and Kuhlthau's (1988) information search process. Other stressful situations worth exploring would include people who are seeking health, legal, or financial information. This theory also has practical implications. For example, if reference librarians under-stood monitoring and blunting behavior and its external cues, they could tailor information to the person's coping style. Monitors may ask for everything in the library about their topic, whereas blunters will ask for "something" on their topic. Their vague request suggests that they do not know much about the topic and do not wish to know a lot about it at this particular time. Being familiar with the M&B theory would allow librar-ians to tailor information to the specific needs of their clients.

Baker, L. M. (1994). *The information needs and information-seeking patterns of women coping with and adjusting to multiple sclerosis* (Doctoral dissertation, University of Western Ontario, London, Canada, 1994). *Dissertation Abstracts International, 56*, 93194.

Dervin, B. (1992). From the mind's eye of the user: The Sense-Making qualitative-quan-titative methodology. In J. D. Glazier & R. R. Powell (Eds.), *Qualitative research in information management* (pp. 61–84). Englewood, CO: Libraries Unlimited.

Krikelas, J. (1983). Information-seeking behavior: Patterns and concepts. *Drexel Library Quarterly, 19*, 5–20

Kuhlthau, C. C. (1988). Developing a model of the library search process: Cognitive and affective aspects. *RQ [Reference Quarterly], 28*(7), 232–242.

Miller. S. M. (1980). When is a little information a dangerous thing? Coping with stressful events by monitoring versus blunting. In S. Levine & H. Ursing (Eds.), *Coping and health* (pp. 145–169). NY: Plenum.

Miller, S. M. (1987). Monitoring and blunting: Validation of a questionnaire to assess styles of information seeking under threat. *Journal of Personality and Social Psychology, 52*(2), 345–353.

Miller, S. M. (1990). To see or not to see: Cognitive informational styles in the coping process. In M. Rosenbaum (Ed.), *Learned resourcefulness* (pp. 95–126). New York: Springer.

Miller, S. M. (1992). Individual differences in the coping process: What to know and when to know it. In B. N. Carpenter (Ed.), *Personal coping: Theory, research, and application* (pp. 77–92). Westport, CT: Praeger.

Steptoe, A. (1989). An abbreviated version of the Miller Behavioral Style Scale. *British Journal of Clinical Psychology, 28*, 183–184.

41
Motivational Factors for Interface Design

Carolyn Watters
Faculty of Computer Science
Dalhousie University, Canada
watters@cs.dal.ca

Jack Duffy
Faculty of Management
Dalhousie University, Canada
J.Duffy@cs.dal.ca

A metalevel analysis of psychological literature on motivation gives some insight into interface design decisions that may consciously or unconsciously affect the motivation of the user and ultimately the success of the system. Usability cannot be considered in isolation of individual user goals, yet little research focuses on design features that integrate psychosocial issues known to impact performance (Preece et al., 2002; Shneiderman, 1997).

Increased motivation has been correlated with enhanced task performance, persistence, and enjoyment (Pinder, 1998) and has been shown to significantly influence overall user satisfaction (Al-Gahtani & King, 1999). Furthermore, task characteristics that have an impact on motivation (e.g., duration, type of goal, and presence of rewards) may influence user evaluations more than interface factors, such as layout and design, use of graphics, and even perceived currency of information (Amabile, 1996).

Motivation is used to refer to those beliefs and attitudes that affect task engagement and learning in various contexts of activity. Motivational constructs in the literature are reviewed from diverse research perspectives. Four motivational theories related to interface design were chosen using the following criteria: widely cited, evidence based, and overlapping core ideas. In other words, an intuitive triangulation approach was

242

used to choose a workable set of theories, namely, self-determination, goal theory, self-efficacy, and attribution theories. The choices are not exhaustive and there are other theories that are also useful for interface design.

Both self-determination and goal theories focus on the reasons for engagement. *Self-determination theory* suggests that people have a basic need to feel competent and that intrinsic motivation results when individuals feel that they are competent and acting in self-determined fashion. This is supported by evidence (Deci et al., 1981; Medway, 1982; Ryan & Deci, 2001) that negative feedback and external pressures reduce intrinsic motivation in tasks. Intrinsic motivation leads to immersive behavior (Csikszentmihalyi, 1990) when the choices for success match the individual's ability to perform, when the skills are relatively high, and the goal relatively challenging.

Goal theory deals with the relationship between goals and behavior in achieving those goals. For example, performance-approach goals (Elliot & Dwek, 1988) are achieved by behavior that engages the individual in activities leading to successful completion while performance-avoiding goals are achieved by risk management behavior that lets the individual disengage and thereby not fail and not "look stupid." There is some evidence that performance-approach goals increase motivation and that higher achieving students have high levels of achievement goals (Wentzel, 1993).

Self-efficacy (Bandura, 1977, 1986) considers self-beliefs of competence as well as feeling a sense of *control* over outcomes. Self-efficacy theory is related to the confidence an individual has in his or her ability to complete some task successfully and may be measured by the strength of this confidence, the breadth of applicability of this confidence, and the difficulty of the task for which this confidence extends. Positive feedback, however, does not necessarily increase these beliefs (Mueller & Dwek, 1998).

Attribution theory integrates competence beliefs and expectancies of success (Eccles & Wigfield, 2002) with incentives to engage in achievement tasks. Attribution theory (Weiner, 1985) puts more weight on the individual's perception of their competency than on other measures in building motivation. This perception comes from a combination of their

Table 41.1   Design implications.

External Indicator	Design Implication	Theories supporting		
Control Related				
Creativity	Choices Multimodal activities	S-D	Goal	
Problem solving	Allow questions, chats	Goal		
Adjusts strategies after setbacks	Include coping models Default sequences	S-E	Attrib	
Error seen as threat	Reduce fear; encourage trying and hints	SE		
Context Related				
Adaptive strategies Effective decision making	Provide credible models Scaffolding	S-E	Attrib	Goal
Bounces back	Lower stress and anxiety Hints and examples	S-E	Goal	
Active participation	Provide rationales	S-D	Goal	
Feedback Related				
Balanced responses Goal management	Acknowledge progress Relate performance to goal	S-E	Attrib	Goal
Accepts feedback	Give competence informing feedback	S-E	Attrib	
Error as opportunity	Treat error as learning opportunity, give hints	S-E		
Persistence	Develop risk tolerance, diaries	Goal		
Defensive to feedback	Acknowledge negative emotions Frustration outlet, chat, email	SE		
Engagement Related				
Collaboration	Encourage collaboration	S-D	Goal	
Personalization	Rules and scenarios	S-D		
Little or no effort Deception	Emphasize rationales	S-E S-D	Attrib Goal	
Passivity Abandonment	Increase choice and control Allow questions	S-D	Attrib	Goal
Task avoidance Disengagement	Support autonomy	S-E-S-D	Attrib	Goal
Disengagement	Encourage collaboration	Goal		
Competency Related				
Takes on challenge Risk taking	Support risk without threat Hints, feedback on attempts	S-E	S-D	
Takes on challenge	Present valid challenge Open ended challenges	S-E	Attrib	
Innovation	Celebrate innovation	S-D	Goal	
High effort for outcomes	Attend to growth Personal progress	S-E	Attrib	Goal

ability to perform the task, effort required to complete the task, the difficulty of the task, and plain luck in completing the task.

Of interest is examining not only the features defined by each of these theories but the convergence of features among these four theories. Also of interest are the implications of the theoretical background on both the internal processes of the users and the external or behavioral indicators stemming from those internal cognitive processes. Uncovering convergence of external indicators helps to identify design features of interfaces that can be used to minimize the effect of negative factors and maximize the effect of positive factors.

In Table 41.1. external indicators were grouped by sorting both positive and negative cognitive processes into five categories (control, context, feedback, engagement, and competency). This typology directly leads to design implications. This general level framework, derived from a metalevel review of the literature, can be used by interface designers to make informed decisions in the design process.

The use of constructs which affect motivation positively and/or prevent discouragement can be integrated with task-specific usability design guidelines to enhance user engagement. This framework is intended to complement and inform interaction design, both as a descriptive and prescriptive template for interface design decisions. Such a framework also functions as an aid in the assessment and evaluation of existing applications, where user motivation plays a significant role in the success of the system. Clearly, these examples by no means exhaust the relevant factors and research is needed into effect size and task dependence.

Acknowledgment

The authors would like to acknowledge the contribution to this work by Isabel Redondo while a MCS student at Dalhousie University.

Al-Gahtani, S. S., & King, M. (1999). Attitudes, satisfaction and usage: Factors contributing to each in the acceptance of information technology. *Behaviour & Information Technology, 18*, 277–297.

Amabile, T. (1996). *The social psychology of creativity.* New York: Springer-Verlag.

Bandura, A. (1977). Self-efficacy: Toward a unifying theory of behavioral change. *Psychological Review, 84*, 191-215.

Bandura, A. (1986). *Social foundations of thought and action: A social-cognitive theory.* Upper Saddle River, NJ: Prentice Hall.

Csikszentmihya, M. (1990). *Flow = The psychology of optimal experience.* New York: Harper & Row.

Deci, E. L., Schwartz, A. J., Sheinman, L., & Ryan, R. M. (1981). An instrument to assess adults' orientations toward control versus autonomy with children: Reflections on intrinsic motivation and perceived competence. *Journal of Educational Psychology, 73*, 642–650.

Eccles, J., & Wigfield, A. (2002). Motivational beliefs, values, and goals. *Annual Review of Psychology, 53*, 109–132.

Elliott, E. S., & Dwek, C. S. (1988). Goals: An approach to motivation and achievement. *Journal of Personality and Social Psychology, 54*, 5–12.

Medway, F. (1982). The efforts of effort feedback and performance patterns on children's attributions and task persistence. *Contemporary Education Psychology, 7*, 26–34.

Mueller, C. M., & Dwek, C. S. (1998). Praise for intelligence can undermine children's motivation and performance. *Journal of Personality and Social Psychology, 75*, 33–52.

Pinder, C. C. (1998). *Work motivation in organizational behaviour.* Upper Saddle River, NJ: Prentice Hall.

Preece, J., Rogers, Y., & Sharp, H. (2002). *Interaction design: Beyond human-computer interaction.* New York: John Wiley & Sons.

Ryan, R. M., & Deci, E. L. (2001). Intrinsic and extrinsic motivations: Classic definitions and new directions. *Contemporary Educational Psychology, 25*, 54–56.

Shneiderman, B. (1997). *Designing the user interface: Strategies for effective human-computer interaction* (3rd ed.). Reading, MA: Addison-Wesley.

Weiner, B. (1985). An attributional theory of achievement motivation and emotion. *Psychological Review, 92*, 548–573.

Wentzell, K. R. (1993). Motivation and achievement in early adolescence: The role of multiple classroom goals. *Journal of Early Adolescence, 13*, 4–20.

42
Network Gatekeeping

Karine Barzilai-Nahon
The Information School
University of Washington, USA
karineb@u.washington.edu

The concept of *gatekeeper* was coined by the social psychologist Kurt Lewin (1947, 1951). His theory of "channels and gatekeepers" was developed as a means of understanding how to produce widespread social changes in communities. Gatekeeping theories have since been applied in various fields. In disciplines such as communication and journalism, the notions of gatekeeping and gatekeepers are used to understand social systems; in the health sciences, operations research, and technology development, the notions are used to augment service practices (Beckman & Mays, 1985; Motoyer-Duran, 1993; Shoemaker, 1991; Shumsky & Pinker, 2003). While traditional gatekeeping theories were mainly applied in communication (Donohue, Olien, & Tichenor, 1989; Gieber, 1956; Shoemaker, 1991; White, 1950), they mainly referred to gatekeeping as a selection process and offered scholars a framework for analyzing, evaluating, and comprehending how communication or news selection occurred and why some items were selected while others were rejected. More generally, they offered a framework to continue Lewin's research on social change, and examine sources for cultural diversity.

As networks, and more specifically, the Internet, became ubiquitous, however, scholars have increasingly used the term *gatekeeper* (Birnhack & Elkin-Koren, 2003; Cornfield & Rainie, 2003; Hargittai, 2000) for illustration rather than referencing a specific theoretical framework. Cyberspace has notably changed both the identity and role of gatekeepers as well the gatekeeping process.

Consistent with the initial course of gatekeeping research—as discussed in the communication literature—Barzilai-Nahon (2004) proposed *network gatekeeping theory* (NGT). Comprising multidisciplinary aspects, including information systems, management, political science, and sociology, NGT offers new definitions of gatekeeping and gatekeepers by adapting traditional concepts to a networked society. Based on an examination of power relations on the Internet and a space of information, NGT conceptualizes the distribution of information and processes of information control. It enables one to analyze centralization in networks, which have a decentralized design, and are commonly viewed as egalitarian spaces. NGT has many ramifications for how we comprehend information dissemination and user behavior on the Internet.

NGT comprises five basic concepts:

1) *Gate* – The entrance to, or the exit from, a network or its sections.

2) *Gatekeeping* – The process of controlling information as it moves through a gate. Activities include selection, addition, withholding, display, channeling, shaping, manipulation, repetition, timing, localization, integration, and disregard and deletion of information.

3) *Gatekeeping Mechanism* – Tool, technology or methodology used to carry out the process of gatekeeping.

4) *Network Gatekeeper* – An entity (person, organization, or governing body) that has the discretion to exercise gatekeeping through a gatekeeping mechanism in networks and can choose the extent to which to exercise it.

5) *Gated* – An entity that is subject to a gatekeeping process.

Gatekeepers in networks have three main functions: 1) to prevent the entrance of undesired information from the outside; 2) to prevent the exit of undesired information to the outside; and 3) to control information inside the network. Table 42.1 summarizes the exclusiveness of NGT compared to traditional gatekeeping theories.

Because the traditional concept of *gatekeeping* was developed mainly as a part of mass communication discourse, the players were conceived as acting in sender-receiver roles. The gatekeeper was conceived as a mass media agent (such as a newspaper, television, or radio station) playing the role of the sender, with the gated, (such as a newspaper reader, television viewer, or radio listener) playing the role of the receiver. The gatekeeper was responsible for editing, producing, and distributing information to be received by the gated.

Table 42.1   Traditional gatekeeping vs. network gatekeeping.

	Traditional Gatekeeping	Network Gatekeeping Theory (NGT)
Gatekeeping process	Mainly a selection process	Information control that includes activities such as selection, addition, withholding, display, channeling, shaping, manipulation, repetition, timing, localization, integration, disregard, and deletion
Focus on gatekeepers	The individual gatekeeper	Focus on two dimensions: authority and functional. Different levels in each dimension (e.g., governments, regulators, search providers, network service providers, organizations, individuals)
Focus on gatekeeping mechanism	Editorial mechanisms	Nine categories are part of gatekeeping mechanisms (e.g., censorship, channeling, infrastructure mechanisms), and one meta-category, the regulation mechanism
Relationship	Relations of sender-receiver	Frequent exchange interaction between gated and gatekeeper
Information	Notion of source-destination	No necessary association between source-destination and gatekeeper-gated
	Only gatekeepers produce and create information freely	The gated also create and produce information
Alternatives	No alternatives to gatekeeping	Possible circumvention of gatekeepers and gatekeeping mechanisms
Power	Gatekeeper has power, the gated has none	The bargaining power of the gated is on the rise. On the other hand, gatekeepers have more mechanisms to control information
Number of gatekeepers	One to a few	A few to many
Types of gatekeepers	One to a few	A few to many

In the context of networks, however, the notion of separate sender-receiver is no longer valid. During any network interaction, the roles of sender and receiver are repeatedly exchanged, with the gatekeeper and the gated playing both roles.

Consistent with the notion of sender-receiver, traditional literature treats information that passes from sender to receiver as having a source-to-destination direction. The source is presumed to be the originator of the information (the gatekeeper) and the information (the gated) is presumed to be the destination. However, in the context of networks, information can also be produced by the gated, and the gated can serve as a source; likewise, the gatekeeper can also serve as a destination point. Furthermore, according to the traditional literature, only gatekeepers create and produce information; the gated audience is not considered capable of producing and creating information freely. The gated only rarely receive the right to create information, in most cases under the control and authorization of the gatekeeper. For example, a newspaper reader asked to react to an article may do so only by means of a column reserved for reader responses, and one of the editors must approve it for publication. NGT argues that in networks, the relationship between gatekeepers and gated is more complex.

It is likely that the gatekeepers create and produce greater volumes of information than the gated because of their vast resources. Nevertheless, the gated can create and produce information independently as well, without having to pass through a content gatekeeper. But when the gated create information independently, its significance is rather low because of the limited exposure it receives compared to information disseminated by the gatekeepers that control most of the audience's attention. The existence of alternative public platforms to gatekeepers is significant in itself because it contributes to a more pluralized cyberspace. Another way of analyzing gated power in networks is by focusing on the production of information rather than on the creation of information. The gated can produce information in networks that was created by gatekeepers, an ability that enhances the power of the gated.

A major deterministic claim put forth by the traditional concept of gatekeeping is that the gated's ability to circumvent the gatekeeping process is minimal. The only alternative is to circumvent a specific gatekeeper by moving to another within the same community, which may well be subject to the same biases and procedures. For example, a reader can switch from one newspaper to another, but the process of gatekeeping through the editorial process continues. NGT shows that in networks the gated can circumvent gatekeeping. For example, through publishing an independent Web site, the gated can respond to events that she cannot respond to through traditional channels of the media and without the intervention of gatekeeping. However, circumvention is not always possible even in networks since often gatekeepers use more than one mechanism, depending on context, which makes the circumvention more difficult.

In traditional literature, relationships between gatekeepers and their audience are mainly uni-directional. This strengthens the gatekeepers' power and their control over their audience. Because of the presumed sender-receiver roles of gatekeeper (sender) and the gated (receiver), the gated are not perceived as possessing any significant power. In a networked environment the situation is significantly more complicated. The gated may have alternatives and the power to create and produce information. Their bargaining position and power are enhanced relative to traditional roles. Consequently, gatekeepers must avoid conditions that encourage the gated to overcome gates that have been posted in networks. On the other hand, gatekeepers have more mechanisms of information control, which they can exercise over the gated (see Figure 42.1).

Traditional gatekeeping researchers usually use ethnographic case study methodologies. In analyzing gatekeeping in a networked context, this might not be sufficient. Barzilai-Nahon (2004) suggests a combination of qualitative and quantitative methodology, using a content analysis of the information combined with quantitative methods, to analyze models as part of the general NGT. NGT allows one to understand information control and to predict patterns of user behavior in the networked environment. For example, it was found that senior members of virtual communities are less likely to post messages that harm the community compared to new members (Barzilai-Nahon, 2004).

In summary, the Internet poses new paradigmatic challenges. On the one hand, it is a more open space than other offline means of communication and allows more diversity in the behavioral modes of users. On the other hand, information control is frequent, and consequently, scholars

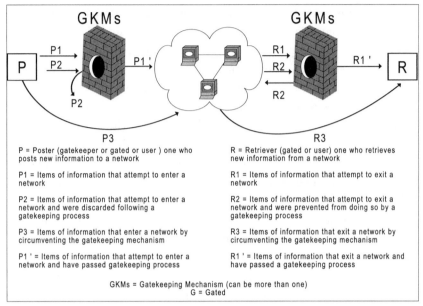

Figure 42.1 Illustrative model of network gatekeeping.

and practitioners should be aware of the importance of analyzing cyber-space through the lens of gatekeeping. NGT enables one to conceptualize and analyze information flow over the Internet, both technically and socially. NGT emphasizes power relationships among relevant actors through information flow, and identifies potential bottlenecks and obstacles. Finally, analyzing the phenomenon of information flow through NGT also helps practitioners and scholars evaluate aspects of virtual communities' cultures through an awareness of the forces that control and provide information to members of online communities.

Barzilai-Nahon, K. (2004). *Gatekeepers and gatekeeping mechanisms in networks.* Unpublished doctoral dissertation, Tel-Aviv University, Tel-Aviv, Israel.

Beckman, L., & Mays, V. (1985). Education community gatekeepers about alcohol abuse in women: Changing attitudes, knowledge and referral practices. *Journal of Drug Education, 15*(4), 289–309.

Birnhack, M., & Elkin-Koren, N. (2003). The invisible handshake: The reemergence of the State in the digital environment. *Virginia Journal of Law and Technology, 8*(2). Retrieved May 20, 2004, from www.vjolt.net/

Cornfield, M., & Rainie, L. (2003). Untuned keyboards: Online campaigners, citizens and portals in the 2002 elections. *Institute for Politics, Democracy & the Internet, Pew Internet & American Life Project*. www.pewinternet.org/PPF/r/85/ report_display.asp

Donohue, G. A., Olien, C. N., & Tichenor, P. J. (1989). Structure and constraints on community newspaper gatekeepers. *Journalism Quarterly, 66*, 807–812.

Gieber, W. (1956). Across the desk: A study of 16 telegraph editors. *Journalism Quarterly, 33*, 423–432.

Hargittai, E. (2000). Standing before the portals: Non-profit websites in an age of commercial gatekeepers. *The Journal of Policy, Regulation and Strategy for Telecommunications Information and Media, 2*, 537–544.

Lewin, K. (1947). Frontiers in group dynamics II: Channels of group life; social planning and action research. *Human Relations, 1*, 143–153.

Lewin, K. (1951). *Field theory in social science: Selected theoretical papers*. NY: Harper & Row.

Motoyer-Duran, C. (1993). Information gatekeepers. In M. Williams (Ed.), *Annual review of information science and technology, 28* (pp. 111–150). Medford, NJ: Learned Information Inc.

Shoemaker, P. (1991). *Gatekeeping*. Newbury Park, CA: Sage.

Shumsky, R., & Pinker, E. (2003). Gatekeepers and referrals in services. *Management Science, 49*, 839–856.

White, D. M. (1950). The "gate keeper": A case study in the selection of news. *Journalism Quarterly, 27*, 383–390.

43
Nonlinear Information Seeking

Allen Foster
Department of Information Studies
University of Wales, Aberystwyth, Wales
aef@aber.ac.uk

Foster's nonlinear model of information-seeking behavior differs from earlier models of information behavior and represents a shift toward a new understanding of user information behavior. The model was first developed within the field of information science by Allen Foster at the Department of Information Studies, University of Sheffield, and continues in the Department of Information Studies, University of Wales, Aberystwyth.

The theoretical model was derived from empirical research exploring the relationship among interdisciplinarity, disciplinarity, behavior, and strategies. The specific focus of inquiry was identification of the activities, strategies, contexts, and behaviors used and perceived to be used by interdisciplinary information seekers, identification of the relationship of the core processes, contexts, and behaviors as part of interdisciplinary information behavior, and the representation of these in an empirically grounded, theoretical model of information-seeking behavior. The naturalistic approach and research methods suggested by Lincoln and Guba (1985) for maximizing credibility, transferability, dependability, and confirmability were adopted (Foster, 2004).

The nonlinear model proposes a theoretical framework within which information behavior may be understood and explored. The nonlinear model of information seeking is represented in terms of three core processes and three levels of contextual interaction as shown in Figure 43.1.

The model suggests that activities remain available throughout the course of information seeking. In viewing the processes in this way, neither start nor finish points are fixed, and each process may be repeated, or lead to any other, until either the query or context determine that information seeking can end. The behavioral relationships are described as concurrent, continuous, cumulative, and looped cycles occurring throughout a research project. The interactivity and shifts described by the model show information seeking to be nonlinear, dynamic, holistic, and flowing. These replace previous interpretations which suggest information seeking exists as a linear process consisting of stages and iterative activities.

The following overview introduces the core processes of *opening, orientation,* and *consolidation* at the center of Figure 43.1, and moves outwards to the three contextual interactions.

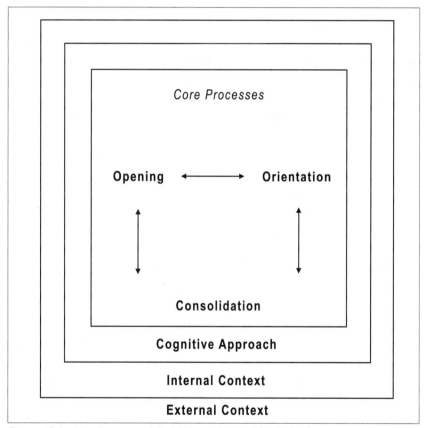

Figure 43.1   Nonlinear model of information-seeking behavior.
Note: From "A nonlinear model of information seeking behaviour" by A. E. Foster, 2004, *Journal of the American Society for Information Science and Technology*, 55, p. 232. Copyright 2003 by Wiley Periodicals. Adapted with permission.

Opening is identified as corresponding to seeking, exploring, and revealing information. Opening represents a collection of activities that interact and inform both further opening activities and the other core processes. Two activities, breadth exploration and eclecticism, are identified as complex in that they involve combinations of other activities to form a larger process. Breadth exploration is identified as a conscious expansion of searching to allow exploration of every possibility. Eclecticism encompasses accepting, gathering, and storing information from a diverse range of both passive and active sources. Other activities identified are networking, keyword searching, browsing, monitoring, chaining, and serendipity (Foster & Ford, 2002).

Orientation processes, or as one interview suggested, "finding which way was up," encompass a diverse range of activities focused on identification and in which direction to look. Activities involve problem definition, which varies from previous interpretations in noting that the process is iterative, cumulative, and repeatedly redefined until the closure of information seeking. Also included are picture building, reviewing, and identifying the shape of existing research, which involve the sub-processes of identifying key names, identifying key articles, and identifying latest opinion in disciplines. Identifying and selecting sources, identifying disciplinary communities, and identifying keywords are the other activities found in orientation.

Consolidation is described as judging and integrating information, and deciding whether further information seeking is necessary. Consolidation is found to be less likely as a first move in information seeking, although consolidation plays a part in every interaction. Key components of consolidation are knowing enough, which emerges as a reiterative process of questioning whether sufficient material to meet the present information need has been acquired. This is closely connected to refining and sifting, which are processes setting and applying relevance criteria and search boundaries to material and sources. Incorporation is identified as a key information organization process. The process of incorporation takes place as a combination of thinking, writing, and discussing with colleagues, and is accompanied by the inclusion of verifying and finishing.

The model views information behavior as integral to the context within which the information seeker works, and includes both internal and external aspects. External influences are labeled *social and organizational, time, the project, navigation issues,* and *access to sources.* Internal influences are summarized in the model as *feelings and thoughts, coherence,* and *knowledge and understanding.*

Cognitive approach describes the mode of thinking observed in the participants, a willingness to identify and use information that might be relevant to an information problem. The model specifies four cognitive approaches: 1) flexible and adaptable, 2) openness, 3) nomadic thought, and 4) holistic.

The model offers a fundamentally different perspective from which to investigate information-seeking behavior. In this, it is of central relevance to the future of information-behavior research. The relationships and interactions found within the model lie at the core of the theory, and it is these that hold the greatest implications for future work.

The theory incorporates internal context and external context, along with individual information-seeking activities, for a holistic view of information-seeking behavior—a view compatible with Ingwersen's cognitive IR model (1996).

The nonlinear model offers a theoretical basis with which to test and reconsider some of the central assertions of early behavioral theories. Specifically, the model offers an alternative to the linear stages offered previously by Kuhlthau (1993), Wilson (1997), and others, as a tool for investigating and interpreting information seeking. The nonlinear theory addresses anomalous patterns of behavior and missed stages noted in the application of previous models, and allows a reconsideration and extension of key concepts previously interpreted only through linear theory.

Beyond the core concepts relevant to information behavior, the theory offers a framework from which to view the creation of an information literate person, a person capable of advanced and successful information behavior. One practical implication of the model points to revising the teaching of information literacy and library skills with a move toward a holistic skills program, including curriculum development and training design.

In its initial form, no claim for generalizability was made, as befits naturalistic inquiry (Foster, 2004); however, the richness of the data and the rigor with which the process was documented allow transferability of the model, and permit further development of the research themes in many directions. The use of naturalistic inquiry has proven valuable in refreshing our understanding of a complex phenomenon, though further developments of the model will benefit from mixed naturalistic and positivistic approaches.

The nonlinear model of information behavior contrasts with earlier theories of information behavior. It offers a potential reinterpretation of information behavior as a dynamic, flowing, holistic process, and points to many lines of future investigation and development.

Foster, A. E. (2004). A nonlinear model of information seeking behavior. *Journal of the American Society for Information Science and Technology, 55*, 228–237.

Foster, A. E., & Ford, N. (2002). Serendipity and information seeking: An empirical study. *Journal of Documentation, 59*, 321–340.

Ingwersen, P. (1996). Cognitive perspectives of information retrieval interaction: Elements of a cognitive IR theory. *Journal of Documentation, 52*, 3–50.

Kuhlthau, C. C. (1993). *Seeking meaning: A process approach to library and information services*. Norwood, NJ: Ablex.

44
Optimal Foraging

JoAnn Jacoby
Education and Social Science Library
University of Illinois at Urbana-Champaign, USA
jacoby@uiuc.edu

Adapted from anthropology (Winterhalder, 1981; Smith, 1983) by way of population biology and behavioral ecology (MacArthur & Pianka, 1966; Stephens & Krebs, 1986), optimal foraging theory has been applied to the information-seeking behavior of scholars (Sandstrom 1994, 1998, 1999, 2001; Cronin & Hert, 1995) and has been used by researchers in human-computer interaction to model Web-browsing behavior (Pirolli & Card, 1995, 1999; Chi et al., 2001). Psychologists have also employed the theory as a corrective to overly mechanistic explanations of learning and memory (Kamil & Roitblat, 1985; Mantovani, 2001).

Optimal foraging theory uses cost-benefit analysis to deconstruct complex processes of selection into their component parts. As Sandstrom (1999, p. 17) explains, "Foraging models include an *actor* choosing among alternatives, a *currency* by which the actor measures costs and benefits, a set of *constraints* limiting behavior, and a *strategy* set specifying the actor's range of available options." The researcher identifies a currency (such as calories or survival rate in ecology; novelty or information value in information science), which provides a scale to measure the net benefits of a particular strategy and predicts resources that will be pursued under certain circumstances (Sandstrom, 1994). By identifying salient factors and then examining them using testable hypotheses, optimal foraging theory provides a method for investigating intricate ecologies, in which many factors are intertwined. Aside from its specific theoretical and methodological precepts, information foraging theory also provides a particularly apt metaphor for information behavior, as Cronin and Hert (1995) recognized. Foraging includes both hunting and gathering, and thus encompasses a broad range of behaviors including everything from highly organized, goal-directed searches to ongoing, ad hoc background activities.

Sandstrom (1994) was the first to apply optimal foraging theory to the information environment, using co-citation analysis to examine information foraging among scholars studying the evolutionary ecology of hunter-gatherer societies. Positing novelty as the currency for scholarly foraging, she suggests that search costs (time spent seeking usable information, on a continuum from directed searching to background monitoring) and handling costs (time required to retrieve, read, and process an item) for information resources can be evaluated to arrive at a cost-benefit analysis from the researcher's point of view (Figure 44.1).

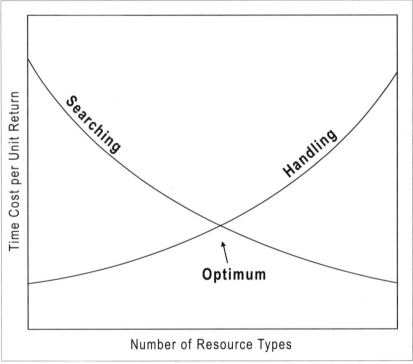

Figure 44.1   Optimal foraging model of an information "diet."

Note: The arrow indicates the optimal mix of resources; pursuing a greater number of resources would cause a greater increase in handling time than decrease in search time.

From "An optimal foraging approach to information seeking and use," by P. E. Sandstrom, 1994, *The Library Quarterly*, 64, p. 426. Copyright 1994 by the University of Chicago Press. Adapted with permission.

Sandstrom found that the resources used by scholars fell into a core-periphery structure, with a "core" of frequently cited sources that represent the scholar's area of research specialization (Figure 44.2). Core resources were usually encountered via interpersonal contact and housed in the researcher's personal collection. Less frequently cited "peripheral" resources were found via more-labor intensive searches and required more handling time because they were unfamiliar. Peripheral resources had higher searching and handling costs, but brought in new ideas from other research areas.

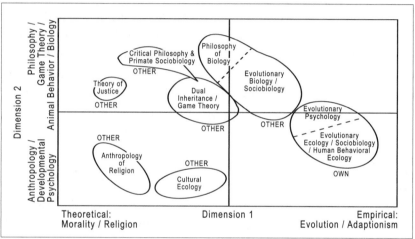

Figure 44.2   Individual resource map of human behavioral ecology scholar showing core-periphery structure.

Note: From "Scholarly communication as a socioecological system," by P. E. Sandstrom, 2001, *Scientometrics*, 51, p. 589. Copyright 2001 by the Kluwer Academic Publishers. Adapted with permission.

Sandstrom also found a continuum of two types of foraging strategies: 1) specialists, who focus on a single high-density "patch" of sources encountered via informal communication or routine monitoring and draw heavily on sources in their personal collections, and 2) generalists who gather sources from a wide variety of patches, a strategy that requires deliberate searching and other labor intensive techniques, as well as handling procedures that involve temporary access to materials rather than ownership. Specialists exhibit a high mean co-citation rate while generalists fall into clusters with relatively low co-citation rates, which are linked to many other widely disparate clusters (Sandstrom, 1994; 1999).

Sandstrom focused on scholarly information behavior and her methods included generating resource maps based on cluster analysis of scholars' co-citation patterns. She then interviewed the scholars to elicit their interpretations of these maps. These methods were well-suited to the academic environment, but optimal foraging theory could easily be applied to information-seeking behavior in other contexts, using other methods. Resource patches could be defined as different types of information sources, including friends, colleagues, and healthcare professionals; or tools such as Google and library catalogs. Currency would also be redefined according to what was salient in a particular context. Optimal foraging theory might also provide some insight into information space from the user's point of view (cf., Case, 1986). Just as Sandstrom mapped research areas as defined by citations, one could map information environments as defined by other (perhaps user-defined) criteria such as the distinction between immediate (personal collection or internet-accessible), adjacent (university library), and outside (interlibrary loan, local bookstores, etc.) information spaces made by the academics in Lee's (2003) recent study.

Optimal foraging theory has also been productively applied to information system design. Taking situationally defined "information value" as the currency, Pirolli and Card's (1995) "information foraging theory" analyzes trade-offs in the value of information gained against the cost of performing particular activities in human-computer interaction tasks. The theory is thus used to analyze "variations in activity afforded by some space of human-system design parameters" (Pirolli & Card, 1995, p. 2). More recently, the foraging metaphor was expanded to include the concept of "information scent," defined as a user's perception of the value and cost of accessing a piece of information based on the perceptual cues available to them (Chi et al., 2001). Information scent is used, in turn, to explain and predict Web surfing patterns. These ideas have been picked up by market researchers and generated a host of more narrowly focused and less interesting studies of online information behavior (e.g., Rajala & Hantula, 2000).

Optimal foraging theory has provided a rich framework for understanding information-gathering behavior in online information environments and among academic researchers. It offers a way to model both the information seeker and the environment as they experience it, allowing systematic examination of the complex interplay between the information environment, people's perceptions of that environment, and the strategies they use to navigate within and between different information spaces. One of the strengths of optimal foraging theory is that it is focused enough to generate testable hypotheses, but nuanced enough to account for the complex interplay of multiple factors. Exploring the extent and limitation of such generalizations could generate a rich body of research along a number of different trajectories. In particular, it would be interesting to see this theory connected with in-situ observation of everyday information behavior so that some of these detailed observational studies could become the basis for explaining the underlying processes that inform information behavior.

Care must be taken, however, to recognize the limits of functionalist theories like optimal foraging. Optimality models are sometimes overextended when researchers slip into the assumption that the behavior they are studying is classically rational. To avoid this pitfall, researchers using this theory need to be mindful that optimal foraging models describe the possibilities of a niche, mediated by many intervening factors, *not* a simple optimum (Pirolli & Card, 1995). As a further corrective, optimal foraging theory could be combined with other methodological approaches such as social network analysis (e.g., Wasserman & Faust, 1994). Such triangulation could provide a more nuanced understanding of how individuals and groups view their information environments, the paths they use to navigate through those spaces, and the underlying principles that guide their information behavior.

Case, D. O. (1986). Collection and organization of written information by social scientists and humanists: A review and exploratory study. *Journal of Information Science, 12*, 97–104.

Chi, E. H., Pirolli, P., Chen , K., & Pitkow, J. (2001). Using information scent to model user information needs and actions and the Web. In *Proceedings of the SIGCHI conference on human factors in computing systems* (pp. 490–497). Seattle, WA: ACM.

Cronin, B., & Hert, C. A. (1995). Scholarly foraging and network discovery tools. *Journal of Documentation, 51*, 388–403.

Kamil, A. C., & Roitblat, H. L. (1985). The ecology of foraging behavior: Implications for animal learning and memory. *Annual Review of Psychology, 36,* 141–169.

Lee, H. (2003). Information spaces and collections: Implications for organization. Library and *Information Science Research, 25,* 419–436.

MacArthur, R. H., & Pianka, E. R. (1966). On optimal use of a patchy environment. *American Naturalist, 100,* 603–609.

Mantovani, G. (2001). The psychological construction of the internet: From information foraging to social gathering to cultural mediation. *CyberPsychology & Behavior, 4,* 47–56.

Pirolli, P., & Card, S. (1995). Information foraging in information access environments. In *Proceedings of the CHI '95 ACM conference on human factors in software* (pp. 1–58). New York: ACM.

Pirolli, P., & Card, S. (1999). Information foraging. *Psychological Review, 100,* 643–675.

Rajala, A., & Hantula, D. (2000). Toward a behavioral ecology of consumption: Delay reduction effects on foraging in a simulated Internet mall. *Managerial and Decision Economics, 21,* 145–158.

Sandstrom, P. E. (1994). An optimal foraging approach to information seeking and use. *The Library Quarterly, 64,* 414–449.

Sandstrom, P. E. (1998). Information foraging among anthropologists in the invisible college of human behavioral ecology: An author co-citation analysis (Doctoral dissertation, Indiana University, 1998). *Dissertation Abstracts International, 60-02,* 276.

Sandstrom, P. E. (1999). Scholars as subsistence foragers. *Bulletin of the American Society for Information Science, 25,* 17–20.

Sandstrom, P. E. (2001). Scholarly communication as a socioecological system. *Scientometrics, 51,* 573–605.

Smith, E. A. (1983). Anthropological applications of optimal foraging theory: A critical review. *Current Anthropology, 24,* 625–651.

Stephens D. W., & Krebs, J. R. (1986). *Foraging theory.* Princeton, NJ: Princeton University Press.

Wasserman, S, & Faust, K. (1994). *Social network analysis: Methods and applications.* Cambridge, UK: Cambridge University Press.

Winterhalder, B. (1981). Optimal foraging strategies and hunter-gatherer research in anthropology. In B. Winterhalder & E. A. Smith (Eds.), *Hunter-gatherer foraging strategies* (pp. 13–35). Chicago: University of Chicago Press.

45
Organizational Sense Making and Information Use

Anu MacIntosh-Murray
Department of Health Policy, Management and Evaluation
Faculty of Medicine, University of Toronto, Canada
anu.macintosh@utoronto.ca

In his classic *Sensemaking in organizations*, Weick (1995) chronicles 100 years of the interdisciplinary literature about sense making, starting with the work of psychologist/pragmatist William James, and continuing with the contributions of many organizational researchers, systems theorists, philosophers, and social scientists. He developed the concept of sense making as a way to understand "a central activity in the construction of both the organization and the environments it confronts" (Weick, 1995, p. 69).

Weick lists seven characteristics of sense making, which set it apart from other explanatory processes such as understanding, interpretation, and attribution. Sense making is understood as a process that is: 1) grounded in identity construction; 2) retrospective; 3) enactive of sensible environments; 4) social; 5) ongoing; 6) focused on and by extracted cues; and 7) driven by plausibility rather than accuracy (Weick, 1995, p. 17).

Weick views organizations as "collections of people trying to make sense of what is happening around them" (Weick, 2001, p. 5). He describes sense making as "less about discovery than it is about invention" because "to engage in sense making is to construct, filter, frame, create facticity, and render the subjective into something more tangible" (1995, p. 14). Weick draws an analogy between sense making and cartography, suggesting that there is no single projection that best represents a true map of preexisting terrain or reality (Weick, 2001, p. 9). There are many useful maps which can be produced, depending on what tools the "cartographer" chooses to use, what portion of terrain he or she focuses on, and for what purpose.

Weick emphasizes that action is crucial to sense making, in that people are part of, and, in fact, create their environment. People bracket and punctuate the continuous flow of experience by noticing some aspects or cues extracted from the environment and imposing labels or categories on them, and ignoring others. Selective perception can result in meaning or sense that may not be accurate: "words approximate the territory; they never map it perfectly. That is why sense making never stops" (Weick, 1995, p. 107).

To understand use or non-use of information, we need to understand what influences people to notice some cues or data and not others as part of sense making. In an organizational or work setting, there may be common influences on ways of perceiving. If there are common labels or categories shared by individuals or groups, these could play a role in determining what sense is made of situations and how information is filtered.

Weick is widely cited in the organizational studies literature, but far less frequently in information science research. For example, organizational researchers have studied sense making as part of strategic learning, "characterized by targeted information gathering that relies on diverse experts for interpretation as well as validation" (Thomas, Sussman, & Henderson, 2001, p. 331). In the field of information science, Choo's (2002) monograph about environmental scanning and information use by managers links theories on organizational and individual information processing and individual information behaviors. Solomon incorporated Weick's organizational view of sense making in his trilogy of articles titled *Discovering information behavior in sense making*, published in 1997.

Researchers using Weick's sense making theory have followed varied methodological paths. Given the importance of language in sense making in organizations, qualitative, interpretive approaches and discourse analysis can be appropriate. For example, MacIntosh-Murray (2003) carried out a case study of information behaviors of healthcare providers and their sense making related to patient safety and adverse events. Her work was based on grounded theory and discourse analysis, guided by Alvesson and Sköldberg's (2000) reflexive methodology. Solomon (1997a, b, c) used ethnography of communication to guide his in-depth, multiyear case study of information behavior in a work planning process.

Two aspects of Checkland's work are relevant to sense making: Soft Systems Methodology (SSM) and Processes for Organizational Meaning (POM). Peter Checkland and his colleagues developed SSM at Lancaster University during the early 1970s in the Department of Systems Engineering. SSM grew from Checkland's dissatisfaction with the applicability of traditional engineering approaches to management problems and issues.

Checkland's SSM offers an alternative to the "hard" systems view that the world is systemic, that is, composed of systems "out there" waiting to be discovered and improved by logical, empirical means by asking "what is the system?" and "what are its objectives?" He describes instead a world made up of many "ill-structured, hard-to-define, 'wicked' problem situations" in which people are trying to take purposeful action without being able to articulate clear, common objectives (Checkland & Holwell, 1998, p. 24). Checkland suggests that it is possible to make sense of such situations by thinking and learning about them in a systematic fashion and modeling them using systems concepts as a guide. In essence, he shifts the "systemicity" from the world to a "process of inquiry into the world" (Checkland, 1999, p. A10).

Underlying the soft systems thinking and approach to understanding situations is an appreciation of how individuals and groups establish meaning and make sense of what is going on around them. Checkland and Holwell devised POM as a visual representation of the processes by which organization meanings are created. They caution that:

> ...it does not purport to be a descriptive account of the organizational process. What it does purport to be is a defensible device with a structure and language which can be used to make sense of life in real organizations and their provision of information systems. Real life itself is always richer and more complex than any of our images of it. Thus, though we would argue that the figure [POM] broadly represents aspects we can observe and analyse, the detailed reality will always be less clear-cut than the model; a terrain is never the same as the map which relates to it. (Checkland & Holwell, 1998, p. 107)

POM highlights the key role of "appreciative settings," which can be interpreted as the values, beliefs, and norms that act as perceptual filters and influence our attention and sense making. This concept can be an important part of understanding sense making and information behaviors and processes.

People (Element 1), as individuals and members of various groups, sense and notice cues from their environments (Element 2). Checkland calls the data they extract and pay attention to "capta." People engage in discourse (Element 3), which is the social act of sense making through discussing, debating, contesting, arguing, persuading, and even manipulating. Examples of this are found in Solomon's (1997a, b, c) and Sonnenwald and Pierce's (2000) studies, and in Weick's (1995) work. Although complete agreement may be rare, some shared meanings and compromises are achieved (Elements 4 and 5), sometimes enough to allow action to be taken (Element 6). Action in turn creates changes in our perceived world. POM can serve as a very useful device to structure exploration of information use by groups in an organizational setting.

Checkland's work is frequently cited in information systems research. Among the few examples in information studies are Brown-Syed's (1996) study of an automated library consortium, and Vakkari's (1999) work integrating studies of information seeking and information retrieval. Chilvers (2000) applied SSM in a case study of the management of digital objects. Although she did not use soft systems methodology per se, MacIntosh-Murray adapted POM to study the construction and use of information by healthcare professionals for improving patient safety in health care organizations (MacIntosh-Murray, 2003; MacIntosh-Murray & Choo, 2004).

Alvesson, M., & Skoldberg, K. (2000). *Reflexive methodology*. London: Sage.

Brown-Syed, C. (1996). Soft systems methodology: Its origins and use in librarianship. In *From CLANN to UNILINC: An automated library consortium from a soft systems perspective*. Retrieved on October 4, 2003, from http://valinor.ca/ssm3.html

Checkland, P. (1999). *Systems thinking, systems practice*. Chichester, UK: John Wiley & Sons.

Checkland, P., & Holwell, S. (1998). *Information, systems, and information systems: making sense of the field*. Chichester, UK: John Wiley & Sons.

Chilvers, A. (2000). Critical issues in the use of Soft Systems Methodology: A case study in the long-term management of digital data objects. *Journal of Librarianship and Information Science, 32*(4), 167–177.

Choo, C. W. (2002). *Information management for the intelligent organization: The art of scanning the environment* (3rd ed.). Medford, NJ: Information Today.

MacIntosh-Murray, A. (2003). *Information behaviour of health care providers for improving patient safety.* Unpublished doctoral dissertation, University of Toronto, Canada.

MacIntosh-Murray, A., & Choo, C. W. (2004). *Information behaviour in the context of improving patient safety: Part 1. Sense making and information roles.* Manuscript submitted for publication.

Solomon, P. (1997a). Discovering information behavior in sense making. I. Time and timing. *Journal of the American Society for Information Science, 48*, 1097–1108.

Solomon, P. (1997b). Discovering information behavior in sense making. 2. The social. *Journal of the American Society for Information Science, 48*, 1109–1126.

Solomon, P. (1997c). Discovering information behavior in sense making. 3. The person. *Journal of the American Society for Information Science, 48*, 1127–1138.

Sonnenwald, D. H., & Pierce, L. G. (2000). Information behavior in dynamic group work contexts: Interwoven situational awareness, dense social networks, and contested collaboration in command and control. *Information Processing and Management, 36*, 461–479.

Thomas, J. B., Sussman, S. W., & Henderson, J. C. (2001). Understanding "strategic learning": Linking organizational learning, knowledge management, and sensemaking. *Organization Science, 12*(3), 331–345.

Vakkari, P. (1999). Task complexity, problem structure, and information actions: Integrating studies on information seeking and retrieval. *Information Processing and Management, 35*, 819–837.

Weick, K. (1995). *Sensemaking in organizations.* Thousand Oaks, CA: Sage.

Weick, K. E. (2001). *Making sense of the organization.* Oxford: Blackwell.

46
The PAIN Hypothesis

Harry Bruce
The Information School
University of Washington, USA
harryb@u.washington.edu

The PAIN hypothesis explicates, in five propositions, the concept of *personal anticipated information need*. The attributes of this concept are derived from elaborations of the concepts *information need* and *anticipated information need* (in particular, Taylor's four levels of information need, Belkin's ASK hypothesis, Dervin's Sense-Making theory, Kuhlthau's uncertainty principle, and Erdelez's information encountering). PAIN is introduced as the motivation and underpinning framework for information behavior that relates to personal information management, specifically, to the thoughts and actions of building and maintaining a personal information collection (PIC behaviors). The PAIN hypothesis articulates the foundation for selected behaviors associated with personal information management. Each proposition is introduced as a framework for further study and for elaboration, empirical validation, or correction by researchers who focus on the behavior of personal information management.

A personal information collection is defined as the space that individuals turn to first when they need information to do a task or pursue an interest. The term *personal information collection* refers broadly to a personal organization of and perspective on information. It includes content in various forms (documents, Web pages, mail, notes, calendars, address books, etc.), structures for representing and organizing this information (folder hierarchies, piles, lists, etc.), and pointers to information (people, links, favorites, etc.). It is an idiosyncratic and dynamic personal construct that individuals take with them into, and out of, the various information events that frame their daily working and personal lives. This construct is an artifact of three processes: 1) selecting, 2) keeping, and 3) maintaining information sources and channels that the individual has located, been given, or encountered.

Each process of personal information collection (selecting, keeping, and maintaining) is underpinned by an individual's anticipation of a future use for information sources or channels. This construct is called personal anticipated information need (PAIN). The basic assumption of personal information collection and the PAIN hypothesis is that individuals are capable of assessing (with varying degrees of accuracy and endurance) the relevance and application of information sources and channels to predicted or potential needs or tasks. PAIN is explicated by the following five propositions.

1) *Personal anticipated information need is triggered by information events.* When an individual locates, encounters, or is given an information source or channel, a number of information use and evaluation behaviors occur. The information source or channel is evaluated against the individual's motives for seeking information (information need). These evaluations may result in immediate information use. But, contact with an information source or channel (intentional or incidental) may also lead to evaluations that acknowledge the usefulness of the information but delay information use to another point in time—an anticipated moment of information use, hypothesized by the individual. Attributes of the information source or channel are used by the individual to make these assessments in relation to his or her sense of task, work-based or recreational information needs. The information source or channel is an amalgam of stimuli that evoke this assessment of PAIN within the information event.

2) *Individuals have differential sensitivity and reactions to personal anticipated information need.* An individual's sensitivity and reactions to PAIN are affected by variables associated with the time and space of each information event. Reactions to an information source or channel are based upon the individual's ability to make sense of the information source or channel—to apply it effectively to an information need; to use it to make a decision, to do a task, or to address an interest; to understand its future value; and to organize it for later access and use. The abilities of an individual to react to PAIN and his or her repertoire of reactions to the stimuli of the information source or channel will differ. The processes of building and managing a personal information collection depend on an individual's ability to make sense of an information source or channel and then to predict its function in his or her life in relation to future tasks or

information needs. This requires acceptance of the information (a form of assessment and evaluation) and an understanding of the implications of delayed access to, and perhaps processing of, the information.

3) *Personal anticipated information need predicts, but does not guarantee, future information use.* PAIN assigns value to an information source or channel at a particular point in space and time. This value may change as the individual moves forward with his or her life. Anticipated applications, tasks, decisions or interest levels may not eventuate. An anticipated need simply may not occur. In other words, individuals make mistakes when they anticipate their future needs for information, and changing situations may affect an individual's abilities to make accurate and enduring PAIN assessments. When an individual creates a personal information collection, he or she is attempting to select and keep (or at least to insure the availability of) useful information (a hit) and to ignore useless information (a correct rejection). PAIN is not free of error, however. People sometimes keep information that turns out to be useless (a false positive); and they sometimes take no steps to keep information that turns out to be useful (a miss).

4) *Personal anticipated information need informs the investments and valuations that underpin the processes of personal information collection.* The selecting, keeping, and maintaining processes of personal information collection require an investment of cognitive effort and time. The extent of these investments by an individual will depend on his or her perception of the relationship between anticipated information need and the information found or encountered. The goal of the personal information collection is to maximize the potential benefit of selecting and keeping an information source or channel while at the same time minimizing the cognitive effort and time that this requires. When an individual chooses to include an information source or channel in the personal information collection, this means that he or she has accepted the relative value of the investment of time and cognitive effort required to achieve the benefit of having the information source or channel readily accessible. In cases where the PAIN is well defined, the individual may need to invest very little cognitive effort and time to translate the selected information source or channel into representations that position it in the personal information collection. In cases where the PAIN is less well

defined, selecting and keeping processes require an increased investment of cognitive effort and time.

5) *Sensitivity to personal anticipated information need is critical information literacy.* The challenge of finding and using information in our working and everyday lives has drawn increasing attention to the set of skills and literacies that individuals need for leading efficient and satisfying lives in an information age. Individuals must be effective users of information. They must also be skillful builders and managers of their personal information collection where they collect, organize, and store the information that they need to refer to on a regular basis. The personal information collection should be cultivated and well-managed, but many are overloaded and disorganized. They are often a source of frustration, anxiety, stress, and embarrassment. The processes that construct the personal information collection rely fundamentally upon the individual's sensitivity to his or her information needs and anticipated information needs. The key to an effective personal information collection, therefore, rests with the accuracy and endurance of an individual's PAIN. Enhancing our sensitivity and appropriate responses to PAIN is, therefore, a key literacy.

In sum, personal information management includes a set of behavior that attempts to bring order—the processes of selecting, keeping, and maintaining the information sources and channels that comprise the personal information collection. These processes are underpinned and informed by each individual's ability to understand the information he or she needs for immediate and deferred purposes, work-based or recreational PAIN. The qualities of the personal information collection will firstly depend upon how well each individual understands his or her PAIN and secondly on how effectively he or she translates this understanding into the processes of selecting, keeping, and maintaining the information sources and channels that comprise the personal information collection.

Belkin, N. J., Oddy, R. N., & Brooks, H. M. (1982). ASK for information retrieval: Part I. Background and theory. *Journal of Documentation, 38*(2), 61–71.

Dervin, B. (1992). From the mind's eye of the 'user': The Sense-Making qualitative-quantitative methodology. In: Glazier, J. D., & Powell, R. R. (Eds.), *Qualitative research in information management* (pp. 61–84). Englewood, CO: Libraries Unlimited.

Erdelez, S. (1999). Information encountering: It's more than just bumping into information. *Bulletin of the American Society for Information Science, 25*(3), 25–29.

Kuhlthau, C. C. (1993). A principle of uncertainty for information seeking. *Journal of Documentation, 49*(4), 339–355.

Taylor, R. S. (1968). Question-negotiation and information seeking in libraries. *College and Research Libraries, 29*, 178–194.

47

Perspectives on the Tasks in which Information Behaviors Are Embedded

Barbara M. Wildemuth and Anthony Hughes
School of Information and Library Science
University of North Carolina at Chapel Hill, USA
wildem@ils.unc.edu and ahughes@unc.edu

People undertake an almost infinite variety of information behaviors. In almost all cases, these information behaviors are undertaken within the context of some other purpose, goal, or activity. In other words, the person's information behaviors are situated within the context of some larger task or set of tasks. For example, the students involved in Kuhlthau's (1991) seminal study engaged in information seeking while completing a school assignment to write a research paper, and the municipal administrators studied by Byström (2002) engaged in a variety of information behaviors while responding to new matters registered with the city government. Though the same term—tasks—is used in the literature, the tasks in which information behaviors are embedded should be distinguished from the specific search goals undertaken or the search tasks assigned to study participants. Of primary concern here are the tasks that form the context for information behaviors. These tasks have direct as well as indirect interactions with people's information-seeking activities and are a primary but under-studied phenomenon. Several theories that do address such tasks are briefly reviewed here.

Allen (1996, 1997) proposed a person-in-situation approach to our understanding of information needs. As he noted, "information needs happen to individuals who are embedded in a range of social situations" (Allen, 1996, p. 88). Allen considered four sources of influence on an individual's information needs (and, thus, on an individual's information-seeking behavior). The four sources of influence include individual influences (i.e., knowledge structures and perceptions), situational/social influences on the individual's needs, individual influences on a group's needs (based on the assumption that a group has information needs beyond those of its individual members), and situational/social influences on a group's needs.

Allen's model is consistent with Dervin's (1999) and Savolainen's (1993) more process-oriented view of information behaviors, in which people are engaged in making sense of their world. When someone experiences a discontinuity in his or her sense making activities, additional information may be sought to resolve that discontinuity. This discontinuity is bridged by asking questions, forming ideas, obtaining resources, and, finally, developing strategies that allow the effective use of these ideas and resources. Thus, in Dervin's view, it is the interaction of the person with his or her world that motivates and shapes information behaviors.

While Allen's and Dervin's work points in an appropriate direction, further investigation is needed to more fully understand how people's experiences of information needs and their information behaviors are embedded within their accomplishment of other tasks. In their exposition of information foraging theory, Pirolli and Card (1999) describe these as the "task environment" or "embedding task" of information seeking (p. 644). They argue that the embedding task motivates someone to seek information and that the outcomes of the information-seeking process will be evaluated in relation to their effects on the outcomes of the embedding task. For example, in planning a vacation, one might want to find out more about sites in central Europe. Thus, the embedding task for this particular search is vacation planning. It seems likely that the information-seeking process will be affected by the searcher's emotional responses, personal history of travel, and expectations concerning the preferences of travel partners, as well as the match between an information source's content and the searcher's topic. In addition, the outcomes of the search will be evaluated in relation to the outcomes of the vacation planning process.

Empirically grounded theories related to information behaviors' embedding tasks are needed. The embedding tasks should be the focus of our studies rather than a minor consideration in studies focusing on information behaviors. As we gain a better understanding of the types of embedding tasks that provide the context for particular information behaviors, we will be better able to understand the processes of information seeking and use.

Studies of embedding tasks, varying in the degree of realism with which the embedding task is incorporated, might be conducted in the environment in which the tasks normally occur, as simulations of naturalistic behaviors, or as experiments that manipulate aspects of a particular task to investigate the effects of those manipulations on information behaviors (Vakkari, 2003). Field studies, such as the Kuhlthau (1991) and Byström (2002) studies mentioned earlier, are the most realistic. Borlund and Ingwersen (1997) explored the value of simulated search goals, in which the researcher fabricates a description of a realistic (though not real) task that could motivate information seeking. Experimental designs are much more common in information retrieval studies and should incorporate aspects of some embedding tasks as experimental manipulations (Beaulieu, Robertson, & Rasmussen, 1996).

Regardless of a study's level of realism, there are several facets of embedding tasks that should be taken into account. The granularity of the embedding task is one such facet. Either the overall task or any of its subtasks may be the embedding task for information behavior. For example, the process of working on a dissertation is an overall task that may motivate information seeking, and the process of seeking a particular citation to include in a particular portion of the dissertation literature review is a subtask that may motivate information seeking.

The affective component of the embedding task must also be taken into account. While Kuhlthau's (1991) work examined students' affective reactions to the information-seeking process, she did not study their affective reactions to the embedding task. It is likely that someone's affective reactions to an embedding task will have noticeable effects on the information behaviors triggered by that embedding task. For example, they may affect someone's level of motivation to seek information, which sources may be considered sufficiently trustworthy, and/or satisfaction with the outcomes of a search.

For study designs in which the researcher wishes to exert some control over the embedding task, two other aspects of the search goal should be taken into account. The first is the complexity of the search goal and the second is whether the search goal is closed-ended or open-ended (Bilal, 2002). Past studies have usually defined a search goal's complexity as the number of facets it suggests (Bilal, 2001) or its *a priori* determinability (Byström, 2002; Vakkari, 1999). The distinction between closed-ended and open-ended search goals is typically defined in terms of whether the target of the search is a single item or a small set of items (closed-ended), or a larger target with a scope that is more vague. For example, typical closed-ended search goals are fact finding searches and known item searches; typical open-ended searches are topic/subject searches that are expected to yield a number of relevant items. Both the complexity and open or closed-endedness of embedded tasks are facets that have been included in earlier studies (e.g., Marchionini et al., 1993; Large et al., 1994), but should now be moved to center stage, as the primary focus of future studies.

The studies of the embedding tasks that form the context for information behaviors may be undertaken at varying degrees of realism. They should take into account the granularity of the embedding task and the study participant's affective reactions to it. In more controlled studies, the effects of the search goals' level of complexity and their open or closed-ended nature also deserve further investigation. To further our understanding of information behaviors, we must begin to take into account the larger context and situation within which the information behaviors occur.

Allen, B. (1997). Information needs: A person-in-situation approach. In Vakkari, P., Savolainen, R., & Dervin, B. (Eds.), *Information seeking in context: Proceedings of an international conference on research in information needs, seeking and use in different contexts*. (pp. 111–122). London: Taylor Graham.

Allen, B. L. (1996). *Information tasks: Toward a user-centered approach to information systems*. San Diego: Academic Press.

Beaulieu, M., Robertson, S., & Rasmussen, E. (1996). Evaluating interactive systems in TREC. *Journal of the American Society for Information Science, 47*, 85–94.

Bilal, D. (2001). Children's use of the Yahooligans! Web search engine. II. Cognitive and physical behaviors on research tasks. *Journal of the American Society for Information Science & Technology, 52*, 118–136.

Bilal, D. (2002). Children's use of the Yahooligans! Web search engine. III. Cognitive and physical behaviors on fully self-generated search tasks. *Journal of the American Society for Information Science & Technology, 53*, 1170–1183.

Borlund, P., & Ingwersen, P. (1997). The development of a method for the evaluation of interactive information retrieval systems. *Journal of Documentation, 53*, 225–250.

Byström, K. (2002). Information and information sources in tasks of varying complexity. *Journal of the American Society for Information Science & Technology, 53,* 1170–1183.

Dervin, B. (1999). On studying information seeking methodologically: The implications of connecting metatheory to method. *Information Processing & Management, 35,* 727–750.

Kuhlthau, C. C. (1991). Inside the search process: Information seeking from the user's perspective. *Journal of the American Society for Information Science, 42,* 361–371.

Large, A., Beheshti, J., Breuleux, A., & Renaud, A. (1994). A comparison of information retrieval from print and CD-ROM versions of an encyclopaedia by elementary school students. *Information Processing & Management, 30,* 499–513.

Marchionini, G., Dwiggins, S., Katz, A., & Lin, X. (1993). Information seeking in full-text end-user-oriented search systems: The role of domain and search expertise. *Library & Information Science Research, 15,* 35–69.

Pirolli, P., & Card, S. (1999). Information foraging. *Psychological Review, 106,* 643–675.

Savolainen, R. (1993). The Sense-Making theory: Reviewing the interests of a user-centered approach to information seeking and use. *Information Processing & Management, 29,* 13–28.

Vakkari, P. (1999). Task complexity, problem structure and information actions: Integrating studies on information seeking and retrieval. *Information Processing & Management, 35,* 819–837.

Vakkari, P. (2003). Task-based information searching. *Annual Review of Information Science & Technology, 37,* 413–464.

48
Phenomenography

Louise Limberg
Swedish School of Library and Information Science
University College of Borås and Göteborg University, Sweden
louise.limberg@hb.se

Library and information science (LIS) researchers have acknowledged the dilemma in information behavior research between person-
centered outcomes and outcomes that are valid for more general patterns
of information behavior (Hjørland, 1997). The purpose of this article is
to present a theory of variation, *phenomenography*, as a theoretical
framework for combining studies of individuals' information behavior
with collective patterns of information seeking and use.

The object of phenomenography is the variation of human experience
of the world. It is grounded in empirical research in education on variation in students' learning outcomes and was initially developed during
the 1970s by a group of researchers led by Ference Marton at Göteborg
University in Sweden. Phenomenography has gradually developed as
regards philosophical foundations and theoretical thinking on variation,
and it has spread to disciplines outside education, and to other parts of
the world. For this article, three authoritative texts have been used as
primary sources (Marton, 1981, 1994; Marton & Booth, 1997). For the
discussion of phenomenographic research on information behavior, three
LIS authors will be cited: Christine Bruce (1997, 1999), Joyce Kirk
(2002), and Louise Limberg (1999a, 1999b, 2000). It is worth noting
that these researchers are located in Göteborg, Sweden, and in Australia,
which seems to reflect the fact that phenomenography has thrived
through close contacts between education researchers at Göteborg
University and researchers at various Australian universities.

Phenomenography is a qualitative research approach, mostly conducted through interviews. During data analysis, interviews are pooled,
that is, they are not tied to individual informants. Analysis focuses on the
manifest content of what has been said and the similarities and differences between what was said about the same topic as expressed in the

interviews. The content and structure of various experiences are put in different categories. The aim of analysis is to present patterns of variation through a limited number of categories of description. Together, the categories of description form the outcome space, which is a kind of map of various ways of being aware of a particular phenomenon, for example, information use.

The study of variation implies an interest in capturing various facets or dimensions of a phenomenon. The aim is to describe the phenomenon of research interest through a limited number of descriptive categories. This means that the research takes as its point of departure human individuals, but that the main focus is the phenomenon under study, information use. Consequently, the categories forming the outcome space group a limited number of experiences of "information seeking," which together constitute the phenomenon of information use.

It is important to note that the categories do not group the *persons* involved in the study, but rather their *ways of experiencing* the phenomenon under study. In phenomenography, ways of experiencing or conceptions are seen as relationships between a person and a specific phenomenon in the world. The research subject, the person experiencing something, and the object (that which is experienced), are not viewed as separate entities. The way in which the subject experiences the object forms a relationship between the two. This is why phenomenographic research has also been labeled a relational approach (Bruce, 1997; Limberg, 2000).

Experiencing a phenomenon is a way of being aware of something. It should be obvious that the theoretical thinking underpinning phenomenography has been inspired by phenomenology (Marton & Booth, 1997). Both have human experience as the research object (Van Manen, 1990). However, the aim of phenomenology is to capture the essence of a phenomenon. This is different from the phenomenographic research interest in investigating and describing phenomena through the variation of people's experience. Ways of experiencing something, its parts, and the relationship between these parts, constitute various dimensions of the phenomenon—for example, relevance or bias in information seeking.

Since the late 1990s, some major phenomenographic research has been conducted within the area of information behavior research. Bruce (1997) investigated the concept of information literacy through the experiences of those in higher education. The findings of her study were presented in *The Seven Faces of Information Literacy*. Three of these facets were not considered in previous research on information literacy. Limberg (1999a, b) studied high school students' various experiences of information seeking and use during a learning assignment. Three major ways of experiencing information seeking and use were identified and described. The students' various experiences reflected their approaches to information seeking and use. Variation in experiences of information seeking coincided with variation in students' learning outcomes.

With a focus on information use, Kirk (2002) identified and described five different ways managers experience information use related to their work environment and occupational tasks. These five different ways of experiencing information use are related in a hierarchy that reflects three different views of information: as an object, as a construct, and as a transformative force.

Phenomenography has been criticized for not taking context into account, although several studies indicate that a combination of contextual and situational particularities with a phenomenographic approach is perfectly viable (Kirk, 2002; Limberg, 1999a, b).

The focus on variation instead of on the general allows new dimensions of phenomena to appear. The consistent user perspective is common to, for instance, that of Kuhlthau's model of the information search process. However, the varying experiences of information seeking and use as described in phenomenographic studies are not apparent in a general model. The focus on experience instead of persons allows researchers to direct attention toward a phenomenon of interest, and not to cognitive styles or mental models linked to particular individuals. The weakness of methodological individualism in some person-centered studies (Hjørland, 1997) is avoided through the focus on the collective dimensions of experiences. The three theses referred to indicate that new dimensions, such as information use, become apparent in information literacy (Bruce, 1997) as well as in information seeking (Limberg, 1999a, b). Kirk claims that phenomenography was particularly appropriate to study information use, which has received little attention in information behavior research. Thanks to rich descriptions of variation, research outcomes may have implications for developing information systems as well as methods for information literacy education or the quality of information services.

Phenomenography allows freedom of choice for researchers as regards concepts or situations to be explored, but requires rigor in analysis in order to develop categories that are founded in the empirical material, and yet expand our theoretical understandings. The object of variation provides potential for deeper understandings of concepts germane to information-behavior research. The overall strength is that the phenomenographic approach firmly combines empirical studies with a theory of variation and the epistemological stance focusing on human experience.

Bruce, C. (1997). *The seven faces of information literacy.* Adelaide: Auslib Press.

Bruce, C. (1999). Phenomenography: Opening a new territory for library and information science research. *New Review of Information and Library Research, 5,* 31–47.

Hjørland, B. (1997). *Information seeking and subject representation: An activity-theoretical approach to information science.* London: Greenwood Press.

Kirk, J. (2002). *Theorising information use: Managers and their work.* Unpublished doctoral dissertation, University of Technology, Sydney, Australia.

Limberg, L. (1999a). Experiencing information seeking and learning. *Information Research: An International Electronic Journal, 5*(1). Retrieved March 21, 2004, from http://informationr.net/ir/5-1/paper68.html

Limberg, L. (1999b). Three conceptions of information seeking and use. In T. D. Wilson, & D. K. Allen (Eds.), *Exploring the contexts of information behaviour* (pp. 116–135). London: Taylor Graham.

Limberg, L. (2000). Phenomenography: A relational approach to research on information needs, seeking and use. *New Review of Information Behaviour Research, 1,* 51–67.

Marton, F. (1981). Phenomenography: Describing conceptions of the world around us. *Instructional Science, 10,* 177–200.

Marton, F. (1994). Phenomenography. In T. Husén, & T. N. Postlethwaite (Eds.), *The international encyclopedia of education,* 2nd ed., Vol. 8 (pp. 4424–4429). Oxford, UK: Pergamon.

Marton, F., & Booth, S. (1997). *Learning and awareness.* Mahwah, NJ: Lawrence Erlbaum.

Van Manen, M. (1990). *Researching lived experience: Human science for an action sensitive pedagogy.* Albany, NY: SUNY Press.

49
Practice of Everyday Life

Paulette Rothbauer
Faculty of Information Studies
University of Toronto, Canada
paulette.rothbauer@utoronto.ca

The scholarship of Michel de Certeau (1925–1986) cuts across the disciplinary fields of historiography, social sciences, semiotics, philosophy, and religious studies (see Buchanan, 2000). Discussion of his ideas also appears in an impressive array of disciplines including theology, anthropology, literary criticism, media studies, and cultural studies (see Ahearne, 1995). *The Practice of Everyday Life* (1984), an expression of his ideas regarding the unstable domain of everyday life, is proposed as a work of particular interest to researchers investigating everyday life information behavior. Two key ideas from Certeau's text frame this proposal: everyday life is constituted of the *tactics* of individuals and groups in response to the *strategies* of dominant social institutions; and an emphasis on the informal, routine, mundane operations and activities of daily life.

Strategies and tactics, the foundational elements of Certeau's conceptualization of everyday life, have much to offer the growing field of everyday life information studies. Recognized or legitimized ways of using and engaging with social institutions that create and define representations of users, audiences, consumers, readers, etc., are termed "strategies" by Certeau. Strategies can issue only from what counts as official practice and legitimate identity; relationships between users and systems are always circumscribed by these strategies (Certeau, 1984, p. xix). Certeau emphasizes the institutions of the military, education, business, and government, but the key point is that a recognizable place of social power must be established before strategies are deployed to deal with others. Strategies both create and control where and when everyday life occurs, and hence, everyday life information behavior can occur.

For example, the public library is a recognizable formal institution due to its visibility as a social, historical, and material presence.

Everyday life information behavior, especially when defined in opposition to scholarly and professional information behavior with recognized sites of practice, is transported across social and historical places, occurring everywhere (and perhaps nowhere) at once. "Ordinary" information seekers have no place of their own, and following Certeau, they must grab hold of the resources distributed by existing and visible information systems and structures. "Tactics" signify resistance to categorization by extant systems of power (see Driscoll, 2002, and Morris, 1990 for critique and discussion). Unlike the strategies deployed from official places of practice, tactics are the "hidden production" of users of these systems: tactical products are fleeting and manifest themselves not as products of use but rather through "ways of using" (Certeau, 1984, pp. xii–xiii). Following Certeau, researchers must first acknowledge and delimit the structures and logics of the systems that produce and distribute information services and resources used in an everyday context by the subjects of their research.

Certeau's conceptualization of everyday life encompasses questions related to ways of using all information resources. He asks, "The thousands of people who buy a health magazine, the customers in a supermarket, the practitioners of urban space, the consumers of newspaper stories and legends—what do they make of what they "absorb," receive, and pay for? What do they do with it?" (Certeau, 1984, p. 31). Questions about the role of libraries and other gatekeepers, use and non-use of media, and the influence of book retailers, publishers, and educators in the information behavior of individuals invites an application of Certeau's practice of everyday life.

One of the most compelling areas in which to do this concerns readers and reading, an area of everyday life practice, or "way of making do," clearly articulated by Certeau and significantly understudied in library and information science (Wiegand, 1997). The act of reading is a tactic dependent on the structure and spaces created for reading and readers by the strategies of official institutions such as libraries, schools, publishers, and bookstores. According to Certeau, reading allows readers to wander through an imposed system—that of the text, but also of the circuit of writing, publishing, distribution, and reception of texts that is itself enmeshed in still larger networks. The practice of reading cannot be totally constrained by textual forms or institutional strategies, nor can the meaning that readers make from texts be entirely deduced backward from the texts themselves.

In a study of voluntary reading influenced by Certeau, Rothbauer (in press) found that young women negotiating non-mainstream sexualities used a variety of apparently trivial methods to search for meaningful reading materials, such as naïve Internet searches, casual bookstore browsing, and random remote use of library catalogues. However, these routine information-seeking methods possessed an important symbolic function that signified entry into larger social communities—despite the evaluation of information materials, services, and tools as unsatisfactory and poor.

Reading is but one case of media use that lends its forms and meanings to an analysis using Certeau's theory of everyday life. His insistence on the impermanence and transience of the products created by users as they engage with reified social systems directs researchers to pay deep attention to *how* users tactically appropriate imposed strategies. In the context of information behavior studies this means investigating modes of information searching and use, and the forms of information services and information texts by looking at techniques of use, or "ways of operating," that are situated in taken-for-granted practices of daily life. Through an elucidation of techniques and with a careful mapping of movement through and among systems, resources, and services, mundane and taken-for-granted information practices emerge from an invisible background of empty routine to take on new possibilities for the creation of meaning in everyday life.

Certeau's practice of everyday life maps to the emerging field of everyday life information studies of ordinary people, those operating in non-scientific, non-professional, and non-elite contexts. A full review of relevant studies is not possible here, but studies by Savolainen (1995) and Chatman (see 2000 for an overview) are significant works that brought attention to everyday life information behavior. A special issue of *Library & Information Science Research* (Spink & Cole, 2001) provides a useful introduction to this area of inquiry. Four themes from LIS studies of everyday life are consistent with Certeau's ideas:

1) Information behavior is situated in non-work contexts.

2) Information seeking is a process capable of satisfying needs associated with everyday coping.

3) Although information seeking is frequently conceived of as purposeful, some researchers focus on non-purposeful, incidental behavior (see Erdelez, 1997; Williamson, 1998).

4) Methods of inquiry tend to be qualitative with an emphasis on ethnographic approaches (see McKechnie, 2000; Pettigrew, 1999).

Certeau's theory of the practice of everyday life invites an analysis of social "places" whose strategies lend stability to a set of recognized procedures, but importantly, it also insists on an investigation of the everyday actions of those who inhabit and travel those spaces. His ideas allow researchers to privilege the potentially banal information practices of ordinary people without neglecting the necessary constraints imposed by information systems of all kinds nor by the forms and fashions of informational texts themselves.

Ahearne, J. (1995). *Michel de Certeau: Interpretation and its other*. Cambridge, UK: Polity.

Buchanan, I. (2000). *Michel de Certeau: Cultural theorist*. London: Sage.

Certeau, M. de. (1984). *The practice of everyday life*. S. Rendell (Trans.), Berkeley, CA: University of California Press.

Chatman, E.A. (2000). Framing social life in theory and research. *New Review of Information Behaviour Research, 1*, 3–17.

Driscoll, C. (2002). The moving ground: Locating everyday life. *South Atlantic Quarterly, 100*(2), 381–397.

Erdelez, S. (1997). Information encountering: A conceptual framework for accidental information discovery. In P. Vakkari, R. Savolainen, & B. Dervin (Eds.), *Information seeking in context: Proceedings of an international conference on research in information needs, seeking and use in different contexts* (pp. 412–421). London: Taylor Graham.

McKechnie, L. (E. F.). (2000). Ethnographic observation of preschool children in the public library. *Library & Information Science Research, 22*, 61–76.

Morris, M. (1990). Banality in cultural studies. In P. Mellencamp (Ed.), *Logics of television: Essays in cultural criticism* (pp. 14–43). Bloomington, IN: Indiana University.

Pettigrew, K. E. (1999). Waiting for chiropody: Contextual results from an ethnographic study of the information behaviour among attendees of community clinics. *Information Processing & Management, 35*, 801–817.

Rothbauer, P. (in press). "People aren't afraid anymore, but it's hard to find books:" Reading practices that inform the personal and social identities of self-identified lesbian and queer young women. *Canadian Journal of Information and Library Science, 28*(3).

Savolainen, R. (1995). Everyday life information seeking: Approaching information seeking in the context of "way of life." *Library & Information Science Research, 17*(3), 259–294.

Spink, A., & Cole, C. (2001). Introduction to the special issue: Everyday life information-seeking research. *Library & Information Research, 23*(4), 301–304.

Wiegand, W. (1997). Out of sight, out of mind: Why don't we have any schools of library and reading studies? *Journal of Education in Library and Information Science, 38*, 314–326.

Williamson, K. (1998). Discovered by chance: The role of incidental information acquisition in an ecological model of information use. *Library & Information Science Research, 20*(1), 23–40.

50
Principle of Least Effort

Donald O. Case
College of Communications and Information Studies
University of Kentucky, USA
dcase@uky.edu

The so-called *principle of least effort* (PLE) is sometimes referred to as *the law of least effort* or *Zipf's law*. It originally appeared in a book by George Zipf (1902–1950) of Harvard University, whose area of expertise was philology—what today we would call linguistics. The book, published in 1949, was entitled *Human behavior and the principle of least effort: An introduction to human ecology*. Zipf initially developed the PLE through statistical analysis of word occurrence in documents, and by analyzing other artifacts of human activity, such as the census and other government records. Zipf intended to develop a broad explanation for human activity.

The PLE's premise is that, in performing tasks (e.g., writing or speaking) individuals adopt a course of action that will expend the *probable least average* of their work—the least effort. Many propositions can be derived from the basic premise. One example (among several dozen offered by Poole, 1985) is this: "Information channel use is a function of user awareness." A number of empirical studies have found that, as knowledge of a source, its potential contents and capabilities increases, the use of that source tends to increase; that is, humans tend to return to the sources that they have used in the past in strong preference to trying out new sources of information.

The theory found early adherents in computer science (e.g., Knuth, 1973; Simon, 1955) to achieve efficiencies in dealing with data and computer files, and in linguistics (see Tsonis et al., 1997) to explain language usage. Buckland and Hindle (1969) made an early argument for its applicability to libraries and information work.

Zipf's principle of least effort has been the subject of fruitful research in linguistics for over a half-century. It has also been applied in general computer science applications (e.g., searching) and in bibliographic applications (e.g., index preparation) for several decades. Mann (1993), Gratch (1990), and Bierbaum (1990) have advocated its use in library research aimed to understanding users and their uses. It is especially relevant to studying the *lack* of use of libraries and library materials. Speaking methodologically, the PLE is a prime example of "unobtrusive" research—it relies on traces of human behavior, especially what people leave behind in the way of records or texts. Thus, it lends itself to methods like content analysis, or descriptive statistical analysis.

The PLE was originally developed through content analysis of natural language texts (e.g., of Joyce's *Ulysses*), and later extended to analysis of other distributions (e.g., human population dispersion, resource usage, and personal interactions). Colin Cherry's (1966, pp. 103-109) classic overview relates the PLE to other "statistical studies of language 'form'." More generally, Adamic and Huberman (2002) demonstrate that the PLE is similar to other "power laws," like Pareto's Law regarding income distributions.

The PLE is certainly related to psychological theories that posit the avoidance of "pain" as an instinctual urge. For instance, Sigmund Freud's (1922) "pleasure principle" encapsulates the view that both social and psychological activities stem from a need to reduce emotional tension—a type of "drive reduction." People seek pleasure in order to alleviate unpleasant internal states—painful feelings or felt desires— and thus reduce tension. Donohew, Nair, and Finn (1984), for example, believe that the acquisition of information is an automatic response in us, and typically brings pleasure. Since information seeking implies that people take action in response to some disquieting internal state (e.g., an "anomalous state of knowledge," or "visceral need"), the pleasure principle could be said to apply universally to information seeking. Yet, perhaps because it is common sense that people seek pleasure and avoid pain, Freud is rarely cited in information behavior research.

Although it is not really a theory, the *cost-benefit paradigm* found in decision sciences is sometimes conflated with the PLE, even though it has markedly different assumptions (see Hardy, 1982). The cost-benefit approach is more *normative* in its assumptions, and it is applied toward conscious decisions regarding the expenditure of effort to achieve some goal. The cost-benefit paradigm proposes that as people seek information they select information channels based on their expected benefits weighed against likely costs. Under this paradigm, information seeking is highly rational and emphasizes a calculation of the benefits to be gained from obtaining the most complete and accurate information. An example is the doctor who considers whether she can render an immediate diagnosis based on the symptoms that are presented by the patient, or whether it is worth the time and money to run further laboratory tests before deciding on a treatment plan. The doctor must estimate the likely value of the information yielded by the tests versus the monetary cost and any potential dangers due to a delay in treatment.

In contrast, the PLE, which is chiefly pragmatic and not at all optimal (at least in the short term), predicts that seekers will minimize the effort required to obtain information, even if it means accepting a lower quality or quantity of information. While the cost-benefit approach suggests a continual focus on resource utilization in the short term, PLE may ignore the need to have optimal results on every occasion. However, perhaps there is some long-term benefit in this kind of behavior.

The major strength of the PLE is also its chief weakness: It is a very general theory and tries to explain much of human behavior. Thus, while it can be applied to many phenomena, it lacks specificity and tends to reduce the complexity of human behavior into one explanation that ignores context and individual differences.

The PLE has been most recently applied as an explanation in the use of electronic resources, most notably Web sites (Adamic & Huberman, 2002; Huberman et al., 1998) and citations (White, 2001). In the future it could be fruitfully used to study the tradeoff between the use of documentary sources (e.g., Web pages) and human sources (e.g., through e-mail, listserves, and discussion groups); since both types of sources (documentary and human) are now located conveniently on our desktops, the question becomes: When will we choose one over the other, given that the difference in effort has lessened?

Adamic, L., & Huberman, B. (2002). Zipf's law and the Internet. *Glottometrics* 3, 143–150.

Bierbaum, E. (1990). A paradigm for the '90s. *American Libraries, 21*, 18–19.

Buckland, M., & Hindle, A. (1969). Library Zipf. *Journal of Documentation, 25,* 54–57.

Cherry, C. (1966). *On human communication: A review, a survey and a criticism* (2nd ed.). Cambridge, MA: MIT Press.

Donohew, L., Nair, M., & Finn, S. (1984). Automaticity, arousal, and information exposure. In R. Bostrom, & B. Westley (Eds.), *Communication Yearbook 8* (pp. 267–284). Beverly Hills, CA: Sage.

Freud, S. (1922). *Beyond the pleasure principle* (C. Hubback, Trans.). London: International Psycho-Analytic Press.

Gratch, B. (1990). Exploring the principle of least effort and its value to research. *C&RL News, 51*, 727–728.

Hardy, A. (1982). The selection of channels when seeking information: Cost/benefit vs. least effort. *Information Processing & Management 18*, 289–293.

Huberman, B., Pirolis, P., Pitkow, J., & Lukose, R. (1998). Strong regularities in World Wide Web surfing. *Science, 280*, 95–97.

Knuth, D. (1973). *The art of computer programming, volume three: Sorting and searching.* Reading, MA: Addison-Wesley.

Mann, T. (1993). The principle of least effort. In *Library research models: A guide to classification, cataloging and computers* (pp. 91–101). New York: Oxford University Press.

Poole, H. (1985). *Theories of the middle range.* Norwood, NJ: Ablex.

Simon, H. (1955). On a class of skew distribution functions. *Biometrika 42*, 425–440.

Tsonis, A., Schultz, C., & Tsonis, P. (1997). Zipf's Law and the structure and evolution of languages. *Complexity, 2*(5), 12–13.

White, H. (2001). Authors as citers over time. *Journal of the American Society for Information Science and Technology, 52*(2), 87–108.

Zipf, G. K. (1949). *Human behavior and the principle of least effort: An introduction to human ecology.* Cambridge, MA: Addison-Wesley.

Zipf, G. (1965). *Psycho-biology of languages.* Cambridge, MA: MIT Press.

51
Professions and Occupational Identities

Olof Sundin and Jenny Hedman
Swedish School of Library and Information Science
Göteborg University and University College of Borås, Sweden
olof.sundin@hb.se and jenny.hedman@hb.se

The significance of professionals' information behavior has attracted increased attention during the last few decades in library and information science (LIS). Great effort has been put into exploring information needs, seeking, and use by various occupational groups (e.g., Leckie, Pettigrew, & Sylvain, 1996). This text aims to complement previous research by means of *theory of professions*.

Throughout the 20th century a tradition of theory of professions has been developed and used within the social sciences, primarily in sociology, but also in LIS. This development should be understood in the context of increasing specialization in working life combined with the acceleration of institutionalized expertise in society. Theory of professions focuses on the relations between occupational groups, theoretical knowledge, and the possibilities for practitioners to exclusively apply such knowledge within their occupational practice. Applying such a perspective to the field of information behavior demonstrates that the traditional focus at the two levels of individual and workplace is not always sufficient for a study of information behavior in occupational practices. Instead, workplaces and their concomitant occupational groups should also be related at a societal level. The workplace is a meeting place, not just for practitioners and their clients, but also for competing professional interests, power relations, and occupational identities.

Until the 1970s theorists of professions often held a strong interest in comparing the traits of occupational groups in order to distinguish professions from other occupational groups (MacDonald, 1995). This direction has been characterized as *essentialistic* as it presupposes a certain essence within these professions. Some of the distinguishing traits are that professional practice should be conducted with a starting point in systematic theory, that the intended occupational group is recognized as an authority within its domain, that society sanctions the enterprise in question, that the practitioners work in accordance with ethical codes, and that the professional body controls its own training program. The essentialistic approach has been criticized for, among other things, its view of society as rationalistic and free from conflict, where professionals work altruistically without group interests, solely for the benefit of their clients and thereby for the best interest of society (MacDonald, 1995).

Since the 1970s, research on professions has taken a new focus, namely to study the professional aspirations among occupational groups, or in other words, their *professional project* (e.g., Larson, 1977). Defining professions in order to distinguish them from other occupational groups thereby becomes less significant. Instead, great interest has been directed toward studying the strategies used by different groups to achieve a certain social status as a "profession." The essentialistic traits have come to be regarded as ambitions held by less established professions, such as nurses, social workers, and librarians, rather than as manifestations of a professional core. Within such projects, considerable symbolic significance is attributed to the theoretical knowledge of the occupational groups in question (Collins, 1979). To consider the symbolic significance of knowledge, the users' relation to, and interaction with, information—such as bibliographical databases, online professional communities, and journal articles—often plays a major part (Sundin, in press).

In LIS, theory of professions has principally been used to explore changes in librarianship over time, the development of its knowledge system, and its relation to other occupational groups (e.g., Harris, 1992; Hjørland, 2000; Tuominen, 1997; Winter, 1988; cf. Abbott, 1988). However, theory of professions has also been used in order to understand the information behavior of other professionals (Sundin, 2002, in print; Wilson, 1983). Sundin explicitly applies the theory of professions within his research on nurses' information behavior, and thereby shows how the "relevance" of information and information "needs" are defined in competition between, or within, different professional knowledge domains. By combining interviews and document studies he demonstrates that nurses' professional information, as well as the significance of their information seeking and use, may be seen as part of their professional project (Sundin, 2002, in print). One pertinent concept related to the theory of professions is that of *cognitive authority*, as developed by Patrick Wilson. In his use of this concept Wilson proposes that both the status assigned to information as well as the kind of professional solutions that are considered socially appropriate are negotiated by experts in different professional domains (Wilson, 1983). Wilson expresses this in the following way: "What one needs to know also depends in part on what others expect one to know" (Wilson, 1983, p. 150).

In the brief overview presented above the role of norms, values, and expectations connected to professionals' information needs, seeking and use has been emphasized. In recent research a promising direction of theory of professions stresses the importance of how the use of a *discourse of professionalism* affects individual occupational practitioners (Evetts, 2003; Fournier, 1999). Such processes may be analyzed in accordance with the concept of *occupational identity*. As a practitioner of an occupation, the individual relates to an identity on a collective level, which, to a varying degree, affects the individual's physical and discursive actions. The professional discourse, formed out of prevailing interests, thereby exerts a disciplinary logic that influences individual practitioners' information needs, seeking, and use by mediating a suitable collective occupational identity.

During training for a profession, students not only learn to master a set of intellectual and practical skills; they also become part of a community with specific norms, values, and expectations concerning personal conduct. Different approaches to information behavior may therefore be seen as expressions of occupational identities. Consequently, it is here proposed that the concept of *information needs* should be complemented with the concept of *information interests*. Thereby it is stressed that information behavior should not merely be regarded as expressions of individuals' subjective demands; it is also, in part, something that is negotiated on a social arena. Occupational identities are, from this point of view, not conceived as stable essences within individuals. Rather, they serve as arenas for a diversity of, sometimes conflicting, approaches to one single phenomenon (McCarthy, 1996).

Theory of professions, together with the concepts of *cognitive author-ity*, *occupational identity*, and *information interest*, contributes to a deeper understanding of issues concerning how practitioners' information behavior is formed, maintained, and mediated in society. This theory can be criticized for its lack of interest in the micro level. Research issues studied from this perspective therefore benefit from being complemented with ethnographically oriented studies that include consequences of professional projects for individuals and their actions. In this way, different levels of analysis may be included and interrelated, which makes for a more profound understanding of the information seeking of professionals.

Abbott, A. D. (1988). *The system of professions: An essay on the division of expert labor*. Chicago: University of Chicago Press.

Collins, R. (1979). *The credential society: An historical sociology of education and stratification*. New York: Academic Press.

Evetts, J. (2003). The sociological analysis of professionalism: Occupational change in the modern world. *International Sociology, 18*, 395–415.

Fournier, V. (1999). The appeal to "professionalism" as a disciplinary mechanism. *The Sociological Review, 47*(2), 280–307.

Harris, R. (1992). *Librarianship: The erosion of a woman's profession*. Norwood, NJ: Ablex.

Hjørland, B. (2000). Library and information science: Practice, theory, and philosophical basis. *Information Processing & Management, 36*, 501–531.

Larson, M. S. (1977). *The rise of professionalism*. Berkeley: University of California Press.

Leckie, G. J., Pettigrew, K. E., & Sylvain, C. (1996). Modeling the information seeking of professionals: A general model derived from research on engineers, health care professionals, and lawyers. *The Library Quarterly, 66*, 161–193.

MacDonald, K. M. (1995). *The sociology of the professions*. London: Sage.

McCarthy, E. D. (1996). *Knowledge as culture: The new sociology of knowledge*. London: Routledge.

Sundin, O. (2002). Nurses' information seeking and use as participation in occupational communities. *New Review of Information Behaviour Research, 3*, 187–202.

Sundin, O. (in press). Towards an understanding of symbolic aspects of professional information: An analysis of the nursing knowledge domain. *Knowledge Organization*.

Tuominen, K. (1997). User-centered discourse: An analysis of the subject positions of the user and the librarian. *The Library Quarterly, 67*, 350–371.

Wilson, P. (1983). *Second-hand knowledge: An inquiry into cognitive authority.* Westport, CT: Greenwood Press.

Winter, M. F. (1988). *The culture and control of expertise: Towards a sociological understanding of librarianship.* New York: Greenwood.

52
Radical Change

Eliza T. Dresang
School of Information Studies
Florida State University, USA
edresang@mailer.fsu.edu

The *theory of radical change*, developed in the last decade of the 20th century by Eliza T. Dresang, is based on the premise that many aspects of information behavior and the design of information resources in the digital age can be explained by what Dresang identifies as digital age principles: *interactivity, connectivity,* and *access.* The striking changes in information behavior (including approach to learning) and information design in the 21st century can often be explained or understood only when taking into consideration these principles that dominate and are facilitated by a microchip-saturated society:

- *Interactivity* refers to dynamic, user-initiated, nonlinear, nonsequential, complex information behavior, and representation.

- *Connectivity* refers to the sense of community or construction of social worlds that emerge from changing perspectives and expanded associations.

- *Access* refers to the breaking of long-standing information barriers, bringing entrée to a wide diversity of opinion and opportunity.

These same principles explicate facets of information behavior as well as the presentation of information in both handheld and electronic or Web-based resources.

The roots of this theory go back to Dresang's dissertation research (1981), which gave students varying levels of involvement in choice of topics and resources in a specific learning situation. In addition to a quasi-experiment pretest-posttest design, Dresang employed Dervin's micro-moment interviewing technique to extract meanings from the students' information behavior. The results from both quantitative and qualitative analyses demonstrated the powerful effect of what have evolved into and been identified as the radical change digital age principles of interactivity, connectivity, and access.

The theory was originally developed by Dresang to explain observed changes in information behavior and information resources, particularly for youth in the digital age (Dresang, 2003, 1999a, 1999b, 1997; Dresang & McClelland, 1999). The radical change theory has been used to identify three ways in which the information behavior of youth has changed in the digital age:

1) How they think, learn, give, receive and create information

2) How they perceive themselves and others

3) How they access information and seek community

The theory has identified three concomitant changes in contemporary handheld books:

1) Changing forms and formats

2) Changing perspectives

3) Changing boundaries

This interaction of digital age information seekers with digitally designed resources that bridge the print/digital divide has been described as "rhizomorphic reading" (Burnett & Dresang, 1999).

Working with Melissa Gross and Leslie Holt, Dresang has also applied radical change to a three-year Institute of Museum and Library Services–funded research project studying information behavior of youth in the use of computers in a public library setting. The counterintuitive, to some, social nature of children's computer use, on- and offline, is one of a number of aspects of their information behavior explained by the radical change theory. A series of articles, one of which will focus on an examination of the findings through the "lens" of radical change, was initiated in 2004 (Gross, Dresang, & Holt, in press). A paradigm change proposed by Dresang for the study of information seeking of youth on the Internet, one that is less adult-proscribed and grows more out of the affinity youth have for computers, can also be analyzed from the perspective of radical change (1999b). This perspective is noted in Agosto's model for young people's decision making in using the Web (2002).

The theory of radical change has been applied in the disciplines of Information Studies/Science, Education, English, and in studies of human computer interaction. Researchers who have used radical change to explain information behavior include Dawlene Hammerberg (2001), University of Wisconsin–Madison, who used radical change in her study of young children's "hypertextual" writing behavior. Sylvia Pantaleo (2002), University of Alberta, applied radical change in research studies to understand first-grade children's information behavior when confronted with non-linear texts. Another application of this theory occurs in a dissertation submitted by Marta J. Abele (2003), Capella University. She used radical change to elucidate preservice teachers' changes in information behavior when exposed to non-traditional books. Perry Nodelman, Professor of English, University of Winnipeg, described Dresang as one of "two significant theorists" who have developed explanatory frameworks for changes in contemporary literature for youth (Nodelman & Reimer, 2003, p. 212). John Zbikowski, University of Wisconsin–Waterwater, used radical change to explicate "the relationship between information and communication technologies and literacy development in and out of schools" (personal communication, March 2, 2004), and Judith Ridge, University of Sydney, found it useful in exploring creative writing (personal communication, February 18, 2004).

Radical change has connections with several other information behavior theories or models. For example, aspects of radical change relate to social constructionism; reader response theory; information literacy; Dervin's Sense-Making; Vygotsky's zone of proximal development; and the hybrid information-seeking Web model. The similarities to these theories and models include environmental influence on information behavior, situational sense making, interpretation of information based on perspective, role of adults in youth information seeking, new illiteracies, and interaction of information behavior and resource design.

No specific research design or data collection or analysis methodology accompanies application of the radical change theory. The appropriate design and analysis depends on the context of the investigation. Research designs employing participant observation and case-study methodologies have been used on several occasions in connection with radical change. One frequently used tool is content analysis, applied to resource narratives and visuals and to text collected from open-ended interview questions and from recordings of focus groups.

The potential applications of the radical change theory have not yet been fully explored. The theory is young, but promises to be useful in many circumstances. Shortly before her death, Elfreda Chatman suggested that the theory of radical change had far greater explicative power than had been tapped and that researchers should and would move beyond its current applications to various other aspects of information behavior. One of the strengths of the theory lies in its versatility. Since its applications to date explain information behavior of young children, adolescents, and adults, it appears pertinent to virtually any information seekers in a wide range of information environments.

Another strength is its applicability to contemporary information behavior. Radical change fills a gap in explaining phenomena that have become prevalent in the digital age in a way that no other theory does. The major weakness related to radical change is that it is not yet well known in arenas where it would be useful. Researchers struggle to explain the very information behavior that radical change explicates without awareness that this appropriate theoretical framework exists. Time and further applications will remedy this.

Radical change does what a theory purports to do; it makes sense of what otherwise does not seem easily explicable. It applies the digital age principles of interactivity, connectivity, and access to explain many different aspects of contemporary information behavior and resources. Perhaps its digital age principles make it seem more logically applied to the online environment, but it is equally useful on and offline. The theory started with looking at system design in the technology of the book and has moved on to explaining systems of information behavior.

Abele, M. (2003). Responses to Radical Change children's books by preservice teachers (Doctoral dissertation, Capella University, 2003). *Dissertation Abstracts International, 64,* 2025.

Agosto, D. (2002). A model of young people's decision-making in using the Web. *Library & Information Science Research, 24*(4), 311–341.

Burnett, K., & Dresang, E. (1999). Rhizomorphic reading: The emergence of a new aesthetic in literature for youth. *The Library Quarterly 69*(4), 421–25.

Dresang, E. (1981). Communication conditions and media influence on attitudes and information uses (Doctoral Dissertation, University of Wisconsin-Madison, 1981). *Dissertation Abstracts International, 43,* 294.

Dresang, E. (1997). Influence of the digital environment on literature for youth: Radical Change in the handheld book. *Library Trends, 45*(4), 639–663.

Dresang, E. (1999a). Informal information seeking behavior of youth on the Internet. *Journal of the American Society for Information Science, 50,* 1123–1124.

Dresang, E. (1999b). *Radical Change: Books for youth in a digital age.* New York: H.W. Wilson.

Dresang, E. (2003). Controversial books and contemporary children. *The Journal of Children's Literature, 29*(1), 1–13.

Dresang, E., & McClelland, K. (1999). Radical change: Digital age literature and learning. *Theory into Practice 38*(3), 160-168

Gross, M, Dresang, E., & Holt, L. (in press). Children's in-library use of computers in an urban public library. *Library & Information Science Research, 25.*

Hammerberg, D. (2001). Reading and writing 'hypertextually': Children's literature, technology, and early writing Instruction. *Language Arts, 78*(5), 207–217.

Nodelman, P., & Reimer, M. (2003). *The pleasures of children's literature* (3rd ed.). Boston: Allyn and Bacon.

Pantaleo, S. (2002). Grade 1 students meet David Wiesner's three pigs. *Journal of Children's Literature, 28*(2), 72–84.

53
Reader Response Theory

Catherine Sheldrick Ross
Faculty of Information and Media Studies
The University of Western Ontario, Canada
ross@uwo.ca

M. H. Abrams once argued in *The Mirror and the Lamp* (1953) that the "situation" of the literary text could be understood in terms of four basic coordinates or relations: the *expressive*, which is the relation of the text to its author; the *pragmatic*, which is the relation of text to audience; the *mimetic*, which is the relation of text to the world; and the *objective*, which is the relation of the text to itself as a self-contained autonomous object. The attention given to these various relations has fluctuated as new models and paradigms of reading and criticism displace what went before. Reader-response criticism emphasizes the pragmatic relation of text to audience and came into prominence in the 1970s and 1980s as a rejection of the *new criticism*, a theory of reading that had previously dominated literature teaching in the English Departments of North American universities. This reader-oriented approach has been given emphasis in a number of studies written within the library and information science (LIS) field (Pawley 2002; Ross 1999; Vandergrift 1986; Wiegand 1998). It has also been used as the theoretical framework for studies such as Janice Radway's *Reading the Romance* (1984) or Elizabeth Long's *Book Clubs* (2003), which have been adopted within LIS as key texts in the ethnography of reading..

For LIS researchers interested in the relation between readers and texts, reader-response criticism is valuable because it foregrounds the activity of the reader who constructs meaning from black marks on the page. Research performed within the framework of reader-response theory asks questions about the agency of the reader: What is the reader doing when she reads? What is the relation between the reader and the text? What happens in the process of the reader's making sense of texts? This emphasis on the active reader distinguishes reader-response theory from the theoretical framework used in earlier reading studies conducted in the library field. When the Graduate Library School was established at the University of Chicago in 1928, for example, reading research was selected as a field of particular importance for librarianship and pursued with energy by the School's faculty such as Douglas Waples, Leon Carnovsky, and Louis R. Wilson (Karetsky 1982, pp. 50–52). The tacit assumption underlying their work was that good literature had good effects on readers, hence the importance of judicious book selection and energetic steps to direct readers toward the best books. This text-active theory of reading takes it for granted that the text is comprised of fixed and determinate textual features that are undeniably *there* and have predictable effects on readers; that is, meanings inhere within the text itself and get swallowed whole like a pill. This model is encapsulated in the title of one of Waples's co-authored books, *What Reading Does to People* (1940).

The text-active model of reading that undergirded the sociological studies of reading within the library field in the 1930s and '40s was compatible with the new criticism, which dominated departments of English Literature. The new criticism was interested in what Abrams (1953) called the "objective relation," the attention to the text as a self-contained autonomous object. For the new criticism, the production of meaning was the result of the impersonal operation of a system of signs organizing the form of the text. The proper way to read was the "close reading" of formal elements of the text—its images, themes, patterns of sound, and use of literary conventions—with a view to uncovering the text's unity.

The undermining of this text-active model of reading by reader-response criticism has involved a replacement of the construct of the determinate text by the construct of the reader actively involved in making sense of the text. Influential theorists such as Wolfgang Iser, Hans Robert Jauss, Norman Holland, David Bleich, Stanley Fish, and others wrote about the role of the reader in studies that came to be called reader-response criticism or reception theory. By 1980, three influential books focusing on reader-response signaled that a marked shift of attention had occurred from the autonomous text to the active reader (Fish 1980; Suleiman & Crosman 1980; Tompkins 1980). "The words *reader* and *audience*," writes Susan Suleiman, in her introduction to one of these collections of reader-oriented critical articles, "once relegated to the status of the unproblematic and obvious, have acceded to a starring role" (Suleiman & Crosman, 1980, p. 3). Now the text's meaning is thought to be constituted by the reader's activity in bringing certain horizons of expectations to the text, in selecting which features of the text to attend to, and in responding to these features. Wolfgang Iser (1978) thought of the text as a set of instructions for meaning production, which readers will follow according to their competencies. Even with competent readers, however, variations in interpretations occur because there are always "gaps" in the text that readers have to fill in by drawing on their own experience and imagination.

Others went further in shifting power to the reader and in questioning the notion of the reader as a passive consumer swallowing the whole meanings produced by others. In an influential essay entitled "Reading as Poaching," Michel de Certeau (1984, pp. 169-170) argued that the reader "invents in texts something different from what [their authors] 'intended'. . . . He combines their fragments and creates something unknown. . . . Whether it is a question of newspapers or Proust, the text has a meaning only through its readers; it changes along with them; it is ordered in accord with codes of perception that it does not control." Similarly, in the field of cultural studies, Stuart Hall (1980) has also been interested in readers' compliance with, or resistance to, hegemonic texts and has identified "dominant," "negotiated," and "oppositional" styles of reading.

One drawback for LIS researchers who want to consider reading as a species of information behavior is that most of these reader-oriented theorists were not interested in actual, empirical readers. They focused instead on the role of idealized implied readers, intended readers, mock readers, competent readers, and so on, all of whom had to be inferred from the text. Researchers interested in studying actual readers have found more help from Louise Rosenblatt whose classic text *Literature as Exploration* (1938/1995) outlines a persuasive theory of reading as a transaction. This book, neglected for many years and now rediscovered, has been influential, especially among educational researchers. In it, Rosenblatt described the readers' processes of engagement as they use an array of strategies to construct meaning from the black marks on the page. She claims that the reader "brings to the work personality traits, memories of past events, present needs and preoccupations, a particular mood of the moment, and a particular physical condition. These and many other elements, in a never-to-be-duplicated combination, determine his response to the peculiar contribution of the text" (Rosenblatt, 1995, pp. 30-31).

For those researchers who are interested in the reading behaviors of real readers, the choice among theories of reading has implications for the research questions asked and the research methodologies chosen. Reader-response criticism put an emphasis on what readers do when reading and shifted the emphasis from the self-contained text to the relationship between text and reader. A fruitful area for reading studies has opened up that goes beyond close readings of texts and large-scale surveys of readers to include intensive interviews with individual readers and ethnographies of reading.

Abrams, M. H. (1953). *The mirror and the lamp: Romantic theory and the critical tradition.* New York: Oxford University Press.

Certeau, M. de. (1984). *The practice of everyday life.* Berkeley, CA: University of California Press.

Fish, S. (1980). *Is there a text in this class? The authority of interpretive communities.* Cambridge, MA: Harvard University Press.

Hall, S. (1980). Encoding/decoding. In S. Hall et al. (Eds.), *Culture, media, language: Working papers in cultural studies* (pp. 1972–1979). London: Hutchison University Library.

Iser, W. (1978). *The act of reading: A theory of aesthetic response.* London: Johns Hopkins University Press.

Karetzky, S. (1982). *Reading research and librarianship to 1940: A history and analysis.* Westport, CT: Greenwood Press.

Long, E. (2003). *Book Clubs: Women and the uses of reading in everyday life.* Chicago: University of Chicago Press.

Pawley, C. (2002). Seeking 'significance': Actual readers, specific reading communities. *Book History 5,* 143–160.

Radway, J. (1984). *Reading the romance: Women, patriarchy and popular literature.* Chapel Hill: University of North Carolina Press.

Rosenblatt, L. (1938/1995). *Literature as exploration* (5th ed.). New York: Modern Languages Association.

Ross, C. S. (1999). Finding without seeking: the information encounter in the context of reading for pleasure. *Information Processing & Management 35,* 783–799.

Suleiman, S. R., & Crosman, I., Eds. (1980). *The reader in the text: Essays on audience and interpretation.* Princeton, NJ: Princeton University Press.

Tompkins, J. P., Ed. (1980). *Reader-response criticism: From normalism to post-structuralism*. London: Johns Hopkins University Press.

Vandergrift, K. E. (1986). Using reader response theory to influence collection development and program planning for children and youth. In J. Varlejs (Ed.), *Information seeking: Basing services on users' behaviors* (pp. 53–66). Jefferson, NC: McFarland & Co.

Waples, D., Berelson, B., & Bradshaw, F. R. (1940). *What reading does to people: A summary of evidence on the social effects of reading and a statement of problems for research*. Chicago: University of Chicago Press.

Wiegand, W. A. (1998). Introduction: theoretical foundations for analyzing print culture as agency and practice in a diverse modern America. In J. P. Danky, & W. A. Wiegand (Eds.), *Print culture in a diverse America* (pp. 1–13). Chicago: University of Illinois Press.

54
Rounding and Dissonant Grounds

Paul Solomon
School of Information and Library Science
University of North Carolina at Chapel Hill, USA
solomon@ils.unc.edu

The idea of *rounding* follows from Elfreda Chatman's theoretical work, which builds on her studies of retired women (1992), persons participating in a job training program (1986), and janitors (1987). Chatman's theoretical ideas are expressed particularly in her *JASIS* articles, "The impoverished life-world of outsiders" (1996) and "A theory of life in the round" (1999). Chatman's theoretical work is further founded in her fascination with the notion of information poverty, which she came to realize was not necessarily linked to economic poverty. This realization led her to identify four conceptions—deception, risk-taking, secrecy, and situational relevance, which are developed in her 1996 article to attack intellectual dilemmas that she faced in interpreting anomalous information behaviors by the participants in her studies. Her 1996 article also posits a theory of information poverty consisting of six propositions, which form the four conceptions into a conceptual framework, which explains how the social may influence information behavior to the point of leading people to avoid information seeking.

Her 1999 article provides a further fascinating glimpse into the evolution of her theoretical thinking with regard to human information behavior as it added data collected in a study of women incarcerated in a maximum-security prison. She notes that: "In its small-worldness a prison, for many, is not an uncomfortable place to be" (p. 207) in recognition of the accommodations that her subjects made to *round* their activities to make their lives bearable. Chatman noted several conceptions as coming into play with a life lived in the round. These include small world, social norms, world view, and social types. These conceptions are woven together into a theoretical framework consisting of six propositions:

1) A small world conception is essential to a life in the round because it establishes legitimized others . . . within that world who set boundaries on behavior.

2) Social norms force private behavior to undergo public scrutiny. It is this public arena that deems behavior—including information-seeking behavior—appropriate or not.

3) The result of establishing appropriate behavior is the creation of a worldview. This worldview includes language, values, meaning, symbols, and a context that holds the worldview within temporal boundaries.

4) For most of us, a worldview is played out as life in the round. Fundamentally, this is a life taken for granted. It works most of the time with enough predictability that, unless a critical problem area arises, there is no point in seeking information.

5) Members who live in the round will not cross the boundaries of their world to seek information.

6) Individuals will cross information boundaries only to the extent that the following conditions are met: 1) the information is perceived as critical; 2) there is a collective expectation that the information in relevant; and 3) a perception exists that the life lived in the round is no longer functioning. (Chatman, 1999, 214)

There is a fundamental insight resulting from Chatman's body of empirical and theoretical work, which is highlighted by the term *rounding*: life in the round is about making life manageable. Could it be that the way that we manage information in our lives is by *rounding* what we consider to be information, what strategies we employ to find information, which people and other sources we rely on for information, what conditions lead us to seek information, and so on? Thus, overall, *rounding* seems to capture the difference between a focus on information seeking alone, which expresses a disciplinary norm in information science, and the idea of discovering information in context (Solomon, 2002), which tries to express the *rounding* that takes place as people interact with the people, information, and technology that they find situationally relevant. This later view adds a dimension to the work of information professionals that involves helping people find the information that they want rather than solely providing them with the information we think they ought to need.

Chatman's theoretical ideas do not just apply to the marginalized in society. These patterns of behavior that Chatman found in the various contexts she studied are evident in the contexts of everyday life and work as well. For example, Solomon's studies of work planning in a governmental organization (1997) and exploration of information behaviors as patterns of action that structure among people engaged in work planning, writing a college paper, and travel planning (1999) all found evidence of rounding as well as departures from the rounding when life in the round was no longer working. In a negative sense rounding may lead to the absence of relevant information (from the point of view of the information professional) as the continuity of rounding works as a structure that helps people manage their lives in ways that are comfortable for them. In a positive sense the structures that allow rounding may be abandoned when they no longer work or continuity is lost. Yet, rounding works for us as a means of simplifying our lives by including what seems to work for us and leaving out the rest. Thus, the positive and negative of these two statements expresses a tension between the structures and actions that we constantly confront in the information field (Solomon, 2000). Perhaps a way of managing this tension is to recognize that people may break out of the round when their rounding no longer enables them to act satisfactorily. An implication for practice may be to design systems and services that support learning. The result would be direct support of both information seeking and information encountering (Erdelez, 1997) as people live life in the round.

This presentation of rounding has a largely individual or personal flavor to it, but this is not necessarily so. Certainly, the various conceptions that Chatman develops in connection with her theories of information poverty and life in the round (e.g., secrecy, social norms) concern the social pressures that others place on individual and group action. Solomon's studies of work planning (1997), college students (1999), and with Hara (2004) of collaboration of chemists and chemical engineers have explored rounding at the social level of people in work/research teams, task interaction across units of an organization, and collaboration across disciplines and time and space. It seems that there is a common pattern across these contexts of *dissonant grounds*. The basic idea is that rounding is "bigger" than any individual, but encompasses ways of thinking, especially with regard to specifying, seeking, and giving meaning to information related to tasks and functions of social units and types. The *ground* is, thus, the social construction, which shapes the individual rounding of its members and, thus, gives meaning to the activities of a social unit. There is a strong potential for grounds to become dissonant when people from different grounds come together to engage in activities that involve coordination or interaction. Thus, in the collaboration of chemists and chemical engineers, dissonance occurred when people utilized seemingly common terms in different technical ways, when chemists with a strong research ethic came together with engineers with a strong problem-solving ethic, and when the scope of activity of the chemical processes under consideration differed in terms of scale (i.e., what works in the laboratory versus what works in the factory).

Rounding and dissonant grounds, thus, seem to be different views of the same phenomena. Organizations round, albeit in more complex ways, just as individuals. Recognizing (and expecting) dissonance as teams, units, or other organizational forms come together (or not) to accomplish activities has important implications for both understanding information behavior and the practice of information professionals.

Chatman, E. A. (1986). Diffusion theory: A review and test of a conceptual model in information diffusion. *Journal of the American Society for Information Science*, *37*, 377–386.

Chatman, E. A. (1987). The information world of low-skilled workers. *Library & Information Science Research*, *9*, 265–283.

Chatman, E. A. (1992). *The information world of retired women*. Westport, CT: Greenwood Press.

Chatman, E. A. (1996). The impoverished life-world of outsiders. *Journal of the American Society for Information Science*, *47*, 193–206.

Chatman, E. A. (1999). A theory of life in the round. *Journal of the American Society for Information Science*, *50*, 207–217.

Erdelez, S. (1997). Information encountering: A conceptual framework for accidental information discovery. In P. Vakkari, R. Savolainen, & B. Dervin (Eds.), *Information seeking in context* (pp. 412–421). London: Taylor Graham.

Hara, N., & Solomon, P. (2004). *Collaboration in a multi-institutional scientific research center: Understanding sense making during the formative period of an organization.* Manuscript submitted for publication.

Solomon, P. (1997). Discovering information behavior in sense making. II. The social. *Journal of the American Society for Information Science, 48,* 1109–1126.

Solomon, P. (1999). Information mosaics: Patterns of action that structure. In T. D. Wilson, & D. K. Allen (Eds.), *Exploring the contexts of information behaviour* (pp. 150–175). London: Taylor Graham.

Solomon, P. (2000). Exploring structuration in knowledge organization: Implications for managing the tension between stability and dynamism. *Advances in Knowledge Organization, 7,* 254–260.

Solomon, P. (2002). Discovering information in context. *Annual Review of Information Science and Technology, 36,* 229–264.

55
Serious Leisure

Jenna Hartel
Department of Information Studies
University of California, Los Angeles, USA
jhartel@ucla.edu

Serious leisure is a constellation of insights about the activities that happen within leisure time. It is useful for studying information behavior in the leisure parts of everyday life, where few research precedents exist, notwithstanding such notable exceptions as Hektor (2001), Julien & Michels (2004), Kari (2001), Pettigrew (2000), Pettigrew, Durrance, & Unruh (2002), Ross (1999), and Savolainen (1995).

Though leisure is personally cherished and socially important, it may also seem nebulous, unstructured, and marginal to information behavior investigators, who have traditionally focused on academic or professional settings. A key insight of serious leisure is that leisure is not homogenous in character but takes two forms: *serious* and *casual*. The *serious* kind of leisure is highly informational and involves knowledge acquisition. Hence the most important feature of serious leisure is that it establishes a mandate for the library and information studies field to explore certain leisure realms. Further, serious leisure supplies definitions, descriptions, and classes that make leisure a more approachable research topic.

Serious leisure was coined in 1982 by Robert Stebbins and is based upon wide-ranging ethnographic research. Though a sociologist, Stebbins considers serious leisure to be interdisciplinary, for it draws from nearly every social science. Conveniently, Stebbins recently summarized the literature on serious leisure in the landmark, *New directions in the theory and research of serious leisure* (Stebbins, 2001). Serious leisure was introduced into library and information studies in 2004 by Hartel who sees it as a call to action and cornerstone for a research program on the informational dimensions of leisure (Hartel, 2004).

A starting point for this concept is to view the day as comprised of four types of activity: paid work, unpaid work, self-care, and free time (Robinson & Godbey, 1997). Leisure happens in this last segment, and is

313

the "uncoerced activity undertaken in free time" (Stebbins, 2002, p. 15). Next, leisure is divided into two forms: serious and casual, which differ markedly. Serious leisure is "the systematic pursuit of an [activity] participants find so substantial and interesting that in the typical case they launch themselves on a career centered on acquiring and expressing its special skills, knowledge, and experience" (Stebbins, 2001, p. 3). The word "serious" in this usage implies concentration and dedication, not gravity, for serious leisure is largely fun. Serious leisure has three varieties: *amateurism*, *volunteering*, and *hobbies.*

The counterpart to serious leisure is *casual leisure*, "the immediately and intrinsically rewarding, relatively short-lived, pleasurable activity requiring little or no special training to enjoy it" (Stebbins, 2001, p. 58). Put another way, casual leisure is, "doing what comes naturally" and it is one of life's simple joys. Napping, watching television, or kissing a sweetheart are prime examples. There are six types of casual leisure: *play, relaxation, passive entertainment, active entertainment, sociable conversation,* and *sensory stimulation.* Because casual leisure does not require knowledge acquisition (one needn't *learn* how to nap!) it may be a less-compelling subject for information behavior research, but is mentioned to bring the distinct qualities of serious leisure into relief.

Stebbins has identified six essential qualities to all serious leisure pursuits. These qualities supply background insights while also suggesting good information-related research questions. To start, serious leisure involves proactive acquisition of knowledge and skill. It is likely this process of knowledge acquisition and its resources that information behavior scholars will seek to explicate. Second, serious leisure includes an occasional need to persevere, as when a cook searches doggedly for the ideal recipe. Third, there is a leisure version of a career that proceeds in stages: beginning, development, establishment, maintenance, and decline. The evolution of information phenomena over the arc of the career is an important and unexplored issue. Fourth, serious leisure has 10 durable benefits, which are personal and social rewards (see Stebbins, 2001, pp. 13–15). Next, participants in serious leisure have a strong identification with their community, which may manifest in displays of affiliation such as a style of dress. Finally, there is a unique ethos or culture to serious leisure realms.

Serious leisure also has a relative intensity scale. Here, imagine the nonchalant and occasional sailor, versus one who is "gung-ho." Those with low levels of involvement are participants, while the ultra-passionate are devotees. Doing serious leisure sporadically (outside of the career stages) is dabbling and is performed by dabblers.

Research on serious leisure can occur at five possible levels of analysis: the personal, interactional, mesostructural, structural, and sociocultural (see Stebbins, 2001, pp. 21–25). Generally speaking, this echoes the "micro" to "macro" poles common to research in the social sciences. Along this axis, the disciplinary emphasis shifts, as would the theoretical approach to information behavior research. The personal level is the province of psychology, and in information behavior may involve a cognitive orientation, such as that of Kuhlthau (1993). The mesostructural level looks at the dynamics of groups and orients sociologically, akin to Chatman's work on prisoners (1999) and the elderly (1996). The most abstract stratum, the sociocultural, engages sociology and anthropology; it is manifest in bibliometrics or domain analysis (Hjorland & Albrechtsen, 1995).

The set of analytical devices just reviewed applies to any of the three forms of serious leisure: amateurism, volunteering, and hobbies. Hartel (2004) argues that hobbies are the plum starting point for information behavior research because of their prevalence. Here, amateurism and volunteering will be tabled so that hobbies can be reviewed in detail.

By definition, a hobby is "the systematic and enduring pursuit of a reasonably evolved and specialized free-time activity" (Stebbins, 2003). Stebbins' research into hobbies has identified five general classes: collectors, makers and tinkerers, activity participants, players of sports and games, and liberal arts enthusiasts (Stebbins, 2001, p. 5). Stamp collecting, knitting, ballroom dancing, playing checkers, and following politics, respectively, are popular examples of individual types of hobbies within the broad classes.

The classes are self-explanatory, except for the liberal arts enthusiasts, who become fascinated with a subject and learn about it incessantly. These hobbyists may amass impressive collections of books and gain reputations as lay experts (see Stebbins, 2001, pp. 27–40). Members of this hobby class should be of particular interest to the information behavior community because of their fervor for information.

Scholarship under the umbrella of serious leisure is sometimes enhanced with the theory of *social worlds* (Unruh, 1980). Social worlds are communities held together by a shared interest. According to Stebbins, the social unit that forms amidst serious leisure is a social world. Additional insights and instruments can be brought to bear on a research project by applying social worlds theory (see Unruh, 1980).

It is important to note that serious leisure and social worlds are not metatheories or theories of information; nor do they determine research design or methods for information behavior projects. Rather, they are interdisciplinary constructs that illuminate features of everyday life and leisure. Per sociologists Wagner & Berger (1985, p. 703) they are "unit theories," a set of concepts specified into a concrete setting (i.e., leisure). Information behavior researchers must adopt theories that matches their research questions. Hartel (2004), for example, paired serious leisure with domain analysis (Hjorland & Albrechtsen, 1995) to study the information forms of hobby cooking.

In some forms of leisure, serious leisure beckons the information behavior community to take leisure seriously. Its descriptive and classificatory elements illuminate, isolate, and stabilize serious leisure subjects so that information behavior research can occur rigorously and systematically. This opens up an exciting and virtually unexplored frontier for the library and information studies field.

Chatman, E. A. (1996). The impoverished life-world of outsiders. *Journal of the American Society of Information Science, 47*, 193–206.

Chatman, E. A. (1999). A theory of life in the round. *Journal of the American Society for Information Science, 50*, 207–217.

Hartel, J. (in press). The serious leisure frontier in library and information studies: Hobby domains. *Knowledge Organization*.

Hektor, A. (2001). *What's the use? Internet and information behavior in everyday life.* Linkoping, Sweden: Linkoping University, Tema.

Hjorland, B., & Albrechtsen, H. (1995). Toward a new horizon in information science: Domain analysis. *Journal of the American Society for Information Science, 46*, 400–425.

Julien, H., & Michels, D. (2004). Intra-individual information behavior. *Information Processing and Management, 40*, 547–562.

Kari, J. (2001). *Information seeking and interest in the paranormal: Towards a process model of information action.* Unpublished doctoral dissertation, University of Tampere, Finland.

Kuhlthau, C. C. (1993). A principle of uncertainty for Information seeking. *Journal of Documentation, 49*(4), 339–355.

Pettigrew, K. E. (2000). Lay information provision in community settings: How community health nurses disseminate human services information to the elderly. *The Library Quarterly, 70,* 47–85.

Pettigrew, K. E., Durrance, J. C., & Unruh, K. T. (2002). Facilitating community information-seeking using the Internet: Findings from three public library-community network systems. *Journal of the American Society for Information Science & Technology, 53,* 894–903.

Robinson, J. P., & Godbey, G. (1997). *Time for life: The surprising ways Americans use their time.* University Park, PA: Pennsylvania State University Press.

Ross, C. (1999). Finding without seeking: the information encounter in the context of reading for pleasure. *Information Processing and Management, 35,* 783–799.

Savolainen, R. (1995). Everyday life information seeking: Approaching information seeking in the context of way of life. *Library & Information Science Research, 17*(3), 259–294.

Stebbins, R. A. (2002). Choice and experiential definitions of leisure. *LSA Newsletter, 63,* 15–17.

Stebbins, R. A. (2001). *New directions in the theory and research of serious leisure: Mellen Studies in Sociology, vol. 28.* Lewiston, NY: Edwin Mellen Press.

Stebbins, R. A. (2003). Hobbies. In *Encyclopedia of leisure and outdoor recreation.* London: Routledge.

Unruh, D. R. (1980). The nature of social worlds. *Pacific Sociological Review, 23,* 271–296.

Wagner, D., & Berger, J. (1985). Do sociological theories grow? *American Journal of Sociology, 90,* 697–728.

56
Small-World Network Exploration

Lennart Björneborn
Department of Information Studies
Royal School of Library and Information Science, Denmark
lb@db.dk

On the Web, so-called small-world network properties are concerned with short distances along link paths through intermediate Web pages and Web sites. Small-world link structures deal with core library and information science issues such as *navigability* and *accessibility* of information across vast document networks on the Web. For instance, short connectivity distances along link paths on the Web affect the speed and exhaustivity with which Web crawlers can reach and retrieve Web pages when following links from Web page to Web page. Further, small-world link topologies of the Web may have implications for the way users surf the Web and the ease with which they gather information (Adamic, 1999).

Small-world theory stems from research in social network analysis on short distances between two arbitrary persons through intermediate chains of acquaintances (Milgram, 1967; Pool & Kochen, 1978/1979; Kochen, 1989), popularized by the notion of "six degrees of separation" (Guare, 1990).

Watts & Strogatz (1998) revived small-world theory by introducing a small-world network model characterized by a combination of highly clustered network nodes and short average path lengths between pairs of nodes. Watts and Strogatz showed that in a small-world network it is sufficient to have a small percentage of "long-range" connections functioning as shortcuts connecting "distant" nodes of the network. Subsequent research has revealed small-world network properties in a wide variety of networks, including biochemical, neural, ecological, physical, technical, social, economical, and informational networks (e.g., Albert & Barabási, 2002). For instance, scientific collaboration networks and semantic networks may show small-world features. The coincidence of high local clustering and short global separation (Watts, 1999) means that small-world networks simultaneously consist of small local and global distances, enabling high efficiency in propagating information, ideas, contacts, signals, energy, viruses, etc., both on a local and global scale in different networks.

Small-world link topologies have been identified in large areas of the hypertextual document networks of the Web (e.g., Adamic, 1999; Albert, Jeong, & Barabási, 1999; Broder et al., 2000). The Web is constructed through *collaborative weaving* by millions of local link creators (Björneborn, 2004). From their micro-level positions, the link creators cannot see how their links fit into the self-organizing macro-level aggregations of link clusters as there exists no global registry and mapping of the Web.

Logically, the distributed knowledge organization of the Web affects options for users' information behavior. In other words, the ways information resources are organized and interconnected on the Web influence the ways in which the Web may be navigated and exploited by users who access information by searching, browsing, serendipitous encountering, or combinations of these different information behaviors (e.g., Catledge & Pitkow, 1995; Erdelez, 2000).

Convergent goal-directed search behavior may identify central points of information that subsequently may function as points of departure for more divergent behavior including browsing and serendipity (Björneborn, 2004). Correspondingly, information that is serendipitously encountered may lead to a need for more focused search strategies. Users moving through an information space may thus change direction and behavior several times as their information needs and interests may develop or get triggered, depending on options and opportunities encountered on their way.

Serendipity—the attentive ability to find unexpected but useful information—typically occurs when users engage in exploratory, browsing information behavior (e.g., Bates, 1986; Cove & Walsh, 1988; Chang & Rice, 1993; Erdelez, 2000; Toms, 2000). Such behavior may help researchers and others to discover information that they did not know they needed, or that they did not know existed. In other words, serendipity may occur when the interest space of a user—i.e., the multitude of tasks, problems, and interests, which are more or less urgent or latent in the user's life and related to work, leisure, etc.—is triggered when the user traverses an information space (e.g., a city, a library, the Web) and encounters contents, options, and pointers offered by this information space (Björneborn, 2004).

The Web was developed as a tool to facilitate easy access to networked information sharing and browsing. Web links may function as subject access points and guiding tools that may help users to discover optional and alternative directions and "loopholes" to encounter information. Traversal options and access points to information on the Web depend on *where* and *where to* millions of Web constructors have placed and targeted links. A human Web surfer or digital Web crawler exploring the Web by following links from Web page to Web page has the possibility to move from one topic cluster to another topically distant cluster by following a single cross-topic link on, for example, a personal link list, as a small-world shortcut.

The shorter the link distances are between Web pages and Web sites belonging to different topical domains, the larger the probability of encountering unexpected information while traversing these link structures. However, there are no straightforward causal relations between small-world knowledge organization and serendipitous possibilities. As stated by several researchers, (e.g., Kleinberg, 2000; Adamic et al., 2001; Menczer, 2002) it is difficult to identify shortest link paths across a Web space if only information about *local* link topologies is available, as is the case for human Web surfers or digital Web crawlers following links.

Special decentralized algorithms have been developed that utilize local connectivity information for identifying short paths through a network if no global link data are vacant. In particular, well-connected hub-like nodes may be exploited in such decentralized algorithms. Findings by Björneborn (2004) on what types of links, Web pages, and sites function as cross-topic connectors in a small-world academic Web space suggest that, for instance, the rich diversity of inlinks and outlinks to and from computer-science Web sites and link lists on personal Web pages could be utilized for such computer-aided navigation along small-world shortcuts.

As academic Web spaces increasingly include self-presentations and link creations by scholars, the sociology of science may employ small-world approaches including the concepts of *weak ties* (Granovetter,

1973) and *betweenness centrality* (Freeman, 1977) for automatic detection of informal social networks or "invisible colleges" (Crane, 1972) and central "gatekeepers," as well as for tracking interdisciplinary connections across scientific domains (Björneborn & Ingwersen, 2001; Björneborn, 2004).

Finally, future visualization tools of Web search engines may get more sophisticated, for instance, with zoomable maps of topical Web clusters and cross-topic small-world shortcuts. Such maps might facilitate the aforementioned complementarities of *convergent* goal-directed searching and *divergent* serendipitous browsing and information encountering (Björneborn, 2004).

Adamic, L. A. (1999). The small world Web. *Lecture Notes in Computer Science, 1696*, 443–452.

Adamic, L. A., Lukose, R. M., Puniyani, A. R., & Huberman, B. A. (2001). Search in power-law networks. *Physical Review E, 64*, 46135.

Albert, R., & Barabási, A. L. (2002). Statistical mechanics of complex networks. *Reviews of Modern Physics, 74*(1), 47–97.

Albert, R., Jeong, H., & Barabási, A. L. (1999). Diameter of the World Wide Web. *Nature, 401*, 130–131.

Bates, M. J. (1986). An exploratory paradigm for online information retrieval. In: Brookes, B.C. (Ed.), *Proceedings of the 6th international research forum in information science (IRFIS 6)* (pp. 91-99). Amsterdam: North-Holland.

Björneborn, L. (2004). *Small-world link structures across an academic Web space: A library and information science approach.* Doctoral dissertation, Royal School of Library and Information Science, Copenhagen, Denmark. Available: www.db.dk/lb/phd/phd-thesis.pdf

Björneborn, L., & Ingwersen, P. (2001). Perspectives of Webometrics. *Scientometrics, 50*(1), 65–82.

Broder, A., Kumar, R., Maghoul, F., Raghavan, P., Rajagopalan, S., Stata, R., Tomkins, A., & Wiener, J. (2000). Graph structure in the Web. *Computer Networks, 33*, 309–320.

Catledge, L. D., & Pitkow, J. E. (1995). Characterizing browsing strategies in the World-Wide Web. *Computer Networks and ISDN Systems, 26*(6), 1065–1073.

Chang, S. J., & Rice, R. E. (1993). Browsing : a multidimensional framework. *Annual Review of Information Science and Technology, 28*, 231–276.

Cove, J. F., & Walsh, B. C. (1988). Online text retrieval via browsing. *Information Processing & Management, 24*(1), 31–37.

Crane, D. (1972). *Invisible colleges: Diffusion of knowledge in scientific communities*. Chicago: University of Chicago Press.

Erdelez, S. (2000). Towards understanding information encountering on the Web. *Proceedings of the 63rd ASIS Annual Meeting, 37*, 363–371. Medford, NJ: Information Today.

Freeman, L. C. (1977). A set of measures of centrality based on betweenness. *Sociometry, 40*(1), 35–41.

Granovetter, M. S. (1973). The strength of weak ties. *American Journal of Sociology, 78*(6), 1360–1380.

Guare, J. (1990). *Six degrees of separation: A play*. New York: Vintage.

Kleinberg, J. M. (2000). Navigation in a small world. *Nature, 406*, 845.

Kochen, M., Ed. (1989). *The small world*. Norwood, NJ: Ablex.

Menczer, F. (2002). Growing and navigating the small world Web by local content. *Proceedings of the National Academy of Sciences, 99*(22), 14014–14019.

Milgram, S. (1967). The small-world problem. *Psychology Today, 1*(1), 60–67.

Pool, I. de S., & Kochen, M. (1978/1979). Contacts and influence. *Social Networks, 1*, 5–51.

Toms, E. G. (2000). Serendipitous information retrieval. *Proceedings of the First DELOS Network of Excellence Workshop on Information Seeking, Searching and Querying in Digital Libraries, Zurich, Switzerland*. Available: www.ercim.org/publication/ws-proceedings/DelNoe01/3_Toms.pdf

Watts, D. J. (1999). *Small worlds: The dynamics of networks between order and randomness*. Princeton, NJ: Princeton University Press.

Watts, D. J., & Strogatz, S. H. (1998). Collective dynamics of "small-world" networks. *Nature, 393*, 440–442.

57
Nan Lin's Theory of Social Capital

Catherine A. Johnson
School of Information Studies
University of Wisconsin–Milwaukee, USA
johnson@sois.uwm.edu

The notion of social capital was popularized during the early 1990s by scholars working in several different fields, and different lenses for viewing social capital thus abound. For instance, sociologist James Coleman and political scientist Robert Putnam consider social capital to be a collective resource and it is the strong interconnections between individuals which foster "sturdy norms of generalized reciprocity and encourage the emergence of social trust" (Putnam, 1995, p. 66). Other researchers, such as Nan Lin of Duke University, view social capital as an individual resource. Lin's theory of social capital is rooted in the concepts of social network analysis, which provides methodological tools for investigating the relationships or ties between individuals. The network of relationships comprises the social network. Social resources are the goods possessed by individuals in the network and can consist of intangible goods such as social status, research collaboration, and information as well as material goods, such as money or a car. These goods are considered social resources because they are available to an individual through his or her social relationships. Access to these resources depends on the relationship with the individual possessing the resource and where one is located in the social structure.

Social capital, therefore, is defined by Lin (2001b, p. 12), as "resources embedded in a social structure which are accessed and/or mobilized in purposive actions." The theory explains how the quality of social resources available to an individual within his or her social network influences the success of achieving desired outcomes or goals. People with better social capital are more likely to get ahead than people with poorer social capital. The theory of social capital grew out of Lin's social resources theory (Lin & Dumin, 1986). The impetus for the theory was to better define what social capital is and provide a method for measuring it.

Lin's work has mainly focused on status attainment and how social capital affects access to better jobs and hence higher status.

In sociology, social capital theory has mainly been used to explain how social structure affects access to better jobs. Studies have also investigated how social capital affects the job search of poor, urban African Americans (Smith, 2003), Internet use (Wellman & Haythornthwaite, 2003), and the search for information (Johnson, 2003).

Social capital theory and methods of social network analysis can be used effectively to understand the structural and relational dimensions of information behavior. For instance, although it is well-known that people prefer personal sources of information over more formal sources, it is not generally known who gets chosen and how ties (relationships) and social structure affect the choice of an information source. Using the methods of social network analysis it is possible to determine the relationship between the information seeker and information source, and the social position of the information source in relation to the information seeker as well as in relation to other people in the information seeker's network. Knowing how social structure affects information seeking may help to explain why people in certain social groups are less able than others to acquire the information they need. Using Lin's position generator, outcomes of information-seeking episodes can be evaluated in terms of social capital.

Names of members of an individual's social network can be elicited in a number of different ways (Flap, Snijders, Volker, & van der Gaag, 2003). In many social network studies, the common method used to elicit names of members of an individual's social network is the *name generator*. The name generator elicits names by asking respondents who of their acquaintances, friends, or relatives they would call upon in certain situations, usually involving an exchange of some sort—a conversational exchange (e.g., with whom do you discuss personal matters?) or exchanges involving help to carry out tasks or providing access to resources. The name generator also elicits names by asking respondents about the emotional content of relationships—for example, "who are your closest friends?" A problem with the name generator, however, lies with the difficulty of eliciting comparable network samples when the questions used to elicit the networks are either subjective or refer to exchange relationships that cannot be systematically sampled.

The *position generator* was developed by Lin and Dumin (1986) to provide a more systematic way of eliciting network members in order to measure the social capital of an individual. It consists of a list of ordered structural positions that are salient to the society or organization being studied. These structural positions can be occupations, authorities, work units, classes, or any other positions that can represent the hierarchical structure of the social group or society of interest. The positions are assigned a prestige score and then ranked. Study respondents are asked to name people they know in each of these occupations or positions. Social capital is measured based on how high up the position generator the respondent can reach (*reach*), the difference between the highest and lowest position accessed (*range*), and how many different occupations in which they know people (*diversity*). Reach, range, and diversity are the measures of social capital obtained from the position generator.

Social capital theory dovetails nicely with several established frameworks for studying information behavior. Regarding Chatman's information poverty (1996, 2000), findings from past studies indicate that social capital is related to education and income. Since the poor tend to prefer informal sources (i.e., people) over more formal sources of information, their difficulties in finding the information they need may be related to their lack of social capital. On a different note, social capital theory complements Erdelez's (1997) information encountering, since social capital and social structure may explain passive acquisition of information: Those with better social capital have better quality social resources and therefore are more likely to be in a position to encounter useful information either directly or by proxy. Similarly and regarding Savolainen's (1995) everyday life information-seeking framework, as part of daily life people search for information that cuts across a variety of sectors, for instance health, education, finances, and employment. Having a greater variety of people in one's social network, with high-quality resources such as education and jobs, may make it more likely that they will find the information they need. Finally, considering Pettigrew's (1999; Fisher, Durrance, & Hinton, 2004) information grounds theory, people who get together in diverse groups are more likely to meet people from different social or work backgrounds. This gives people the opportunity to interact with others who have access to different and presumably better resources and thus add to their social capital. The findings that certain information grounds may be more conducive to information acquisition than others may be explained by the level of social capital present.

Social capital theory provides a useful framework for examining information behavior. It provides a way of understanding how the social structure affects both access to information and the flow of information between members of social groups or organizations. The main strength of the theory is that it provides a method for measuring social capital which can be assessed against information-seeking outcomes.

The measurement of social capital also is one of the more problematic elements of the theory. Since the position generator and the theory of social capital is based on a hierarchical depiction of society, when the groups being studied are not obviously hierarchical it may be difficult to identify ranked positions. For instance, members of an academic department or of a poor neighborhood may not vary appreciably in their access to social resources. While occupations usually have prestige rankings assigned to them, other positions chosen to represent structural locations may not have prestige scores and therefore the researcher will have to do additional research to develop reliable rankings. Overall, social capital theory can be fruitfully applied to information behavior when attempting to understand how social context or social factors affect people's ability to find the information they need.

Chatman, E. A. (1996). The impoverished life-world of outsiders. *Journal of the American Society for Information Science, 47,* 193–206.

Chatman, E. A. (2000). Framing social life in theory and research. *The New Review of Information Behaviour Research, 1,* 3–18.

Coleman, J. S. (1988). Social capital in the creation of human capital. *American Journal of Sociology, 94,* S95–S120.

Davenport, E., & Snyder, H. W. (2004). Managing social capital. In B. Cronin (Ed.), *Annual Review of Information Science & Technology, 39* (pp. 517–550) Medford, NJ: Information Today.

Erdelez, S. (1997). Information encountering: A conceptual framework for accidental information discovery. In P. Vakkari, R. Savolainen, & B. Dervin (Eds.), *Information seeking in context: Proceedings of an international conference on research in information needs, seeking and use in different contexts* (pp. 412–421). London: Taylor Graham.

Fisher, K. E., Durrance, J. C., & Hinton, M. B. (2004). Information grounds and the use of need-based services by immigrants in Queens, NY: A context-based, outcome evaluation approach. *Journal of the American Society for Information Science & Technology,* 55. 754–766.

Flap, H., Snijders, T., Volker, B., & van der Gaag, M. (2003). Measurement instruments for social capital of individuals. Retrieved February 28, 2004, from www.xs4all. nl/~gaag/work/SSND.pdf

Johnson C. A. (2003). *Information networks: Investigating the information networks of Mongolia's urban residents.* Unpublished doctoral dissertation, University of Toronto.

Lin, N. (2001a). *Social capital: A theory of social structure and action.* Cambridge, UK: Cambridge University Press.

Lin, N. (2001b). Building a network theory of social capital. In N. Lin, K. Cook & R. S. Burt (Eds.), *Social capital: Theory and research* (pp. 3-29). New York: Aldine de Gruyter.

Lin, N., & Dumin, M. (1986). Access to occupations through social ties. *Social Networks 8,* 365–385.

Lin, N., Fu, Y.- C., & Hsung, R.- M. (2001). The position generator: Measurement techniques for investigations of social capital. In N. Lin, K. Cook & R. S. Burt (Eds.), *Social capital: Theory and research* (pp. 3–29). New York: Aldine de Gruyter.

Pettigrew, K. E. (1999). Waiting for chiropody: Contextual results from an ethnographic study of the information behavior among attendees at community clinics. *Information Processing & Management, 35,* 801–817.

Putnam, R. D. (1995). Bowling alone: America's declining social capital. *Journal of Democracy,* 6(1), 65–78.

Savolainen, R. (1995). Everyday life information seeking: Approaching information seeking in the context of "way of life." *Library and Information Science Research, 17,* 259–294.

Smith, S. S. (2003). Exploring the efficacy of African American's job referral networks: A study of the obligations of exchange around job information and influence. *Ethnic & Racial Studies 26,* 1029–1046.

Wellman, B., & Haythornthwaite, C., Eds. (2002). *The Internet in everyday life.* Oxford: Blackwell Publishers.

58

The Social Constructionist
Viewpoint on Information Practices

Kimmo Tuominen
The Library of Parliament, Finland
Kimmo.Tuominen@eduskunta.fi

Sanna Talja and Reijo Savolainen
Department of Information Studies
University of Tampere, Finland
Sanna.Talja@uta.fi and Reijo.Savolainen@uta.fi

Social constructionism (constructionism) focuses on talk, interaction, and language use in various contexts. In information studies, constructionism provides a dialogic viewpoint to study the assumptions and implicit theories that people draw on when they engage in information practices and produce accounts of them. This kind of *discursive information research* (DIR) aims at capturing the socially and culturally shaped ways of understanding information practices, that is, the practices of seeking, accessing, creating, using, and sharing information.

From the constructionist viewpoint, the concept "information practice" is preferred over "information behavior," since the former assumes that the processes of information seeking and use are constituted socially and dialogically, rather than based on the ideas and motives of individual actors. All human practices are social, and they originate from the interactions between the members of a community.

A common assumption of information behavior research is that information seeking and retrieval are affected by cognitive, affective, and task-related factors. From the constructionist viewpoint, people's accounts of their "innermost" emotions and thoughts draw upon historically formed discourses and vocabularies (Tuominen, Talja, & Savolainen, 2002). People's talk about their experiences and emotions is oriented toward making their own and others' acts meaningful and understandable. People thus not only describe but also produce and build

328

their experience, emotions, identities, and social worlds through dialogue and discourse.

Constructionism is, in the widest sense, a synonym for "the linguistic turn" in the human and social sciences. It is not a single theory but a bundle of theoretical frameworks that have been influenced by the work of classical figures such as Mihail Bakhtin (1981), Valentin Volosinov (1986), Harold Garfinkel (1984), and Michel Foucault (1972). Common to all these theorists is an emphasis on the essential role of language use in the production of social reality. In the 1920s and 1930s, Bakhtin and Volosinov criticized individualistic and mentalistic assumptions of knowledge construction, and formulated theoretical premises that research approaches such as cultural studies and discursive psychology later built upon.

The most commonly used research methods in social constructionist research are conversation analysis and discourse analysis. In the 1960s, Garfinkel founded the ethnomethodological research tradition that aims at capturing the ways in which everyday life is routinely and intersubjectively accomplished. Leaning on the work of Garfinkel, Harvey Sacks (1996) developed the conversation analytic research method that concentrates on fine details of interactive talk—such as turn-takings, hesitations, and sequential patterns—to understand the contextual functions and action-orientation of utterances. Foucault was the first to systematically outline the discourse analytic approach that focuses on how reality is represented in talk and texts, and on the consequences of different ways of representing reality. Later, Jonathan Potter (1996), Margaret Wetherell (Wetherell & Potter, 1996), Ian Parker (2002), Derek Edwards (1997), and others, many of whom are founding members of the Discourse and Rhetoric Group (DARG, 2004), developed methods such as the analysis of interpretive repertoires that combine features of the conversation analytic tradition and Foucauldian discourse analysis. Kenneth Gergen (2001), Rom Harré (1994), and John Shotter (1993) wrote important constructionist works on knowledge production, the formation of selves and identities, and the role of mental vocabularies in social life.

Related to conversation and discourse analytic research traditions is the sociology of scientific knowledge (SSK), a research program promoted by figures such as Bruno Latour (Latour & Woolgar, 1981), Steve

Woolgar (1988), and Karin Knorr Cetina (1981). In an ethnomethod-ological spirit, SSK aims at capturing the taken-for-granted practices of collective knowledge construction in scientific fields. This tradition has generated insightful analyses on how everyday scientific practices often radically diverge from the textbook model of how objective research results should be generated. Empirical studies undertaken in SSK commonly apply ethnographic methods, which are as applicable in constructionist studies as conversation and discourse analytic methods.

In science and technology studies, the social shaping of technology (SST) perspective (Bijker et al., 1987) is important from the viewpoint of information practice research, as it extends the scope of research from social issues of information seeking and technology use to the formation and nature of technical artifacts. In SST, neither information technology nor its uses are understood as stable, uncontested phenomena. The social constructionist theory of technology (SCOT) widens the analytical perspective even further by focusing on "the regimes of truth which surround, uphold, impale, and represent technology" (Grint & Woolgar, 1997, p. 32).

Constructionist studies analyze information, information technology, and information users as conversational constructs produced within the boundaries of specific discourses and epistemic positions. Constructionists start from the assumption that when we study information needs, users' sense making, or relevance criteria, we are always concerned with practices of language use that are "overt, public, disciplined, and institutionalized" (Frohmann, 2001). Contributions by Talja (1997), Talja, Keso, and Pietiläinen (1999), Tuominen (1997, 2001), and Tuominen and Savolainen (1997) discuss the potentials and implications of constructionism as a theoretical and methodological framework in the study of information practices. Pettigrew's (1999) empirical study showed how sensitive issues like information sharing in clinical services can be analyzed by utilizing a constructionist understanding of information as an interactional accomplishment. Julien and Given (2003) discuss how academic librarians construct the identities of faculty members and how these constructions might be detrimental for the attempt to build collaborative relationships with the faculty.

In the field of everyday life information seeking, Given (2002), McKenzie (2003), and Tuominen (2001) have undertaken empirical studies focusing on participants' accounts of their information practices. These studies bring into sight the presuppositions or "moral narratives" related to information seeking and use and demonstrate the influence of these narratives on information practices and information seekers' identities. Information practices look different and reveal new sides when looked at from the viewpoint of DIR.

Constructionism opens up multiple potential research venues to pursue. Through its focus on situated action and interaction, constructionism can, for instance, inform the analysis of collaborative information seeking and retrieval. Recently, Tuominen, Talja, and Savolainen (2003) have applied constructionist ideas in digital library research by suggesting a way of designing digital libraries as places of collective knowledge construction.

Studying how information practices, actors, and technologies are constructed in discourse and conversation provides a broader sociological perspective for understanding information seeking and information technology use. As discourses mediate much of our understanding of the world, the "regimes of truth" prevailing in institutional and everyday contexts also have practical implications. Therefore, an increased understanding of such implicit theories and their implications makes it possible to adopt new approaches in research and design aimed at supporting people's mundane information practices.

Bakhtin, M. M. (1981). *The dialogic imagination: Four essays*. Austin, TX: University of Texas Press.

Bijker, W. E., Hughes, T. P., & Pinch, T. J. (1987). *The social construction of technological systems: New directions in the sociology and history of technology*. Cambridge, MA: MIT Press.

Discourse and rhetoric group (DARG). Retrieved February 23, 2004, from www.lboro.ac.uk/departments/ss/centres/dargindex.htm

Edwards, D. (1997). *Discourse and cognition*. London: Sage.

Foucault, M. (1972). *The archaeology of knowledge*. London: Routledge.

Frohmann, B. (2001). Discourse and documentation: Some implications for pedagogy and research. *Journal of Library and Information Science Education, 42*, 13–28.

Garfinkel, H. (1984). *Studies in ethnomethodology*. Cambridge: Polity Press.

Gergen, K. J. (2001). *Social Construction in context*. London: Sage.

Given, L. M. (2002). Discursive constructions in the university context: Social positioning theory and mature undergraduates' information behaviour. *The New Review of Information Behaviour Research, 3*, 127–142.

Grint, K., & Woolgar, S. (1997). T*he machine at work: Technology, work and organization*. Cambridge, UK: Polity Press.

Harré, R. (1994). *The discursive mind*. Thousand Oaks, CA: Sage.

Julien, H., & Given, L. M. (2003). Faculty-librarian relationship in the information literacy context: A content analysis of librarians' expressed attitudes and experiences. *The Canadian Journal of Information and Library Science, 27*, 65–87.

Knorr-Cetina, K. D. (1981). *The manufacture of knowledge: An essay on the constructivist and contextual nature of science*. Oxford: Pergamon Press.

Latour, B., & Woolgar, S. (1981). *Laboratory life: The social construction of scientific facts*. Beverly Hills, CA: Sage.

McKenzie, P. J. (2003). Justifying cognitive authority strategies: Discursive strategies of information seekers. *The Library Quarterly, 73*, 261–288.

Parker, I. (2002). *Critical discursive psychology*. Basingstoke: Palgrave Macmillan.

Pettigrew, K. E. (1999). Waiting for chiropody: Contextual results from an ethnographic study of the information behavior among attendees at community clinics. *Information Processing & Management, 35*, 801–817.

Potter, J. (1996). *Representing reality: Discourse, rhetoric and social construction*. London: Sage.

Sacks, H. (1996). *Lectures on conversation*. Oxford: Blackwell.

Shotter, J. (1993). *Conversational realities: Constructing life through language*. London: Sage.

Talja, S. (1997). Constituting "information" and "user" as research objects: A theory of knowledge formations as an alternative to the information man theory. In P. Vakkari, R. Savolainen, & B. Dervin (Eds.), *Information seeking in context: Proceedings of an international conference on research in information needs, seeking and use in different contexts* (pp. 67–80). London: Graham Taylor.

Talja, S., Keso, H., & Pietiläinen, T. (1999) The production of "context" in information seeking research: A metatheoretical view. *Information Processing & Management, 35*, 751–763.

Tuominen, K. (1997). User-centered discourse: An analysis of the subject positions of the user and the librarian. *The Library Quarterly, 4*, 350–371.

Tuominen, K. (2001). Tiedon muodostus ja virtuaalikirjaston rakentaminen: konstruktionistinen analyysi [Knowledge formation and digital library design: A constructionist analysis]. Espoo: CSC - Scientific Computing Ltd. Retrieved, February 26, 2004, from http://acta.uta.fi/pdf/951-44-5112-0.pdf

Tuominen, K., & Savolainen, R. (1997). Social constructionist approach to the study of information use as discursive action. In P. Vakkari, R. Savolainen, & B. Dervin (Eds.), *Information seeking in context: Proceedings of an international conference on research in information needs, seeking and use in different contexts* (pp. 81–96). London: Graham Taylor.

Tuominen, K., Talja, S., & Savolainen, R. (2002). Discourse, cognition and reality: Toward a social constructionist metatheory for library and information science. In H. Bruce, R. Fidel, P. Ingwersen, & P. Vakkari (Eds.), *Emerging frameworks and methods* (pp. 271–284). Greenwood Village, CO: Libraries Unlimited.

Tuominen, K., Talja, S., & Savolainen, R. (2003). Multiperspective digital libraries: The implications of constructionism for the development of digital libraries. *Journal of the American Society for Information Science & Technology, 54,* 561–569.

Volosinov, V. N. (1986). *Marxism and the philosophy of language.* Cambridge, MA: Harvard University Press.

Wetherell, M., & Potter, J. (1992). *Mapping the language of racism: Discourse and the legitimation of exploitation.* New York: Harvester/Wheatsheaf.

Woolgar, S. (1988). *Science: The very idea.* Chichester: Horwood.

59
Social Positioning

Lisa M. Given
School of Library and Information Studies
University of Alberta, Canada
lisa.given@ualberta.cs

Social positioning theory examines the influences of contextual dis-cursive practices on individuals' lives. This theory allows researchers to explore poststructural notions of identity construction, and is grounded in a postmodern tradition where personal identity is relative, socially constructed, contextual, and highly individual. Although research exploring information behavior is well established in library and infor-mation science, few studies have examined the influence of social dis-courses on individuals' actions. When discursive stereotypes inform librarians' service and policy decisions, for example, the end result may be practices that meet the needs of very few people. Social positioning theory offers a framework for the development of individualized models of service and research by facilitating the examination of social dis-courses within informational contexts, with a focus on the social com-plexities that inform individuals' information behaviors.

Social positioning theory represents a dynamic extension of role the-ory. Although role theory is well established in the social sciences (Greenberger & O'Neil, 1993; Menaghan, 1989), it has been criticized for its inability to examine complexities across roles. Once a woman has a child, for example, society assigns her the "mother" role and dictates cer-tain responsibilities. While role theory exposes conflicts (e.g., between "mother" and "worker"), it ignores the interplay between roles where individuals construct new social positions (e.g., "mother-worker-spouse") by accepting or rejecting elements of each role. Social positioning theory allows for the exploration of such complexities in the development of indi-viduals' identities.

Self-positioning was first explored in psychology, in Hollway's (1982) examination of gender differences in heterosexual relationships, and the social practices that reinforce male and female identities. Hollway

(1998) has identified several discursive tenets related to the positions men and women take up (or discard) in determining gender identities:

- Discourses make available positions for individuals to take up or disregard; these positions are placed in relation to other people through the meaning a particular discourse makes available (e.g., "the woman submits to the man").

- In some cases, taking up particular positions is not equally available to all social group members (e.g., "the man submits to the woman" may not be possible given a traditional discourse).

- Practices and meanings have histories that are developed and reproduced throughout individuals' lives.

Hollway's work has evolved into social positioning theory, which posits that individuals are active developers of their identities (e.g., Davies & Harré, 1990). van Langenhove and Harré (1999) detail the modes of positioning as discursive practice:

- *First and second order positioning* – First order positioning refers to the ways individuals locate themselves and others discursively by using several categories and storylines (e.g., a younger student says to a mature student: "You remind me of my mother. Can you help me with this assignment?"; this positions the older student as helpful due to her age or mother-like qualities, not her academic abilities); second order positioning occurs when an individual questions how they have been positioned and negotiates a new position (e.g., the mature student replies: "Why? I'm not that old!").

- *Performative and accountive positioning* – Second order positioning, when occurring within the conversation with the person who has positioned another person in the first order, is called performative positioning; when second order positioning occurs with a third party (e.g., the mature student says to a friend: "That younger student wanted my help because I reminded her of her mother—can you believe that?"), this renegotiation of the position is called accountive or third order positioning.

- *Moral and personal positioning* – People can be positioned with regard to the moral orders in which they perform social actions; it is often sufficient to refer to the roles people occupy within a given moral order or to certain institutional aspects of social life to understand their positions.

- *Self and other positioning* – Within a conversation, each participant always positions the other while simultaneously positioning him or herself; in this way, positioning is a discursive practice, where individuals accept or renegotiate the positions on offer.

- *Tacit and intentional positioning* – Most first order positioning is tacit, where individuals will not position themselves or others in an intentional or even a conscious way; however, where an individual is teasing or lying to another, the first order positioning can be intentional (e.g., the younger student makes the connection to her mother to make the mature student feel uncomfortable); second and third order positionings are always intentional, especially where a tacit first order positioning has occurred.

In addition to these general modes of positioning, there are four categories of intentional positioning, where individuals actively choose discursive positions:

1) *Deliberate self-positioning* – This occurs in every conversation where one expresses his/her personal identity; the stories people tell differ according to how they want to present themselves to others.

2) *Forced self-positioning* – This differs from deliberate self-positioning in that the initiative for self-positioning lies with someone else; often, this occurs in institutions, where individuals are classified so that they may act in the way they are expected to act within the organization (e.g., a librarian asks: "Are you a student?," forcing the individual to position him/herself as a student or not a student).

3) *Deliberate positioning of others* – This occurs in either the

presence or absence of the individual being positioned; when the person is present this can take the form of a moral reproach; when the person is absent, this takes the form of gossip.

4) *Forced positioning of others* – This also occurs in either the presence or absence of the person being positioned, where a third party is forced to position him/herself in relation to the individual being positioned.

Social positioning theory has been applied in various research contexts, including health, education, and social psychology, and to improve human services (e.g., Carbaugh 1999; Sabat & Harré, 1995). In library and information science, Given (2002, 2000) first applied this theory in an examination of mature university students' social identities and academic information behaviors. This research revealed the influence of discursive positioning on students' activities and interactions with others in pursuing informational goals. The study found, for example, that tacit positioning of all university students as young high school graduates adversely affected mature students' information-seeking strategies. In addition, intentional positioning of mature students as outsiders in the classroom silenced these students in their interactions with peers and instructors—two major sources of academic information. McKenzie and Carey (2000) have since used positioning theory to explore the implications of discursive constructions of physician and patient for information-seeking. Overall, the application of this theory in library and information science remains underutilized.

Social positioning theory offers a framework to expose the effects of stereotypical presumptions on informational encounters. Although people may react quite differently to the social positions offered (from outrage and active resistance of others' perceptions, to quiet complicity), studies of these experiences can lead to service practices that best meet individuals' needs. The concrete effects of social positioning (e.g., silencing a mature student in the classroom) shape information practice. This theory adds a necessary level of complexity to information behavior research and enhances understandings of individuals' needs and the informational activities that support those needs.

Carbaugh, D. (1999). Positioning as display of cultural identity. In R. Harré & L. van Langenhove (Eds.), *Positioning theory: Moral contexts of intentional action* (pp. 160–177). Oxford: Blackwell.

Davies, B., & Harré, R. (1990). Positioning: The discursive production of selves. *Journal for the Theory of Social Behaviour, 20*, 43–63.

Given, L. M. (2002). Discursive constructions in the university context: Social positioning theory and mature undergraduates' information behaviours. *The New Review of Information Behaviour Research, 3*, 127–141.

Given, L. M. (2000). *The social construction of the "mature student" identity: Effects and implications for academic information behaviours.* Unpublished doctoral dissertation, the University of Western Ontario, London, Canada.

Greenberger, E., & O'Neil, R. (1993). Spouse, parent, worker: Role commitments and role-related experiences in the construction of adults' well-being. *Developmental Psychology, 29*, 181–197.

Hollway, W. (1982). *Identity and gender difference in adult social relations.* Unpublished doctoral dissertation, University of London, England.

Hollway, W. (1998). Gender difference and the production of subjectivity. In J. Henriques, W. Hollway, C. Urwin, C. Venn, & V. Walkerdine (Eds.), *Changing the Subject: Psychology, Social Regulation, and Subjectivity* (pp. 227–263). London: Routledge.

McKenzie, P.J., & Carey, R. F. (2000). "What's wrong with that woman?": Positioning theory and information-seeking behaviour. In A. Kublik (Ed.), *CAIS 2000: Dimensions of a global information science: Proceedings of the 28th annual conference of the canadian association for information science, Edmonton, Alberta, Canada.* Retrieved June 11, 2004, from www.cais-acsi.ca/proceedings/2000/mckenzie_2000.pdf

Menaghan, E. G. (1989). Role changes and psychological well-being: Variations in effects by gender and role repertoire. *Social Forces, 67*, 693–714.

Sabat, S. R., & Harré, R. (1995). The construction and deconstruction of self in Alzheimer's disease. *Ageing and Society, 12*, 443–461.

van Langenhove, L., & Harré, R. (1999). Introducing positioning theory. In R. Harré & L. van Langenhove (Eds.), *Positioning theory: Moral contexts of intentional action* (pp. 14–31). Oxford: Blackwell.

60

The Socio-Cognitive Theory of Users Situated in Specific Contexts and Domains

Birger Hjørland
Department of Information Studies
Royal School of Library and Information Science, Denmark
bh@db.dk

The domain analytic theory (DA) was introduced in information sci-ence by Hjørland and Albrechtsen (1995) and Hjørland (2002a). Although DA emphasizes domains, as opposed to individuals, as units of analysis in information science, it nevertheless also has a view of users' individual cognitive processes. This view is termed *the socio-cognitive view* (cf., Hjørland, 2002b).

A basic assumption in the socio-cognitive view is that small children's cognition is mainly determined by biological principles. When children learn language and symbols the cognitive processes are increasingly mediated by signs, meaning, and symbols, which are internalized in the individual and then reprogram the way cognitive processes work. Such systems of signs and symbols are first developed externally, in a culture. They are culture-specific and partly social- and domain specific.

People's use of information may be partly biologically determined. Some people like music much more than others and therefore they use more information about music. Some people have a flair for mathematics, others try to avoid it. When we speak of people's relevance criteria in relation to IR, they are, however, mainly determined by cultural factors. They may, for example, be determined by trends or "paradigms" in knowledge domains, as demonstrated by Hjørland (2002) in psychology. When searching for literature about a topic, say schizophrenia, the rele-vance criteria are implied by the theory, tradition, or "paradigm" to which the searcher subscribes or belongs. Psychoanalysts prefer psycho-analytical papers, cognitivists prefer cognitivistic papers, etc. Relevance criteria are socialized into the individual from the academic tradition in which he has been raised (and to which he may himself add, modify, or change relevance criteria). It should be obvious that people seeking information about, for example, music, are similarly socialized into specific cultures and preferences: people tend to prefer music that other people in the same culture or subculture prefer.

What is the difference between the socio-cognitive view and traditional cognitive views? Gärdenfors (1999, pp. 29–30) wrote:

> The role of culture and society in cognition was marginalized in early cognitive science. These were regarded as problem areas to be addressed when an understanding of individual cognition had been achieved. . . .
>
> However, when the focus of cognitive theories shifted away from symbolic representations, semantic and pragmatic research reappeared on the agenda . . .
>
> . . . a second tradition turns the study programme up-side-down: actions are seen as the most basic entities . . .

The socio-cognitive view thus turns the traditional cognitive program upside down. It emphasizes the internalization of culturally produced signs and symbols and the way cognitive processes are mediated by culturally, historically, and socially constructed meanings. Less priority is given to "hardware" whether in brains or computers.

Domain analysis consequently does not conceive users in general, but sees them as belonging to different cultures, to different social structures, and to different domains of knowledge. Information producers, intermediaries, and users are more or less connected in communities that share common languages, genres, and other typified communication practices. They share meanings to different degrees: There are different *semantic distances* between the agents.

DA and the socio-cognitive view are based in a kind of philosophical realism, termed *pragmatic realism* (cf. Hjørland, 2004a). What are the implications of pragmatic realism for information science? Basically, the implication is that it becomes important to distinguish carefully between objective and subjective knowledge, where studies of users are seen as studies of subjective knowledge.

When users seek information, they always do it on the basis of their subjective knowledge. They may or may not be familiar with the objective possibilities for searching. For example, users may not know about citation indexes and they may thus miss an important search opportunity that exists objectively (cf. Hjørland, 2000a). When studying users' information-seeking behavior (which is, of course, based on the users' subjective knowledge of information sources), information scientists need to interpret such studies based on knowledge about the objective possibilities. One may say, of course, that *nobody* knows the objective possibilities. The argument is, however, that information scientists should know them better than the users that they are investigating. Information scientists, more than the users, should know about possibilities and limitations in search engines, citation indexes, thesauri, controlled vocabularies, etc. They should advise the users on how to exploit those possibilities. Consequently, when studying users' behavior this should be interpreted on the basis of some kind of model of the objective possibilities, e.g., the UNISIST model (see Fjordback Søndergaard, Andersen, & Hjørland, 2003). Such a model is based on the information scientists' subjective view (and could possibly be wrong or unhelpful). Such models must be introduced, discussed, and refined in the scientific literature if information science is going to make progress. A given piece of knowledge is always subjective, but it is supposed that some answers are more correct or fruitful than other, and the only way to find out is to consider the arguments that support a given view.

Pragmatic realism is also important in order to understand relevance in information science. Whether or not a certain substance is relevant as a cure for cancer is ultimately decided in medical research, not by asking patients or users of medical services. It is of course always legitimate to be skeptical about a knowledge claim. This will lead into a discussion about the basis for that claim and ultimately to epistemological discussions. A thing is relevant for a given purpose if it contributes to reaching the goal—whether or not the user thinks so. In a similar way is the validity, and thus the relevance, of a document claiming that a certain substance is relevant as a cure for cancer also ultimately decided in medical research, not by asking users of information services.

In some domains, e.g., rock music, the users may be "experts," at least until this field is properly represented in musicology. In other fields, such as child psychology, experienced mothers may have adequate competencies for which a degree in developmental psychology cannot be a substitute. This last example is related to different epistemologies, i.e., to different views of how to obtain knowledge. Developmental psychology has mainly been dominated by a "positivist" epistemology, while other epistemologies give a higher status to the kind of experiences that motherhood represents. In both cases the realist view applies: A given document may or may not be relevant to a given purpose, whether or not the user believes this to be so. Of course, a document is not relevant in a situation if the user cannot understand it. In higher education an attempt is typically made to provide students with the knowledge necessary in order to study the documents that are deemed to be relevant. In the sciences one learns mathematics and in theology one learns Greek, Latin, and Hebrew. The underlying philosophy is that the relevant texts presuppose these kinds of learning. Again, different opinions may exist. Different views of what is relevant may exist as different "paradigms" in all subjects. A user's information behavior should be interpreted on the basis of such paradigms.

Domain analysis is thus an approach to information science that has important implications for studies of information behavior. Its strength is that it represents a more correct and fruitful theory about cognitive processes compared to traditional cognitive views. It may contribute to the development of information systems that are specific to different groups of users. Its drawback is that it is more difficult to carry out user studies because they should be interpreted on the basis of a model of the objective search possibilities.

Fjordback Søndergaard, T., Andersen, J., & Hjørland, B. (2003). Documents and the communication of scientific and scholarly information: Revising and updating the UNISIST model. *Journal of Documentation, 59*(3) 278–320.

Gärdenfors, P. (1999). Cognitive science: From computers to anthills as models of human thought. *Human IT, 3*(2). Retrieved February 20, 2004, from www.hb.se/bhs/ith/2-99/pg.htm

Hjørland, B. (2000a). Information seeking behavior: What should a general theory look like? *The New Review of Information Behaviour Research, 1*, 19–33.

Hjørland, B. (2002a). Domain analysis in information science: Eleven approaches - traditional as well as innovative. *Journal of Documentation, 58*, 422–462.

Hjørland, B. (2002b). Epistemology and the socio-cognitive perspective in information science. *Journal of the American Society for Information Science and Technology, 53*, 257–270.

Hjørland, B. (2004a). Arguments for philosophical realism in library and information science. *Library Trends, 52*, 488–506.

Hjørland, B. (In press). Domain analysis in information science. In M. A. Drake (Ed.), *Encyclopaedia of Library and Information Science (2nd ed.)*. New York: Marcel Dekker.

Hjørland, B., & Albrechtsen, H. (1995). Toward a new horizon in information science: Domain analysis. *Journal of the American Society for Information Science, 46*, 400–425.

61
Strength of Weak Ties

Christopher M. Dixon
Human Resources and Skills Development
Government of Canada
cmdixon@magma.ca

In 1973 social network scholar Mark Granovetter wrote his first article on strength of weak ties (SWT) to focus on what he considered to be "a fundamental weakness of current sociological theory," specifically social network theory (Granovetter, 1973, p. 1360). He felt there had been excellent research into micro-level interactions and revealing large-scale studies concerning macro-phenomena, but a methodology relating micro-level findings to a macro scale had yet to be created. To overcome this deficiency, Granovetter proposed an analysis of the social dynamics that occur among the different ties within an egocentric network. He began with a discussion on the nature of strong, weak, and absent ties. Granovetter reasoned that the stronger the tie between two individuals, the more they had in common with each other and, therefore, that they were part of the same social network. Granovetter also contended that an individual's social network could be made up of strong and weak ties, but only weak ties could serve as links or "bridges" to another social network (Granovetter, 1973, p. 1365).

To support this assertion, Granovetter introduced the findings of a labor market study he had recently completed. This study focused on how individuals in a Boston suburb acquired job information and from whom they procured this information. Granovetter first assessed whether the information provider was a strong or weak tie, basing this appraisal on the frequency of contact between the provider and recipient. Subsequently, he devised corresponding categories to reflect the strength of the tie. A strong tie existed if a person saw his/her contact "often or at least twice a week; a weak tie was present if a person encountered his/her contact occasionally or more than once a year, but less than twice a week; and an extremely weak tie or, possibly, an absent tie existed if a person rarely met his/her contact, i.e. once a year or less" (Granovetter, 1973, p. 1371).

The data collected indicated that 16.7 percent of the respondents saw their contacts often, 55.6 percent saw their contacts occasionally, and 27.8 percent saw their contacts rarely. Granovetter interpreted these results as an indication that, in most cases, job information from the weak ties led to a change for the individual (Granovetter, 1973; Granovetter, 1982). For Granovetter, this example demonstrated that weak bridging ties are "the channels through which ideas, influences, or information socially distant from the ego may reach him[/her]" (Granovetter, 1973, p. 1370-71). Additionally, Granovetter argued that an individual's knowledge of the world becomes "encapsulated" without access to ties beyond his/her own social network.

To complete his theory of SWT and to demonstrate that his analysis of a micro-level egocentric network could be extrapolated to a larger entity, Granovetter presented a case study of an Italian community in Boston that was destroyed because it was unable to mobilize itself to prevent "urban renewal" within its locality. Granovetter attributed the community's inability to succeed to the lack of weak bridging ties among many cliques within the area neighbourhoods. He surmised that the community leaders would have been able to gain the community's trust and motivate its members towards a common cause had they developed "bridges" into these cliques (Granovetter, 1973, p. 1374). Additionally, without weak ties to one another, these cliques caused crucial information to remain isolated, thus preventing an exchange of knowledge among socially distant community members.

It should be noted that Granovetter was not the first scholar to draw attention to SWT. Liu and Duff (1972) utilised the notion of SWT to account for their research findings concerning how family planning information was shared among the lower and middle economic classes within particular neighbourhoods located in a city in the Philippines. Unfortunately, their results were inconclusive as they were unable to explain certain social interactions and could not "trace the channels of information flow from the contextual data" (Liu & Duff, 1972, p. 366).

There are few qualitative secondary resources for SWT since none of the articles published by social network scholars in response to Granovetter's first article could substantiate his theory. According to

Granovetter, the most comprehensive test of his theory was conducted by Friedkin, who studied the responses given by the "faculty members of seven biological science departments of a large American University" about each other (Granovetter, 1983, p. 217). Information behavior scholars might consider the Friedkin study to be useful as it addresses "the need for greater precision and type of information transmitted through different kinds of ties" (Granovetter, 1983, p. 219).

To date there has been a modest amount of research devoted to Granovetter's theory. There was an initial response among social network scholars immediately following the 1973 article, but as Granovetter stated in his 1982 work, the studies that addressed his work either used his hypothesis to explain their findings or could not provide conclusive empirical evidence. Granovetter was content to leave empirical testing to other scholars, maintaining that his key purpose for writing about SWT was to generate discussion among his fellow social network scholars.

Within the information behavior field, there has been some interest in Granovetter's work. Chatman's (1992) study on the information-seeking behaviour of older citizens and Haythornthwaite's (1996) summary of social network analysis both incorporated aspects of Granovetter's SWT in their respective works, but only within the larger context of social network theory. Pettigrew (1998, 2000) is the only scholar to have used Granovetter's theory prominently in her work.

Despite the lack of interest in Granovetter's SWT, it still has the potential to be a powerful explanatory tool for information behaviour scholars. For example, if Granovetter's hypothesis regarding the transmission of novel information through weak bridging ties is true, it might lead to an explanation as to why some individuals or groups of individuals remain information poor. This supposition could also provide insight into why certain information sources, such as libraries or government agencies, consistently remain underused despite their ability to provide pivotal information to a number of people.

Before information behavior scholars consider using Granovetter's hypothesis as a research framework or explanatory tool, they should be cognisant of some of the deficiencies of this theory. These include:

- The broad criteria Granovetter used to determine the strength of a tie

- The lack of strong empirical evidence to support his premise
- His use of a single information event to support his theory as opposed to multiple information events, which would provide more opportunities to test his supposition
- His tendency to define for the individual what is information, rather than, as prominent information behaviour scholars suggest, permitting the individual to define what is information for him or herself (Dervin, 1983; Dervin & Nilan, 1985; Harris & Dewdney, 1994)
- His overemphasis on weak ties as information sources at the expense of strong ties (Commentary..., 1974; Friedkin, 1980; Granovetter, 1982; Marsden & Campbell, 1984)

The potential for Granovetter's theory to be an explanatory tool for information behavior scholars remains unknown. A comprehensive empirical study on the information transferred between different ties within a variety of social networks could support or refute his suppositions.

Chatman, E. A. (1992). *The information world of retired women.* New York: Greenwood Press.

Commentary and Debate: Gans responds to Granovetter's 'strength of weak ties'; Granovetter responds to Gans; Gans responds to Granovetter. (1974). *American Journal of Sociology, 80*(2), 524–532.

Dervin, B. (1983). Information as a user construct: The relevance of perceived information needs to synthesis and interpretation. In S. A. Ward, & L. J. Reed (Eds.), *Knowledge structure and use: Implications for synthesis and interpretation* (pp. 155–183). Philadelphia: Temple University Press.

Dervin, B., & Nilan, M. (1986). Information needs and uses. *Annual Review of Information Science and Technology, 21,* 3–33.

Friedkin, N. E. (1980). A test of the structural features of Granovetter's 'Strength of Weak Ties' theory. *Social Networks, 2,* 411–422.

Granovetter, M. S. (1973). The strength of weak ties. *American Journal of Sociology, 78,* 1360–1380.

Granovetter, M. S. (1982). The strength of weak ties: a network theory revisited. In P. V. Marsden, & N. Lin (Eds.), *Social structure and network analysis* (pp. 105–130). Beverly Hills, CA: Sage.

Granovetter, M. S. (1983). The strength of weak ties: A network theory revisited. *Sociological Theory, 1,* 201–233.

Harris, R., & Dewdney, P. (1994). *Barriers to information: How formal help systems fail battered women.* Westport, CT: Greenwood.

Haythornthwaite, C. (1996). Social network analysis: An approach and technique for the study of information exchange. *Library and Information Science Research, 18,* 323–342.

Liu, W. T., & Duff, R. W. (1972). The strength in weak ties. *Public Opinion Quarterly, 36*(3), 361–366.

Marsden, P. V., & Campbel, K. E. (1984). Measuring tie strength. *Social Forces, 63*(2), 482–501.

Pettigrew, K. E. (1998). The role of community health nurses in providing information and referral to the elderly: A study based on social network theory. (Doctoral dissertation, University of Western Ontario, London, Ontario, Canada, 1998). *Dissertation Abstracts International, 59,* 3683.

Pettigrew, K. E. (2000). Lay information provision in community settings: How community health nurses disseminate human services information to the elderly. *Library Quarterly, 70*(I), 47–85.

62
Symbolic Violence

Steven Joyce
School of Library and Information Studies
University of Alberta, Canada
steve.joyce@ualberta.ca

Before discussing Pierre Bourdieu's *symbolic violence*, it is first necessary to sketch an outline of his sociology. While symbolic violence has been treated as a theory in its own right (Bourdieu, 1997,1991; Swartz, 1997), it finds a better fit as a theoretical concept within Bourdieu's better known, larger cultural theory of action in which one develops a *habitus* (an internalized set of dispositions) on a field of struggle (a network that constitutes the distribution of capital and power). The field is where individuals, situated according to habitus, attempt to acquire and mobilize various forms of capital. Bourdieu (1986) generally treats four types of capital: *economic* (money and property), *cultural or informational* (cultural goods and services), *social* (friendships, acquaintances, and social networks), and *symbolic*.

Symbolic capital is different from the other forms in that it accrues from them, and it provides the means to legitimate the exercise of power. When one accumulates sufficient economic, cultural, and social capital, one can set the rules of the game. Further, symbolic capital (or symbolic power—Bourdieu uses the terms interchangeably) is a key ingredient of symbolic systems, which perform three distinct yet interrelated functions: cognition, communication/social integration, and social differentiation. First, symbolic systems are "structuring structures" (Bourdieu, 1991, p. 164–165). As such, they exercise a cognitive function in that different modes of knowledge structure different ways of apprehending the world. For instance, the scientist may understand the world very differently than the humanist. Symbolic systems also constitute "structured structures" (pp. 164–166) whereby deep structures of meaning are shared by all members of a culture and dictate what is possible to know or do within that culture. Bourdieu argues that these "structured structures" provide not only instruments of knowledge but also instruments of communication. Thus, in facilitating communication, symbolic systems exercise a function of social integration. Finally, symbolic systems serve as instruments of domination. Through knowledge and communication, a dominant symbolic system integrates all the members within that system, establishes a hierarchical order for less dominant systems, and legitimizes the distinctions of social rankings by the "fictitious integration of society as a whole" (p. 167). This integration Bourdieu calls symbolic violence.

For Bourdieu, the exercise of power almost always entails some form of legitimation. This legitimation comes in the form of symbolic violence, which is the imposition of symbolic systems on groups such that the imposition is disguised and taken for granted. Symbolic systems exercise symbolic power "only with the complicity of those who do not want to know that they are subject to it or even that they themselves exercise it" (164). As such, symbolic violence is hegemonic in that dominated groups accept as legitimate the condition of their domination: it "is the violence which is exercised upon a social agent with his or her complicity" (Bourdieu & Wacquant 1992, p. 167). However, Bourdieu makes clear that it does not constitute a Gramscian form of hegemony because it does not involve the negotiated construction of ideological consensus.

> Legitimation of the social order is not... the product of a deliberate and purposive action of propaganda or symbolic imposition; it results... from the fact that agents apply to the objective structures of the social world structures of perception and appreciation which are issued out of these very structures and which tend to picture the world as evident. (Bourdieu, 1989, p. 21)

As such, symbolic violence is not necessarily imposed from above.

> Social agents are knowing agents who, even when they are subjected to determinisms, contribute to producing the efficacy of that which determines them insofar as they structure what determines them. And it is always in the "fit" between determinants and the categories of perception that constitute them as such that the effect of domination arises. (Bourdieu & Waquant, 1992, pp. 167–168)

To this end, as social agents reproduce their social worlds, they also reproduce their own domination.

The capacity to impose the "legitimate vision of the social world and... its divisions" constitutes what Bourdieu (1987) calls worldmaking power, which rests on the concept of misrecognition. In order for an exercise of power to be recognized as legitimate, it must first be misrecognized as disinterested. "Activities and resources gain in symbolic power, or legitimacy, to the extent that they become separated from underlying material interests and hence go misrecognized as representing disinterested forms of activities and resources" (Swartz, 1997, p. 90). Bourdieu (1990) noted that "even 'economic' capital cannot act unless it succeeds in being recognized through a conversion that can render unrecognizable the true principle of its efficacy" (p. 118). In other words, legitimacy obtains through a misrecognition of the logic of interest as the logic of disinterest.

As a theoretical perspective, symbolic violence has rarely been used in IB research (one example is Joyce 2003). Why, then, is it important for such research? First, it has the potential to provide novel insights into information behaviors and the social discourses that elicit such behaviors. By gaining an understanding of the nature of symbolic systems and how they are imposed on groups, one may come to have a better understanding of how individuals' information needs are produced in the first place. Further, symbolic violence as a concept can be operationalized in service of other theories to produce insights into, for example, the role it plays in social positioning theory (Harré & van Langenhove, 1999), the strategies and tactics of resistance employed against it (Certeau, 1984), and how it helps to sustain a normative existence in a life lived in the round (Chatman, 1999).

Second, no one is immune to symbolic violence. As such, we can examine the impact of symbolic violence on librarians and how such impact affects access, collections, and services. If, as Bourdieu argues, all action is interested but the exercise of world-making power is misrecognized as disinterested, then one might well ask just how balanced library collections are. Such examination may have great appeal for activist librarians and critical researchers alike. Indeed, while Bourdieu focused much of his work on the production of symbolic power, he viewed his sociology as a tool in the struggle against various forms of symbolic violence.

Third, symbolic violence, in conjunction with Bourdieu's *oeuvre* as a whole, can help to provide a metatheory or worldview within which the researcher can place his or her work. Virtually all science is carried out with a particular if implicit worldview. Because scientists are aware of the underlying assumptions, the worldview need not be articulated. On the other hand, social science often employs theories and methods that stem from disparate worldviews the underlying assumptions of which do *not* go without saying. Symbolic violence can help provide a metatheoretical framework within which researchers can situate their work, and it can be linked to and extended by other theoretical perspectives such as, for example, Habermas's theory of communicative action, Giddens's structuration theory, or the tenets of social constructionism.

The methodological approaches associated with symbolic violence can be either quantitative or qualitative. While Bourdieu's own methods often leaned to the quantitative, Joyce (2003) used purely qualitative methods to examine emergent interpretative repertoires to see how symbolic violence and the acquisition of informational capital mediate the coming out process in gay youth. Either way, however, symbolic violence is best used with research that has a critical edge. Critical research strives to expose social flaws and promote actions that would help eliminate those flaws (Rubin & Rubin, 1995, p. 35). Further, critical research is self-reflexive, and this is particularly important because if, as Bourdieu argues, symbolic violence applies to all forms of symbolic representations, then how can one practice social science, itself a symbolic enterprise, without reproducing the effects of social distinctions? Bourdieu's answer is a call for the "reflexive practice" of sociology (Bourdieu & Waquant, 1992). "Every sociological inquiry requires a simultaneous critical reflection on the intellectual and social conditions that make the inquiry possible. If sociology is the science of social conditions determining human practices, it must also be the science of social conditions determining intellectual practices, including sociology" (Swartz, 1997, p. 270). Indeed, the incorporation of symbolic violence into one's worldview, or its employment as either concept or theory, requires a level of reflexivity that can only improve the quality of research.

Bourdieu, P. (1977). *Outline of a theory of practice*. Cambridge, UK: Cambridge University Press.

Bourdieu, P. (1986). The forms of capital. In J. G. Richardson (Ed.), *Handbook of theory and research for the sociology of education* (pp. 241–258). New York: Greenwood.

Bourdieu, P. (1989). Social space and symbolic power. *Sociological Theory, 7,* 14–25.

Bourdieu, P. (1990). *The logic of practice.* Cambridge, UK: Polity Press.

Bourdieu, P. (1991). *Language and symbolic power.* Cambridge, MA: Harvard University Press.

Bourdieu, P., & Waquant, L. J. (1992). *An invitation to reflexive sociology.* Cambridge, UK: Polity Press.

Certeau, M. (1984). *The practice of everyday life.* Berkeley: University of California Press.

Chatman, E. A. (1999). A theory of life in the round. *Journal of the American Society for Information Science & Technology, 50,* 207–217.

Harré, R., & van Langenhove, L., Eds. (1999). *Positioning theory: Moral contexts of intentional action.* Oxford: Blackwell.

Joyce, S. (2003). *The discursive construction of lesbian, gay, and bisexual identity: How symbolic violence and informational capital mediate the coming out process.* Unpublished doctoral dissertation, The University of Western Ontario, Ontario, Canada.

Rubin, H. J., & Rubin, I. S. (1995). *Qualitative interviewing: The art of hearing data.* Thousand Oaks, CA: Sage.

Swartz, D. (1997). *Culture & power: The sociology of Pierre Bourdieu.* Chicago: University of Chicago Press.

63
Taylor's Information Use Environments

Ruth A. Palmquist
Graduate School of Library and Information Science
Dominican University, USA
rpalmq@dom.edu

Robert S. Taylor describes the moment in 1953 when he realized that information use was comprised of the basic processes of gathering, orga- nizing, retrieving, analyzing, and communicating (Taylor, 2001). Furthermore, he realized that it was necessary to identify these processes more completely in order to construct any system that could deliver the information needed at the time the user's need was to be met. Despite the regularity of this sequential process, Taylor recognized that the user's environment or situation had a critical effect upon the nature of the information needed. During Taylor's career he had been a newspa- per reporter, a sports editor, an intelligence agent, a college librarian, and finally a university professor and dean at the Syracuse University School of Information Studies. So while he recognized that the process for seek- ing information was composed of a fairly predictable set of processes, he knew that use environments were relatively unstudied.

Taylor's first seminal publication came in 1968 and presented two key notions. First, he identified the idea that the user must express to an information system not what is known, but the very thing that is not known. Second, Taylor (1968) also suggested that the experience of user's information need could be viewed as proceeding through four basic cognitive levels: visceral, conscious, formalized, and compromised. Taylor's concern about the conversational give and take between the user and the system gave rise to many efforts to formalize his ideas. However, it should be noted that Taylor himself did not try to test methodologically any of his theoretical ideas. Always modest in his assertions about what might be called his multi-decade "thought experiment" to postulate

354

about the characteristics of various information use environments (IUEs), he always hoped that others would do so.

Many efforts in the late 1970s and throughout the 1980s were influenced by Taylor's focus on the user's cognitive state when thinking about his or her problem/information need. Key among them were Dervin's Sense-Making work (1983), which is largely qualitative in method, and Belkin's (1980) Anomalous States of Knowledge (ASK) work followed by Belkin, Oddy, and Brooks's (1982a and 1982b) design study for a simple measure to develop a semantic network of the user's problem. This measure was tested with a quasi-experimental by Oddy, Palmquist, and Crawford (1986). Taylor's own efforts (MacMullin & Taylor, 1984) moved forward with an effort to develop a list of information traits and dimensions that might be added to a document description along with subject descriptors to more fully describe information relevant to a user's problem. These dimensions included, for example, whether a problem was likely to be well or ill-structured; whether a problem was likely to be simple or complex; whether the user came from a work environment where assumptions were well understood and agreed upon or one in which this was not the case. For each of these environments, different types of information responses were identified.

With the sponsorship of the National Science Foundation, Taylor (1986) began to develop a framework for examining information use environments (IUE) by considering the differences existing for major groups of information users. His intent was to suggest components that once identified could be assembled to create information systems that could then provide the value-added processes tailored to a particular use environment. To quote Taylor (1986, p. 204), the "principal strength of the value-added model lies in its stress on the user and on the needs and dimensions of the information environment as a major element in the design and evaluation of systems." Essentially, he wanted to understand the forms of information, preferred modes of access, and the kinds of enhancements or signals that could enrich the system so that use might be improved in a particular context or use environment (Taylor, 1986). He saw that only the *potential* for value was carried by the information; it was in the head of the user or in the use of the information that a message had value.

Taylor's (1991) lengthy essay improves the articulation of his theory of information behavior by beginning to think about users as groups. It is with this effort that his view of Information Use Environments (IUE) emerged. The primary groups Taylor examines are engineers, legislators, and practicing physicians. He also attempts to describe the conscious and unconscious assumptions for these groups as to what makes information useful and valuable within each context. Taylor returns to the considerations of information traits and dimensions pursued in MacMullin and Taylor (1984) in thinking about the typical problems that occur in the groups he is considering. He felt the need to look at groups precisely because these traits and dimensions may be more easily identified when they are examined within the information valued by a particular group.

Each context he examined differed markedly from the others. For example, Taylor (1991) describes the engineer's approach to an information source as very different from the usual package of a paper, a report, or a book. Engineering consumes information, he states, and transforms it, producing a product or a system that itself is information bearing, however, not in verbal form. So, an engineer often extracts information from the physical inspection of such a product or by direct personal contact with other engineers. Taylor's article is soundly backed by the literature of others who have thought about these groups from non-information use perspectives and the combination of Taylor's insights with these additional perspectives make the whole particularly rich and thought provoking.

While many others have added to our collective understanding that the culture, the environment in which a group operates, greatly influences that group's information behavior and use, it was the thinking of Robert S. Taylor that played a major role in developing this path initially. It probably should be said that Taylor did not foresee a time when we would study the information behavior of what he called "special socio-economic groups" (Taylor, 1991). He believed we would concentrate upon the information use of the professions and the business entrepreneurs. It is to his credit that he identified such groups, however, and recognized them as a unique division in the effort to identify information use environments (Taylor, 1991).

Belkin, N. J. (1980). Anomalous states of knowledge as a basis for information retrieval. *Canadian Journal of Information Science, 5,* 133–143.

Belkin, N. J., Oddy, R. N., & Brooks, H. M. (1982a). ASK for information retrieval: Part I: Background and theory. *Journal of Documentation, 38,* 61–71.

Belkin, N. J., Oddy, R. N., & Brooks, H. M. (1982b). ASK for information retrieval: Part II: Results of a design study. *Journal of Documentation, 38,* 145–164.

Dervin, B. (1983). Information as a user construct: The relevance of perceived information needs to synthesis and interpretation. In S. A. Ward & L. J. Reed (Eds.), *Knowledge structures and use: Implications for synthesis and interpretation* (pp. 153–184). Philadelphia: Temple University Press.

Kuhlthau, C. C. (1991). Inside the search process: Information seeking from the user's perspective. *Journal of the American Society for Information Science, 5,* 361–371.

MacMullin, S. E., & Taylor, R. S. (1984). Problem dimensions and information traits. *The Information Society, 3*(I), 91–III.

Oddy, R. N, Palmquist, R. A., & Crawford, M. (1986). Representation of anomalous states of knowledge in information retrieval. *Proceedings of the 49th ASIS annual meeting,* 248–254.

Taylor, R. S. (1968). Question negotiation and information seeking in libraries. *College & Research Libraries, 29*(3), 178–194.

Taylor, R. S. (1986). *Value-added processes in information systems.* Norwood, NJ: Ablex.

Taylor, R. S. (1991). Information use environments. In B. Dervin & M. J. Voigt (Eds.), *Progress in communication sciences* (pp. 217–255). Norwood, NJ: Ablex.

Taylor, Robert. (2001). For whom we design systems. Retrieved April 5, 2004, from www.libsci.sc.edu/bob/ISP/taylor2.htm

64
Taylor's Question-Negotiation

Phillip M. Edwards
The Information School
University of Washington, USA
pme2@u.washington.edu

Robert S. Taylor, a historian and librarian by training, is generally recognized as an influential pioneer in the characterization of individuals' expressions of information need through question formulation. In a highly cited article published in 1968, Taylor derives a model of the information-seeking process in libraries that is frequently "cited in the work of [information behavior researchers] who explicitly identify their orientation with the cognitive viewpoint" (Pettigrew, Fidel, & Bruce, 2001, p. 47). This model consists of three major components:

1) Four stage model for the expressions of individuals' information needs

2) Process model for prenegotiation decisions made by the inquirer

3) Five filters through which a question passes during negotiation

The first component, the four stage model for the expression of individuals' information needs, originally appeared in an earlier publication by Taylor (1962). He refines and clarifies this concept in his 1968 article: "An inquiry is merely a micro-event in a shifting non-linear adaptive mechanism" (p. 179). This mechanism involves transitions between several stages in the mind of the inquirer:

QI—the actual, but unexpressed need for information (the visceral need)

Q2—the conscious, within-brain description of the need (the conscious need)

Q3—the formal statement of the need (the formalized need)

Q4—the question as presented to the information system (the compromised need) (p. 182)

The primary assumption underlying this construct is that an information need is "something distinct and traceable" (Taylor, 1962, p. 392). Furthermore, Taylor considers a transition between stages via question negotiation with an intermediary to be "a form of communication" (Taylor, 1968, p. 183). These themes—identifiable information needs and negotiationascommunication—persist in much of the literature on information behavior relating to intermediation.

One of the novel propositions in Taylor (1968) is the placement of negotiation with an intermediary in a larger context of informationseeking behavior. In his process model for prenegotiation decisions made by the inquirer, Taylor diagrams a sequence of decision points through which users attempt to satisfy their information needs. This proposes that users engage in information gathering activities—e.g., engaging in original experimentation/observation, searching the literature, asking colleagues, consulting personal files, interacting with library resources, and independently forming search strategies (i.e., "selfhelp")—long before consulting with a librarian. Taylor focuses the remainder of the 1968 article on the inherent complexity associated with the subsequent librarianpatron negotiation process: "In [question negotiation], one person tries to describe for another person not something he knows, but rather something he does not know" (1968, p. 180). In order to address this complexity, Taylor (1968) proposes five filters that may be employed by librarians to approximate the higherlevel information needs of individuals:

1) Determination of the subject

2) Objective and motivation

3) Personal characteristics of the inquirer

4) Relationship of inquiry description to file organization

5) Anticipated or acceptable answers (p. 183)

This portion of the model is based upon limited empirical evidence—a small number of openended and unstructured interviews with special librarians—suggesting that the characteristics of the process of negotiation can be the subject of research.

Many researchers have directly adopted various aspects of Taylor's model to frame the results of their work. Pettigrew (2000), for example, uses Taylor's stages of information need to characterize interactions of nurses and elderly patients in neighborhood foot clinics. Researchers addressing relevance issues often refer to Taylor's five filters as a starting point for discussing their studies. However, early criticisms of this model and its direct adoption do appear in the literature. Taylor's proposed model is largely based upon his experience in libraries and a limited number of interviews. Acknowledging partial support derived from other published studies, Markey (1981) questions the validity of Taylor's model:

> It is clear that Taylor's theory remains untested and unchallenged but subsequent reports appear to support and reinforce his work....Taylor's theory remains untested, or perhaps, unchallenged in the literature, so that subsequent studies stimulated by his work rest on mere acceptance rather than evidence. (pp. 217, 223)

The impact of Taylor's model may be more pronounced for the development of subsequent information behavior theories; the dialogue enabled as a result of Taylor's writings may be more significant than the original model itself. Notable explicit and implicit extensions of Taylor's (1962, 1967, 1968) information-seeking model include Markey (1981), Belkin, Oddy, and Brooks (1982), Dervin and Dewdney (1986), Kuhlthau (1988, 1991), and Gross (1995).

Markey (1981) draws partial empirical verification for Taylor's model of information needs from a review of the reference interview literature; she also extends Taylor's model to accommodate the information needs of *both* actors during presearch negotiation and interviews. In her conceptualization of the extended model, "the librarian becomes, in a sense, a surrogate to the client, restructuring the client's question into a form acceptable to the system and consonant with the expressed information need" (Markey, 1981, p. 218).

Belkin, Oddy, and Brooks (1982) make reference to Taylor's model in their discussion of the Anomalous State of Knowledge (ASK) model. Dervin and Dewdney (1986) similarly reference Taylor (1967) in their discussion of Sense-Making and neutral questioning. Kuhlthau (1988, 1991) places Taylor's model in the context of other information-seeking models and extends these constructs to the six-stage Information Search Process model. The relationship between these three models and Taylor's information seeking model is discussed at length by Morris (1994).

Gross (1995) uses Taylor's levels of question formation to frame her own theory of the imposed query; she derives a six stage model—initiated stage, query transfer to an agent, interred stage, agent's query is negotiated, processed stage, evaluated stage—by extending Taylor's stages of question formulation. Gross (1995) also reflects that, as seen in Taylor's prenegotiation process model, "it is very common for flowcharts and models to show [asking another person] as a preliminary step in that it occurs before consultation with an information-providing institution" (p. 293). Taylor (1967, 1968) was the first author to firmly establish the question negotiation process/reference interview as a *researchable* concept. One substantive yet largely overlooked methodological recommendation to address issues associated with Taylor's model was published by Wildemuth (1990). Empirically verifying and extending Taylor's model and constructs is essentially an attempt to refine and "develop an empirically grounded model of a multistage nondeterministic process" (Wildemuth, 1990, p. 337). Wildemuth's approach involves the collection of qualitative data on processes, derivation of event histories, coding the process data based on induced categories, and analyzing the coded data for patterns and sequences of events over time.

Belkin, N. J., Oddy, B. N., & Brooks, H. M. (1982). ASK for information retrieval: Part I. Background and theory. *Journal of Documentation, 38*(2), 61–71.

Dervin, B., & Dewdney, P. (1986). Neutral questioning: A new approach to the reference interview. *RQ, 25,* 506–513.

Gross, M. (1995). The imposed query. *RQ, 35,* 236–243.

Kuhlthau, C. C. (1988). Developing a model of the library search process: Cognitive and affective aspects. *RQ, 28,* 232–242.

Kuhlthau, C. C. (1991). Inside the search process: Information seeking from the user's perspective. *Journal of the American Society for Information Science, 42,* 361–371.

Markey, K. (1981). Levels of question formulation in negotiation of information need during the online presearch interview: A proposed model. *Information Processing & Management, 17(5)*, 215–225.

Morris, R. C. T. (1994). Toward a user-centered information service. *Journal of the American Society for Information Science, 45*, 20–30.

Pettigrew, K. E. (2000). Lay information provision in community settings: How community health nurses disseminate human services information to the elderly. *The Library Quarterly, 70(1)*, 47–85.

Pettigrew, K. E., Fidel, R., & Bruce, H. (2001). Conceptual frameworks in information behavior. In M.E. Williams (Ed.), *Annual Review of Information Science and Technology, 35*. Medford, NJ: Information Today.

Taylor, R. S. (1962). The process of asking questions. *American Documentation, 13*, 391–396.

Taylor, R. S. (1967). *Question-Negotiation and information seeking in libraries* (Studies in the man-system interface in libraries, Rep. No. 3). Bethlehem, PA: Center for the Information Sciences, Lehigh University.

Taylor, R. S. (1968). Question-negotiation and information seeking in libraries. *College & Research Libraries, 29(3)*, 178–194.

Wildemuth, B. M. (1990). A method for inducing process models from qualitative data. *Library & Information Science Research, 12*, 329–340.

65
Transtheoretical Model of Health Behavior Change

C. Nadine Wathen
Department of Psychiatry and Behavioural Neurosciences
McMaster University, Canada
wathenn@mcmaster.ca

Roma M. Harris
Faculty of Information and Media Studies
The University of Western Ontario, Canada
harris@uwo.ca

A key goal of health advocates and professionals is to help people live healthier lives. This often involves encouraging people to give up their actively unhealthy behaviors (e.g., smoking, over-eating), adopt healthy behaviors (exercise), or better manage a number of behaviors to improve health and well-being. Health promotion activities, from individual counseling to mass media campaigns, are essentially "information interventions." In fact, principles and theories from communication and related fields, including information behavior studies, are often used to understand how best to develop effective approaches to informing people about their health.

The transtheoretical model (TTM), also called "stages of change" and "readiness to change," evolved primarily from the addictions field as a way to understand how people change their smoking behavior (Prochaska & DiClemente, 1983). Initially, the authors of the approach wanted to explain not only the "basic processes of change" (Prochaska et. al., 1988, p. 520), but also to determine whether people moved through these processes in a staged fashion, in the hope of assisting researchers and clinicians to develop and provide interventions matched to stage, thereby increasing the potential for positive change. The TTM, from the mid-1980s to the present, has been tested and applied to a remarkable extent, not only in the addictions field, but in a number of health and non-health areas.

The basic premise of the TTM is that discrete stages of behavior change exist, and that people progress through these in a more or less linear fashion, although with frequent stops along the way, some of which are merely pauses in the journey, while others may result in permanent or temporary regression to an earlier stage. The model, therefore, was conceived as a spiral (Figure 65.1), with a strong temporal dimension (Figure 65.2).

The TTM comprises 10 processes of change that occur differentially more than five stages, and a number of measures have been developed for applying the TTM to a range of health-related behaviors (available at www.uri.edu/research/cprc/measures.htm). As seen in Figures 65.1 and 65.2, the five stages are:

1) *Precontemplation* – the person has no intention to change the problem, and in fact may be unaware that her/his behavior is a problem.

2) *Contemplation* – the person is aware that s/he has a problem and is starting to think seriously about changing it, but has not yet committed to taking action. A key aspect of this phase is that the person actively starts to weigh the pros and cons of the problem and its solution.

3) *Preparation* – the person is ready for change, and in fact

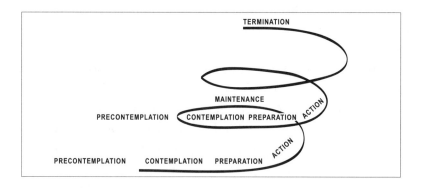

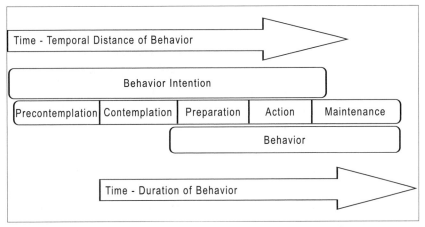

Figure 65.2   The temporal dimension as the basis for the stages of change.

Note: From "Smoking cessation and stress management: Applications of the transtheoretical model of behavior change," by W. F. Velicer, J. O. Prochaska, J. L. Fava, G. L. Norman, & C. A. Redding, 1998, *Homeostasis in Health and Disease*, 38, p. 218. Copyright 1998 by Pergamon Press. Adapted with permission.

may have started making some changes, such as small reductions in their problem behavior.

4) *Action* – the person is actively making changes to her/his behavior, experiences and/or environment to address the problem. They are "working on it," but have yet to solve the problem.

5) *Maintenance* – the person is working to prevent a relapse and consolidate the gains made in the action phase.

As a person tracks through these stages, s/he engages in "experiential" (cognitive-affective) and "behavioral" "processes of change." The 10 processes are described in detail in a number of publications (e.g., Prochaska et. al., 1992). Further evolutions of the TTM have incorporated mediating and moderating variables, including self-efficacy, resistance to temptation, and decisional balance.

From an information behavior perspective perhaps the most interesting aspect of the TTM is the implicit and explicit reliance on becoming informed as an initial step of the change process. This is especially evident during "consciousness raising," when a person is actively "increasing *information* about self and problem [employing] observations, confrontations, interpretations, *bibliotherapy*" (italics added) (Prochaska et al., 1992, p. 1108). It is noteworthy that this cognitive-affective process happens first, before the transition from the precontemplation to the contemplation stage.

A number of information behavior theories are germane to the TTM's description of how people in the information-intensive phases of change become aware of and seek to address their problems. For instance, social constructionism provides useful insights into "problem behaviors" and their "solutions" as does Dervin's Sense-Making theory; Miller's theory of monitoring and blunting is useful when considering the "stages of change." For example, monitoring and blunting may be situational, with people in the precontemplation stage blocking information they are not yet ready to consider, but becoming more active information monitors as they move to the contemplation and preparation stages of change. Further examination of the intersection of these theories is required.

Some authors have argued that the "consciousness-raising" process may be engaged at several different stages depending on the type of behavior being modified. In his meta-analysis of TTM studies, Rosen (2000) found that this process was among those that varied most by stage, and was used primarily in the contemplation and preparation stages for smoking cessation and psychotherapy, but during the action and maintenance stages for substance abuse, exercise, and diet behaviors. Clearly, understanding when, why, and how people require information as they seek to change health-related behaviors is a key aspect of designing appropriate "information interventions" to help them, a finding borne out in a randomized field trial by Dijkstra et al. (1999) using tailored vs. non-tailored information materials with a group of "low readiness" smokers, and in an overview analysis by Spencer et al. (2002). In a direct application of approaches from communications theory and information science, Velicer and colleagues (1993) argue that "[i]ntervention efficacy can be increased when the treatment is maximally matched to the needs of the client. One means of achieving such matching is through use of an expert system, a computer-based decision-making system designed to utilize client information to produce unique, matched information and interventions" (p. 269). Additional research in this area is required.

While there is evidence that the stages of change are robust for certain health behaviors, the evidence is mounting that the TTM is not necessarily applicable as a research or clinical approach for all types of behaviors, with a main criticism being that the concept of discrete stages is not always borne out (Sutton, 2001). Recent analyses have called for reassessment of specific aspects of the model (Littell & Girvin, 2002; Rosen, 2000; Sutton, 2001). As Rosen states "[t]he TTM's most original contribution is the premise that different strategies facilitate progress at various points in the process of lifestyle change" (Rosen, 2000, p. 599). From an information behavior perspective, the important lesson of the transtheoretical model is the value of tailoring information and matching interventions to a person's "readiness to change." Understanding how best to achieve this should remain a key goal of research based on this model.

Dijkstra, A., De Vries, H., & Roijackers, J. (1999). Targeting smokers with low readiness to change with tailored and nontailored self-help materials. *Preventive Medicine, 28*, 203–211.

Littell, J. H., & Girvin, H. (2002). Stages of change: A critique. *Behavior Modification, 26*, 223–273.

Prochaska, J. O., & Diclemente, C. C. (1983). Stages and processes of self-change of smoking: Toward an integrative model of change. *Journal of Consulting & Clinical Psychology, 51*, 390–395.

Prochaska, J. O., DiClemente, C. C., & Norcross, J. C. (1992). In search of how people change: Applications to addictive behaviors. *American Psychologist, 47*, 1102–1114.

Prochaska, J. O., Velicer, W. F., DiClemente, C. C., & Fava, J. (1988). Measuring processes of change: Applications to the cessation of smoking. *Journal of Consulting & Clinical Psychology, 56*, 520–528.

Rosen, C. S. (2000). Is the sequencing of change processes by stage consistent across health problems? A meta-analysis. *Health Psychology, 19*, 593–604.

Spencer, L., Pagell, F., Hallion, M. E., & Adams, T. B. (2002). Applying the transtheoretical model to tobacco cessation and prevention: A review of literature. *American Journal of Health Promotion, 17*, 7–71.

Sutton, S. (2001). Back to the drawing board? A review of applications of the transtheoretical model to substance use. *Addiction, 96*, 175–186.

Velicer, W. F., Prochaska, J. O., Bellis, J. M., Diclemente, C. C., Rossi, J. S., Fava, J. L., & Steiger, J. H. (1993). An expert system intervention for smoking cessation. *Addictive Behaviors, 18*, 269–290.

Velicer, W. F., Prochaska, J. O., Fava, J. L., Norman, G. L., & Redding, C. A. (1998). Smoking cessation and stress management: Applications of the Transtheoretical Model of behavior change. *Homeostasis in Health and Disease, 38*, 216–233.

66
Value Sensitive Design

Batya Friedman and Nathan G. Freier
The Information School
University of Washington, USA
batya@u.washington.edu and nfreier@u.washington.edu

Human values impact people's information behavior. Imagine, for example, that a young Muslim man is interested in exploring the historical roots of jihad for a term paper. Imagine, too, that his library logs all digital reference interactions, and has a policy that if subpoenaed, such logs can be made available to law enforcement agencies. Under such conditions, this man might well decide to seek relevant information by other means, as he seeks to balance the value of access to information with other competing values such as privacy, consent, personal safety, security, and religious freedom. Despite the clear importance of values in human information behavior, the information behavior field does not yet have a comprehensive way of approaching this area. Value Sensitive Design offers one such approach.

Value Sensitive Design (VSD) emerged in the 1990s as an approach to the design of information and computer systems that accounts for human values throughout the design process (Friedman & Kahn, 1992; Friedman, 1997; Friedman, Kahn, & Borning, 2002). Two overarching goals motivate VSD: 1) to be proactive about human values in system design, and 2) to do so in a manner that is principled, comprehensive, and systematic.

VSD particularly emphasizes values with moral import, including privacy, trust, human dignity, respect for person, physical and psychological well-being, informed consent, intellectual property, access, universal usability, freedom from bias, moral responsibility, and moral accountability. While emphasizing the moral perspective, VSD also accounts for usability (e.g., ease of use), conventions (e.g., standardization of technical protocols), and personal predilections (e.g., color preferences within a graphical interface). Key features of VSD involve its

368

interactional perspective, tripartite methodology, and emphasis on direct and indirect stakeholders.

VSD is an interactional theory: values are viewed neither as inscribed into technology (an endogenous theory) nor as simply transmitted by social forces (an exogenous theory). Rather, people and social systems affect technological development, and new technologies shape (but do not rigidly determine) individual behavior and social systems.

VSD systematically integrates and iterates three types of investigations: conceptual, empirical, and technical. *Conceptual investigations* comprise philosophically informed analyses of the central constructs and issues under investigation. For example, how does the philosophical literature conceptualize certain values and provide criteria for their assessment and implementation? What values have standing? How should we engage in trade-offs among competing values in the design, implementation, and use of information systems (e.g., access vs. privacy, or security vs. trust)? *Empirical investigations* focus on the human response to the technical artifact, and on the larger social context in which the technology is situated. The entire range of quantitative and qualitative methods used in social science research may be applicable, including observations, interviews, surveys, focus groups, experimental manipulations, measurements of user behavior and human physiology, contextual inquiry, collection of relevant documents, and interaction logs. *Technical investigations* focus on the design and performance of the technology itself. It is assumed that technologies in general, and information and computer technologies in particular, provide values that follow from properties of the technology. For example, an online calendar system that displays individuals' scheduled events in detail readily provides information about employees' availability, but makes privacy difficult. Technical investigations can involve either retrospective analyses of existing technologies or the design of new technical mechanisms and systems. The three types of investigations—conceptual, empirical, and technical—are employed iteratively in a way that the results of one type of investigation are integrated with those of the others, which, in turn, influence additional investigations.

Direct stakeholders refer to parties who interact directly with the computer system or its output. Indirect stakeholders refer to all other parties who are otherwise affected by the use of the system. For example, computerized medical records systems impact not only the direct stake-holders, such as doctors, nurses, insurance companies, and hospitals, but an especially important group of indirect stakeholders: the patients.

Recent projects that have successfully drawn on VSD have focused, for example, on (a) network security; (b) the design of technological interactions to support informed consent; (c) bias in computer systems; (d) autonomy and privacy in hardware design; (e) the human-robotic relationship (with populations ranging from preschool children through the elderly); (f) privacy in public places that house Web cams; (g) military weapon information systems and the possibility of a just war; and (h) large scale urban simulation of land use and transportation planning. Thus, from this growing body of research and design (see, for example, Friedman, 1997; Friedman, Howe, & Felten, 2002; Friedman & Kahn, 1992, Friedman, Kahn, & Borning, 2002; Hagman, Hendrickson, & Whitty, 2003; Kahn, Friedman, Perez-Granados, & Freier, 2004; Tang, 1997) there is evidence that VSD can be applied to a wide range of populations in diverse contexts, using diverse information systems.

Having emerged within the field of human-computer interaction, VSD currently lacks an explicit model of information behavior. That said, even at this point in its development, VSD can contribute to the field of information behavior in some key ways:

- *Explicit values analyses* – VSD—particularly through its conceptual investigations—can provide a framework for identifying the value components of a given information behavior theory or a specific information interaction.

- *Stakeholder analyses* – Many information behavior theories focus on the information seeker and the information giver but may ignore others impacted by these activities. For example, when caregivers seek medical information for a family member with AIDS, the family member may not want certain inquiries made (to protect privacy). Thus, by unduly focusing on the information behavior of the direct stakeholder (the caregiver seeking medication information), the researcher may miss important impacts of the information interaction.

- *Value conflicts within the individual* — It is clear from the psychological literature that people not only have multiple values, but these values often conflict internally (e.g., access versus privacy) (Turiel, 1998). VSD is committed to uncovering and representing heterogeneity and conflict within individual value analyses.

- *Value conflicts within systems* — Many times information behavior involves conflicts between individuals and systems. For example, online access to court records increases the convenience of public access to court records but may unduly expose the victims of crimes to unwanted or psychologically harmful publicity.

- *Values in context* — VSD maintains that how values play out in a particular culture at a particular point in time can vary, sometimes considerably. For example, privacy plays a central role in human development; yet what counts as private (financial information, first name) and how one signals privacy (facing the wall of an igloo, as the Inuit do) varies across contexts. Information systems sensitive to human values must account for these contextual dimensions.

- *Integration of system design with information behavior* — VSD offers an explicit approach to integrating empirical investigations of people's information behavior with the design of information systems responsive to that behavior.

The theory and methods of VSD are to be used in concert with other existing theories and methods. Ultimately, value-sensitive design requires that we broaden the goals and criteria for judging the quality of information systems to include those that advance human values.

Note: This material is based upon work supported by the National Science Foundation under Grant No. 0325035.

Friedman, B. (Ed.). (1997). *Human values and the design of computer technology.* New York: Cambridge University Press.

Friedman, B., Howe, D. C., & Felten, E. (2002). Informed consent in the Mozilla browser: Implementing value-sensitive design. *Proceedings of HICSS-35, IEEE Computer Society.*

Friedman, B., & Kahn, P. H., Jr. (1992). Human agency and responsible computing: Implications for computer system design. *Journal of Systems Software, 17,* 7–14.

Friedman, B., Kahn, P. H. Jr., & Borning, A. (2002). *Value sensitive design: Theory and methods.* University of Washington Computer Science & Engineering Technical Report 02-12-01, December 2002.

Hagman, J., Hendrickson, A., & Whitty, A. (2003). What's in a barcode: Informed consent and machine scannable driver licenses. In *CHI 2003 Extended Abstracts of the Conference on Human Factors in Computing System* (pp. 912–913). New York: ACM Press.

Kahn, P. H., Jr., Friedman, B., Perez-Granados, D. R., & Freier, N. G. (in press). Robotic pets in the lives of young children. *Extended Abstracts of CHI 2004.* New York: ACM Press.

Tang, J. C. (1997). Eliminating a hardware switch: Weighing economics and values in a design decision. In B. Friedman (Ed.), *Human values and the design of computer technology* (pp. 259–269). New York: Cambridge University Press.

Turiel, E. (2002). *The culture of morality: Social development, context, and conflict.* Cambridge, UK: Cambridge University Press.

67
Vygotsky's Zone of Proximal Development

Lynne (E. F.) McKechnie
Faculty of Information and Media Studies
The University of Western Ontario, Canada
mckechnie@uwo.ca

Lev Vygotsky was a prominent Soviet developmental psychologist. A contemporary of Jean Piaget, his work was produced from 1924 until his untimely death in 1934. It was not accessible to Western scholarship until fairly recently; first, because it was suppressed in the Soviet Union, and subsequently, because it was not translated from Russian into English and other languages until the late 1960s and 1970s.

The general propositions of Vygotsky's developmental theory are that action creates thought, development results from dialectical processes, and development occurs in historical and cultural contexts (Thomas, 1992). Vygotsky's approach, like those of Bruner's scaffolding, Bandura's social learning theory, and Kaye's child-as-apprentice, is interactionist (Winter & Goldfield, 1991). To explain the relationship between learning and development, Vygotsky used the theoretical construct of the zone of proximal development (ZPD), which he defined as:

> the distance between the actual developmental level as determined by independent problem solving and the level of potential development as determined through problem solving under adult guidance or in collaboration with more capable peers. (Vygotsky, 1978, p. 86)

Vygotsky postulated that new cognitive skills are first practiced by children in social interaction with a more experienced individual until the skill is mastered and internalized and the child is able to exercise the skill independently.

373

Every function in the child's cultural development appears twice: first, on the social level, and later, on the individual level; first between people (interpsychological) and then inside the child (intrapsychological) (Thomas, 1992, p.57).

Learning is constituted as an interactive process wherein the adult guides the child's participation so that the child may function comfortably at a challenging level by providing bridges between what the child knows and needs to know, providing structures to organize problem solving, and gradually transferring responsibility for managing problem solving to the child.

Vygotsky presented his ideas in two key monographs: *Mind in society: The development of higher psychological processes* (1978) and *Thought and language* (1986). His work has been interpreted and developed, with Wertsch's (1985) collection of essays being a particularly authoritative source. More succinct summaries of Vygotsky's theory are found in Thomas (1992, pp. 319–346) and McKechnie (1997) who describes the relevance of the ZPD to library and information science (LIS), especially as it relates to children's use of libraries and their information behavior.

Vygotsky's theory has been used most heavily in the disciplines of education (for an overview see Callison, 2001) and psychology (for representative examples see Rogoff, Ellis, & Gardner, 1984; Wertsch, McNamee, McLane, & Budwig, 1980). However, it has also begun to influence the work of LIS scholars. Kuhlthau's five zones of intervention, times in the information search process when a person needs assistance to move forward, arise from Vygotsky's ZPD (Kuhlthau, 2004, pp. 127-144). Cooper's study of the information-seeking behavior of seven-year-olds in school library media centers suggests that understanding the "significance of a supportive human or virtual intermediary" (2002, p. 921) within the ZPD will be helpful in designing more child-centered information systems. McKechnie's (2000) study of the use of public libraries by preschool children found that the ZPD was useful to explain and analyze children's behavior as parents, other adult caregivers, and library staff were observed mediating and scaffolding the children's interaction with library space, services, and materials.

While use within LIS has focused on the information behavior of children, the concept of the ZPD has been used in other disciplines to study the behavior of individuals of any age when confronted with an unfamiliar task or situation. It would be particularly useful in LIS research for exploring information behaviors associated with novice information seekers of any age or information activities occurring in a collaborative context. Areas where it could be applied appropriately include studies of information literacy acquisition, studies of reference and reader's advisory work, studies of information intermediaries such as librarians and gatekeepers, and studies of informal information giving and sharing.

With its emphasis on interpersonal interaction, the ZPD has been most frequently associated with qualitative research methods. McKechnie (2000), for example, used ethnographic observation to capture the naturally occurring interaction between preschool age children, mothers, and library staff. Kuhlthau (2004) used a combination of observation, interview, and think-aloud methods in her studies of the information search process of high school students. Cooper (2002) used both qualitative and quantitative methods in her case study of young children's information-seeking behavior in a school library media center, with data derived from observation, videorecording, and member checking being analyzed through quantitative content analysis.

Vygotsky's claim that learning occurs within the social realm is congruent with much of the current work in information behavior, which emphasizes interpersonal contexts and the ZPD is, therefore, very suited to IB research. However, one could argue that non-human tools such as computer interfaces and cataloguing and classification schemes also scaffold learning by providing bridges and structures to organize an individual's thought. One weakness of the ZPD therefore, is that it is not very helpful for looking at IB in information retrieval studies unless a human intermediary is involved with the use of textual and/or technological information access tools.

Vygotsky's ZPD has the potential to address an important gap in our understanding of information behavior. As human thought and behavior changes and matures through life, it is reasonable to assume that human information behavior also develops as one proceeds through childhood and adolescence to adulthood. Through examining emerging information behaviors in children as they interact with more skilled adult caregivers in information contexts and activities, it may be possible to uncover developmental information behaviors which underlie and set the foundation for more mature adult information behavior.

Callison, D. (2001). Scaffolding. *School Library Media Activities Monthly*, *17*(6):37–39.

Cooper, L. Z. (2002). A case study of information-seeking behavior in 7-year-old children in a semistructured situation. *Journal of the American Society for Information Science & Technology*, *53*, 904–922.

Kuhlthau, C. C. (2004). Chapter 8 - Zones of intervention in the process of information seeking. In *Seeking meaning: A process approach to library and information services* (2nd ed.) (pp. 127–144). Westport, CT: Libraries Unlimited.

McKechnie, L. (1997). Vygotsky's zone of proximal development: A useful theoretical approach for research concerning children, libraries, and information. *Journal of Youth Services in Libraries 11*(1), 66–70.

McKechnie, L. (2000). Ethnographic observation of preschool children. *Library & Information Science Research*, *22*(1), 61–76.

Rogoff, B., Ellis, S., & Gardner, W. (1984). Adjustment of adult-child instruction according to child's age and task. *Developmental Psychology*, *20*(2), 193–199.

Thomas, R. M. (1992). Vygotsky and the Soviet tradition. In *Comparing theories of child development* (3rd ed.) (pp. 319–346). Belmont, CA: Wadsworth.

Vygotsky, L. S. (1978). *Mind in society: The development of higher psychological processes*. Cambridge, MA: Harvard University Press.

Vygotsky, L. S. (1986). *Thought and language* (A. Kozulin, Trans.). Cambridge, MA: MIT Press.

Wertsch, J. V. (1985). *Vygotsky and the social formation of mind*. Cambridge, MA: Harvard University Press.

Wertsch, J. V., McNamee, G. D., McLane, J. B., & Budwig, N. A. (1980). The adult-child dyad as problem-solving system. *Child Development*, *51*, 1215–1221.

Winter, J. A., & Goldfield, E. C. (1991). Caregiver-child interaction in the development of self: The contributions of Vygotsky, Bruner, and Kay to Mead's theory. *Symbolic Interaction*, *14*(4), 433–447.

68

Web Information Behaviors of Organizational Workers

Brian Detlor
DeGroote School of Business
McMaster University, Canada
detlorb@mcmaster.ca

The theory of Web information behaviors of organizational workers is based on an exploratory investigation of how organizational workers utilize various Web-based information systems, such as enterprise portals, departmental Web sites, and the World Wide Web, for knowledge creation, distribution, and use purposes (Detlor, 2000). Empirical evidence gathered from the study shows how organizational workers are engaged in an information needs-seeking-use cycle of Web activity within the information environment of the firm. Two primary sources for the theory are Detlor (2003) and Detlor (2004). The theoretical model is based on two key works from the Information Studies field dealing with information use and information environments. The first is Choo's (1998) *general model of information use*, which explains the process of how humans seek and use information. The second is Taylor's (1986, 1991) *value-added approach*, which describes the structure of *information use environments* and their application to system design.

Drawing upon Choo's (1998) and Taylor's (1986, 1991) theoretical components, the theory presents a formulation of how organizational workers utilize Web-based systems as an information source to help resolve typical work-related problem situations. In this respect, Web use is defined to be the whole iterative cycle of information needs, seeking, and use applied to Web-based systems within the context of the information environment of the firm.

Figure 68.1 illustrates the workings of the theory. Foremost is the identification of the information environment construct which comprises, among other things, users and Internet-based information systems. Step I refers to the *information needs* stage. Here, users are confronted with discrete problem situations typically faced in their work settings; each problem situation has certain characteristics called problem dimensions. It is these characteristics that determine the types of information needed to help users resolve their problems. Users in this stage become aware of a gap in their knowledge to resolve the problem situations they face.

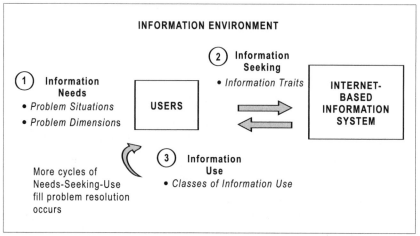

Figure 68.1   Web information behaviors of organizational workers.
Note: From "Internet-based information systems use in organizations: An information studies perspective," by B. Detlor, 2003, *Information Systems Journal*, 13(2), p. 121. Copyright 2003 by Blackwell Publishing. Adapted with permission.

Step 2 is the *information seeking* stage where users turn to an Internet-based information system to obtain the requisite information to help resolve their problems. In this stage, users examine information outputs presented to them from the Internet-based interface. The information traits of these outputs determine the effectiveness of the system. An Internet-based information system (IS) is useful if it appropriately signals the potential value of an information output.

Step 3 is the *information use* stage. This step starts when the user has completed a scan of the information sources available from the

Internet-based IS. In this stage, the user selects and processes the information according to various classes of information use. As a result of this action, the use of the information obtained from the Internet-based IS changes the problem situation, such that the situation is resolved or modified. If the modified situation, the information needs-seeking-use cycle repeats again until the problem situations become resolved in the minds of the users.

This iterative cycle reflects the dynamic nature of organizational information environments. They are in a constant state of flux as users go about addressing and readdressing their problem situations. In this way, the model illustrates how the information environment influences Internet-based IS use and how such use, in turn, influences the structure of the information environment itself.

As this theory is relatively new, it has yet to be used by other information behavior researchers. The theory can be used to study scenarios of Web-based use in organizations. For example, the case study exemplified in Detlor (2004) identified a core set of problem situations for which Web-based systems are used (search, browse, and explore) and, more importantly, that specific scenarios of problem dimension, information trait, and information use patterns are associated with each of these problem situations. It would be useful if further studies could identify patterns of Web use at more refined levels of problem situations, such as across various types of work tasks, or across a range of urgent and less critical information needs.

Findings from such studies would offer certain implications for designers of organizational Web-based systems. First, designers would become more aware of the various problem situations for which users primarily turn to Web-based systems for answers, and thus could offer functionality in Web-based systems designs which directly support end users in these information behaviors. Designers could do this by presenting and highlighting information on Web-based interfaces according to each problem situation's associated information traits as a means of emphasizing the importance and value of this information to users. Different information displays could be presented to users based on their problem situations. Further, designers could create features and functions in their Web-based designs that facilitate or match the predominant information uses of these systems for each problem situation scenario.

The previous description suggests strong implications for the way Internet-based IS in organizations are designed. Rather than building systems primarily for the retrieval of subject-specific information, as is typically done now, Internet-based IS may be better designed if they were made to respond to the information needs-seeking-use cycle in which employees utilize these systems. That means systems would need to focus on problem situation identification and place an emphasis on the presentation of information based on problem situation scenarios. The theory suggests that a user's problem situation influences how and what information needs to be displayed in an Internet-based IS. Having systems explicitly designed to handle such scenarios would benefit users and increase the usability of these systems in organizations.

Future studies could also look at the impact various information environment structures have on the information needs-seeking-use cycle of behavior organizational workers. Likewise, studies could examine the reciprocating effect of how the information behaviors of organizational workers in relation to their Web-based IS use impacts the structure of the information environment itself.

To assess how organizational participants fare in their information needs-seeking-use cycles with Internet-based IS, a variety of research methods would likely be required. For instance, tracking participant Web usage via computer log files would be needed to provide an accurate account of the frequency and type of Web applications and sites visited. One would then have to assess the information traits of the outputs presented by these Web applications and sites. To investigate the problem dimensions that prompt users to utilize Web information systems and the uses of the information obtained from them, in-depth interviews with participants would likely be required.

In addition to the models from which this theory was derived, Wilson's (1999) model of information behavior is relevant. Wilson recognizes the problematic situation that drives user needs and the situated context in which people engage in a cyclical process of information-seeking behavior.

There are two primary strengths for the proposed theory for studying information behavior problems: 1) the theory acknowledges the cyclical process in which organizational workers interact with Web-based information systems; and, 2) it raises awareness for the need to match the way information is presented on Web sites (information traits) with the specific task or problem situation at hand (problem dimensions). The limitation of the model is that there have been few empirical investigations that have confirmed the existence of discrete sets of problem dimensions and information traits, and even fewer that have attempted to identify problem scenarios which match preferred information traits to specific problem dimensions. More research and testing is needed to discover the best ways to display information on Internet-based systems to help resolve the problems typically faced by organizational participants in their day-to-day work tasks.

Choo, C. W. (1998). *The knowing organization.* New York: Oxford University Press.

Detlor, B. (2000). Facilitating organizational knowledge work through Web information systems: An investigation of the information ecology and information behaviours of users in a telecommunications company (Doctoral dissertation, University of Toronto, Ontario, Canada, 2000). *Dissertation Abstracts International 61,* 4211.

Detlor, B. (2003). Internet-based information systems use in organizations: An information studies perspective. *Information Systems Journal, 13*(2), 113–132.

Detlor, B. (2004). *Towards knowledge portals: From human issues to intelligent agents.* Dordrecht, The Netherlands: Kluwer.

Taylor, R. S. (1986). *Value-added processes in information systems.* Norwood, NJ: Ablex.

Taylor, R. S. (1991). Information use environments. In B. Dervin, & M. J. Voigt (Eds.), *Progress in Communication Sciences, Vol. 10* (pp. 217–255). Norwood, NJ: Ablex.

Wilson, T. D. (1999). Models in information behaviour research. *Journal of Documentation, 55*(3), 249–270.

69
Willingness to Return

Tammara Combs Turner
The Information School
University of Washington, USA
tcombs@u.washington.edu

Joan C. Durrance
School of Information
University of Michigan, USA
durrance@umich.edu

The concept of willingness to return began as a new and user-focused indicator of library reference success; it is the result of an insight that emerged from Durrance's 1980s qualitative study of the reference interview from the perspective of the user. At that time, accuracy, a variable relatively easy to measure (without the need to bother the user), was the key indicator of reference success. The first unobtrusive studies of reference accuracy were published by Terence Crowley and Tom Childers in the early 1970s (Crowley & Childers, 1971). By the mid 1980s this had become the standard method of evaluating the success of the reference interview (Hernon & McClure, 1987). The implied assumption behind accuracy as the key factor in reference success was simply that all identical questions had identical answers that could be determined from the resources of the collection. Typically researchers were assigned groups of specific questions (with known answers and approaches) to administer to public and academic libraries. Most studies showed that librarians had approximately a 55 percent accuracy rate. At that time researchers reasoned that if librarians increased their accuracy rates, reference service would be improved.

Durrance, on the other hand, suggested that a questioner's willingness to return to a staff member another time might be a powerful indicator of success—from the perspective of the user (Durrance, 1989, 1995). The insights that resulted in the willingness to return measure were influenced by the emerging knowledge gains from research on information seeking and use and the work of a variety of researchers (Dervin et al., 1976; Dervin & Nilan, 1986).

The first willingness to return studies were conducted periodically by Durrance and graduate students at the University of Michigan. Similarly to the earlier studies designed to determine accuracy rates, these studies used unobtrusive methods. Unlike the accuracy studies where researchers were assigned questions, willingness to return researchers selected questions that were meaningful to them or to a proxy who accompanied them to the observation site, typically a medium- to large-sized public or academic library. Observer-researchers completed a standard checklist and examined key factors associated with reference success. The approaches used were quite similar to those used by Dewdney, Michell, and Ross at the University of Western Ontario (Dewdney & Ross, 1994; Dewdney & Michell, 1996).

In order to understand willingness to return as it applies to the reference interview one must understand the nature of this interaction that occurs in a public desk or environment that is generally characterized by anonymity and where a questioner brings a query to someone he/she is not likely to know. The interaction itself (often not an interview) typically lasts about three minutes (Lynch, 1978; Dewdney, 1986). These short, typically anonymous encounters are often very basic interactions between a professional and a user.

The early willingness to return studies showed that users were likely to return to librarians who were effective communicators and who used open questions; they also learned that questioners were more likely to return to those who appeared idle when approached, who could be observed working with other users, and who were identified by name. Willingness to return studies also showed that approachability was even more important than the first group of factors as was the librarian's ability to successfully negotiate the question. Finally, this research showed that the most successful interactions from the perspective of the user were those where the librarian showed a great deal of interest in the question, possessed very good listening skills, used open questions very effectively, and determined the need behind the initial question (Durrance, 1995).

Dewdney, Michell, Nilsen, and Ross have incorporated the concept of willingness to return into their series of studies of reference effectiveness

(Dewdney, 1986; Dewdney & Ross, 1994; Ross & Nilsen, 2000). Their reference research has added considerably to the knowledge base and understanding of what happens in the reference interview. For example, they have shown, from the perspective of the user, how particular communication approaches and behaviors boost the effectiveness of the reference interview. In addition, they have contributed to the theoretical base associated with reference (Dervin & Dewdney, 1986; Dewdney & Michell, 1996).

Findings of studies of reference by various researchers that have incorporated willingness to return have been used to foster more effective reference service, not only by focusing on building strength in areas associated with a person's willingness to return but also by identifying problem areas associated with avoiding further contact with the professional. The basic willingness to return framework can be seen as one of the many building blocks developed through the research and theoretical approaches of a number of researchers, such as those discussed above, and theoreticians such as Dervin (Dervin & Dewdney, 1986).

The most effective work in translating both this small conceptual contribution to understanding reference success and other, considerable knowledge gains based on research into practice has been conducted by Ross and Dewdney and more recently by their colleague Nilsen (Ross & Dewdney, 1998; Ross, Nilsen, & Dewdney, 2002). These reference researchers have made theory and research accessible to practicing librarians.

The shelf-life of willingness to return has been extended due to its application by researchers to other situations. More recently researchers have incorporated this user-focused concept into studies of digital reference. (Janes, Hill, & Rolfe, 2001; Mon & Janes, 2004; Nilsen, 2004). Turner (unpublished) incorporated this framework into a pilot study of leaders of online peer-to-peer technical support groups to determine why they had been willing to return to the same set of newsgroups at a later time to ask more questions. The results identified a number of factors that contribute to participants returning behavior to gain help and support. In general, users noted many of the same factors that questioners noted in the library setting.

Willingness to return has been incorporated into a study of consumer health information behavior and use of a major consumer health information site (NCHealthInfo, www.nchealthinfo.org) by Durrance and Fisher. This study is part of the broader Information Behavior in Everyday Context (IBEC) project, involving a joint research team from the Information School at the University of Washington and the School of Information at the University of Michigan. An additional use of willingness to return may be in an area such as online peer-to-peer groups in which many of the same factors that occur in the reference interaction also occur. Its use is likely to be limited to basic interactions, where anonymity and short interactions are the norm, rather than to value-added services which require different theoretical constructs.

Crowley, T., & Childers, T. (1971). *Information service in public libraries: Two studies*. Metuchen, NJ: Scarecrow Press.

Dervin, B., & Dewdney, P. (1986). Neutral questioning: A new approach to the reference interview. *RQ, 25*, 506–513.

Dervin, B., & Nilan, M. (1986). Information needs and uses. *Annual Review of Information Science & Technology, 21*, 3–33.

Dervin, B., Zweizig, D., Banister, M., Gabriel, M., Hall, E. P., & Kwan, C. (1976). *The development of strategies for dealing with the information needs of urban residents: Phase I: The citizen study*. Washington, DC: U. S. Office of Education. (ERIC Document Reproduction Service No. ED 125640)

Dewdney, P. (1986). *The effects of training reference librarians in reference skills: A field experiment*. Unpublished doctoral dissertation, University of Western Ontario, London, Canada.

Dewdney, P., & Michell, G. (1996). Oranges and peaches: Understanding communication accidents in the reference interview. *RQ, 35*, 520–536.

Dewdney, P., & Ross, C. S. (1994). Flying a light aircraft: Reference service evaluation from a user's viewpoint. *RQ, 34*(2) 217–230.

Durrance, J. C. (1989) Reference success: Does the 55% rule tell the whole Story?. *Library Journal, 114*, 31–36.

Durrance, J. C. (1995). Factors that influence reference success: What makes questioners willing to return? *The Reference Librarian, 49/50*, 243–265.

Hernon, P., & McClure, C. R. (1987). *Unobtrusive testing and library reference*. Norwood, NJ: Ablex Publishing.

Janes, J., Hill, C., & Rolfe, A. (2001). Ask-an-expert services analysis. *Journal of the American Society for Information Science & Technology, 52*, 1106–1121.

Lynch, M .J. (1978). Reference interviews in public libraries. *The Library Quarterly, 48*, 119–142.

Mon, L., & Janes, J. (2004). The thank you study: User satisfaction with digital reference service. *Research Report*. 2003 OCLC/ALISE Research Grant. Retrieved, March 19, 2004, from www.oclc.org/ca/fr/research/grants/reports/janes/jj2004.pdf

Nilsen, K. (2004) The library visit study: User experiences at the virtual reference desk. *Information Research, 9*(2). Retrieved March 19, 2004, from http://informationr.net/ir/9-2/paper171.html

Ross, C. S., & P. Dewdney. (1998). *Communicating professionally: A how-to-do-it manual for library applications* (2nd ed.). New York: Neal Schuman.

Ross, C. S., & Nilsen, K. (2000). Has the Internet changed anything in reference? The library visit study, Phase 2. *Reference & User Services Quarterly, 40*(2) 147–155.

Ross, C. S., Nilsen, K., & Dewdney, P. (2002). *Conducting the reference interview: A how to do it manual for librarians*. New York: Neal Schuman.

Turner, Tammara. (unpublished). Willingness to return in online communities: Samples from developer newsgroups.

70
Women's Ways of Knowing

Heidi Julien
School of Library and Information Studies
University of Alberta, Canada
heidi.julien@ualberta.ca

Feminist theories abound, and have much to offer research in library and information studies (LIS), informing work in the organization of knowledge (Olson, 2001), in analyses of the profession of librarianship (Harris, 1992), and in library management (Turock, 2001). Within the diversity of feminist theories, Belenky et al.'s *women's ways of knowing* (WWK) articulated in *Women's ways of knowing: The development of self, voice, and mind* (Belenky et al., 1986) serves as an intriguing exam-ple. The WWK theory has yet to significantly inform work in LIS or, more specifically, information behavior (IB), but it offers interesting potential.

Situated firmly within the social constructionist epistemological tra-dition, the intent of the theory's authors was to challenge the construc-tion of only particular people (i.e., white males) as "valid and respected knowers" (Goldberger, 1996, p. 3) and to complement Perry's (1970) work, in which he "describes how students' conceptions of the nature and origins of knowledge evolve and how their understanding of them-selves as knowers changes over time" (Belenky et al., 1986, p. 9). Although Perry included women in his study sample, their voices remained unarticulated in the book arising from his research. Thus, Belenky et al. set out to express those missing female voices. Goldberger (1996), in her introduction to a second volume, *Knowledge, difference, and power: Essays inspired by women's ways of knowing*, makes a famil-iar argument: that "...ways of knowing identified as historically femi-nine...(intuitive knowing ... *connected knowing*) have been devalued and discouraged..." (Goldberger, 1996, p. 9). As one of the original authors of WWK, Goldberger states that their theory was based on the premise "that gender is a major social, historical, and political category that affects the life choices of all women in all communities and cultures.

387

We (implicitly) asked, How were Western social constructions of gender and authority affecting women's sense of self, voice, and mind?" (Goldberger, 1996, p. 4). The research study that led to WWK was based on extensive interviews with ordinary women with a diverse range of ethnic and demographic backgrounds, and was focused on family and school as social institutions that defined for women how and what they are to know. Belenky et al. articulated five epistemological perspectives among the women they interviewed:

- *Silence*, or not knowing, where the individual feels powerless, mindless, and voiceless. This situation appears to result from a social context of isolation, that discourages conversation and discussion.

- *Received knowing*, in which knowledge and authority are the sources of truth, and are understood to be outside the self, and in which one learns from powerful others through listening.

- *Subjective knowing*, where knowing is "personal, private, and based on intuition and/or feeling states" (Goldberger, 1996, p. 5).

- *Procedural knowing*, a place where "techniques and procedures for acquiring, validating, and evaluating knowledge claims are developed and honored" (Goldberger, 1996, p. 5). This way of knowing can be further subdivided into *separate* knowing (characterized by skepticism and distance) and *connected* knowing (which is more empathetic and associative).

- *Constructed knowing*, in which "truth is understood to be contextual; knowledge is recognized as tentative, not absolute; and it is understood that the knower is part of (constructs) the known…constructed knowers [value] multiple approaches to knowing (subjective and objective, connected and separate) and [insist] on bringing the self and personal commitment into the center of the knowing process" (Goldberger, 1996, p. 5).

WWK has generated interest in "psychology, philosophy, education, women's studies, diversity and culture studies, humanities, law and feminist jurisprudence, nursing, theology, and communication" (Goldberger, 1996, p. 2). It has informed discussions of embodiment, intersubjectivity, the construction of knowledge within communities, and postcolonial studies. Like most feminist theories, WWK has been criticized as essentialist, but the authors maintain that this oversimplifies their work. They do, however, acknowledge the validity of another common criticism aimed at feminist theories, that WWK does not explicitly address issues of race or class (despite the diversity of women in their original study). However, the classic charges of antirationalism and subjectivism are soundly rejected by the authors in favor of "alternative ideals of reason" (Goldberger, 1996, p. 9). There also has been debate about whether the theory is developmental, in the sense that knowers "ought" to move through the forms of knowing in "stages." Although she expresses concern about establishing "developmental endpoints," Goldberger argues that "constructed knowing can be considered 'superior' in its flexibility and in the sense that it represents a meta perspective on knowing" (Goldberger, 1996, p. 13).

Within the field of information behavior, WWK has yet to make a significant impact. The theory was invoked in one LIS doctoral dissertation (Julien, 1997), in which the "self" was recognized as a potential information source for adolescents making career decisions, and where "authority" of information sources was explored. More recently, Ford (2004) refers to WWK in a discussion of critical thinking as he develops a model of learning. Ford situates WWK in a section on various "information behavioral responses to learning tasks" (p. 188), a decidedly rationalist, cognitive approach within his overall argument for the importance of context. This use of the theory is slightly ironic; WWK clearly falls within a qualitative, emic, critical, tradition of valuing the voices of ordinary people and seeking to destabilize the Western empirical, rationalist tradition.

WWK has great potential within the "IB in daily life" research stream, particularly as approached from qualitative perspectives. Primarily, WWK does suggest the value of the "self" as "informational," as one source of help to which people turn as they construct their responses to the world. Perhaps even more obviously, WWK highlights the value of gender as a potentially significant variable in IB. Indeed, most IB work could benefit from a more critical approach, bringing explicit attention to contextual variables such as gender, race, and class. These variables do not figure overtly in current models of IB, except as relatively unexplored (and therefore marginal) aspects of "situation" or "context." When an understanding of "context" is expanded to include the way in which individuals construct their own gender/race/class, the implications for IB research are truly opened up. For example, these variables would seem to fit with the "intervening variables" component of Wilson's (2000) model of information behavior (i.e., psychological, demographic, role-related or interpersonal variables). Interestingly, however, the gender/race/class triad, either as an individual or a social construction, has not yet generated a great deal of interest on the part of IB researchers.

Whether such considerations might have relevance to system design is an open question, particularly if "system" is narrowly construed to mean computerized information retrieval systems. If "system" is more broadly interpreted as information help in a larger context, then greater understanding of differences in the ways people of varying genders, races, or cultural backgrounds, for example, construct "authority" or value various approaches to "knowing," could clearly inform the work of information service providers. What questions, both practical and theoretical, might ensue by asking how a "received knower" and a "subjective knower" might differ in their information behavior in a formal information setting, such as a public library?

Any critical theory, including feminist theories such as WWK, has potential to expand current understandings of IB, based as they are on research that, for the most part, has heretofore overlooked variables such as the roles of self-reflection, or gender differences. These gaps are ripe for attention, and may demand some urgency, if IB research is to move forward with contemporary work in the other social sciences and humanities.

Belenky, M. F., Clinchy, B. M., Goldberger, N. R., & Tarule, J. M. (1986). *Women's ways of knowing: The development of self, voice, and mind.* New York: Basic Books.

Ford, N. (2004). Towards a model of learning for educational informatics. *Journal of Documentation, 60*, 183–225.

Goldberger, N. R. (1996). Introduction: Looking backward, looking forward. In N. R. Goldberger, J. M. Tarule, B. M. Clinchy, & M. F. Belenky (Eds.), *Knowledge, difference, and power: Essays inspired by women's ways of knowing* (pp. 1–21). New York: Basic Books.

Harris, R. (1992). *Librarianship: The erosion of a woman's profession*. Norwood, NJ: Ablex.

Julien, H. (1997). How does information help? The search for career-related information by adolescents (Doctoral dissertation, University of Western Ontario, London, 1997). *Dissertation Abstracts International, 59*, 2227.

Olson, H. A. (2001). Patriarchal structures of subject access and subversive techniques for change. *Canadian Journal of Information and Library Science, 26*, 1–29.

Perry, W. G. (1970). *Forms of intellectual and ethical development in the college years*. New York: Holt, Rinehart & Winston.

Turock, B. J. (2001). Women and leadership. *Journal of Library Administration, 32*, 111–132.

Wilson, T. D. (2000). Human information behavior. *Informing Science, 3*, 49–55.

71
Work Task Information-Seeking and Retrieval Processes

Preben Hansen
Swedish Institute of Computer Science, Sweden
preben@sics.se

It is essential that professionals today both stay informed and inform their work environments to be competitive, effective, and innovative. Managing the flow of information (i.e., gathering, assimilating, and creating information) is becoming increasingly complex. The information-seeking and retrieval (IS&R) processes we as individuals engage in are becoming more specialized and less amenable to standard theoretical tools. Studies in information seeking (e.g., Allen, 1977; Kuhlthau, 1993; Marchionini, 1995) and information retrieval (e.g., Belkin et al., 1995; Ingwersen, 1996; Saracevic, 1996) attempt to describe these processes. In information science as well as in human-computer interaction and system design (Hansen, 1999), the concept of *work task* has become a fundamental contextual aspect affecting the IS&R process.

The rationale for developing a framework for work task information seeking and retrieval is grounded in a belief that IS&R should not be treated in isolation, but rather as embedded in a larger task context. In order to understand the dynamic nature of IS&R processes, one needs to adopt a broader perspective, both situationally and contextually, which includes the tasks people perform (Hansen & Järvelin, 2000). There are, however, several issues of concern:

- IR systems still have problems supporting both tasks and users.

- The context of the tasks is vague and not well understood.

- Relatively few studies empirically connect the work task to IS&R in order to investigate user behaviour and seeking strategies.

392

The basic theoretical framework is focused on three types of task per-formance processes (Figure 71.1). A *work task* may be considered to be the situation in which a need for information emerges. The work task is in turn embedded in a larger context. An important concept is that infor-mation-seeking tasks and/or information retrieval tasks are embedded within the work task itself. This is vital to understanding how and why people use and adopt information-seeking behaviours and strategies.

Another important concept is the relationship between the different task levels and other components within a work environment. The IS&R phenomena are investigated from the point of how these tasks levels are interrelated, how they interact and influence the overall IS&R process, and how knowledge about the task and task characteristics may influ-ence the design of IR tools and systems (Hansen, 1999; Hansen & Järvelin, 2000; Byström & Hansen; 2002).

The empirical research in work task IS&R is based on ethnographic data collection. Studies have been performed in real-life professional environments, such as a patent office (Hansen & Järvelin, 2000), a news-paper (Hansen et. al., 2002), and, currently, in software development. One feature of the methodology is the use of combined qualitative and

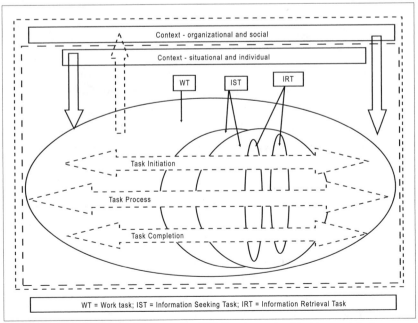

Figure 71.1   Conceptual framework of IS&R tasks embedded in work task.

quantitative data collection methods (Hansen & Järvelin, 2000). In Kabel et al. (2004), the conceptual framework described above is used as a starting point in an experiment on IR and task-related indexing of documents.

The framework was originated by Hansen (1997) from within an interdisciplinary context in relation to the design of user interfaces. These ideas have been developed further into a conceptual framework as a result of practical and theoretical work at the intersection of information science and computer science (Hansen, 1999; Hansen & Järvelin, 2000; Byström & Hansen, 2002). The framework is related to a number of existing and emerging theories—for example, the cognitive information retrieval (IR) model developed by Ingwersen (1996), which involves the user, the user's situational characteristics, the system, and the domain. Byström & Järvelin (1995) discuss the complexity of tasks as an important aspect of information seeking. Wilson (1999) also discusses the information retrieval process as a sub-task of the information-seeking process. Borlund (2000), simulating a real query situation, uses a similar approach to enhance the traditional experimental setting for IR evaluation.

The strength of this framework lies in the use of real-life settings for data collection and analysis. This allows the investigation of what people actually are doing. Based on data from real-life settings and work tasks, it is possible to construct scenarios and task descriptions that might be used to describe processes and to develop experiments. The strength of the approach is simultaneously its weakness: In order to develop and utilise the theoretical framework, one needs to perform fairly ambitious data collection, which typically will be complex both conceptually and practically. It may also be hard to find a setting or domain that will provide meaningful and necessary data in order to investigate the research questions at hand. Furthermore, data collection and data analysis can be very cumbersome and time-consuming.

The theoretical and conceptual framework presented has been used to explain the relationship between different types of work tasks and the performance of IS&R activities in different domains. The framework has been used as a theoretical basis for conceptual discussions (Hansen, 1999; Byström & Hansen, 2002), and it has been used empirically for constructing task descriptions, developing scenarios, and in the design of a series of interactive IR evaluation experiments (Karlgren & Hansen,

2003). Finally, the framework may be helpful for investigating different domains and work settings to gain a better understanding of information handling processes, as well as to inform the design of tools and systems for information access.

Allen, T. J. (1977). *Managing the flow of technology: Technology transfer and the dissemination of technological information within the R&D organization.* Cambridge, MA: MIT Press.

Belkin, N. J., Cool, C., Stein, A., & Thiel, U. (1995). Cases, scripts, and information-seeking strategies: On the design of interactive information retrieval systems. *Expert Systems with Applications, 9*(3), 379–396.

Bennett, J. L. (1972). The user interface in interactive systems. *Annual Review of Information Science and Technology 7,* 159–196.

Borlund, P. (2000). Evaluation of Interactive Information Retrieval Systems. Unpublished doctoral dissertation, Åbo Academi, Åbo, Finland.

Byström, K., & Hansen, P. (2002). Work tasks as unit for analysis in information seeking and retrieval studies. In Bruce, H., Fidel, R., Ingwersen, P., and Vakkari, P. (Eds.), *Proceedings of the fourth international conference on Cconceptions of library and information science* (pp. 239–251). Greenwood Village, CO: Libraries Unlimited.

Byström, K., & Järvelin, K. (1995). Task complexity affects information seeking and use. *Information Processing & Management, 31*(2), 191–213.

Hansen, P. (1997). *An exploratory study of IR interaction for user interface design: An interdisciplinary approach.* Unpublished master's thesis, University College of Borås, University of Göteborg, Sweden.

Hansen, P. (1999). User Interface Design for IR Interaction: A Task-Oriented Approach. In T. Aparac, T. Saracevic, P. Ingwersen, & P. Vakkari (Eds.), *Digital libraries: Interdisciplinary concepts and opportunities. Proceedings of the third international conference on conceptions of library and information science* (pp. 191–205). Zagreb, Croatia: Naklada Benja.

Hansen, P., Petrelli, D., Karlgren, J., Beaulieu, M., & Mark Sanderson, M. (2002). User-centered interface design for cross-language information retrieval. In *Proceedings of the twenty-fifth annual international ACM SIGIR conference on research and development in information retrieval, SIGIR 2002, Tampere, Finland* (pp. 383–384).

Hansen, P., & Järvelin, K. (2000). The information seeking and retrieval process at the Swedish Patent and Registration Office: Moving from lab-based to real life work-task environment. In *ACM-SIGIR 2000 Workshop on Patent Retrieval, Athens, Greece* (pp. 43–53).

Ingwersen, P. (1996), Cognitive perspectives of information retrieval interaction: Elements of a cognitive IR theory. *Journal of Documentation, 52,* 3–50.

Kabel, S., de Hoog, R., Wielinga, B., & Anjewierden, A. (2004). The added value of task and ontology-based markup for information retrieval. *Journal of the American Society for Information Science and Technology, 55,* 348–362.

Karlgren, J., & Hansen, P. (2003). Cross-language relevance assessment and task context. In *Third workshop of the cross-language evaluation forum, CLEF 2002. Rome: Italy, September 2002, LNCS 2785 Rome, Italy* (pp. 383–391).

Kuhlthau, C. (1993). *Seeking meaning. A process approach to library and information services.* New York: Ablex.

Marchionini, G. (1995). *Information seeking in electronic environments. Cambridge Series on Human Computer Interaction 9.* Cambridge: Cambridge University Press.

Saracevic, T. (1996). Relevance reconsidered '96. In P. Ingwersen, & N.O. Pors (Eds.), *Proceedings of the second international conference on conceptions of library and information science (CoLIS4)* (pp. 201–218). Copenhagen, Denmark: The Royal School of Librarianship.

Wilson, T. D. (1999). Models in information behaviour research. *Journal of Documentation, 55,* 249–270.

72
World Wide Web Information Seeking

Don Turnbull
School of Information
University of Texas at Austin, USA
donturnbull@ischool.utexas.edu

A significant number of the contributions of information-seeking theory and models are based on assumptions or smaller-scale studies of user information needs and searching (Belkin, Oddy, & Brooks, 1982a; Belkin, Oddy, & Brooks, 1982b; Kuhlthau, 1991). These models suppose cognitive activity and the feedback given by the information search environment. With the more recent focus on World Wide Web browsing and searching, a new set of data collection and user-modeling studies are possible. While these new Web-based models can be primarily based on detectable patterns in either individual interest (content) or situational activity (context), it is hoped that it may be possible to generalize a set of habits from these patterns that can then be either integrated with existing information-seeking models or to form a new basis for information-seeking studies.

It is possible that by combining these previous studies with new data collection methods and accounting for newer information-seeking technologies such as the Web, we may be able to discover, measure, and compare information seeking and information retrieval patterns. Over the last few years Choo, Detlor, and Turnbull (1998, 1999, 2000a, 2000b) have worked on a hybrid information-seeking framework (based on Ellis, 1989 and Aguilar, 1967) that has potential to be extended or mapped to other information-seeking activities such as information search.

To extend this model, it may be possible to add yet another model dimension that is more quantitative as seen in studies like Huberman et al.'s (1998) *law of surfing* study of aggregate Web use or toward the *information foraging* work championed by Pirolli and Card (1995) that focuses more on individual users and their general information-seeking behaviors.

Are these fruitful directions to move in, in light of the significant previous research into information seeking? Is there anything new to discover in information seeking or is it best to apply existing models to Web environments?

This more behavioral-oriented research shows that habits and routines are dominant in terms of information (seeking) behavior and it may be useful to explore the efficacy of the above models towards more finitely describing user behavior, be it assumptions about cognitive activity or noting the impact of various information technologies. One technique increasingly employed in the recent years is the highly quantitative, *knowledge discovery in databases* (KDD), which includes *data mining*, to analyze large-scale datasets of Web use activity. It would be useful to address the applicability of these techniques to either extend or confirm existing information seeking and use models or devise altogether new models.

One barrier to understanding such large datasets is in visualization methods to make sense of quantitative information-seeking data, including new metaphors for envisioning and presenting results or new models now more possible due to advances in multidimensional or real-time visualization (Card, 1996; Card, Mackinlay, & Shneiderman, 1999). One application that may have merit is taken from ideas relating to faceted classification, where different views of the same data may be viewed according to context, confirmation of habits, prediction, content identification and classification or by individual or aggregate use. Also, at a simpler level, since much information behavior is repetitive and iterative, it may be possible to visualize both individual and aggregate information seeking sessions as a spiral model, where the user slowly gets to a centered "target" or solution to the information-seeking problem at hand. Additionally, it would be useful to address and formalize a set of standards for data collection, analysis, and presentation to make it possible to compare studies of Web information seeking. The current variety of presentation and (path) graphing formats, not to mention the variability of data collection methods and datasets, makes any comparison and consensus about Web information seeking problematic. Past information seeking research focuses on two main directions: discernable types of user communities and insights into unique types of user behavior. Why not combine both directions to study Web information seekers and their behaviors as bounded by possible Web-based interactions as defined by the Web browser technology in use? KDD methods may prove to be the primary method to combine these two directions of study.

Recently, there has been an increased focus on modeling information retrieval activity, more specifically Web searching. As Web information retrieval technology improves (and browsing technology stands relatively still), users become habituated to conducting a search as the initial step in information seeking. By focusing first on Web searching, some of the above questions may be answered in an approachable manner and then be built upon for more complex, open-ended information-seeking activities. These Web search studies show that users do have particular patterns of search use and yield insight into user mental models of search (Jansen, Spink, Bateman, & Saracevic, 1998; Silverstein, Henzinger, Marais, & Moricz, 1998). It is possible that a system that can identify and track an individual user's search behavior in comparison to aggregate patterns, and begin to build a profile of interests and habits, can be used to personalize search results and interfaces to augment information-seeking sessions (Pitkow et al., 2002). This type of observation leads to an approach that has potential to both confirm or leverage current information-seeking models or help to unveil altogether new models, that may be either general (e.g., an information-seeking episode) or contextual (e.g., e-Commerce or content topic specific) to a particular user, a particular situation, or as generally applicable to any information seeker. However, the true strength of these new avenues and methods may be to combine with existing information-seeking models to provide glimpses into human information seeking combined with the World Wide Web information environment.

Aguilar, F. J. (1967). *Scanning the business evironment*. New York: Macmillan.

Belkin, N. J., Oddy, R. N., & Brooks, H. M. (1982a). ASK for information retrieval: Part I. Background and history. *Journal of Documentation, 38*, 61–71.

Belkin, N. J., Oddy, R. N., & Brooks, H. M. (1982b). ASK for information retrieval: Part II. Results of a design study. *Journal of Documentation, 38*, 145–164.

Card, S. K. (1996). Visualizing retrieved information: A survey. *IEEE Computer Graphics and Applications, 16*(2), 63–67.

Card, S. K., Mackinlay, J. D., & Shneiderman, B. (1999). *Readings in information visualization: Using vision to think*. San Francisco, CA: Morgan Kaufmann.

Choo, C. W., Detlor, B., & Turnbull, D. (1998). A behavioral model of information seeking on the web: Preliminary results of a study of how managers and IT specialists use the Web. *Proceedings of the 61st Annual Meeting of the American Society of Information Science, 35*, 290–302.

Choo, C. W., Detlor, B., & Turnbull, D. (1999). Information seeking on the Web: An integrated model of browsing and searching. *Proceedings of the 62nd Annual Meeting of the American Society of Information Science, Washington, 36*, 3–16.

Choo, C. W., Detlor, B., & Turnbull, D. (2000a). *Web work: Information seeking and knowledge work on the World Wide Web*. Dordrecht, Netherlands: Kluwer Academic Publishers.

Choo, C. W., Detlor, B., & Turnbull, D. (2000b). *Working the Web: An empirical model of the Web use*. Paper presented at the 33rd Hawaii International Conference on System Science (HICSS), Maui, HI.

Ellis, D. (1989). A behavioural model for information retrieval system design. *Journal of Information Science, 15*(4), 237–247.

Huberman, B. A., Pirolli, P. L. T., Pitkow, J. E., & Lukose, R. (1998). Strong regularities in World-Wide Web surfing. *Science, 280*, 95–97.

Jansen, B. J., Spink, A., Bateman, J., & Saracevic, T. (1998). Real life information retrieval: A study of user queries on the web. *ACM Special Interest Group on Information Retrieval (SIGIR) Forum, 32*, 5–18.

Kuhlthau, C. C. (1991). Inside the search process: Information seeking from the user's perspective. *Journal of the American Society of Information Science, 42*, 361–371.

Pirolli, P., & Card, S. (1995). *Information foraging in information access environments*. Paper presented at the Conference on Human Factors in Computer Systems, CHI-95, Denver, Colorado, USA.

Pitkow, J., Schutze, H., Cass, T., Cooley, R., Turnbull, D., & Edmonds, A. (2002). Personalized search: A contextual computing approach may prove a breakthrough in personalized search efficiency. *Communications of the ACM, 45*(9), 50–55.

Silverstein, C., Henzinger, M., Marais, H., & Moricz, M. (1998). Analysis of a very large web search engine query log. *ACM Special Interest Group on Information Retrieval (SIGIR) Forum, 33*, 6–12.

About the Editors

Dr. Karen E. Fisher (née Pettigrew) is an associate professor at the Information School of the University of Washington, USA, where she teaches information behavior, qualitative research methods, community analysis, and outcome-based evaluation. Her BA (English and Russian, 1989) is from Memorial University of Newfoundland, and her MLIS (1991) and PhD in library and information science (1998) from the University of Western Ontario. Her research addresses information behavior in everyday contexts (IBEC). The author of more than 50 articles and books, her current research is funded by the Institute of Museum and Library Services, and the National Science Foundation. She received the 1995 ALISE Jane Anne Hannigan Award, the 1999 ALISE Research Award, and the 2005 ALA Jesse H. Shera Award for Distinguished Published Research. She is a member of several editorial boards as well as the Permanent Program Committee of the Information Seeking in Context (ISIC) Conference series, and is the 2004–05 chair of ASIST SIG USE. For more information about Dr. Fisher, visit ibec.ischool.washington.edu.

Dr. Sanda Erdelez is an associate professor at the School of Information Science and Learning Technologies at the University of Missouri–Columbia, USA where she directs the Information Experience Laboratory (http://ielab.coe.missouri.edu/) for a study of information behavior in an electronic environment. Dr. Erdelez teaches human information behavior, research methods, business information resources, and online information searching. She obtained LLB (1982) and LLM (1986) from University of Osijek, Croatia; and PhD in Information Transfer (1995) from Syracuse University, where she studied as a Fulbright Scholar. Dr. Erdelez's research in accidental aspects of information behavior, especially information encountering (www.infoencountering.com), has been funded by SBC Communication and Dell Inc. She is the 2003–2004 chair of ASIST SIG USE.

Dr. Lynne McKechnie is associate dean and an associate professor at the Faculty of Information and Media Studies at the University of Western Ontario in London, Ontario, Canada where she teaches library services and literature for children and young adults, research methods, reference, and everyday life information behavior. She holds a BA (Anthropology, 1972) from the University of Manitoba, an MLS (1979) from the University of Toronto and a PhD (LIS, 1996) from the University of Western Ontario. She has been the recipient of ALA's Baber Research Award (2003), ALISE Research Grant (1999), and a grant from the Social Sciences and Humanities Research Council of Canada (1998–2002). Dr. McKechnie has served as elected Treasurer of ALA's Library Research Round Table and is currently the editor of the *Canadian Journal of Information and Library Science* and chair of the ALISE Research Committee.

Index

Page numbers in *italics* refer to figures or figure legends.
Page numbers in bold refer to chapters contributed by the author cited.

A

Abbott, A. D., 158, 294
Abele, Marta J., 300
Abrams, M. H., 303, 304
access, principle of, 298
accessibility, of information, 4, 6, 77, 205, 318
accidental acquisition of information, 179
accommodations, rounding and, 308
accountability, 105, 368
accountive positioning, 335
Ackerman, M. S., 14
action chains, 109
action research, need for, 51
actions, interplay of, 231
Adamic, L. A., 290, 291, 318, 319, 320
addictions, 363–364
administrative authority, 83
affective behavior, 40, 277
affective factors, 55
affective load theory (ALT), 39–43, 115
affective states, 39
age/aging, 208, 346, 360. *see also* children
Aguilar, F. J., 397
Ahearne, 284
Al-Gahtani, S. S., 242
Albert, R., 318, 319
Albrechtsen, H., 12, 89, 123, 315, 316, 339
Allen, J. F., 13

Allen, Thomas, 123, 174, 392
allied game theoretic models, 95
Alreck, P., 34
Alvesson, M., 266
Amabile, T., 242
amateurism, 314, 315
ambiguity, 50, 51
American Society for Information Science & Technology (ASIS&T), xxii, xxiii
Andersen, J., 341
Anderson, J. R., 7
Angulo, J. de, 80
Annual Review of Information Science & Technology, xxii, 58
anomalous state of knowledge (ASK), concept of, 44–48, 128, 165, 270, 290, 355, 360
anomaly, definition, 44–45
anonymity, increases in, 205
anxiety, 235–238
Appleby, J., 10
archival intelligence, 49–53
archives
  of film, 89
  navigation of, 50–51
area scanning, 61
Armstrong, C. J., 58
art, information properties, 115
artificial intelligence, 13
Artz, J. M., 156
AskERIC users, 55

assessment, 65
Association of Library and Information
    Science Education (ALISE),
    xxii
associative memory, 46
attribution theory, 243–244, *244*
Auramäki, E., 100
author searching, 61
authority
    administrative, 83
    claims of, 223
    cognitive, 83–87, 126, 296
    gatekeeping and, 251–252
    source selection and, 229
authors, text relation to, 303
authorship, 84, 126
autonomy, 370
autotelic experiences, 156
avoidance and vigilance, theory of, 239
awareness
    action and, 155
    flow theory and, 155
    of information, 161–162, 204
    information channel use and, 289
    lack of, 171
    maintenance of, 139
    raising of, 380
    study of, 121

B

Baeza-Yates, R., 101
Baker, Lynda M., **239–241**, 240
Bakhtin, Mihail, 11, 329
Bandura, Albert, 34, 39, 54–57, 373
bandwidth, consumption of, 95
Bar-Ilan, J., 10
Barabási, A. L., 318, 319
Barkow, J. H., 7, 14
Barzilai-Nahon, Karine, **247–253**
Barzun, J., 10
baseline measures, 199
Bateman, J., 217, 399
Bates, J. A., 10

Bates, Marcia J., xxiii, **1–24**, 9, 10, 13,
    14, 49, **58–62**, 123, 124, 125,
    128, 130, 319
Bateson, Gregory, 5
Baxter, Graeme, **204–209**
Bayma, T., 126
Beaulieu, M, 277
Beckman, L., 247
Beckman, S., 13
behavioral approaches, 140
behaviorial characteristics, 34
behaviorism, 8
behaviorists, 7
Belenky, M. F., 387
Belkin, Nicholas J., 13, 39, **44–48**,
    128, 165, 215, 270, 355, 360,
    392, 397
Belnap, N., 133
Benoît, Gerald, **99–103**
Berger, J., 316
Berger, P. L., 2, 8, 11, 131
Berkenkotter, C., 12
Berkowitz, R. E., 63, 64, 66
berrypicking theory, 49, 58–62
Between Facts and Norms
    (Habermas), 99
betweenness centrality, 321
Beyer, J., 198
Bhavnani, Suresh, 61
biases
    cultural, 108
    gatekeepers and, 251
    inherent, 108
    value-sensitive design and, 370
bibliographic applications, 289–290
bibliographic databases, 50
bibliometric approaches, 13
bibliotherapy, 366
Bierbaum, E., 290
Big6™ skills, 63–68, *65*
Bilal, D., 217, 277, 278
biological science department, 346
Birnhack, M., 247

Bishop, A. P., 12
Björneborn, Lennart, **318–322**
Black, J. B., 133
black students, 237
Blair, D. C., 11
Bleich, David, 304
blocking, of information, 366
blogs, carrying capacity, 95
Bok, Sessela, 76
Book Clubs (Long), 303
BookHouse, 89
books
    cognitive authority of, 84
    fiction, 89
    handheld, 299
    non-traditional, 300
    system design in, 301
Booth, S., 280, 281
Borlund, P., 218, 277, 394
Borning, A., 368, 370
Bostick, S. L., 236
boundaries
    life in the round and, 308, 309
    radical change and, 299
    setting of, 81
    social, 8
    studies of, 106
    temporal, 81, 309
Bourdieu, Pierre, 143, 158, 349, 350,
        351, 352
Bowers, F. T., 12
Bradford, S. C., 13
Bradford Distribution, 61
bricolage, concept of, 115
Briggs, L. J., 39
Broder, A., 319
Brookes, B. C., 13, 198
Brooks, H. M., 45, 46, 355, 360, 397
Brown, C. D., 120
Brown, M. K., 63
Brown-Syed, C., 268
browsing
    behaviors, 319

definition, 138
framework for, *70*
human-computer interfaces and, 61
levels of, 69
model of, 69–74
for recreation, 73
searching using, 125
taxonomy of, 69–70, 72
techniques, 60
Bruce, Christine, 280, 281, 358
Bruce, Harry, xxi, xxii, 10, 147,
        270–274
Bruner, J., 373
Brush, T., 67
Buchanan, J., 284
Buckland, M., 289
Budd, J. M., 11
Budwig, N. A., 374
Burnett, K., 299
business leaders, 156
Button, G., 3
Byström, Katriina, **174–178**, 217,
        275, 277, 278, 393, 394

C
Callahan, E., 108
Callison, D., 374
Campbell, M., 211, 212, 213, 347
Campos, J., 182
capital
    conversion of, 351
    cultural, 146, 349
    economic, 349
    informational, 352
    knowledge, 96
    social, 78, 96, 323–327, 324, 325
    symbolic, 349
    types of, 349
Capps, L., 116
Carbaugh, D., 337
Card, S. K., 49, 259, 263, 276, 397,
        398
career development, 314

caregivers, 370
Carey, R. F., 337
Carlin, M., 111
Carmichael, J.V.J., 12
Carnovsky, Leon, 304
Carroll, J. M., 14
Carver, C. S., 40
Case, Donald O., xxi, 10, 12, 170, 225, 262, **289–292**
casual leisure, 314
catalogs, online, 59
Catledge, L. D., 319
Certeau, Michel de, 284–287, 305
chaining, 125, 138
Chang, Shan-Ju L., **69–74**, 319
change
    processes of, 364–365
    spiral model of, *364*
    transtheoretical model, 363
channels, gatekeepers and, 247
Chatman, Elfreda. A., xxi, 12, 121, 147, 150, 158, 186, 308, 310, 315, 325, 346, 351
    concept of rounding and, 308
    on radical change theory, 301
    theory of information poverty, 75–78
    theory of life in the round, 79–82
Checkland, P., 115, 267
chemical engineers, 310
chemists, 139, 310
Chen, C., 227
Chen, H., 156
Chen, L.L.J., 4
Cherry, Colin, 13, 290
Chi, E. H., 259, 262
child-as-apprentice, 373
Childers, Tom, 382
children
    cognitive web IR patterns, 217
    use of libraries, 374
Chilvers, A., 268
Chomsky, N., 7

Choo, C. W., 268, 377, 397
Chowdury, G. G., 13
Chu, C. M., 12
citation indexes, 341
citation rates, 261–262
citation searching, 60–61, 138
Clark, L., 199
class distinctions, 76, 77, 121
cognitive approaches, 13, 217, 256
cognitive authority
    filters, 85
    resource selection and, 126
    theory of, 83–87
    theory of professions and, 296
cognitive behavior, 40
cognitive information retrieval theory, 174, *216*
cognitive intents. *see* information intents theory
cognitive load, 41
cognitive operations
    affective load and, 39, 40, 41
    goal direction and, 41
    motivation and, 41
cognitive psychology, 39, 46
cognitive science, 7, 13
cognitive skills, childhood, 373
cognitive systems/work analysis, 174
cognitive triggers, 171
cognitive viewpoints, 46
cognitive work analysis (CWA), 88–93, 90, *90, 91*
Cole, C., 49, 286
Coleman, James S., 95, 96, 323
collaborations
    information resources and, 194
    as social resources, 323
collaborative weaving, 319
COLLATE project, 89
collection stage, 231
collective action dilemma, 94–98
collectivism, 110
collectivity, 105

Collins, R., 294
communication
    channels of, 119
    collaborations, 194
    control of, 44
    control through, 99
    diffusion theory and, 119
    domain analysis and, 340
    effective, 44
    elicitation and, 133–137
    ethnography of, 266
    of innovation, 118
    institutional dialog and, 136
    interpretive repertoires, 221–224
    level of context in, 109
    literacy development, 300
    observation of, 27
    physical, 13
    reciprocation of greetings, 110
    relevance of, 55
    shared stories, 105
    social isolation and, 205
    speed of messages, 109
    symbolic systems, 350
    systems of, 45
    technology, 120
    theory of, 165
    threats to face, 150
    types of, 170–171
    willingness to return and, 383
communicative action, theory of,
    99–103, 352
communities
    bridging ties, 345
    identification with, 314
    interactions within, 328
communities of practice, 104–107,
    170, 224
Communities of Practice (Wenger),
    104
competency, 243, 244, 245
competition, 96
computerization, 299

concentration, focused, 155
Conceptions of Library and
    Information Science (CoLIS4),
    xxii
conceptual graphs, 46, 199
conceptual investigations, 369
connected knowing, 387
connectivity
    local, 320
    principle of, 298
consciousness raising, 366
consolidation processes, 256
constancy, across time-space, 28
constraints
    analysis of, 91
    information horizons and, 191
constructed knowing, 388
constructionist approaches, 11, 85,
    221–224, 328–333. see also
    specific theories
constructivist approaches, 11
constructivist learning theory, 34
constructs, reading, 304
consumers
    adaptation of innovation, 118
consumption, models of, 144, 146
content analysis, 40, 290
context
    analysis and, 147
    browsing, 70
    currency and, 262
    design implications, 244
    elicitation and, 133
    emergent factors and, 151
    framework for, 150–151
    influence of, 216–217
    information grounds and, 186, 187
    information horizons and, 192–193
    information seeking and, 114, 257
    of interactions, 150
    level of, 109
    lifecycle of imposition, 165
    nonlinear model and, 255–256

context (*cont.*)
    patterns of behavior and, 310
    values conflict, 371
    zone of proximal development and,
        373
contributions
    group affiliation and, 96
    predictions and, 95
control
    design implications, *244*
    gatekeeping and, 251
    potential for, 155
    self-efficacy and, 243
convenience, diffusion theory and, 119
conversation, 224, 314. *see also* com-
    munication; language
conversation analytic research method,
    329
Cool, C., 10, 12
Cooper, L. Z., 374, 375
Cooper, W. S., 11
cooperation
    boundaries and, 106
    computer-supported, 100
    human capacity for, 97
    predictions and, 95
    sustaining, 96
coping assistance services (CAS), 39
coping strategies, uncertainty and, 41
Cornfield, M., 247
Cosijn, E., 218
Cosmides, L., 7, 14
cost-benefit paradigms, 290–291
costs, of searching, 260
counseling interventions, 42
Covi, L., 123, 125
Cox, D., 139
Crabtree, A., 10
Crane, Diana, 123, 321
Cranfield, M., 217
Crawford, M, 355
creative writing, 300
creativity, flow theory and, 153

credibility, cognitive authority and,
    83–84
critical incident interview techniques,
    195
critical theory approaches, 11–12
criticism, reader-response, 303
Croft, W. B., 13, 218
Cromwell, R. L., 85
Cronin, B., 106, 259
Crosman, I., 304, 305
crowding, resource use and, 95
Crowley, Terence, 382
Csikszentmihalyi, M., 153, 154, 156,
    243
cultural capital, 146, 349
cultural diversity, 247
cultural studies scholars, 124
culture
    mastery of life and, 146
    models of, 108–112, 115
    values and, 368
    zone of proximal development and,
        373
currency, context and, 262
curriculum development, 64
cyberspace, gatekeeping in, 247–248.
    see also World Wide Web
Czech Republic, film archives, 89
Czerwinski, M., 183

D

Dahlbom, B., 13
daily activities, types of, 313–314
Dalrymple, P. W., 113
data analysis, 55
data collection, 55
data mining, 398
databases
    adoption of, 124
    bibliographic, 61, 294
    knowledge discovery in, 398
    subject searching, 60
    vendors of, 59

Daubman, K. A., 40
Davenport, E., 105, 106, 170
Davies, B., 335
Davies, Elisabeth, **104–107**
Davis, D. G., 10
Day, R. E., 12
de Figueiredo, A. D., 182
de Mey, M., 46
De Michelis, G., 100
deception, 76, 308
Deci, E. L., 243
decision making
    computer-based, 366
    innovation and, 119–120
    questions about, *91*
    search behavior and, 49
decision points, 359
Deese, J., 46
degradation of resources, 95
democracy, 99, 205
demographics of sharing, 170
Denzin, N. K., 115
Dervin, Brenda, xxiii, 4–5, 10, 11, 12,
    25–29, 35, 39, 45, **113–117**,
    128, 130, 165, 166, 172, 204,
    225, 240, 270, 276, 298–299,
    300, 347, 355, 360, 366, 383,
    384
descriptive biographies, 12
Detlor, Brian, **377–381**, 397
DeVault, M. L., 210, 211, 212, 213
development, learning and, 373
developmental psychology, 342
Dewdney, P., 165, 166, 347, 360, 383,
    384
Dewey, J., 11
diagrams, modeling and, 4
diaries, task-related, 176–177
Dick, A. L., 10
DiClemente, C. C., 363, 364
Dietz, T., 100
differentiating, definition, 138
diffusion theory, 118–122
Dijkstra, A., 366

Dillon, A., 12, 14
Dillon, J. T., 133, 134, 135
discourse analytic approaches, 11, 221,
    222–223, 329–330
Discourse and Rhetoric Group
    (DARG), 329
discourse of professionalism, 295
discursive information research (DIR),
    328
discursive practice, 335–336
dissonant grounds, rounding and,
    308–312
distance-sensitive co-occurrence analy-
    sis, 46
distributed cognition, 170
Dixon, Christopher M., 344–348
documents
    cognitive authority of, 84
    descriptors, 355
    networks, 318
domain analysis, 12, 123–127, 316
domain analytic theory, 339
domain information, 175
domain searching, 61
Donohew, L., 290
Donohue, G. A., 247
Douglas, J. D., 80
dramaturgy, 149
Dresang, Eliza T., 166, **298–302**
Dretske, F. I., 11
Driscoll, C., 285
Duff, R. W., 345
Duffy, Jack, **242–246**
Dumin, M., 323, 325
Duncker, E., 108
Durrance, Joan C., 183, 185, 186, 313,
    325, **382–386**, 385
Dwek, C. S., 243

E

e-journals, adoption of, 124
e-mail, 95, 120
Eccles, J., 243

ecological model of information seek-
    ing, *129*, 147, 180, 183
ecological psychology, 88
ecological theory of human information
    behavior, 128–132
economic capital, 349
economic poverty, 308
education
    field of, 105
    information literacy, 63–67
    social capital and, 325
    views on information and, 208
Edwards, Derek, 329
Edwards, Phillip M., **358–362**
effort. *see also* principle of least effort
    (PLE)
    estimates of, 6
    self-efficacy and, 54
Egli, U., 133
egocentric networks, 344
Eisenberg, Michael B., **63–68**, 218
elderly patients, 360
electronic discussion groups, 120
electronic resources, 237
elicitation as micro-level information
    seeking, 133–137
elicitation process, *134*
Elkin-Koren, N., 247
Ellis, David, 10, 12, 13, 34, 126,
    138–142, 397
Ellis, S., 374
Ellis's model of information seeking
    behavior, 138–142
emancipatory knowledge, 100
embedding tasks
    foraging theory, 276
    granularity of, 277, 278
    grounded theories and, 276–277
emergency dispatchers, 150
empirical investigations, 369
empiricism, 102
end-users. *see* users
energy expenditure, 54. *see also* costs;
    effort

enforcement of norms, theory of, 95
engagement
    design implications, *244*
    motivation and, 243
    reading and, 305
engineering approaches, 13, 356
engineers, 139, 140
English literature researchers, 139
entertainment, 314
environmental biology scholars, 124
environmental maps, 226
environments
    face threats and, 151–152
    information-providing, 166
    Internet-based, 169–173
    questions about, *91*
    role definition within, 151
    synergistic, 185
epistemology
    communities of practice as, 104
    orientation of discourse, 222
    perspectives, 388
    schools of, 124
Erdelez, Sanda, 34, 115, 128, 167,
    169, 170, **179–184**, 186, 270,
    287, 310, 319, 325
ethical codes, professional, 294
ethnographic approaches, 12
    gatekeeping and, 251
    serious leisure and, 313
ethnography of communication, 266
ethnomethodology, 3, 329
European information policy, 204
evaluations
    of cognitive authority, 86
    cognitive work analysis, 88–93
    consolidation and, 256
    flow of, *193*
    of information retrieval, 102
    judgment of quality, 208
    of reference interviews, 382
evaluative browsing, 71

Evers, V., 111
everyday life information seeking
(ELIS) model, 143–148, 183,
284–288, 330–331
concept of, 114
framework, *145*
social capital and, 325
women's ways of knowing and, 389
Evetts, J., 295
evolutionary psychology, 7
Exland-Olson, S., 96
experience
categories of, 281
focus on, 282
historic context of, 217
library anxiety and, 237
network competence and, 55
experience sampling method (ESM),
154, 156
experimental approaches, 6, 45, 281
experts, role definition, 151
exploration stage, 231, 319
expressive relations, 303
external forces, constraint by, 29
extracting, definition, 139

F

"face," cultural value of, 110
face threat, theory of, 149–153
fact/value dichotomy theory, 102
family planning information, 345
Faust, K., 263
Fava, J. L., 365
feedback, design implications, *244*
feelings, interplay of, 231
Felten, E., 370
feminine orientation, cultural, 110
feminist theories, 387–391
Ferreria Novellino, M. S., 101
fiction retrieval systems, 89
Fidel, Raya, xxi, xxii, 10, **88–93**, 147,
174, 358
field size, search methods and,
124–125

Fielding, N., 12
fill-in item instruments, 40
film archives, 89
Finland, ELIS in, 146
Finn, S., 290
first-order positioning, 335
Fish, Stanley, 304
Fisher, Karen E. (Pettigrew), xxii, 10,
12, 77, 147, 159, *160*, 161,
170, 183, 185, **185–190**, 186,
188, 287, 293, 313, 325, 330,
346, 358, 360, 385
Fjordback, Søndergaard, 341
Flap, H.J., 324
Flores, F., 100
flow
definition, 154
experience of, 155–156
theory of, 153–157
focus, concentration and, 155
focus browsing, 71
Fogg, B. J., 86
Folkman, S., 34
foot clinics, 185, 360
footnote chasing, 50
foraging theory
archival intelligence theory and, 49
embedding tasks, 276
optimal foraging theory, 259–264
task environments, 276
World Wide Web and, 397
Ford, D. P., 111, 140, 182, 204
Ford, N., 182, 256, 389
Foreman-Wernet, L., 26
formulation stage, 231
Foster, Allen, 182, **254–258**
Foucault, M., 11, 158, 329
Fournier, V., 295
France, librarianship in, 121
free rider problem, 94–95
free time activities, 313

Freedom of Information legislation, U.K., 208
Freeman, L. C., 321
Freier, Nathan G., **368–372**, 370
Freud, S., 290
Friedkin, N. E., 346, 347
Friedman, Batya, **368–372**
Friedman, E., 96
Fritch, J. W., 85
Frohmann, B., 11, 330
Fuller, S, 11
Fulton, Crystal, **79–82, 225–229**
fundamental equation of information science, 198

G

Gaines, B. R., 4
Galambo, J., 133
Gale, J, 34
games
    strategic, 95
    theories, 95–96
gap bridging
    information search process, 232
    monitoring and blunting theory, 239
    in reading, 305
    Sense-Making and, 27, 128
Garcia, L., 101
Gärdenfors, P., 340
Gardner, W., 374
Garfield, E., 13
Garfinkel, Harold, 11, 39, 211, 329
Garvey, William, 123
gated, concept of, 248
gatekeeping
    central, 321
    concept of, 248
    function of, 248
    mechanism of, 248
    network, 247–253
    traditional *vs.* network, *249*
gates, concept of, 248

gender
    cultural norms, 110
    feminist theories, 387–391
    library anxiety and, 237
    self-positioning and, 334–335
    social life and, 210
    women's ways of knowing and, 387–391
gender identities, 335
general model of the information seeking professionals, 158–164
generalists, foraging strategies, 261
Gergen, Kenneth, 329
Germany, film archives, 89
Gibson, James J., 88
Giddens, A., 158, 352
Gieber, W., 247
Gilovich, T., 5
Gintis, H., 94
Girvin, H., 367
Given, Lisa M., 10, 147, 330, **334–338**, 337
Glaser, B. G., 12, 140
goal-determined behaviors, 35
goal theory, 243, *244*, 277
goals
    of browsing, 71
    closed-ended, 278
    directionality, 41
    levels of, 54
    modification during searches, 55
    multiple levels of, 56
    open-ended, 278
    of searches, 277–278
Godbey, G., 313
Goffman, Erving, 39, 133, 149, 150, 151
Goldberger, N. R., 387, 388, 389
Goldfield, E. C., 373
"good citizen" information, 205
Goodstein, L. P., 88
Gorgolione, J. M., 40
Gould, E., 111

government information sources, 55,
    346
government workers, 310
Graessar, A. C., 133, 199
Graff, H. F., 10
Granovetter, M. S., 78, 320, 344, 345,
    346, 347
graphical user interfaces, 89
Grasso, M. A., 100
Gratch, B., 290
Greenberger, E., 334
Gregor, F., 211, 212, 213
Griesdorf, H., 217
Griffin, D., 5
Grint, K., 330
Gross, Melissa, **164–168**, 170, 299,
    360, 361
grounded theory
    approaches, 140
    context development and, 151
    embedding tasks and, 276–277
    library anxiety, 235
group affiliations, 96, 105. *see also spe-*
    cific groups
group solidarity, theories of, 95
Guare, J., 318
Guba, E. G., 107, 254

H

Habermas, J., 99, 100, 101, 352
habits, 28, 41
habitus, 143, 349
Hagman, J., 370
Hall, E. T., 105, 108–112, 115, 170
Hall, K., 139
Hall, Stuart, 305
Hamilton-Pennell, C., 65
Hammerberg, Dawlene, 300
Hansen, Preben, 174, 177, **382–396**
Hantula, D., 262
happiness, flow theory and, 153–154
Hara, B, 106, 310
Hardin, G., 94, 95

hardware design, 370
Hardy, A., 290
Hargittai, E., 247
Harmon, G., 192
Harper, D. J., 13
Harré, Rom, 329, 335, 337, 351
Harris, Michael, 12
Harris, Roma M., 12, 158, 212, 294,
    347, **363–367**, 387
Hartel, Jenna, 6, **313–317**
Harter, S. P., 58
Hathaway, R. S., 115
Haugan, M., 12, 139
Hawk, W. B., 217
Hayles, N. K., 11
Haythornthwaite, C., 324, 346
health advocates, goals of, 363
health behavior change, transtheoreti-
    cal model of, 363–367
health information, 384–385
healthcare providers
    cost-benefit paradigms, 291
    goals, 363
    information behaviors, 266
Hechter, M., 95, 96
Hedman, Jenny, **293–297**
hegemony, 350
Hektor, A., 313
Henderson, J. C., 266
Hendrickson, A., 370
Hendry, D. G., 13
Henefer, Jean, **225–229**
Henzel, Herbert, 123
Henzinger, M., 399
hermeneutics, 102
Herner, S., 69
Hernon, P., 227, 382
Hersberger, Julie, **75–78**, 77, 79
Hert, C. A., 259
Hertzum, M., 89
Hildenbrand, S., 10
Hill, C., 384
Hindle, A., 289

Hindreth, C. R., 14
Hinton, M. B., 183, 185, 186, 325
historical approaches, 10
history scholars, 124
Hjørland, Birger, 10, 12, 123, 124,
    280, 282, 294, 315, 316,
    339–343
hobbies, 144, 314, 315
Hofstede, G. H., 108–112
Holland, Norman, 304
Hollway, W., 334
Holquist, M., 11
Holt, L. E., 166
Holt, Leslie, 299
Holwell, S., 267
homeless persons, 79
Howe, D. C., 370
Huberman, B. A., 95, 290, 291, 397
Huckin, T. N., 12
Hughes, Anthony, **275–279**
Hultgren, F., 192
human behavioral psychology, *261*
human-computer interaction
    cooperative work and, 100
    radical change theory and, 300
    tasks, 262
    value-sensitive design and, 370
    work task IS&R, 392
human-computer interfaces, 61, 170
*Human Effort and the Principle of
    Least Effort* (Zipf), 289
human-robotic relationships, 370
humanities, idiographic approach, 9
humanities scholars
    information-seeking behaviors, 59
    search methods, 125
    Web browsing, 126
Hummert, M. L., 130
Hunt, L., 10
hybrid information-seeking Web model,
    300
hyperlinks, 318, 319. *see also* connec-
    tivity

hypothesis testing, 6–7

I

IBEC Life in the Round Project, 79
idiographic, definition, 9
idiographic approaches, 8–9, 12
Iivoneen, M., 10, 108
imaging, conceptual graphs, 46
immersive behavior, 243
imposed query model, 164–168
impression management, 149
incentives, contributions and, 96
incidental information acquisition,
    128, 129
income, social capital and, 325
indicative browsing, 72
individualism, 110, 282
individuality, 205–206, 271–272
individuals, innovativeness of, 119
industrial research scientists, 139, 140
influence, sources of, 275–276
information
    definition of, 225
    electronic, 179
    frames of reference for, 150
    manipulation of, 179
    spaces, 319–320
    traits, 355
    users of (*see under* users)
information acquiring-and-sharing
    (IAS&S), 169–173
information agents, 170
information behavior in everyday con-
    text (IBEC), 385
information behavior modeling, 31–36,
    172, 174, 180
information encountering
    browsing and, 73
    ecological theory and, 128
    functional model of, *181*
    IA&S and, 169
    Internet environments, 170, 319,
        320

life in the round and, 310
OAI and, *180*
PAIN hypothesis and, 270
passive attention mode and, 34
scholars and, 126
social capital and, 325
study methodologies, 182
theory of, 115, 179–184
information fraging, 397
information giving, 225–229
information grounds theory, 185–190,
    187, 325–326
information horizons, 191–197, *195*
information intents theory, 198–203,
    201
information interchange, theory of,
    204–209
information literacy
    action research on, 52
    Big6™ skills and, 63–68
    education in archives, 52
    in higher education, 281–282
    PAIN hypothesis and, 273
    for primary sources, 49
information poverty
    economic poverty and, 308
    key concepts, 76
    rounding and, 310
    theory of, 75–78
*Information Processing and
    Management*, 33
information processing approaches, 7
information retrieval (IR)
    berrypicking, 58–62
    bit-at-a-time, 60
    children's, 217
    components, 101
    cultural influences on, 111
    early research, 58–59
    elicitation theory and, 135
    integrative framework for informa-
        tion seeking and, 215–220
    speech act theory and, 101

systems for fiction, 89
    systems of, 45–47
    tasks, 177
information scent, 262
Information Science and Knowledge
    Management, 105–106
information search process, 230–234,
    231, 282, 361. *see also* search
    strategies
information-seeking and retrieval
    processes
    framework for, 393–394
    work task-related, 392–396
information-seeking behaviors
    barriers, 28
    boundaries and, 81
    description, 5
    ecological model of, *129*
    Ellis's model of, 138–142
    facilitators, 28
    general model of, *34*
    integrative framework for, 215–220
    Kirkelas's model of, 225–229, *227*
    micro-level, 135–136
    need and, *33*
    protective behaviors and, 77
    social class and, 146
    universe of knowledge, *32*
    varying factors, 124
Information Seeking in Context (ISIC)
    Conferences, 75, 140
information-seeking model, 240
information service providers, 82
information skills process
    models of, *64*
    stages, 64
information technology, 300
information use environments (IUEs),
    174, 354–357, 377
informational capital, 349
informed consent, 370
informedness, survival and, 205
Ingwersen, Peter, 47, 174, **215–220**,
    218, 256, 277, 321, 394

INISS Project, 31, 34
initiation stage, 230–231
innovations
    characteristics, 119
    diffusion theory, 118–122
inquiry, definition, 358
insiders, 79
institutional ethnography (IE), theory
        of, 210–214
institutions
    cognitive authority of, 84
    search strategies and, 51
    strategies of, 284
    work of, 211
instruments, cognitive authority of, 84
integration, affective norms and, 41
integrative framework for information
        seeking and interactive infor-
        mation retrieval, 215–220
intellective skills, 51
intentional positioning, 336, 337
interactive information retrieval (IIR),
        215–220
interactivity, principle of, 298
interests
    information needs and, 295
    information search process, 233
interface design, 242–246, 244, 379.
        see also human-computer
        interaction
Internet
    children's use of, 299–300
    collective good, 95
    environment of, 169–173
    gatekeeping and, 251–252
    impact of, 8
    information systems, 377, 378
    innovations, 120
    online communities, 96
    peer-to-peer support groups, 384
    self-efficacy and, 55
    SIF-FOW, 169
    surrogate collections, 51

use, 324
user self-preservation, 151
interpersonal behaviors
    face threats and, 149–152
    information acquisition-and-
        sharing, 172
    institutional ethnography and, 212
    interaction order of, 149
    life in the round and, 309
    queries and, 164–165
    zone of peripheral development
        and, 375
interpretive repertoires, 221–224
interpretive research, 115
interview methods
    construction, 28–29
    critical incident techniques, 195
    information horizon maps, 195,
        195–196
    micromoment, 298–299
    neutral strategy for, 113
    open-ended, 116
    telephone interviews, 55
    time-like strategy, 113
interviews
    by 911 calltakers, 150
    context and, 147
    electronically-assisted, 205
    as face threats, 150
    faculty attitudes, 120
    information horizons and, 191
    place in phenomenography,
        280–281
    reference-type, 360, 361, 382, 384
    transcripts, 196
intuitive knowing, 387
invisible colleges, 321
invitational browsing, 72, 73
Irving, A., 63
Isen, A. M., 40
Iser, Wolfgang, 304, 305
ISI Web of Knowledge, 61

J

Jacob, E. K., 12
Jacob, M., 10
Jacobs, N., 223
Jacoby, JoAnn, **259–264**
James, L., 39, 77
James, William, 265
Janes, J., 384
janitors, study of, 308
Jansen,B. J., 399
Janson, M. A., 100
Järvelin, K., 174, 215, *215*, 217, 392,
        393, 394
Jauss, Hans Robert, 304
Jeong, H., 319
Jiao, Q. G., 236, 237
job searches, 324
job training programs, 308
Johnson, Catherine A., **323–327**
Johnson, D., 66
Jones, W., 183
Jones, W. G., 49
Journal of Documentation, 33
*Journal of the American Society for
        Information Science*, 75
journal runs, 61
Joyce, Steven, **349–353**, 351, 352
Julien, Heidi, 313, 330, **387–391**

K

Kabel, S., 394
Kahn, P. H., Jr., 368, 370
Kahneman, D., 5
Kamil, A. C., 259
Karetsky, S., 304
Kari, J., 130, 313
Karlgren, J., 394
Katopol, Patricia, **235–238**
Kaye, K., 373
Kearsley, G. P., 133
Kekäläinen, J., 218
Kelly, George, 11, 230

Keso, H., 114, 330
Kincheloe, J. L., 115, 117
King, M., 242
Kintsch, W., 46
Kirk, Joyce, 280, 282
Kiss, G., 46
Kleinberg, J. M., 320
Kling, R., 12, 123, 125
Knorr-Cetina, Karin, 330
knowing, ways of, 387–391
knowledge
    generation of, 100
    mapping, 199
    organizational, 170
    persuasion and, 120
    symbolic significance, 294
    types of, 100
knowledge, sociology of, 75
Knowledge and Human Interests
        (Habermas), 99
knowledge discovery in databases
        (KDD), 398
Knuth, D., 289
Kochen, M., 318
Kollock, P., 96
Komlodi, A., 14, **108–112**, 111
Kraft, D. H., 13
Krebs, J. R., 259
Krikelas, J., 225–229, 240
Krikelas's model of information seek-
        ing, 225–229, 227
Kuhlthau, Carol Collier, 11, 34, 39, 63,
        114, 128, 158, 171, 174, 200,
        204, 217, **230–234**, 240, 256,
        270, 275, 277, 282, 315, 360,
        361, 374, 375, 392, 397
Kuhn, Thomas, 2, 25–26
Kwasitsu, L., 162
Kwasnik, B. H., 12, 45, 46

L

labels, sense making and, 266
Lajoie-Paquette, Darian, **118–122**

Lance, K. C., 65
land use planning, 370
language
    cognitive authority and, 85
    communicative action and, 99–103
    constructionist viewpoint, 328–333
    dissonant grounds and, 311
    institutional dialog and, 136
    interpretive repertoires, 221–224
    principle of least effort and, 289
    social reality and, 11, 329
    uses of, 330
    worldview and, 80
Large, J. A., 58, 278
Larson, M. S., 294
Latour, Bruno, 158, 329
Lave, C. A., 2
Lave, Jean, 104
learned affective norms (LANs), 41
learning
    development and, 373
    forging theories, 259
    social theory of, 105
    support for, 310
least effort, principle of, 289–292
Leckie, Gloria J., 10, **158–164**, 159,
    160, 161, 293
Lee, H., 262
legitimation, symbolic violence and,
    350
Lehtinen, E., 100
leisure, 313, 314
levels of information need, theory of,
    270
Lewin, Kurt, 247
librarians
    children's, 213
    impact of social violence on, 351
    as intermediaries, 59, 213
    library anxiety and, 235–238
    as surrogates, 360
librarianship, changes in, 294–295
libraries

anxiety about, 167, 235–238
computers in, 299
as formal institutions, 284–285
media centers, 165
underuse, 346
use by children, 374
willingness to return, 382
library anxiety scale, 236
Liddy, E. D., 13
life in the round, theory of, 79–82, 308
lifelong learning, 50
Limberg, Louise, 280, **280–283**, 281,
    282
Lin, Nan, 78, 323, 324, 325
Lincoln, Y. S., 107, 115, 254
linguistic tokens, decontextualized,
    101
linguistic turns, 239
listening skills, 383
literacy, development, 300
Literature as Exploration
    (Rosenblatt), 305
literature scholars, 124
Littell, J. H., 367
Liu, M., 236
Liu, W. T., 345
Liu, Ying-Hasng, 135–136
local settings, data collection in, 211
Long, Elizabeth, 303
long-term orientation, cultural, 110
low-income environments, 121
Lowe, Carrie A., **63–68**
Luckmann, T., 11, 131
Lukose, Rajan M., 95
Lynch, M. J., 383
Lyytinen, K., 100

M

Maack, M. N., 10, 121
MacArthur, R. H., 259
MacDonald, K. M., 293, 294
MacIntosh-Murray, Anu, **265–269**
MacIsaac, D., 100

Mackinlay, J. D., 398
MacMullin, S. E., 355, 356
Madden, A. D., 14
"making do," 285
Manaszewicz, R., 131
Mann, T., 290
Mantovani, G., 259
Marais, H., 399
Marcella, Rita, **204–209**
March, J. G., 2
Marchionini, G., 14, 278, 392
Marcus, A., 111
Markey, K., 360
Marsden, P. V., 347
Marshall, J., 120
Martin, B., 39
Marton, Ference, 280, 281
Marx, K., 211
masculine orientation, cultural, 110
mastery of life, types of, 144–147
matching items instruments, 40
Maula, H., 124, 126
Maynard Smith, J, 94
Mays, V., 247
McAdam, D., 96
McCain, K. W., 13
McCarthy, E. D., 295
McClelland, K., 299
McClure, C. R., 10, 382
McCoy, L., 210, 211, 212, 213
McCreadie, M., 70
McGill, M. J., 13
McKechnie, Lynne (E. F.), xxi, xxii,
    287, **373–376**
McKenzie, Pamela J., 85, 86, 147,
    221–224, 330, 337
McKim, G., 13, 123
McLane, J. B., 374
McNamee, G. D., 374
Mead, George Herbert, 99
meaning
    construction of, 81
    negotiation of, 105

pragmatic, 134
semantic, 134
social theory of learning and, 105
theories of, 100
media centers, 165
Medway, R., 243
Mellon, Constance, 167, 235, 236, 237
membership, communities of practice
    and, 105
memory, forging theories, 259
Menaghan, E. G., 334
Menczer, F., 320
mental constructs, 226
mental states, 171
mental vocabularies, 329
Merton, R. K., 79
messages, speed of, 109
metacognition, 64
metaphore, terms in, 27
metatheories
    definition, 1–2
    in LIS, 10–14
    sources of, 7–8
methodology, theory and, 25–29
Metoyer-Duran, C., 4
Michels, D., 313
micro-behaviors, 40
micro-level information seeking
    (MLIS), 135–136, 344
middle class groups, 146
Milgram, S., 318
military weapons, 370
Miller, G. A., 13
Miller, Suzanne M., 115, 239, 240, 366
Miller behavioral style scale (MBSS),
    240
mimetic relations, 303
*Mind in society: The development of
    higher psychological processes*
    (Vygotsky), 374
Minsky, M. L., 13
Mirror and the Lamp, The (Abrams),
    303

mistrust, information poverty and, 76
Mitchell, G., 383, 384
Miwa, Makiko, **54–57**
Mizzaro, S., 86
models
    definition, 2
    formulation of, 49
    theory development and, 3
Mokros, H., 150
Mon, Lorri, **149–153**, 384
monitoring, definition, 138
monitoring and blunting (M&B) theory,
        115, 239–241, 366
monitoring browsing, 72
monochronic time, 109
mood, information search process, 233
Moore, N., 205
moral narratives, 331
moral positioning, 336
Morgenstern, O., 94, 95
Moricz, M., 399
Morris, M., 285
Morrison, E., 237
Mote, L.J.B., 125
motivation
    constructs affecting, 245
    engagement and, 243
    interface design and, 242–246
    social cognitive theory, 54–57
motivational factors for interface
        design, 242–246
Motoyer-Duran, C., 247
Mueller, C. M., 243
Mullins, L. S., 150
multi-processing in information behav-
        ior, 183
multidimensional library anxiety scale,
        236
multiple-choice instruments, 40
municipal administrators, 275
Murnighan, J. K., 96
Murray, A. D., 227
music scholars, 120

N

Nahl, Diane, **39–43**, 115
Nair, M., 290
name generators, 324
narratives, context and, 147
National Science Foundation, 355
natural language processing, 13
naturalistic inquiry, framework for, 55
Naumer, Charles, **153–157**
navigability, of information, 318
needs
    continuous, 228
    definition of, 226
    discrete, 228
    information interests and, 295
    nature of, 227–228
negotiation, 358–362
network competence, 55
network gatekeeping, 248, 249
network gatekeeping theory (NGT),
        247–253, 252
network security, 370
Neumann, L. J., 106
neutral questioning, 361
New South Wales Department of
        Education, 63
New Zealand, librarianship in, 121
Newell, A., 13
newspapers, as gatekeepers, 250
Nichols, D. M., 167
Nielsen, J., 14
Nilan, M., 114, 128, 130, 218, 225,
        347, 383
Nilsen, K., 383, 384
Nilsson, G. B., 13
911 calltakers, 150
Nodelman, Perry, 300
nomothetic approaches, 8–9, 12
nonlinear model of information-seeking
        behavior, 254–258, 255
Norcross, J. C., 364
Norman, D. A., 14
Norman, G. L., 365

normative behavior, theory of, 147
Norvig, P., 13
nurses, interactions with, 360
nursing science scholars, 124
Nussbaum, J. F., 130
Nyce, J. M., 10

O

objective relations, 303
observation
    of communication, 27
    context-specific, 81–82
    diffusion theory and, 119
observational approaches, 6
occupational identities
    concept of, 295
    professions and, 294
    theory of professions and,
        293–297, 296
Ochs, E., 116
Oddy, R. N., 13, 45, 46, 355, 360, 397
office work, communicative action and,
    100
older citizens, information-seeking
    behavior, 346
Olien, C. N., 247
Olson, H. A., 387
Olson, M., 94, 95
O'Neil, R., 334
online groups, 95
online search interfaces, 60
Onwuegbuzie, A., 236, 237
opening processes, 256
opinion leadership, 121. *see also*
    innovations
opportunistic acquisition of informa-
    tion (OAI), 179–183
opportunistic browsing, 71, 72
optimal foraging theory, 259–264, *260*
optimality models, limits of, 263
organizational analysis, *91*
organizational information environ-
    ments, 379

organizational knowledge, 170
organizational meaning, process for
    (POM), 267–268
organizational workers, 377–381, 378
organizations
    cognitive authority of, 84
    rounding by, 311
    sense making theory, 265–269
orientation processes, 256
orienting strategies, 8–9
Orlikowski, W. J., 12
Ostrom, E., 95
other positioning, 336, 337
outcomes expectations, 55, 161
outsiders, 79
Over, P., 13

P

Packer, K. H., 125
Paice, C. D., 167
PAIN hypothesis, 270–274
Paisley, William, 12, 44, 123
Palmer, C. L., 13, 123, 124
Palmour, V. E., 227
Palmquist, Ruth A., **354–357**
Pantaleo, Sylvia, 300
paradigms, 7
Parker, E. B., 44
Parker, E. W., 123
Parker, Ian, 329
passive attention mode, 34
Paulson, R., 96
Pawley, C., 303
payoffs, contingent, 95
peer-assessment, 65
peer-reviewed articles, 125–126
Peirce, Charles S., 99
Pejtersen, Annelise Mark, **88–93**, 174
Pendleton, V. E., 80
Peregren, J., 101
Perez-Grandos, D. R., 370
performative positioning, 335
Peritz, B. C., 10

Perry, W. G., 387
persistence
    cultural value of, 110
    learned affective norms and, 41
    self-efficacy and, 54
person-in-context, 34, 35
person-in-situation approaches, 174,
    275
personal anticipated information need.
    see PAIN hypothesis
personal construct theory, 230
personal existence, concept of, 130
personal information collection (PIC),
    270, 271, 272
personal information management, 183,
    273
personal positioning, 336
persuasion, knowledge and, 119
Petry, F. E., 13
Pettigrew, Karen E. see Fisher, Karen
    E. (Pettigrew)
phenomena
    cognitive explanations, 45
    radical change theory explanations,
        301
    study of, 3
phenomenography, 280–283
phenomenology, 102
philosophical-analytic approaches, 11
Philosophical Discourse of Modernity,
    The (Habermas), 99
physicists, information seeking by, 139
Pianka, E. R., 259
Picard, Rosalind, 39
Pierce, J. R., 13
Pierce, L. G., 268
Pietiläinen, T., 114, 330
Pinder, C. C., 242
Pinker, E., 247
Pirolli, P., 49, 262, 263, 276, 397
Pitkow, J. E., 319, 399
Pitts, J., 63
places of worship, 188

plausibility, 84, 265
play, 314
pleasure principle, 290
political activism, 213
Pool, I de S., 318
Poole, H., 4, 6, 289
position generators, 325
positioning theory, 223
positive feedback, 243
positive psychology, 39, 153
potential memory, 171
Potter, Jonathan, 221, 222, 223, 329
poverty, social capital and, 324
Powell, R. R., 10
power
    elicitation and, 135
    of gamekeepers, 249
    gatekeeping and, 252
    information and, 80
    legitimation, 350
    loci within society, 99
    social theory of learning and, 105
    tactics and, 285
    worldmaking, 351
power distance, cultural, 110
power/energy flow, 27, 28
powerlessness, silence and, 388
practical knowledge, 100
practice of everyday life, 284–288
pragmatic realism, 340, 341
pragmatic relations, 303
pragmatics, 102, 134
Preece, J., 242
pregnant women, 85
preparatory browsing, 72–73
presentation stage, 231
prestige
    authorship and, 126
    ranking, 326
    of sources, 125
Price, D.J.D., 13
primary sources
    archival research, 49

digitized, 50
    environments of, 52
    information literacy for, 49
primitive terms, 27
principle of least effort (PLE), 4, 6, 7,
    182–183, 228–229, 289–292
print/digital divide, 299
priorities, questions about, *91*
prisoners, face threats to, 150
prisoner's dilemma, 95
prisons, women inmates, 79–80, 308
privacy, 370
probablilistic and plausible inference
    network models, 218
problem dimensions, 378
problem identification, 35
problem recognition, 35
problem resolution, 35
problem solving
    Big6™ model, *65*
    mastery of life and, 146
    search behaviors, 41
    search episodes and, 35
    self-efficacy and, 56
    skills, 64
    stages of, 35
    steps, 63
problem statements, 46
"problematic situation," theory of, 45
problems, structuring of, 51
procedural knowing, 388
process for organizational meaning
    (POM), 267–268
process mapping, 31, 233
Prochaska, J. O., 363, 364, 365, 366
professional projects, 294, 295
professionalism, 158, 295
professionals, 159, *160*
professions, definition, 294
professions and occupational identities,
    theory of, 293–297
"proof of concept" work, 13
protective behaviors, 77

proto-theories, 3
protocol analysis, 40
proxy searching, 170
public libraries, 284–285, 299
publishers, cognitive authority of, 84
pursuit of truth theory, 102
Putnam, H., 102
Putnam, Robert, 323

Q

quality control, 85–86, 208, 291
Quek, F., 101
queries. *see also* questions
    evolution of, 60
    information retrieval and, 46
    modification, 59
    types of, 164
    varied search strategies, 51
question-negotiation theory, 358–362
questions, 164, 165, 383. *see also*
    queries
Quine, W. V., 102

R

Raber, D., 11
Rabin, M., 94
Radford, G. P., 12
radical change, theory of, 298–302,
    299–301
Radway, Janice, 303
Rainie, L., 247
Rajala, A., 262
ranking, 46, 101
Rasmussen, E., 277
Rasmussen, J., 88, 89, 92
rational actor model, 95
Rayward, W. B., 10
reader-response theory, 102, 303–307,
    304–305
readers, reading and, 285–286
readiness to change, 363
reading, 286, 304

reading as transaction theory, 305
Reading the Romance (Radway), 303
received knowing, 388
reception theory, 304
recordkeeping practices, 51
records, search strategies and, 51
Redding, C. A., 365
redundancy, 233
reference interviews, 360, 361, 382, 384
references, digital logs of, 368
reflections, flow of, *193*
reflexive methodology, 266
"regimes of truth," 331
Reitman, W. R., 51
relationships, communities of practice and, 105
relaxation, 314
relevance
    cognitive authority and, 86
    cultural factors and, 339–340
    dynamic nature of, 218
    judgment of, 55, 166
    language and, 330
    life in the round and, 310
    perception of, 81
    situational, 308
    weighted frequencies, 101
Ren, W., 55
"render unto Caesar" hypothesis, 29
representations
    online surrogates, 51
    understanding of, 50
reputation
    cognitive authority of, 84
    cultural value of, 110
    dilemma situations and, 96
    source selection and, 229
    threats to face, 149–153
research, nature of, 7
research design, 27
research methods, 29
Resnick, P., 96

resources
    design, 300
    digital, 120
    electronic, 291
    free rider problem, 94–95
    individual consumption of, 95
    optimal foraging theory, *260*
    patches, 262
    questions about, *91*
    relationships between, 193
    scanned, 71
    social, 323
    willingness to return, 382
retired women, 308
Reynolds, P. D., 2
Riberio-Neto, B., 101
Rice, R. E., 69, 70, 319
Ridge, Judith, 300
Rieh, Soo Young, **83–87**
Rioux, Kevin, 167, **169–173**, 182
risk management behavior, 243
risk-rewards theory, 34
risk-taking, 76, 308
Ritzer, G., 3, 11, 12
rivalness, 95
Robertson, S., 277
Robinson, J. P., 313
Robyns, M. C., 50
Rochester, M. K., 121
Rodney, M. J., 65
Rogers, E. M., 118, 119, 120
Rogers, Y., 14
Rogoff, B., 374
Roitblat, H. L., 259
Rolfe, A., 384
Rosen, C. S., 366, 367
Rosenblatt, Louise, 305, 306
Ross, Catherine Sheldrick, **303–307**, 313, 383, 384
Roth, A. E., 96
Rothbauer, Paulette, **284–288**
rounding, dissonant grounds and, 308–312

Rubin, H. J., 352
Rubin, I. S., 352
Ruesch, J., 5
Russell, S. J., 13, 49
Ruthven, I., 218
Ryan, R. M., 243

S

Sabat, S. R., 337
Sacks, H., 329
sailors, serious leisure, 315
Salton, G., 13
Sanderson, P. M., 92
Sandstrom, A. R., 9, 10, 12
Sandstrom, P. E., 9, 10, 12, 14, 75,
    259, 260, 261, 262
Saracevic, T., 150, 217, 392, 399
satisficing, 4, 5–6
Savolainen, Reijo, 10, 11, 55, 113, 114,
    129, 130, **143–148**, 183, 185,
    221, 223, 224, 276, 286, 313,
    325, **328–333**
Saxton, M., 170
Saye, J., 67
scanning, definition, 71
scatter within domains, 125
Schamber, L., 218
Scheier, M. F., 40
Schleichert, H., 133
scholars
    human behavioral psychology, *261*
    information practices, 123–127,
        285
    social networks, 346
    Web spaces, 320–321
Schutz, A., 11, 205
science, nomothetic approach in, 9
scientific collaboration networks, 318
Scott, J., 77, 78
screening techniques, 73
search engines, 321
search goals, 277
search processes, 60

search strategies. *see also* information
        search process
    decision points, 359
    domain analysis and, 123–127
    interruptions, 41
    micro-behaviors in, 40
    principle of least effort and, 289
    questions about, *91*
    serendipity and, 319
    structuring problems, 51
    terminations, 41
    types of foraging, 261
    Web-based, 397–400
search techniques, 58
Searle, John, 39, 102
*Second-Hand Knowledge: An Inquiry
        into Cognitive Authority*
        (Wilson), 83
second-order positioning, 335
secrecy, 76, 150, 308
Seeger, T., 44
selection stage, 231
self-assessment, 65
self-care activities, 313
self-consciousness, 155
self-determination theory, 243, *244*
self-efficacy, theory of, 34, 54, 55, 56,
        243, *244*
self-knowledge, 100
self-monitoring techniques, 40
self-positioning, 334, 336
self-preservation, 151
self reports, search behaviors, 41
self-rewarding experiences, 156
Seligman, Martin, 39
semantic distances, 340
semantic networks, 318, 355
sender-receiver relationships, *249*, 250
sense making, theory of, 49, 113, 303,
        330
    characteristics of, 265
    discontinuity in, 276
    in organizations, 265–269
    situational, 300

Sense-Making theory, 165, 240, 270,
    355, 361, 366
  central metaphor of, 28
  concept of, 4–5
  gap-bridging and, 45
  imposed queries and, 166
  IS&R and, 218
  knowledge gaps and, 35
  methodology, 25–29
  radical change theory and, 300
  theory of, 113–117
sensory stimulation, 314
serendipity
  acquisition of information, 179
  behaviors, 319
  information encountering and,
    169–170
  information seeking and, 166–167
serious leisure, theory of, 313–317
Settle, R. B., 34
Seven Faces of Information Literacy
    (Bruce), 282
shadows of the future, 96
shame, cultural value of, 110
Shannon, Claude, 13, 165
sharing, demographics of, 170
Shaw, D., 12
Shaw, M.L.G., 4
Shneiderman, B., 242, 398
Shoemaker, P., 247
short-term orientation, cultural, 110
Shotter, John, 329
Shumsky, R., 247
SIF-FOW (sharing information found
    for others on the Web), 169
silence, 388
Silverstein, C., 399
Simon, H. A., 4, 6, 13, 289
Situated Learning: Legitimate
    Peripheral Participation
    (Wenger), 104
situated learning, theory of, 104
situational browsing, 71, 72

situational relevance, 76, 308
situational variation, 28
"six degrees of separation," 318
Skinner, B. F., 7
Sköldberg, K., 266
Small, H., 13
small business managers, 55
small world concept, 80, 81
small-world network exploration,
    318–322
Smith, Dorothy, 210, 211, 212
Smith, E. A., 259
Smith, K., 139
Smith, M., 96
Smith, Marc, 94–98
smoking behaviors, 363
Snijders, T., 324
Snow, D., 96
Snyder, C. R., 153
social-behavioral psychology, 39–40
social capital, theory of, 78, 146,
    323–327
social classes, 146
social cognitive theory, 54–57
social constraints, 56
social constructionist theory, 130–131,
    300, 328–333, 352
social constructionist theory of tech-
    nology (SCOT), 330
social dilemmas, 94
social informatics, 12–13
social integration, 350
social interactions, 170
social isolation, 205
social learning theory, 39
social network analysis, 77–78, 323,
    324
social networks, 191–192, 321
social norms, 80, 81, 308
social order, 350
social positioning theory, 334–338, 351
social power, 135

social reality, 11, 329
social resources, 323
social roles, 80
social scientists, 59, 123, 369
social shaping of technology (SST), 330
social sharing, 170
social spaces, 95
social status, 294, 324
social studies, 66–67
social systems, 120
social theory of learning, 105
social types, 80
social workers, 33–34
social worlds, theory of, 316
socio-cognitive approaches, 12
socio-cognitive theory, 339–343
socio-technical networked systems, 96
sociolinguistics, 39
sociology, definition, 352
sociology of knowledge, 75
sociology of scientific knowledge
        (SSK), 329–330
Soergel, D., 125
soft systems methodology (SSM), 267,
        268
software engineers, *194*
Solomon, Paul, 266, 268, **308–312**
solution statements, 35
Sonnenwald, Diane H., 10, **191–197**,
        191–197, 268
sources
    assessing quality of, 85–86
    categories, 175
    of influence, 275–276
    of information, 226
    information-seeking success and,
        161
    primary, 49
    selection of, 228–229
Special Interest Group on Information
        Seeking and Use (ASIS&T
        SIG USE), xxii, xxiii
specialists, foraging strategies, 261

specificity, browsing behaviors, 71
speech act theory, 100, 101
speech acts and society theory, 102
Spencer, L., 366
Spink, A., 140, 183, 217, 286, 399
Spitzer, K., 66
stages of change, 363
stakeholder analyses, 370
stakeholders, 369–370
Star, S. L., 12
Starkweather, W. M., 120
statistical properties of information, 13
status, 110, 119, 294
steadiness, personal, 110
Stebbins, Robert, 313, 314, 315
Steel, T., 133
Steele, C., 237
Steffe, L., 34
Steig, M., 49
Steinwachs, K., 111
Stenstrom, A. B., 133
Stephens, D. W., 259
Steptoe, A., 240
stereotype threat, theory of, 237
Stooke, Roz, **210–214**
stories, shared repertoire of, 105
strategic interactive games, 95
strategies, origins of, 284
Strauss, A., 12, 140
Streatfield, D. R., 12, 31, 159
strength of weak ties (SWT) theory,
        344–348
stress-coping strategies, 34, 239–241
Stripling, B., 63
Strogatz, S. H., 318
strong and weak ties, theory of, 78
structuration theory, 352
"structuring structures," 349
*Student Learning Through Ohio
        School Libraries* (Todd,
        Kuhlthau), 200
students
    affective reactions, 277

students (*cont.*)
   digital age changes, 298–299
   information seeking, 275
   interviews with, 165
   library anxiety, 235–238
   middle school, 67
   of professions, 295
   rounding by, 310
   social sciences, 66–67
subject chasing, 50
subjective knowing, 388
subjectivity, social theory of learning
   and, 105
Suleiman, Susan, 304, 305
Sundin, Olof, **293–297**, *294*
support interventions
   affective load and, 42
   online, 384
   peer-to-peer, 384
surfing, Web, 262, 397
Sussman, S. W., 266
Sutton, S., 367
Swartz, D., 349, 351, 352
Sylvain, C., 159, *160*, 161, 293
symbolic capital, 349
symbolic violence, 349–353
systematic browsing, 71

T

tacit positioning, 336, 337
tactics, categorization and, 285
Talja, Sanna, 10, 11, 114, **123–127**,
   130, 170, 224, **328–333**
Tang, J. C., 370
task analysis, questions about, *91*
task-solving information, 175
tasks
   complexity, 175–176
   definition, 65, 89
   diaries, 176–177
   flow theory and, 154–155
   foraging theory, 276
   goal theory and, 243
   information search process, 230

   model, 232
   performance, 217
   professional work roles and, 159,
      160
   reproductive, 144
   work-related, 174–178
Taylor, Robert S., 45, 165, 174, 270,
   354, 355, 356, 358–362, 360,
   377
Taylor, S., 221
teachers, 146–147, 300
technology
   cognitive work analysis and, 88
   definition of, 32
   faculty attitudes, 120
   innovations, 120–121
   peer-to-peer support groups, 384
   value-sensitive design, 370
Tenopir, C., 217
theories
   definition, 2, 25
   methodology and, 25–29
   protective behaviors, 77
Theory of Communicative Action, The
   (Habermas), 99
thinking skills, promotion of, 50
third-party searching, 170
Thomas, J. B., 266
Thomas, N. P., 10
Thomas, R. M., 373, 374
Thompson, R. H., 13
Thought and Language (Vygotsky),
   374
thoughts, interplay of, 231
threats to face, 149–153
thrift, cultural value of, 110
Tichenor, P. J., 247
Tidline, Tonyia J., **113–117**, 115
time
   altered sense of, 155–156
   budgets, 144
   concepts, 109
   information dispersal, 186
   information search process, 232
time-space moments, 27

Todd, Ross J., **198–203**
Toms, E. G., 179, 182, 319
Tónnies, F., 80
Tooby, J., 7, 14
Torres, D. A., 49, 50
Tracy, K., 150
Tracy, S. J., 150
tradition, cultural value of, 110
tragedy of the commons, 94
transportation planning, 370
transtheoretical model (TTM),
    363–367
travel planning, 310
triadic reciprocal causation, 56
Trice, H., 198
Trosow, S. E., 10
trust
    communities of practice and, 105
    predictions and, 95
    reputation and, 96
truth, pursuit of, 102
Tsonis, A., 289
Tuominen, Kimmo, xii, 10, 11, 151,
    185, 218, 221, 223, 224, 294,
    328–333
Turnbull, Don, **397–400**
Turner, Tammara Combs, **382–386**
Turock, B. J., 387
Turtle, H., 218
Tversky, A., 5
Twidale, M. B., 167

U

uncertainty
    affective load and, 41
    avoidance, cultural, 110
    coping strategies, 41
    definition of, 41
    information and, 225
    information search process and,
        230–231
    reduction of, 128
    strategies for reduction of, 50, 51
uncertainty principle, 232–233, 270
unconscious need, theory of, 45

UNISIST model, 341
United Kingdom, 204
universe of knowledge, *32*
Unruh, D. R., 313, 316
Updike, D. B., 12
usability, 111, 368
Usenet groups, 95
user-centered design approaches,
    13–14
user modeling, 140
user needs research, 31, *33*
users
    affective states, 39
    background interest of, 181
    characteristics of, 27
    clarifying linguistic confusions, 101
    decision points, 359
    demographic attributes, 29
    domain analysis and, 340
    ecological factors, 131
    ecological theory and, *129*
    face threats and, 150
    foreground problem of, 181
    gatekeepers and, 251
    interaction with information, 47
    interest space of, 319
    Internet-based information systems,
        377
    mental models of search, 400
    multichannel use by, 289
    national culture of, 111
    non-librarian, 59
    personal computers, 170
    points of view, 114
    products of, 286
    provider views and, 205, *207*
    queries by, 166
    role definition, 151
    strategies of, 284
    stress-coping strategies, 34
    tactics of, 285
    willingness to return, 382–386

V

vacation planning, 276
Vakkari, P., 2, 162, 174, 215, 217,
    218, 268, 277, 278
value-added approach, 377
value-seeking behaviors, 5, 355
value sensitive design (VSD), 368–372
values
    compatibility with, 119
    conflicts, 371
    cultural, 110
    information behavior and, 368–372
    mastery of life and, 146
    questions about, *91*
    of the self, 389
van der Gaag, M., 324
Van Kampen, D. J., 236
van Langenhove, L., 335, 351
Van Manen, 281
Van Scoyoc, A. M., 237
Vandergrift, K. E., 303
variation, study of, 281–282
Vaughan, M. W., 12
Velicer, W. F., 365, 366
vendors, databases, 59
verbing, 114, 116
viewing patterns, 73
Vincente, K. J., 88
visceral need, 290
visual arts, 115
Volker, B., 324
Volosinov, Vanentin, 329
volunteering, 314, 315
Von Neumann, J., 94, 95
Vygotsky, Lev, 11, 233, 300, 373–376,
    374, 375

W

Wagner, D. G., 2, 8, 316
Wallin, C. C., 120
Walsh, B. C., 31, 33, 319

Walsh, J. P., 126
Walter, V., 213
Wang, P., 4, 10, 217
Waples, Douglas, 304
Waquant, L. J., 350, 352
Warner, E. S., 227
Wasserman, S., 263
Wathen, C. Nadine, **363–367**
Watters, Carolyn, **242–246**
Watts, D. J., 318
"way of life" concept, 143–144
Weaver, W., 13, 165
Web. *see* World Wide Web
Weick, K. E., 265–269
Weiner, B., 243
Welborn, L., 65
Wellman, B., 324
Welser, Howard T., **94–98**
Wenger, Etienne, 104, 105, 106
Wentzel, K. R., 243
Wersig, G., 44, 45
Wertsch, J. V., 374
Westbrook, L., 10
Wetherell, Margaret, 221, 222, 223,
    329
What Reading Does to People
    (Waples), 304
White, D. M., 247
White, H., 291
White, H. D., 13
White, M. D., 4, 108, 120
Whitty, A., 370
Whyte, W. F., 80
Wiberley, S. E., Jr., 49
Wiegand, W. A., 10, 12, 213, 285, 303
Wiemann, J. M., 130
Wiener, N., 13
Wigfield, A., 243
Wildemuth, Barbara M., 192,
    275–279, 361
Wilkinson, M. A., 162
Williamson, Kirsty, **128–132**, 147,
    179, 180, 182, 186, 287
willingness to return, concept of,
    382–386

Wilson, Louis R., 304
Wilson, Patrick, 11, 83–87, 128, 294, 295
Wilson, T. D., xxi, xxiii, 4, 12, **31–36**, 55, 56, 140, 159, 172, 174, 180, 204, 215, 257, 379, 390, 394
Wilson's General Model, 31–36, 55
Wineberg, S., 50
Wingens, M., 198
Winograd, T., 100
Winter, J. A., 373
Winter, M. F., 294
Winterhalder, B., 259
Wolf, S., 67
women
    prisoners, 79–80, 308
    retired, 308
    ways of knowing, 387–391
Woo, C. C., 100
Woolgar, Steve, 158, 329–330
word occurance statistics, 289
work
    communities of practice, 105
    conceptual model, 217
    definition, 212
    documentary, 158
    human-information interactions, 89–92
    least average rate of, 6
    paid, 313
    principle of least effort and, 289
    professional work roles and, *160*
    of reading, 305–306
    rounding and, 310
    social organization of, 213
    understanding of, 158
    unpaid, 313
work knowledge, 100
work tasks
    information activities, 174–178
    IS&R framework for, 393
    IS&R processes, 392–396

working classes, 146
working poor, 121
workplaces, as information grounds, 188
World Wide Web
    browsing by scholars, 126
    cognitive authority of, 84
    hybrid information-seeking model, 300
    information behaviors of organizational workers, 377–381
    information seeking, 397–400
    law of surfing, 262
    manipulation of information, 179
    principle of least effort and, 291
    searching, 61
    sharing tools, 170
    SIF-FOW, 169
    small-world network properties, 318–322
    surfing patterns, 262
    Web cams, 370
    Web clusters, topical, 321
    Web crawlers, 318, 320
worldviews, 80, 81, 205, 308, 309
Wright, R., 14
Wu, Mei-Mei, **133–137**

Y

Yakel, Elizabeth, **49–53**
Yamagishi, T., 94, 95
Yates, J., 12
Yates, S. J., 221

Z

Zbikowski, John, 300
Zipf, George, 6, 7, 13, 182, 289
zone of proximal development (ZPD), 233, 300, 373–376
Zuboff, S., 51
Zurcher, L., 96

More Titles of Interest from Information Today, Inc.

Understanding and Communicating Social Informatics

A Framework for Studying and Teaching the Human Contexts of Information and Communication Technologies

Rob Kling, Howard Rosenbaum, and Steve Sawyer

Here is a sustained investigation into the human contexts of information and communication technologies (ICTs), covering both research and theory. The authors demonstrate that the design, adoption, and use of ICTs are deeply connected to people's actions as well as to the environments in which ICTs are used. They offer a pragmatic overview of social informatics, articulating its fundamental ideas for specific audiences and presenting important research findings.

2005/240 pp/hardbound/ISBN 1-57387-228-8/$39.50

Covert and Overt

Recollecting and Connecting Intelligence Service and Information Science

Edited by Robert V. Williams and Ben-Ami Lipetz

This volume explores the historical relationships between covert intelligence work and information/computer science. The book first examines the pivotal strides to utilize technology in the gathering and dissemination of government/military intelligence during World War II. Next, it traces the evolution of the relationship between spymasters, computers, and systems developers through the years of the Cold War.

2005/276 pp/hardbound/ISBN 1-57387-234-2

ASIST Members $39.60 • Non-Members $49.50

The History and Heritage of Scientific and Technological Information Systems

Edited by W. Boyd Rayward and Mary Ellen Bowden

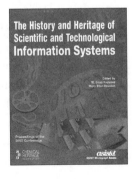

Emphasis for the second conference on the history of information science systems was on scientific and technical information systems in the period from World War II through the early 1990s. These proceedings present the papers of historians, information professionals, and scientists on a wide range of topics including informatics in chemistry, biology and medicine, and information developments in multinational, industrial, and military settings.

2004/440 pp/softbound/ISBN 1-57387-229-6

ASIST Members $36.40 • Non-Members $45.50

Information Representation and Retrieval in the Digital Age

Heting Chu

This is the first book to offer a clear, comprehensive view of Information Representation and Retrieval (IRR). With an emphasis on principles and fundamentals, the author first reviews key concepts and major developmental stages of the field, then systematically examines information representation methods, IRR languages, retrieval techniques and models, and Internet retrieval systems.

2003/250 pp/hardbound/ISBN 1-57387-172-9

ASIST Members $35.60 • Nonmembers $44.50

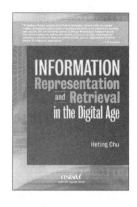

Statistical Methods for the Information Professional

Liwen Vaughan

Author and educator Liwen Vaughan clearly explains the statistical methods used in information science research, focusing on basic logic rather than mathematical intricacies. Her emphasis is on the meaning of statistics, when and how to apply them, and how to interpret the results of statistical analysis. Through the use of real-world examples, she shows how statistics can be used to improve services, make better decisions, and conduct more effective research.

2001/240 pp/hardbound/ISBN 1-57387-110-9

ASIST Members $31.60 • Non-Members $39.50

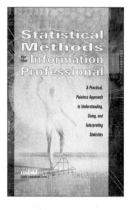

Intelligent Technologies in Library and Information Service Applications

F.W. Lancaster and Amy Warner

In this carefully researched monograph, authors Lancaster and Warner report on the applications of AI technologies in library and information services, assessing their effectiveness, reviewing the relevant literature, and offering a clear-eyed forecast of future use and impact.

2001/214 pp/hardbound/ISBN 1-57387-103-6

ASIST Members $31.60 • Non-Members $39.50

To order or for a complete catalog, contact:

Information Today, Inc.

143 Old Marlton Pike, Medford, NJ 08055 • 609/654-6266
email: custserv@infotoday.com • Web site: www.infotoday.com